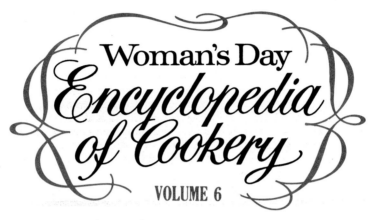

Woman's Day Encyclopedia of Cookery

VOLUME 6

in 12 volumes—over 2,000 pages—
with more than 1,500 illustrations in color,
1,000 entries and 8,500 recipes
1,200 menus, 50 specialty cook books
and a host of delightful features by distinguished food writers.

Prepared and edited by the Editors of Woman's Day
Editor: EILEEN TIGHE
Managing Editor: EVELYN GRANT   *Food Editor:* GLENNA MCGINNIS
Art Consultant: HAROLD SITTERLE   *Photographic Editor:* BEN CALVO
Associates: OLIVIA RISBERG, CHARLOTTE SCRIPTURE,
CAROLYN STORM, JOHANNA BAFARO

SPECIAL PROJECT STAFF
Editor: NIKA STANDEN HAZELTON   *Art Director:* LEONARD A. ROMAGNA
Associates: L. GERALDINE MARSTELLER, HELEN FEINGOLD,
SUSAN J. KNOX, INEZ M. KRECH

FAWCETT PUBLICATIONS, INC.   NEW YORK

Printed in U.S.A. by
FAWCETT-HAYNES PRINTING CORPORATION
Rockville, Maryland

Table of Contents

VOLUME 6

HADDOCK TO KID

Definitions and 740 Recipes
How to buy, store, prepare, cook, and serve •
Nutritive Food Values • Caloric Values

HADDOCK............................845	HUNGARIAN COOKERY.......916
HALIBUT..............................848	ICES......................................924
HAM COOK BOOK 851	ICE CREAM COOK BOOK.....928
HAM AND EGGS..................861	INDIA'S COOKERY..............935
HAMBURGER COOK BOOK. 867	IRISH COOKERY.................943
HARD SAUCE......................877	ITALIAN COOKERY.............950
HASH COOK BOOK..............879	JAM.......................................961
HEAD CHEESE....................882	JAMAICAN SOUPS..............966
HERB COOKERY.................886	JAMBALAYA........................968
HOW TO BUILD AND PLANT AN HERB GARDEN............900	JAPANESE COOKERY.........969
HERRING............................901	JELLIED DISHES................978
HOW TO COOK SUPERBLY: Hollandaise 905	JELLIES...............................981
HOMINY.............................906	JEWISH COOKERY.............985
HONEY...............................908	JULEP..................................996
HORS-D'OEUVRE................912	KABOBS...............................997
HORSERADISH...................913	KALE....................................998
HOT CAKES........................914	KETCHUP............................999
HUBBARD SQUASH............914	100 MENUS.......................1000
HUCKLEBERRIES...............915	

To help you plan more varied meals
with the recipes in this volume.

GENERAL INFORMATION ...1004
COMPLETE RECIPE INDEX ...1005

Foreword

To the best of our knowledge, no work of this magnitude ever has been undertaken by any author, editor, or publisher in America. The editors of Woman's Day, with a special staff of experts, present to you this Encyclopedia of Cookery, a comprehensive and colorful library on all culinary matters. The twelve-volume encyclopedia contains in its 2,000 pages over 8,500 recipes from all over the world, 1,500 food illustrations in color, 1,200 menus, 50 special cook books and over 1,000 food definitions. In addition, there are full details about all foods, their nutritive and caloric values, how to buy, serve, prepare, and cook them. There is a history of food and cooking, articles on nutrition, diet, entertaining, menu planning, herbs and spices. Every topic of culinary interest is covered. Five years of intensive work have gone into its preparation, backed by twenty-five years of food and cookery experience in the publication of Woman's Day.

We think you will find this Encyclopedia of Cookery the most complete and authoritative work ever published on the subject. It is a library for everyone who cares about good food and the fine art of preparing it.

The Editors

HADDOCK—This salt-water fish is one of the most important food fish of the North Atlantic, from Nova Scotia to Cape Hatteras. It is closely related to the cod, but the two fish can easily be told apart; the haddock has a black lateral line and a patch below it and above the pectoral fin. The haddock is much smaller than the cod. In New England waters, haddocks on the average weigh between two and six pounds. Haddock is an all-season fish, and is as popular in northern Europe as it is in the United States.

The flesh is firm and white, with a pleasant flavor which is on the bland side. Smoked haddock is called finnan haddie.

Haddock can be successfully cooked in any desired way. Fillets are a favorite.

Availability and Purchasing Guide—Fresh haddock is available all year round, whole and in fillets. Frozen haddock is available in fillets.

Fresh haddock should be firm-fleshed and have a fresh odor.

Storage—Wrap haddock in moisture-proof covering or place in a tightly covered container. Keep fish in the coldest part of the refrigerator. Plan to use within 2 days.

Frozen haddock should be kept solidly frozen until ready to use. Once thawed, use immediately.

☐ Refrigerator shelf, raw: 1 to 2 days
☐ Refrigerator shelf, cooked: 3 to 4 days
☐ Refrigerator frozen-food compartment, prepared for freezing: 2 to 3 weeks
☐ Freezer, prepared for freezing: 1 year

Nutritive Food Values—Haddock is a very good source of protein and contains phosphorus, potassium, niacin, and thiamine.

☐ 3½ ounces, raw = 79 calories
☐ 3½ ounces, fried = 165 calories
☐ 3½ ounces, smoked = 103 calories

Basic Preparation—Wash fish quickly in cold, salted water. Frozen fish should be thawed in the refrigerator; allow about 8 hours for 1 pound of fish. Haddock may be cooked by dry or moist heat.

☐ **To Freeze**—Haddock can be frozen in steaks, chunks, or fillets. Dip fish into salted water, ¼ cup salt to 4 cups cold water, for 30 seconds. Drain. Wrap in moisture- vapor-proof material, excluding as much air as possible. Seal.

BROILED HADDOCK FILLETS

1½ pounds haddock fillets
 1 teaspoon salt
 ⅛ teaspoon pepper
 ¾ cup small soft bread cubes
 3 tablespoons butter or margarine, melted
 ¼ teaspoon crumbled dried thyme
12 fresh grapefruit sections

Wipe fillets with a damp cloth. Sprinkle both sides of fish with salt and pepper. Place in a shallow buttered baking pan or on buttered broiler rack. Mix bread cubes with 2 tablespoons of the butter and the thyme. Sprinkle over fish. Top with grapefruit sections. Brush with remaining butter. Place under broiler with oven control set to hot (400°F.) and broil for 25 minutes, or until fish is flaky and crumbs are brown. Makes 5 or 6 servings.

Haddock Plaki

FLAKED HADDOCK, NEWBURG
   3 tablespoons butter or margarine
1½ tablespoons flour
   1 teaspoon salt
   ½ teaspoon paprika
   ¼ teaspoon ground nutmeg
     Dash of cayenne
   ¾ cup light cream
   ⅓ cup milk
1½ pounds haddock fillets, cooked
     and flaked
   3 tablespoons sherry
   2 egg yolks
   4 slices of toast

Melt butter and blend in the flour and
seasonings. Add cream and milk slowly;
cook until thickened, stirring constantly.
Add fish and heat. Add sherry mixed
with egg yolks and cook for 2 or 3
minutes longer. Serve at once on hot
toast. Makes 4 servings.

HADDOCK-POTATO PATTIES
   4 medium potatoes
   1 pound haddock fillets, cooked and
     flaked
   1 egg, beaten
   2 tablespoons minced onion
   1 teaspoon poultry seasoning
     Salt and pepper
     All-purpose flour
     Fat for frying

Cook potatoes and mash. Add fish, egg,
onion, poultry seasoning, and salt and
pepper to taste. Shape into 8 flat patties.
Roll in flour and panfry in hot fat until
brown. Makes 4 servings.

HADDOCK PLAKI
   3 tomatoes or about 1 cup canned
     tomatoes
   2 large onions, sliced
   1 garlic clove, chopped
   1 parsley sprig, finely chopped
   ¼ cup olive oil or butter
   1 haddock large enough for 2 persons
   1 lemon, sliced
     Ground sage, salt, and pepper to
     taste
     Bread crumbs
     Lemon juice, if desired

Peel and mash tomatoes; add onion, garlic, and parsley. Add olive oil. Place mixture in shallow pan and let simmer over
low heat until onion is tender. Place fish
in pan and cover with lemon slices. Add
sage, salt, and pepper and sprinkle with
bread crumbs. Cook in oven until fish is
browned. Let the *Plaki* cool and serve
cold. Squeeze a little lemon juice on it,
and you'll find it is an appetizing hot-
weather dish. Makes 2 servings.

HAKE—The hake is a salt-water food fish
which lives in the Atlantic and northern
Pacific. It is a relative of the cod. Hakes
are slender, dark-gray fish with fins on
their backs; the first small and triangular,
the second long and narrow. Their aver-

Poached Halibut Steaks with Curry Sauce

age market weight is between one and four pounds. The meat is soft and white with a delicate flavor.

Hake is marketed whole or filleted, and also fresh, frozen, salted, and smoked. A great deal of it is sold, along with cod, haddock, and other white fish, under the label of "deep-sea fillets." It can be prepared and frozen in any manner suited to cod and haddock.

Caloric Value

☐ 3½ ounces, raw = 74 calories

HAKE CASSEROLE

2 pounds hake fillets
4 potatoes, sliced
3 onions, sliced
Few celery tops
1 bay leaf
4 whole cloves
1 garlic clove
¼ teaspoon dillseed
¼ teaspoon white pepper
2½ teaspoons salt
½ cup butter or margarine
½ cup dry white wine
2 cups boiling water
2 cups light cream
Chopped parsley

Put all ingredients except last 2 in 3-quart casserole. Cover; bake in preheated moderate oven (375°F.) for 1 hour. Add scalded cream. Garnish with parsley. Makes 6 servings.

SESAME BAKED HAKE

2 pounds hake fillets
Salt to taste
Melted butter (about ⅔ cup)
3 cups soft bread crumbs
¼ teaspoon pepper
¼ cup sesame seeds, toasted in moderate oven (350°F.)
½ teaspoon dried thyme

Put fish in a shallow baking dish. Sprinkle with salt and pour on ¼ cup melted butter. Mix 1 teaspoon salt, ⅓ cup melted butter, and remaining ingredients. Spread on fish. Bake in preheated moderate oven (375°F.) for about 30 minutes. Makes 6 servings.

CURRIED HAKE

3 onions, chopped
1 garlic clove, minced
1 small green pepper, chopped
1 tablespoon curry powder
¼ cup butter or margarine
4 whole cloves
1 cinnamon stick
½ cup undiluted evaporated milk
1 pound hake fillets, cubed
Salt
Hot cooked rice

Cook first 4 ingredients in the butter for 5 minutes. Add next 5 ingredients, cover, and simmer for 10 minutes. Season to taste. Serve with rice. Makes 4 servings.

HALF AND HALF

HALF AND HALF—A dairy product consisting of a mixture of milk and cream. The mixture is usually homogenized, and used for coffee or table cream. Half and half, on the average, contains between ten and twelve per cent butterfat. Whole sweet milk contains three and nine-tenths per cent butterfat, light cream twenty per cent, medium cream between thirty-six to forty per cent.

In the British Isles, half and half is the term used for a mixture of mild and bitter draught beer. It is one of the most popular drinks in the pubs which are known as the "workingman's clubs." Playing darts in an English pub, and gossiping with the locals over a glass of half and half, or "'alf and 'alf" as the London Cockney would say, is a pleasing and soothing experience for Englishman and foreigner alike.

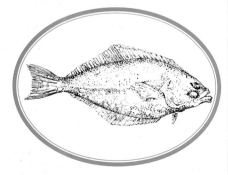

HALIBUT—A cold-water fish which lives in all the seas of the world and is one of the finest and most important of salt-water food fish; there are several varieties. The fish is flat and resembles a gigantic flounder. Female halibuts have been known to weigh as much as 600 pounds; males seldom exceed 100 pounds and more usually weigh around fifty.

The flesh is white and excellent in flavor and texture, but the large female halibuts do not make for the best eating since their flesh is coarse. Chicken halibuts, weighing up to ten pounds, are considered the finest.

Availability—Fresh halibut is available all year round; it is most abundant from March to September. Halibut is also available frozen in steaks and fillets.

Purchasing Guide—Fresh halibut is sold as steak or fillets. It should be firm-fleshed and have a fresh odor.

Storage—Fresh fish should be wrapped in a moisture-proof covering and kept in the coldest part of the refrigerator. Plan to use within 2 days. Frozen fish should be kept solidly frozen until ready to use. Once thawed, use immediately.
- ☐ Refrigerator shelf, raw: 1 to 2 days
- ☐ Refrigerator shelf, cooked and covered: 3 to 4 days
- ☐ Refrigerator frozen-food compartment, prepared for freezing: 2 to 3 weeks
- ☐ Freezer, prepared for freezing: 1 year

Nutritive Food Values—A very good source of protein, low in fat. Halibut liver oil is a rich source of vitamin A.
- ☐ 3½ ounces, raw = 100 calories
- ☐ 3½ ounces, broiled = 171 calories

Basic Preparation—Wash halibut in cold, salted water. Do not allow fish to remain in water as it may lose flavor and nutrients. Frozen halibut should be thawed in the refrigerator; allow about 8 hours for 1 pound of fish. Halibut may be cooked by dry or moist heat; poached, broiled, baked, fried, or used for soufflé or steamed pudding. To freeze at home see Haddock, page 845.

BAKED WHOLE HALIBUT

Stuff whole halibut lightly with well-seasoned bread stuffing. Cut 3 or 4 gashes in skin and insert thin slices of salt pork or bacon. Put a pinch of dried thyme or marjoram, 1 minced onion, 3 tablespoons minced parsley, and 2 tablespoons fat in baking pan. Put fish in pan; bake in pre-heated moderate oven (350°F.) until fish flakes easily with a fork.

POACHED HALIBUT STEAKS WITH CURRY SAUCE

Cut 1½ to 2 pounds halibut steaks into individual pieces. Cover with boiling water; season with a slice of onion, a parsley sprig or a few celery tops, salt, and a few peppercorns. Simmer gently for 10 to 15 minutes, or until fish is tender. Reserve stock and remove fish to hot platter. Serve with Curry Sauce. Makes 3 to 4 servings.

Curry Sauce
- 3 tablespoons butter or margarine
- ½ onion, grated
- 1½ tablespoons flour
- 2 to 4 teaspoons curry powder
- ½ teaspoon salt
- 1¼ cups fish stock (add water if necessary)
- ¼ cup cream or undiluted evaporated milk

Cook onion in butter for a minute or two. Blend in flour and seasonings. Add fish stock gradually; cook until thickened, stirring constantly. Add cream before serving. Makes about 1½ cups.

DEVILED HALIBUT STEAKS

Mix 2 tablespoons prepared mustard, 1 tablespoon salad oil, 2 tablespoons chili sauce, 2 tablespoons prepared horse-radish, and 1 teaspoon salt. Spread half of mixture on 4 halibut steaks (about 2 pounds). Put on greased broiler rack and broil for about 6 minutes under medium heat. Turn fish, spread with remaining sauce, and broil for 5 or 6 minutes longer. Makes 4 servings.

PLANKED HALIBUT STEAKS
- 8 small white onions
- 4 to 6 carrots, cut into strips
- 1 package (10 ounces) frozen broccoli
- 2 pounds halibut steaks (about 1 inch thick)
- Salt and pepper to taste
- Melted butter or margarine
- Juice of 1 lemon
- Paprika and parsley

Cook vegetables separately until almost tender. Meanwhile, if plank is used, oil well and heat in hot oven (400°F.). Sprinkle fish with salt and pepper. Brush with melted butter. Put on heated plank or on greased ovenproof baking dish. Bake in hot oven (400°F.) for 30 to 40 minutes, or until fish flakes easily when tested with a fork. If fish is not browned enough, put under broiler for a few minutes. Brown vegetables lightly in small amount of butter. Arrange around fish. Top fish with butter mixed with lemon juice; sprinkle with paprika and garnish with parsley. Serve on plank. Makes 4 servings.

BARBECUED HALIBUT STEAKS
- 1 small onion, minced
- ½ green pepper, chopped
- 3 tablespoons butter or margarine
- ½ cup chili sauce
- ½ cup ketchup
- Juice of 2 lemons
- 2 tablespoons brown sugar
- ½ cup water
- 1 teaspoon powdered mustard
- 1 tablespoon Worcestershire
- ½ teaspoon each of salt and pepper
- 4 halibut steaks (2 pounds)

Cook onion and green pepper in butter for 5 minutes. Add remaining ingredients except fish and simmer for 10 minutes. Broil halibut until done, brushing from time to time with the sauce. Makes 4 servings.

HALIBUT WITH CREAMY MUSTARD SAUCE
- 1½ pounds halibut steaks
- ¼ cup butter or margarine
- ¼ cup all-purpose flour
- ½ teaspoon powdered mustard
- ½ teaspoon steak sauce
- ¾ teaspoon salt
- Dash of pepper
- 2 cups milk
- 1 tablespoon minced chives
- Paprika

Poach fish in seasoned simmering water to cover until fish flakes. Drain and leave fish in covered pan. Melt butter and blend in flour and seasonings. Add milk and cook until thickened, stirring. Put fish on hot platter and pour sauce over fish. Sprinkle with chives and paprika. Makes 4 servings.

HAM—The rear leg of a hog, from the aitchbone (hipbone) through the meaty part of the shank bone, is called a ham.

The hog has been a domestic animal since prehistoric times and although no one knows for sure just when salt was first used to cure ham, this was one of the earliest methods of food preservation, and cured ham was traditional at the pagan spring festivals which predated the Christian Easter.

Tradition says that Columbus brought eight pigs with him on his second trip to the Americas, and Cortés brought swine to Honduras in 1524. When de Soto landed at Charlotte Harbor, Florida, in 1539, he brought with him 600 soldiers, 350 horses, and thirteen hogs. It did not take the Indians long to find out how good roast pork could be, and records show the whole Spanish encampment was burned twice by the Indians in their efforts to get it. In 1542, the survivors of the expedition killed 700 pigs to provide meat for the return voyage down the Mississippi. Fifty years later, when the French explored the river, the Indians fed the explorers pork raised from the descendants of the original de Soto herd. These, as well as others brought west from the English colonies, especially Virginia, sired the "razorbacks" and "stump rooters" from which the famed country-style hams of Virginia, Georgia, Kentucky, and Tennessee are made today.

The differences in the taste of ham lie in the breed of the hog and the food it is fed. In the case of cured hams, taste is also affected by the flavors of the brines used in curing, and the fuel, such as hickory logs, over which the meat is smoked. Razorbacks forced to forage for their own food produce a different flavor from the corn-fed breeds developed on America's pig farms and agricultural experiment stations. The final effect on taste is, of course, provided by the liquids, spices, and sauces used in cooking, roasting, and basting the ham in the home.

FRESH HAM
(UNCURED LEG OF PORK)

Availability—All year round, with the supply most plentiful at the New Year and Easter. The most common range of weight for a whole fresh ham is 10 to 14 pounds.

Purchasing Guide—The inspection stamp, federal, state, or city, guarantees the wholesomeness of the meat. At the present time U. S. grade identification does not appear on retail cuts of pork, but in high-quality ham the layer of external fat is firm and white; the color of the lean is grayish-pink in young pork, and turns a delicate rose color in older animals; the lean is well marbled with fat; the texture of the lean is firm and fine-grained; bones are porous and pinkish in color.

The cuts of fresh ham most commonly sold, bone-in or boneless, are: whole ham; half ham, shank or butt; ham end, shank or butt; center slice, from ½ to 3 inches thick.

The following rule of thumb may be used for determining the amount to buy:
- ¾ to 1 pound per serving for ham with bone
- ¼ to ⅓ pound per serving for boneless ham

Storage—Loosen or remove market paper; store unwrapped or loosely wrapped in coldest part of refrigerator. If fresh ham cannot be used within time suggested, wrap closely and seal tightly in moisture-vapor-proof material and freeze quickly.

To store cooked ham and gravy, cool quickly, cover tightly, and place in coldest part of refrigerator. Or freeze quickly. Do not refreeze.

- Refrigerator shelf, uncooked: 5 to 6 days
- Refrigerator frozen-food compartment, prepared for freezing, uncooked: 2 to 3 weeks
- Freezer, prepared for freezing, uncooked: 3 to 4 months
- Refrigerator shelf, cooked, with gravy: 4 to 5 days
- Refrigerator frozen-food compartment, cooked, with gravy, prepared for freezing: 2 to 3 weeks
- Freezer, cooked, with gravy, prepared for freezing: 2 to 3 months

Nutritive Food Values—Fresh ham is a very good to excellent source of high-quality protein and thiamine, fair to good source of iron and niacin, and fair source of riboflavin.
- 3½ ounces, fat, roasted = 394 calories
- 3½ ounces, medium-fat, roasted = 374 calories
- 3½ ounces, lean, roasted = 346 calories

Basic Preparation—Fresh ham should be thoroughly cooked to bring out its full flavor, as well as to kill any trichinae organisms present. The cooked lean of fresh ham should be grayish-white without any tinge of pink. This does not mean overcooking, which reduces juiciness, flavor, tenderness, and food value. Low cooking temperatures are recommended.

☐ **To Roast (Bake)**—Place the ham, fat side up, in a shallow open pan, on a rack to keep the meat out of the drippings. Insert a meat thermometer into the center of the meat, making sure the point does not rest on fat or bone. Roast at an oven temperature between 325°F. and 350°F. until the meat reaches an internal temperature of 185°F. A 10- to 14-pound whole ham, bone-in, needs approximately 25 to 30 minutes per pound; a boneless whole ham weighing 7 to 10 pounds needs 35 to 40 minutes per pound; a half ham, bone-in, weighing 5 to 7 pounds needs 40 to 45 minutes per pound.

Boneless half hams, and shank and butt ends which weigh less than 7 pounds vary so in shape that it is impossible to give approximate cooking times per pound for them. Use a meat thermometer, and cook until the meat reaches an internal temperature of 185°F. If you don't have a meat thermometer, check on doneness by cutting into the meat. Roast slices more than 2 inches thick in the same way.

For center slices, bone-in or boneless, calculate cooking time by the thickness of the piece. A 2-inch slice should roast for about 60 minutes. A 1-inch slice takes about 40 minutes.

☐ **To Panbroil Slices**—Only slices 1 inch or less thick should be panbroiled. Trim fat from edge of slices, and rub over heated skillet. Snip fat edges of slices in several places to keep edge from curling. Put in skillet, and panbroil until browned on both sides, about 5 to 10 minutes on each side.

☐ **To Panfry Slices**—Follow directions given for panbroiling, but cook ham in a small amount of fat.

☐ **To Cook in Liquid**—Cover ham with cold water. Season to taste with herbs, onions, etc. Cover. Simmer slowly, that is, cook just *below* or *at* the boiling point. This is important. Allow 25 minutes for each pound of ham. A 10- to 12-pound fresh ham will take approximately 4 to 6 hours.

CURED AND SMOKED HAM

Availability—All year round, cured or cured and smoked, whole and in a variety of cuts, uncooked (cook-before-eating) or fully cooked (ready-to-eat), and as standard or specialty hams.

Cured ham and cured and smoked ham are also available canned. Other canned ham products available include deviled ham and spiced ham.

Purchasing Guide—Standard ham is available in the following cuts: Whole hams, bone-in, semiboneless (the aitchbone and shank bone are removed, leaving only the leg bone to hold the shape), and boneless; half hams, bone-in, shank or butt; ham ends, bone-in, shank or butt; center slices, bone-in, from about ½ inch to 3 inches thick (the thinner slices are also known as ham steaks); ham boned and rolled, from slices of any weight requested to a whole ham, which may weigh as much as 14 pounds; thinly sliced ham, boneless, fully cooked (often called boiled ham).

A wide variety of specialty hams are produced in this country, and Italian, Danish, Polish, German, Czechoslovakian, Hungarian, French Bayonne, and English York hams are imported. Among the best-known of these specialty hams are:

American Country-Style Hams (Georgia, Kentucky, Smithfield, Tennessee, and Virginia)—Heavily cured and smoked, but uncooked, they are generally available as whole hams in the localities in which they are cured, and by mail or in specialty food stores nationally. Some cooked Smithfield hams are found in specialty food stores, too.

Italian Prosciutto and German Westphalian Hams—Cured, pressed, smoked, aged in spices, and ready-to-eat. They are usually sold sliced paper-thin.
Note: Picnic shoulders and shoulder butts are not hams, although often called hams, especially when cured.

Storage—Refrigerate in original wrapper or container. Do not freeze. Country-style hams, uncooked, can be stored in a cool place for several months. Canned hams should generally be refrigerated. Be sure to check label for special instructions.
□ Whole ham, refrigerator shelf, uncooked: 2 weeks
□ Half ham or ham end, refrigerator shelf, uncooked: 1 week
□ Center slices and thinly sliced ham, refrigerator shelf, uncooked or cooked: 3 days
□ Whole ham, half, or end, refrigerator shelf, cooked and covered: 1 week
□ Canned ham, refrigerator shelf, unopened: 1 year, unless label directs otherwise
□ Canned deviled or spiced ham, kitchen shelf, unopened: 1 year
□ Canned ham, deviled, or spiced ham, refrigerator shelf, opened and covered: 1 week

Nutritive Food Values—Cured ham has approximately the same food values as fresh ham. The caloric values of 3½ ounces of various hams are as follows:
□ Standard, fat, baked = 394 calories
□ Standard, medium-fat, baked = 374 calories

□ Standard, lean, baked = 346 calories
□ Boiled = 234 calories
□ Specialty, fat = 460 calories
□ Specialty, medium-fat = 389 calories
□ Specialty, lean = 310 calories
□ Canned = 193 calories
□ Canned deviled = 351 calories
□ Canned spiced = 294 calories

Basic Preparation—Remove rind of uncooked standard whole ham, half ham, or ham end. If necessary, rinse and pat dry before cooking.

Soak, parboil, and remove rind of specialty hams before baking.

Fully cooked hams may be served without heating, or they may be heated to an internal temperature of about 130°F.

□ **To Prepare Specialty Ham for Baking**—Unwrap ham and soak 24 to 30 hours in cold water to cover; drain. Put ham in large kettle, cutting off tip of ham, if necessary. Cover with water; bring to boil and simmer, covered, until tender (allow about 25 to 30 minutes per pound), or until large bone in heavy end of ham becomes loose and protrudes. Remove ham from water, and cut off rind. The ham is now ready to be sliced and eaten, or to be glazed.

□ **To Bake**—For uncooked or fully cooked ham, put ham, fat side up, on rack in open roasting pan. Insert meat thermometer so the bulb is in the center of thickest part and does not touch bone. (Do not add water.) Put in preheated oven and bake as directed in Timetable for Baking, below.

To glaze a ham, remove it from the oven 45 minutes before it is done, score, stud with cloves, and spread with glaze. Return to oven and finish baking.

Specialty hams which have been parboiled are simply scored, spread with a glaze, and baked, glazed-side up, in a preheated slow oven (300°F.) for about 1 hour.

To bake slices, put a 2-inch-thick fully cooked ham slice on a rack in a shallow plan, and bake in a preheated slow oven (325°F.) for 40 minutes. An uncooked ham slice requires 60 minutes. The slice can be studded with whole cloves, and topped with a glaze before baking, if desired.

HAM GLAZES
■ Applesauce—Mix ½ cup corn syrup, 1 cup strained applesauce, and 2 tablespoons prepared mustard.
■ Butterscotch—Mix ¾ cup brown sugar, 2 teaspoons powdered mustard, and small amount of ham fat.
■ Honey—Use ¾ cup strained honey.
■ Jelly—Mash 1 cup cranberry, currant, or other tart jelly.
■ Marmalade—Use ½ cup orange, peach, or apricot marmalade.
■ Molasses—Mix ½ cup each of vinegar and molasses.
■ Mustard—Mix ¼ cup prepared mustard, ½ cup brown sugar, and 2 tablespoons honey.
■ Pineapple—Mix ½ cup crushed pineapple and ¾ cup brown sugar.
■ Sweet Pickle—Use liquid drained from gherkins or other sweet pickles.

□ **To Broil Slices**—Slash the fat edges in several places to prevent curling. Broil 3 inches from unit. A 1-inch-thick slice of fully cooked ham requires 5 minutes per side. Allow 10 minutes per side for uncooked ham slices.

□ **To Panbroil Slices**—Ham slices ¼ to ½ inch thick should be panbroiled. Trim fat from edge of slices, and rub over heated skillet. Snip fat edges of slices in several places to keep edge from curling. Put in skillet, and panbroil until browned on both sides, 2 to 5 minutes on each side for uncooked slices and 1½ to 2 minutes for fully cooked slices.

□ **To Panfry Slices**—Follow directions given for panbroiling but cook ham in a small amount of fat.

TIMETABLE FOR BAKING
UNCOOKED AND FULLY COOKED STANDARD CURED HAM

CUT	APPROXIMATE WEIGHT (POUNDS)	OVEN TEMPERATURE	INTERNAL TEMPERATURE	APPROXIMATE COOKING TIME (MINUTES PER POUND)
Uncooked Ham				
Whole	10 to 14	300°F. to 325°F.	160°F.	18 to 20
Half	5 to 7	300°F. to 325°F.	160°F.	22 to 25
End	3 to 4	325°F.	160°F.	35 to 40
Fully Cooked Ham				
Whole	12 to 16	325°F.	125°F. to 130°F.	10 to 15
Half	6 to 8	325°F.	125°F. to 130°F.	18 to 24

HAM COOK BOOK

The Perennial Pleasure of Ham: A meat for all seasons ∎ A meat for all meals ∎ A meat for young and old ∎

FRESH HAM

ROAST FRESH HAM

1 fresh ham
1 garlic clove, cut
  Salt and pepper to taste
1 tablespoon caraway seed
4 onions, sliced
2 carrots, sliced
2 celery stalks, sliced
1 bay leaf
3 whole cloves
1 cup water
1 cup dry white wine

Allow ½ pound uncooked meat for each serving. Score skin of ham in 2 directions, making a diamond pattern. Rub meat on all sides with garlic, salt, pepper, and caraway seed. Put onions, carrots, celery, bay leaf, and cloves on bottom of large baking pan. Add water. Lay ham, fat side down, on vegetables. Roast, uncovered, in preheated slow oven (325° F.) for 1 hour. Baste frequently with pan juices and wine. Turn meat fat side up and roast until done. Roasting time is about 4½ hours for a 5-pound ham from the time the meat is put in the oven. Or roast to 185°F. on a meat thermometer.

COLD FRESH HAM

Fresh ham, 6 to 7 pounds, boned and rolled
Salt and pepper to taste
Rosemary
2 garlic cloves

Season meat with salt, pepper, and just a little rosemary. Cut each garlic clove in several pieces. Bury each garlic piece just under the surface of the meat by making tiny gashes and inserting pieces. (Remove garlic before serving.) Put on rack in roasting pan, and roast in preheated slow oven (325°F.) for 30 to 35 minutes per pound (185°F. internal temperature on a meat thermometer). Cool, but do not refrigerate. Serve with one of the ham sauces on page 859 and spiced fruit. Makes 6 to 8 servings.

PORK FRICASSEE FILIPINO

1 fresh ham (about 8 pounds)
½ cup soy sauce
  Juice of 1 lemon
2 teaspoons poultry seasoning
1½ teaspoons salt
½ teaspoon pepper
1 teaspoon ground ginger
2 medium onions, chopped
2 cups water
6 tablespoons cornstarch

Have meat sliced into 1-inch slices. Remove bones, trim off fat, and cut slices into pieces about 1 x 1½ inches. Combine remaining ingredients except water and cornstarch. Pour over meat. Let stand for at least 30 minutes. Put in large kettle, add water, and bring to boil. Cover and simmer for 1½ hours, or until tender. Skim fat from broth. Thicken with cornstarch mixed with a little cold water. Simmer for about 5 minutes. Makes 12 servings.

CURED HAM

Note: In the recipes that follow, the ingredients specify fully cooked (ready-to-eat), uncooked (cook-before-eating), or cooked ham. As an ingredient "cooked ham" refers to either fully cooked or uncooked ham which has been baked, broiled, etc., at home. It may also be fully cooked ham, as bought.

APPETIZERS

HAM DIP
1 cup ground cooked ham
3 tablespoons mayonnaise
2 tablespoons chili sauce
1 tablespoon prepared mustard
½ teaspoon each of chili powder and brown sugar

Mix all ingredients well and chill in refrigerator. Serve with hot potato chips. Makes about 1¼ cups.
Note: This keeps well in refrigerator.

HAM AND CHEESE BITES
Remove crusts from 6 slices of white bread. Slice thin 1 package (8 ounces) Mozzarella cheese. On each of 3 bread slices place cheese, a slice of boiled ham, and another layer of cheese. Cover with other 3 slices of bread. Fry gently in butter until golden on both sides. With a sharp knife, cut each sandwich into quarters. Serve hot. Makes 12.

SMITHFIELD HAM CANAPÉS
Make 24 small baking powder biscuits, or heat beaten biscuits from a package. Split biscuits and place bits of cooked Smithfield ham (about ¼ pound altogether), sliced paper-thin, between halves. Serve with a little bowl of Dijon mustard, so the guests may season the canapé if they like. Makes 24.

HAM TURNOVERS
1¼ cups ground cooked ham
1 teaspoon curry powder
1 teaspoon Worcestershire
  Dash of cayenne
  Mayonnaise (2 to 3 tablespoons)
1 box pastry mix
1 egg yolk
1 teaspoon cold water

Mix first 4 ingredients. Add enough mayonnaise to moisten. Roll prepared pastry mix to ⅛-inch thickness. Cut in 3-inch squares. Put about 1 tablespoon of the mixture in one corner of each square. Moisten edges with water and fold over to form a triangle. Crimp edges with fork, and cut 1 or 2 gashes in top to allow steam to escape. Put on baking sheet and brush with egg yolk beaten with 1 teaspoon water. Bake in preheated very hot oven (450°F.) for 15 minutes, or until golden brown. Serve hot. Makes 12 to 14.

HAM-AND-CHEESE APPETIZERS
1½ cups grated process American cheese
¼ cup evaporated milk
1 cup ground cooked ham
¼ cup ketchup
1 teaspoon powdered mustard
6 slices toast

Melt cheese in milk in top part of double boiler over boiling water. Add remaining ingredients, except toast; mix well. Trim crusts from toast; spread one side of slices with mixture. Cut into fingers and reheat in preheated moderate oven (350°F.). Makes 1½ dozen.

SOUP

HAM AND CORN POTATO SOUP
  Baked-ham bone
  Water
4 cups diced potatoes
1 onion, chopped
  About 2 cups (one 1-pound can) cream-style corn
2 cups milk
¼ cup minced parsley
  Salt and pepper to taste
4 slices of rye bread, cubed
¼ cup ham-fat drippings

Break bone at joints; cover and simmer in 6 cups water for 1½ hours. Remove bone and take off meat. Add meat, potatoes, and onion to broth. Cook until potatoes are tender. Add corn, milk, and parsley. Season. Heat. Serve with the bread cubes already browned in drippings. Make 4 large servings.

HAM-LIMA BEAN SOUP
1 box (1 pound) dried Lima beans
10 cups cold water
1 ham bone with scraps
1 onion, peeled and sliced
2 celery stalks, sliced
8 whole black peppercorns
2 carrots, peeled and cut in chunks
¼ teaspoon powdered mustard
1 bay leaf
1 leek, sliced (optional)
3 tablespoons butter or margarine
2 tablespoons all-purpose flour
1½ cups milk

Pick over and wash beans. Put in large kettle and add the water. Bring to boil and boil for 2 minutes. Cover and let

stand for 1 hour. Add next 8 ingredients Bring again to boil, cover and simmer for about 1½ hours. Remove bone and force mixture through sieve or food mill. Or whirl in blender until smooth. Melt butter and blend in flour. Add milk and cook, stirring, until thickened. Add to bean mixture with any ham scraps removed from bone. Heat. Makes 2½ quarts, or 6 to 8 servings.

HAM DUMPLINGS
1 cup ground lean cooked ham
¾ cup all-purpose flour
¼ teaspoon salt
1 teaspoon baking powder
¼ teaspoon each thyme and sage
  Dash of mace
⅓ cup milk
  Chicken broth or other stock or soup

Mix lightly all ingredients, except broth. Drop by teaspoonfuls into boiling broth. Cover and simmer for 10 minutes, or until dumplings are cooked. Makes about 16, or 4 servings.
Note: Try them in split pea soup if you have hearty eaters.

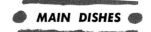

MAIN DISHES

HAM-STUFFED CHICKEN LEGS
8 raw chicken legs
8 cooked ham pieces, about 2 x 1 x 1 inches
2 eggs, slightly beaten
  Fine dry bread crumbs
  Melted butter or margarine

Remove bone from chicken pieces, keeping skin intact. With skin side down, pound chicken to flatten slightly. In center of each put a piece of cooked ham. Fold chicken over, pull skin to cover, and fasten with skewer or strong wooden toothpicks. Dip into eggs and roll in crumbs. Put in shallow baking dish and pour over each a little melted butter. Cover; bake in preheated slow oven (325°F.) for about 1¼ hours. Remove skewers. Serve plain or with gravy made from drippings in baking dish. Makes 4 servings.

BAKED HAM WITH SPICY SAUCE
1 cup orange or pineapple juice
¾ cup light brown sugar, packed
2 teaspoons powdered mustard
¼ teaspoon ground cloves
⅛ teaspoon nutmeg
½ teaspoon ginger
3 teaspoons rum extract
6–pound rolled, boneless fully cooked ham (or 5-pound canned ham)
  Whole cloves
½ cup raisins, plumped in boiling water
1 tablespoon fresh lemon juice
1 tablespoon arrowroot or cornstarch
1 tablespoon water

Mix first 6 ingredients and bring to boil. Simmer, stirring, until sugar is dissolved. Add 2 teaspoons rum extract. Pierce ham several times with fork and cover with marinade. Let stand for 4 hours, basting occasionally with marinade. Remove ham, put on rack in roasting pan and bake in preheated slow oven (325°F.) for 1 hour. Remove from oven and score with knife. Stud with cloves. Increase heat to 425°F. and bake for 30 minutes longer, basting frequently with marinade. Remove ham. Add drained raisins and lemon juice to pan drippings. Blend arrowroot and 1 tablespoon water and stir into mixture. Cook, stirring, until thickened. Add remaining 1 teaspoon rum extract. Serve sauce with ham. Makes 8 to 10 servings.

HAM IN CIDER
    ½ bone-in uncooked ham (about 6 pounds)
    2 large carrots, scraped and sliced
    3 medium onions, peeled and sliced
    3 stalks celery, diced
       Few parsley sprigs
   12 whole cloves
    6 whole black peppercorns
    1 bay leaf
       Cider (about 2 to 3 quarts)

Put ham in kettle and add remaining ingredients, except cider. Add enough cider to cover ham. Bring to boil, cover and simmer for 2 hours, or until tender. Serve hot, or let cool in the broth, remove and chill. Makes 8 servings.

GLAZED COLD HAM
Put ⅔ cup cold water in small bowl; sprinkle with 4 envelopes unflavored gelatin. Put 1 cup sugar in heavy skillet and cook, stirring constantly, until golden brown and syrupy. Remove from heat and very gradually stir in ¼ cup hot water. Then add 1 cup sugar mixed with ⅛ teaspoon ground cloves and 1 teaspoon powdered mustard. Stir and cook for 2 or 3 minutes longer, or until mixture is of the consistency of whipped cream. Remove from heat and add gelatin; stir until dissolved. Add ½ cup cold water; cool. Put scored ham on rack on a tray. Pour glaze over top and sides of ham, spreading evenly with spoon. Add remaining glaze for a second coat. Let ham stand until glaze is firm, about 15 minutes. Canned hams are especially attractive when glazed this way. Makes enough glaze for one 5-pound canned ham or an 8- to 10-pound cooked ham.

HAM-AND-BEAN BAKE
    ⅔ cup chopped baked-ham fat
    1 onion, chopped
    2 tablespoons ketchup
    1 tablespoon molasses
    1 teaspoon powdered mustard
    ½ teaspoon salt
    ⅛ teaspoon pepper
    1 teaspoon Worcestershire
    ¾ cup ground baked ham
       About 2¼ cups (one 1-pound, 4-ounce can) dried Lima beans
       About 2¼ cups (one 1-pound, 4-ounce can) red kidney beans

Fry ham fat until crisp. Pour off drippings. Add onion and cook slowly for 5 minutes. Add remaining ingredients. Pour into shallow baking dish. Bake in preheated moderate oven (350°F.) for 25 minutes, or until thoroughly heated. Makes 4 servings.

HAM BAKED IN CLARET
    1 center-cut fully cooked ham slice, 1 inch thick (about 2 pounds)
    1 teaspoon powdered mustard
    2 cups chopped peeled tart apples
    ½ cup firmly packed brown sugar
    1 cup claret

Put ham in large shallow baking dish. Sprinkle with mustard. Top with apples and sprinkle with brown sugar. Pour claret over ham. Cover; bake in preheated moderate oven (350°F.) for 1 hour. Uncover; bake for 30 minutes longer. Makes 4 servings.

SPICED HAM AND BANANAS
       Few whole cloves
    1 center-cut fully cooked ham slice (about 2 pounds)
       Prepared mustard
       Brown sugar
    ½ cup water
       Juice of 1 lemon
    2 or 3 firm ripe bananas

Insert cloves into fat of ham. Put ham in shallow baking dish and spread with mustard. Sprinkle with brown sugar. Add water and half of lemon juice. Bake in preheated slow oven (300°F.) for about 50 minutes. Peel bananas, cut into halves lengthwise, and arrange on ham. Sprinkle with brown sugar and remaining lemon juice. Bake for 10 to 15 minutes longer, basting bananas several times with the drippings in pan. Makes 4 servings.

STUFFED HAM SLICES
    2 center-cut fully cooked ham slices, 1 inch thick (about 3 pounds)
   24 whole cloves
    ½ pound fresh spinach
       Chopped tops from 1 bunch of green onions
    1 cup chopped celery leaves
    6 parsley sprigs, chopped
    1 teaspoon salt
    ¼ teaspoon pepper
       Dash of cayenne
       Dash of ground mace or nutmeg

Score edges of ham slices and insert 12 cloves into the fat of each. Mix remaining ingredients and use to stuff ham slices, sandwich fashion. Insert several skewers to hold slices together. Put on rack in shallow baking pan and bake in preheated slow oven (325°F.) for about 1½ hours. Makes 6 servings.

HAM AND BROCCOLI CASSEROLE
    1 box (11 ounces) frozen cut-up broccoli
    1 cup diced cooked ham
    1 cup (one 8-ounce can) midget potatoes, drained
    ¼ cup butter
   1¼ cups all-purpose flour
   2⅓ cups milk
    ¼ teaspoon seasoned pepper
    ½ teaspoon steak sauce
    2 teaspoons prepared mustard
    ¼ cup grated Cheddar cheese
       Seasoned salt
   1½ teaspoons baking powder
    ½ teaspoon salt
    2 tablespoons chopped parsley
   2½ tablespoons cooking oil

Cook broccoli until just tender; drain. Combine with ham and potatoes in shallow 1½-quart baking dish. Melt butter and blend in ¼ cup flour. Gradually add 2 cups milk and cook, stirring, until thickened. Add next 4 ingredients and seasoned salt to taste. Mix next 3 ingredients with remaining flour. Mix oil and remaining milk and stir into flour mixture with fork. Drop from tablespoon onto mixture in baking dish. Bake in preheated hot oven (425°F.) for 25 to 30 minutes. Makes 6 servings.

HAM AND GREEN-NOODLE CASSEROLE
    2 cups green noodles, cooked and drained
    1 cup dairy sour cream
    1 cup diced cooked ham
    ½ cup sliced ripe olives
    ½ cup chopped dry-toasted or dry-roasted peanuts
    1 can (3 ounces) chopped mushrooms, drained
    1 teaspoon prepared mustard
    ¼ teaspoon pepper
    1 can Cheddar cheese soup
    1 cup grated sharp Cheddar cheese

Mix well all ingredients, except cheese. Put in shallow 1½-quart baking dish. Sprinkle with cheese. Bake in preheated moderate oven (350°F.) for 25 minutes. Makes 6 servings.

HAM AND POTATOES AU GRATIN
   1½ cups diced cooked ham
    3 cups diced cooked potato
    4 tablespoons margarine
    1 small onion, minced
    3 tablespoons all-purpose flour
    2 cups milk
       Seasoned salt and pepper to taste
    ½ cup grated sharp Cheddar cheese
    2 tablespoons fine, dry bread crumbs

Put ham and potato into shallow 1½-quart baking dish. Melt 3 tablespoons margarine, add onion and cook until golden. Blend in flour. Gradually add milk and cook, stirring until thickened. Season with salt and pepper; pour over ham and potato. Sprinkle with cheese and crumbs. Dot with remaining margarine. Bake in preheated hot oven (400°F.) for about 20 minutes. Makes 4 servings.

BAKED CRANBERRY HAM CUBES
    4 cups diced cooked ham
    3 tablespoons butter or margarine
    ½ cup water
    ½ cup sugar
   1½ cups cranberries
    2 tablespoons grated orange rind
       Salt and pepper

Lightly brown ham in the butter. Bring water and sugar to boil, stirring until sugar is dissolved. Add ¾ cup of the cranberries and simmer, covered, for 15

minutes. Add orange rind and salt and pepper to taste. Mix ham and sauce in shallow 1½-quart baking dish. Bake, uncovered, in preheated moderate oven (350°F.) for 20 minutes. Add remaining cranberries and bake for 10 to 15 minutes longer. Makes 6 servings.

HAM AND SWEETS

    2 cups small slices of cooked ham
      About 2 cups (one 1-pound, 2-ounce
      can) sweet potatoes
    4 slices of canned pineapple
    8 whole cloves
    ½ cup pineapple juice
    2 tablespoons brown sugar
    ¼ teaspoon ground cinnamon
      Dash of ground nutmeg

Arrange ham slices and halved potatoes alternately in shallow casserole or large pie pan, standing ham upright when possible. Cut pineapple slices into halves and arrange on top of ham and potatoes. Insert cloves in ham; pour juice over top. Sprinkle with sugar and spices. Bake in preheated moderate oven (350°F.) for about 25 minutes. Makes 4 servings.

BAKED HAM-AND-PORK BALLS

    ¾ pound ground fully cooked ham
    ½ pound lean pork, ground
    ½ cup milk
    ½ cup cracker crumbs
    ¾ cup brown sugar, packed
    ½ cup vinegar
    ½ cup water
    6 whole cloves
    1 tablespoon powdered mustard

Mix first 4 ingredients and shape in 12 balls about 2 inches in diameter. Put in shallow baking dish. Bring remaining ingredients to boil and pour over ham balls. Bake, uncovered, in preheated slow oven (325°F.) for about 2 hours. Makes 4 servings.

HAM AND CABBAGE WITH TOMATOES

    ½ medium cabbage, shredded
    1 center-cut, uncooked ham slice,
      1 inch thick, cut in 4 serving pieces
    1 can (1 pound) tomatoes
    ½ teaspoon pepper
    ½ teaspoon monosodium glutamate
    1 teaspoon steak sauce
    1 teaspoon sugar

Put cabbage in shallow 1½-quart baking dish. Arrange ham pieces on top. Mix remaining ingredients and spread on ham. Bake uncovered, in preheated moderate oven (350°F.) for about 1 hour. Makes 4 servings.

Note: A fully cooked ham slice can be used in the recipe above. Reduce cooking time to 45 minutes.

CHICKEN IN HAM BLANKETS

    3 cups diced cooked potatoes
    3 tablespoons butter or margarine
    3 tablespoons all-purpose flour
    2 cups milk
    1 cup diced sharp Cheddar cheese
      Salt and pepper
    8 small slices of cooked chicken
    8 slices of boiled or baked ham
      Paprika

Baked Ham with Pineapple Glaze

Put ¾ cup potato in each of 4 flat individual baking dishes. Melt butter in saucepan; blend in flour. Gradually add milk and cook, stirring, until thickened. Add cheese and stir until cheese is melted. Season to taste with salt and pepper. Reserve about ½ cup sauce and pour remainder over potato. Put a slice of chicken at one side of each ham slice and fold ham over to form a triangle. Arrange two on each dish of potato. Top with remaining ½ cup sauce and sprinkle with paprika. Put in preheated hot oven (400°F.) for 10 minutes, or until thoroughly heated. Or broil under medium heat until lightly browned. Makes 4 servings.

HAM AND VEAL LOAF
    1½ pounds ground uncooked ham
    ½ pound ground raw veal
    2 eggs
      Dried bread rolled to make 1½ cups fine crumbs
    1 teaspoon celery salt
    ⅛ teaspoon pepper
    ¾ cup milk
      Creamy Horseradish Sauce (see page 859)

Mix all ingredients except Sauce. Shape into two rolls to fit into two greased No. 2½ cans (3½ cups each). Shake mixture; then press down lightly. Cover each can with foil or several layers of wax paper and tie securely. Put on rack in large kettle; surround with water half the depth of cans. Cover kettle and bring water to boil. Reduce heat and simmer for 3 hours. Turn hot or cooled loaves onto board and slice; cut slices into halves if preferred. Serve hot or cold with Creamy Horseradish Sauce. Makes 8 servings.

HAM CORN-BREAD RING WITH CREAMED PEAS
    ¾ cup yellow cornmeal
    1 cup all-purpose flour
    ¼ cup sugar
    2 teaspoons baking powder
    ½ teaspoon baking soda
    ¾ teaspoon salt
    1 cup dairy sour cream
    ¼ cup milk
    1 egg, beaten
    2 tablespoons margarine, melted
    1 cup ground cooked ham
      Creamed cooked peas

Mix all ingredients, except peas, just to blend. Pour into well-greased 6-cup ring mold, patting mixture down and leveling off top. Bake in preheated hot oven (425°F.) for about 20 minutes. Let stand for 2 or 3 minutes. Then turn out on hot serving plate. Fill center with hot peas. Makes 6 servings.

Note: Other creamed vegetables such as onions, asparagus, broccoli, or mixed vegetables can be substituted for the peas.

HAM BISCUIT ROLL WITH CHEESE SAUCE
    ¼ cup butter or margarine
    ¼ cup all-purpose flour
    2 cups milk
    1½ to 2 cups ground cooked ham
    1 tablespoon instant minced onion
      Salt, pepper, and powdered mustard
      Biscuit dough (recipe using 2 cups flour)
    ¾ cup grated Cheddar cheese

Melt butter and blend in flour. Gradually add milk and cook, stirring, until thickened. Mix ham, onion, ¼ teaspoon each salt and pepper, and ¼ teaspoon powdered mustard. Stir in enough of the first mixture to hold ingredients together. Roll out biscuit dough to form a rectangle about 12 x 10 inches. Spread with ham mixture. Roll up from 10-inch end as for jelly roll. Cut in 1-inch slices and put, cut side down, on greased cookie sheet. Bake in preheated very hot oven (450° F.) for 15 to 20 minutes. Add cheese to first mixture and heat, stirring, until cheese is melted. Season to taste with salt, pepper, and powdered mustard. Serve on ham biscuits. Makes 6 servings.

CURRIED HAM AND FRESH-PORK LOAF
    1 pound boiled ham ends
    1 pound fresh lean pork
    1 garlic clove, minced
    1 small onion, chopped
    3 teaspoons salt
    1 teaspoon pepper
    2 teaspoons curry powder
    1 to 2 teaspoons crumbled dried sage
    1 egg white
    ½ cup evaporated milk
    4 slices of bacon
    2 quarts boiling water
    ¼ cup vinegar

Force meats through food chopper twice, using medium blade. Add garlic, onion, 2 teaspoons salt, the pepper, curry powder, sage, egg white, and evaporated milk. Mix lightly but thoroughly, and shape into a rounded loaf about 9 inches long. Lay bacon out on a square of cheesecloth. Put meat loaf on bacon and roll up in cloth. Tie ends with cord. Put on trivet in large kettle. Add boiling water, vinegar, and remaining salt. Cover and simmer for 2½ hours. Remove from liquid and let stand until cold. Chill, unwrap, and cut in thin slices. Makes 6 to 8 servings.

ORANGE-GLAZED HAM LOAF
    1 pound uncooked ham
    1 pound ground veal
    2 eggs, beaten
    1 cup fresh orange juice
    ½ teaspoon salt
    ¼ teaspoon pepper
    1 cup fine, dry bread crumbs
      Orange Juice Glaze
      Orange slices

Mix lightly ham, veal, eggs, orange juice, salt, pepper, and bread crumbs. Shape in loaf and put in shallow baking pan. Bake in preheated moderate oven (350°

F.) for 1½ hours, basting frequently with half the Orange Juice Glaze. Ten minutes before ham loaf is done, top with orange slices. Serve with remaining Glaze. Makes 6 servings.

Orange Juice Glaze
Combine 3 tablespoons sugar and 1 tablespoon cornstarch in saucepan. Add 1½ cups fresh orange juice and cook, stirring, until slightly thickened.

GLAZED BANANA-HAM ROLLS
Cut 4 firm ripe bananas in half crosswise, then cut each half in 2 lengthwise pieces. Spread one cut side with peanut butter and cover with matching piece, sandwich fashion. Wrap each of the 8 pieces in a long, thin slice of cooked ham. Sauté rolls lightly in hot margarine until browned on both sides. Cover with a glaze of ¼ cup honey and ½ cup fresh orange juice, mixed together. Cook for a few minutes longer, basting with the glaze in the pan. Makes 4 servings.

HAM AND CORN FRITTERS
      About 1 cup (one 8½-ounce can) cream-style corn
    2 eggs
    ¾ cup diluted evaporated milk
    2 teaspoons baking powder
    2 cups all-purpose flour
    1 teaspoon salt
    ¼ pound boiled ham, diced
      Fat for deep frying

Mix all ingredients except fat. Drop by heaping tablespoonfuls into hot deep fat (365°F. on a frying thermometer) and fry until golden brown and done. Serve hot, with applesauce if desired. Makes 4 servings.

HAM CROQUETTES
    ¼ cup butter or margarine
    ¼ cup all-purpose flour
    1 small onion, minced
    1 cup milk
    2 eggs
    1 tablespoon fresh lemon juice
    1½ cups ground cooked ham
      Salt and pepper
      Fine dry bread crumbs
      Fat for deep frying

Melt butter; blend in flour and onion. Add milk and cook, stirring constantly, until very thick. Stir into 1 egg beaten with lemon juice. Add ham and salt and pepper to taste. Pour into a shallow dish; cool. Shape into 4 croquettes. Chill. Dip into crumbs, then into 1 egg beaten with 2 tablespoons water. Dip again into crumbs and let stand for 30 minutes. Fry in hot deep fat (390°F. on a frying thermometer) for 2 minutes, or until done. Serve with a Creamy Horseradish Sauce or Hot Mustard Sauce (page 859). Makes 4 servings.

HAM HAWAIIAN
    ¼ cup butter or margarine
    ½ medium green pepper, chopped
    2 cups slivered cooked ham

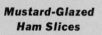

Mustard-Glazed Ham Slices

Glazed Cold Ham

About 4 slices (one 9-ounce can)
of pineapple
2 tablespoons brown sugar
1½ tablespoons cornstarch
1½ tablespoons vinegar
1½ teaspoons prepared mustard
⅛ teaspoon pepper
¾ cup cold water
1⅓ cups packaged precooked rice
⅛ teaspoon ground cloves

Melt half of butter in skillet. Add green pepper and ham; cook for 5 minutes. Drain pineapple, reserving liquid. Cut slices into bite-size pieces. Mix liquid and next 6 ingredients. Stir into ham mixture; cook, stirring, until thickened. Add pineapple; heat. Prepare rice as directed on the package; then add remaining butter and the cloves. Serve with the ham mixture. Makes 4 servings.

HAM À LA CRÈME

6 green onions, chopped fine
¼ cup butter or margarine
¼ cup all-purpose flour
¾ cup each of milk and light cream
2 tablespoons tomato purée
¼ cup white wine
Salt and pepper
8 thin slices of baked or boiled ham

In top part of double boiler over direct heat, cook onions in butter for 5 minutes. Blend in flour. Add milk and cream; cook, stirring, until thickened. Put over boiling water and stir in purée and wine. Add salt and pepper to taste. Cut ham into strips and put in shallow broiler-proof dish. Pour sauce over ham and put under broiler until lightly browned and bubbly. Makes 4 servings.

HAM-ASPARAGUS ROLLS WITH MACARONI AND CHEESE

8 slices boiled ham
16 to 24 spears cooked asparagus
2 tablespoons butter or margarine
1 quart milk
1 tablespoon instant minced onion
2 teaspoons seasoned salt
1 teaspoon powdered mustard
¼ teaspoon pepper
2 cups broken macaroni
2 cups grated Cheddar cheese

Roll each slice of ham around 2 or 3 spears of asparagus. Heat lightly in butter in skillet. Remove and keep warm. Pour milk into skillet, add onion, salt, mustard, and pepper. Bring to boil. Gradually add macaroni, keeping mixture boiling. Cook, uncovered, stirring often, for 20 minutes. Stir in cheese and top with ham rolls. Heat for a few minutes if necessary. Makes 4 servings.

HAM FRIED RICE

1 cup uncooked rice
2 eggs, slightly beaten
¼ cup cooking oil
¼ cup sliced green onions with tops
2 tablespoons soy sauce
½ teaspoon sugar
¼ teaspoon monosodium glutamate
1 cup diced cooked ham

Cook rice without salt until tender. Drain

and cool. Scramble eggs slightly in 1 tablespoon oil; set aside. Heat remaining 3 tablespoons oil in skillet. Add green onion and heat for 1 minute, stirring. Add rice and stir quickly to coat with oil. When heated, stir in remaining ingredients, including eggs. Serve with additional soy sauce, if desired. Makes 4 servings.

HAM KEDGEREE

⅔ cup uncooked rice
1 cup diced cooked ham
2 hard-cooked eggs, chopped
1 teaspoon curry powder
2 tablespoons minced parsley
¼ cup heavy cream (or enough to moisten)
Salt and pepper to taste

Cook and drain rice. Add remaining ingredients and heat, stirring gently. Makes 4 servings.

HAM HASH

4 medium potatoes, peeled and cooked
1 small onion
½ green pepper
1 cup diced cooked ham
¼ teaspoon salt
⅛ teaspoon pepper
Dash of dried thyme
3 tablespoons butter or margarine

Force first 4 ingredients through food chopper, using coarse blade. Stir in seasonings. Heat butter in skillet, add the hash and cook until well browned, stirring frequently. Makes 6 servings.

FRIZZLED HAM WITH PIQUANT SAUCE

In a little margarine in skillet, frizzle enough thinly sliced cooked ham for 4 servings. Put on hot platter. Take skillet off heat and add 3 tablespoons vinegar; 1½ teaspoons prepared mustard; ½ teaspoon sugar; ⅛ teaspoon paprika; and 1 tablespoon guava, currant, grape, or apple jelly. Heat, stirring, until blended. Pour over ham. Makes 4 servings.

BAKED HAM WITH CUMBERLAND SAUCE

Cut cold baked ham into thin slices, arrange on platter, and serve with Cumberland Sauce. To make sauce, mix in saucepan 1 teaspoon powdered mustard, 1 teaspoon paprika, ½ teaspoon ground ginger, a dash of salt, 1 tablespoon water, grated rind of 2 oranges, 2 tablespoons fresh orange juice, and 1 tablespoon fresh lemon juice. Let stand for 30 minutes. Add ¼ cup currant or apple jelly and heat, stirring, until jelly is dissolved. Cool and strain. Add 2 tablespoons port wine and quartered slices of ½ orange. Makes 4 servings.

HAM SALAD

2 cups diced cooked ham
½ cup chopped salted peanuts
1 cup diced celery
Mayonnaise
Salad greens

Mix first 3 ingredients. Moisten with mayonnaise. Serve on greens. Makes 4 servings.

BROILED HAM SALAD

2 cups finely diced cooked ham
1½ cups finely diced celery
¼ cup lightly seasoned French dressing
½ cup salad dressing or mayonnaise
⅓ cup dairy sour cream
¼ cup toasted slivered almonds
2 cups finely crushed potato chips
1 cup grated Cheddar cheese
Salad greens

Marinate ham and celery in French dressing in refrigerator for 1 hour. Add salad dressing and sour cream and mix lightly. Put in 9-inch metal pie pan or 4 individual broiler-proof ramekins. Chill until almost ready to serve. Sprinkle with almonds. Mix potato chips and cheese and press on top of mixture. Put under broiler for 2 or 3 minutes, or until cheese is melted. Tuck greens around edge and serve. Makes 4 servings.

MOLDED HAM SALAD

2 envelopes unflavored gelatin
½ cup water
1 cup pineapple juice
1 tablespoon fresh lemon juice
½ teaspoon salt
1 tablespoon prepared mustard
1 teaspoon sugar
½ teaspoon paprika
1½ cups mayonnaise
1 cup finely diced celery
1 cup finely diced cooked ham
Salad greens
Broiled Ham Salad or fruit salad, optional

Soften gelatin in water. Dissolve over hot water. Add fruit juices and seasonings. Beat in mayonnaise. Chill until slightly thickened. (If mayonnaise is cold, it will not be necessary to chill mixture.) Fold in celery and ham. Pour into 6-cup mold and chill until firm. Unmold on salad greens. If desired, fill center with ham salad, using recipe for Broiled Ham Salad and omitting potato chips and cheese, or fill with fruit salad. Makes 6 servings.

HAM FRUIT SALAD

1 cup diced cooked ham
½ cup diced peeled orange
½ cup diced unpeeled apple
¾ cup diced pineapple or tidbits
½ cup diced banana
Salad greens
Fruit Dressing

Mix lightly all ingredients, except last 2.

Serve on greens with the Fruit Dressing. Makes 4 to 6 servings.

Fruit Dressing

In heavy saucepan mix 2 teaspoons grated orange rind, 1 teaspoon grated lemon rind, juice of 1 orange and 1 lemon (there should be ½ cup; if not enough, add a little water), 1 beaten egg, dash of salt, and ½ cup sugar. Bring to boil, stirring. Cool; then chill. When ready to serve, fold in ¼ cup dairy sour cream.

HOT HAM-CHEESE ROLLS

    8 sandwich rolls
 1½ cups ground cooked ham
    1 cup shredded process American
       cheese
  ¼ cup chopped olives
  ½ cup minced celery
    1 tablespoon prepared mustard
    1 small onion, grated
  ⅛ teaspoon pepper
  ½ cup salad dressing
    1 teaspoon Worcestershire
       Melted butter or margarine

Cut a 1½-inch circle out of each roll so that the part beneath the crust is cone-shape; cut each top into halves. Scoop out some crumbs from each roll. Mix crumbs with remaining ingredients except butter. Fill rolls; replace tops. Brush with butter. Bake on ungreased cookie sheet in preheated slow oven (325°F.) for about 20 minutes. Makes 4 servings.

HAM SALAD BOATS

    2 cups chopped cooked ham
    1 cup diced celery
  ½ cup chopped green pepper
    1 onion slice, minced
    2 hard-cooked eggs, chopped
  ¼ cup chopped sweet pickle
    2 tablespoons prepared mustard
    8 frankfurter rolls
  ¾ cup mayonnaise

Mix all ingredients except last 2. Cut tops from rolls; remove centers. Crumble tops and centers coarsely and add to mixture. Add mayonnaise and mix well. Heap in rolls. Makes 4 servings.

WESTERN LONG BOYS

       French bread
       Butter or margarine
    1 small onion, chopped
  ⅓ cup chopped green pepper
    1 cup chopped cooked ham
    6 eggs, slightly beaten
  ½ cup milk
  ½ teaspoon salt
  ¼ teaspoon pepper
       Ketchup or chili sauce

Cut bread into four 6-inch lengths. Split, butter, and toast. Sauté onion, green pepper, and ham in 3 tablespoons butter in large skillet. Mix eggs, milk, salt, and pepper and pour into skillet. Scramble gently for 2 or 3 minutes, or until set. Top half of each Long Boy with egg mixture. Add top halves. Serve with ketchup. Makes 4.

HAM AND POTATO-SALAD SANDWICHES

Put a slice of baked or boiled ham and a layer of potato salad between slices of bread. Spread both sides of sandwiches with softened butter or margarine. Grill slowly until browned on both sides.

SAUCES FOR HAM
Spicy Cranberry Sauce

Crush 1¾ cups (one 1-pound can) cranberry jelly with fork and beat until smooth. Add ⅛ teaspoon each of ground cloves and cinnamon and 2 tablespoons port or Madeira.

Hot Mustard Sauce

Mix ¼ cup English-type or Dijon prepared mustard, 1 teaspoon powdered mustard, ¼ cup salad dressing or mayonnaise, and 2 tablespoons dairy sour cream.

Creamy Horseradish Sauce

  ½ cup heavy cream
  ½ teaspoon salt
       Dash of cayenne
  ½ teaspoon prepared mustard
    3 tablespoons mayonnaise
    2 to 4 tablespoons prepared
       horseradish

Whip cream until stiff. Stir in remaining ingredients. Serve on ham. Makes about 1 cup.

50 WAYS TO USE LEFTOVER HAM

HAM STRIPS

1. Creamed Potatoes—Combine in skillet 1 quart diced raw potatoes, 2 cups light cream, slivered ham (about 1½ cups), salt and pepper to taste, and dash of ground nutmeg. Simmer, covered, until potatoes are tender. Makes 4 generous servings.

2. Ham-Banana Salad—Combine ham with slivers of celery, bananas, and mustard-mayonnaise dressing for a delicious salad.

3. Ham-Bean Salad—Combine drained canned kidney beans with ham, chopped celery, chopped green pepper, pimiento, capers, salad dressing, and salt and pepper to taste.

4. Ham-Cheese Salad—Mix ham with strips of Swiss cheese and celery. Add wedges of tomatoes and toss with French dressing.

5. Rice—Combine ham with cooked rice, pineapple tidbits, and mayonnaise to taste.

6. Salads—Add ham strips to mixed-vegetable salad, potato salad, chicken salad, or macaroni salad.

7. Sauerkraut—Cook sauerkraut with 1 chopped onion and 1 chopped apple for about 30 minutes. Add ham and cook for 15 minutes longer.

8. Slaw—Mix ham with shredded raw carrots and cabbage; add mayonnaise, salt, pepper, and vinegar to taste.

9. Tomatoes—Combine ham strips with canned tomatoes and hominy. Simmer for about 30 minutes. Season to taste.

10. Tossed Salad—Combine ham with strips of cheese, canned peas, chopped celery, sliced cucumber, head lettuce broken into chunks, wedges of tomato, and French dressing.

HAM CHUNKS OR CUBES

11. Baked Beans—Add ham chunks to baked beans with a little sweet-pickle relish. Sprinkle with brown sugar and heat or bake.

12. Creamed Ham, Eggs, and Mushrooms—For 6 servings, combine 2 cans cream-of-mushroom soup and ¾ cup milk. Add about 1½ cups cubed ham, and heat. Add ½ pound lightly browned mushrooms and 6 quartered hard-cooked eggs; stir lightly. Heat gently. Serve on toast or in patty shells.

13. Curried Ham and Rice—Combine 1 can cream-of-chicken soup with 2 cups cooked rice and 1 cup cubed ham. Season with curry powder. Garnish with chunks and cubes. Makes 3 or 4 servings.

14. Ham-and-Egg Shortcake—Heat cream-of-mushroom soup with a little milk. Add ham and diced hard-cooked eggs; heat. Serve on shortcake made with prepared biscuit mix. Sprinkle with chopped parsley.

15. Ham Creole—Cook 1 chopped onion and 1 chopped green pepper in 2 tablespoons fat for a few minutes. Add 2 cups (one 1-pound can) tomatoes. Simmer for 10 minutes. Add 2 cups ham and cook for 5 minutes longer. Makes 4 servings.

16. Ham Macédoine—Mix 2 cups cooked mixed vegetables with 1 can condensed cream-of-chicken soup, undiluted, and 1½ cups ham chunks. Sprinkle with buttered bread crumbs; bake, uncovered, in preheated moderate oven (350°F.) for about 30 minutes. Makes 4 servings.

17. Ham Pie—Heat canned cream-of-mushroom soup with a little milk. Add ham and cooked peas. Top with mashed potatoes and sprinkle with grated Parmesan cheese. Bake in preheated hot oven (425°F.) until potatoes are brown. Sprinkle with chopped parsley.

18. Ham Succotash—Heat ham with cooked Lima beans and whole-kernel corn. Season with onion and salt and pepper.

19. Kabobs—Alternate chunks of ham with pineapple and green pepper. Sprinkle with brown sugar and broil until lightly browned and hot.

20. **Luncheon Salad**—Combine ham with chunks of hard-cooked eggs, celery, green pepper, mayonnaise, and salt and pepper. Serve on salad greens.

21. **Paprika Ham**—Mix 1 cup tomato sauce with 1 tablespoon prepared mustard, 1 teaspoon paprika, and 1 teaspoon instant minced onion. Add 1½ cups ham; simmer for 10 minutes. Stir in 1 cup dairy sour cream and heat slightly. Serve on noodles. Makes 4 servings.

22. **Rice Casserole**—Add 1 to 1½ cups ham to packaged Spanish rice with canned or cooked shrimps before cooking.

23. **Veal and Ham Stew**—Brown 1 pound stewing veal in 2 tablespoons butter or margarine. Add 1 can cream-of-mushroom soup and 1 cup water. Cover and simmer until tender. Add 1 cup ham, 2 sliced pimientos, and 8 chopped ripe olives. Simmer for about 10 minutes. Serve on noodles or rice. Makes 4 servings.

GROUND OR MINCED HAM

24. **Baked or Stuffed Potatoes**—Cut potatoes into halves; scoop from shell, mash, add ham, and season with salt and pepper. Pile in shell and brown in preheated hot oven (400°F.).

25. **Cabbage Rolls**—Cut core from medium head of cabbage. Cover with boiling water, removing leaves as they become tender. Stuff with 2 cups ham mixed with 2 cups cooked rice, salt, pepper, and onion salt. Add one 1-pound can of sauerkraut, 1 teaspoon caraway seeds, and 1 cup water. Cover and simmer for 1 hour. Makes 4 servings.

26. **Deviled Eggs**—Add ham to filling for deviled eggs; serve on toast with a hot cheese sauce.

27. **Egg-Salad Sandwich Filling**—Combine ham with chopped hard-cooked eggs, chopped olives, prepared mustard, and salad dressing to make a tempting sandwich filling.

28. **Ham and Pickle Sandwich Filling**—Combine ham with chopped sweet pickle, mayonnaise to moisten, and prepared mustard and pepper to taste.

29. **Ham-Broccoli-Noodle Casserole**—Combine 2 cups ham with 1 cup cooked chopped broccoli, 3 cups cooked noodles, and 1 can cream-of-mushroom soup, thinned with ½ cup milk. Sprinkle with shredded cheese and bake in preheated moderate oven (350°F.) for about 15 minutes.

30. **Ham Shirred Eggs**—Put 2 tablespoons ham in bottom of a custard cup and add 2 tablespoons heavy cream and 1 raw egg. Put on rack in skillet with 1 cup water. Cover and cook to desired doneness. Makes 1 serving.

31. **Ham-Stuffed Buns**—Combine minced ham with an equal amount of shredded cheese; moisten with mayonnaise; season with mustard and horseradish. Fill buns, wrap, and heat.

32. **Hash**—Combine ham with chopped cooked potatoes; season with onions and pepper. Fry in small amount of fat until lightly browned.

33. **Hot Ham and Cheese Sandwich**—Mix ham with shredded cheese, chopped olives, minced celery, and mayonnaise to moisten. Season with prepared mustard, pepper, Worcestershire, and onion to taste. Scoop out center from sandwich rolls. Fill with mixture. Bake in preheated slow oven (325°F.) for about 15 minutes.

34. **Pancakes**—Fill pancakes with ham and pour over them hot cream-of-mushroom soup, thinned with a little milk.

35. **Scrambled Eggs**—Mix 1 cup diced process cheese with ½ cup water and 1 cup ham. Bring to boil, stirring. Add 6 slightly beaten eggs and scramble. Add ham to scrambled eggs. Makes 3 or 4 servings.

36. **Sour-Cream Casserole**—Mix 1½ cups ham with 1 cup dairy sour cream, 2 cups cooked noodles, 2 beaten eggs, and chopped parsley. Bake in shallow dish in preheated moderate oven (350°F.) for about 20 minutes. Makes 4 servings.

37. **Stuffed Eggplant**—Parboil eggplant in boiling water for about 10 minutes. Split into halves lengthwise and scoop out pulp. Combine with cooked rice, ham, onion, and salt and pepper to taste. Line a casserole with eggplant shells. Add mixture. Sprinkle with grated Parmesan cheese and bread crumbs; dot with butter. Bake in preheated hot oven (400°F.) for about 30 minutes.

38. **Stuffed Mushrooms**—Chop and cook mushroom stems and a little chopped onion in fat for a few minutes. Combine with ham, bread crumbs, and salt and pepper to taste. Fill mushroom caps. Put in pan with a little water. Bake in preheated moderate oven (375°F.) for about 15 minutes, or until tender.

39. **Stuffed Onions**—Parboil large onions. Remove centers, chop, and mix with ham. Season with salt and pepper. Stuff onions and bake for about 15 minutes. Sprinkle with chopped parsley.

40. **Stuffed Peaches**—Fill canned peach halves with ham; sprinkle with bread crumbs. Bake in preheated moderate oven (375°F.) for about 20 minutes.

41. **Stuffed Peppers**—Combine ham with cooked rice to stuff peppers.

42. **Stuffing**—Add ham to stuffing for breast of veal.

43. **Sweet-Potato Bake**—Add ham to mashed sweet potatoes, sprinkle with brown sugar, and bake in preheated moderate oven (350°F.) until lightly browned.

44. **Waffles**—Add ham to waffle batter before baking.

HAM BONES, SCRAPS, AND FAT

45. **Black Beans and Rice**—Cover ham bones with 2 quarts water. Add 1 pound dried black beans; bring to boil and boil for 2 minutes. Cover and let stand for 1 hour. Cook 1 cup chopped onions, 1 chopped green pepper, and 1 minced garlic clove in ½ cup olive oil for about 5 minutes. Add to beans with 2 bay leaves. Bring to boil and simmer, covered, for 2 hours, or until beans are tender, adding more water if necessary. Add ¼ cup wine vinegar. Serve with rice, chopped hard-cooked eggs, sliced red onions, and chopped parsley. Makes 6 to 8 servings.

46. **Cracklings**—Use cracklings (see Ham Fat, below) in biscuits, corn bread, or muffins.

47. **Ham Fat**—Save scraps of fat from ham. Cut into small pieces and render until pieces of fat are brown and crisp (cracklings). Pour off fat. Use liquid fat for frying eggs or potatoes and for making pastry.

48. **Lentil Soup**—Use directions for Pea Soup (below) adding 2 cups canned tomatoes.

49. **Pea Soup**—Cover ham bones with 2 quarts water. Add 1 onion, 1 celery stalk, and 1 pound split green peas. Simmer, covered, for 2 hours, or until thick. Remove bone and cut off any bits of ham. Add to soup. Season with salt, add more water if necessary, and heat.

50. **Vegetable Dinner**—Cover ham bone with 2 quarts water. Simmer for about 1 hour. Add potatoes, carrots, onions; cook until almost tender. Add wedges of cabbage and cook until all is tender. Remove bone, cut off any bits of ham, and add.

By Helen Evans Brown

"Ham and eggs," says the American as he slides onto a stool at a quick lunch counter. "A grunt and two cackles," echoes the cook in the kitchen behind, and soon two amber-tinged slices of juicy pink ham and two perfectly fried eggs are set before the eager customer. Not far away, at a more exalted restaurant, a waiter discusses the *spécialités de maison:* "*Quiche Bourbonnaise,* perhaps, or *Wiener Eierkuchen?* Eggs Benedict? Very good, sir." And another dish of ham and eggs is polished off with relish.

In France, *soufflé de jambon* and *croque monsieur* are favorites. In China it's eggs fu yung, in Italy *spaghetti alla carbonara;* and so it is the whole world over. Ham weds happily with eggs, in dishes lowly or elegant, but nourishing and delicious every one.

Rule number one in any successful ham and egg dish is that the eggs must be so fresh that when they are broken the white clings closely to the yolk and doesn't run all over the pan. (True, very fresh eggs are hard to peel when cooked, but I have found that the electric egg cookers eliminate that difficulty. If that device is not included among your cooking equipment, make a tiny hole in the pointed end of the egg with a needle before putting it in the simmering water, and plunge the cooked eggs immediately into cold water. Crack the shells gently; peel from the large end.)

Rule number two pertains to the ham. Get a good one, an "old-fashioned" or "country-cured" one, if possible, or a good reliable brand. Or use Virginia-type ham (they're wonderful in North Carolina, too, and Arkansas, and probably many other southern states). Or use a Danish or Polish canned ham, or one of the famous hams of Europe such as Bayonne, Parma, Westphalia, prosciutto, York, or Alsace.

PHILLIP'S HAM AND EGGS

I was once advised by a gastronome, whose business took him around the countryside, that almost any American lunchroom could turn out a good dish of fried ham and eggs; therefore it was always the safest choice. The dish can be truly called gourmet fare if it is prepared with loving care. My husband does ham and eggs this way, and they never fail to make a hit. Allow 2 slices of ham about ¼ inch thick for each serving. Fry them gently in a little butter until they show a touch of golden color, but not until they are tough and dry. Remove them to a warm platter and keep hot. Allow 2 eggs to a serving, and for each egg add another teaspoon of butter to the fat in the pan. Break in the eggs; add 1 tablespoon of water, cover, and cook over very low heat until the eggs are done to your liking. Toward the end baste eggs with the pan juices, or turn if "over easy" is desired. Sprinkle the whites with salt and put on the platter with the ham. Add a little garnish of parsley and some nicely buttered toast.

FRIED EGGS À L'AMÉRICAINE

According to French chefs, this is the way we serve our fried eggs! Well, it's good. Fry eggs as above, place them on pieces of fried ham, sprinkle with French-fried parsley, and serve with tomato sauce.

HUEVOS CON TORTILLAS Y JAMON
(Ham and Eggs with Tortillas)

The Mexicans do ham and eggs this way for a goodly snack, with a glass of their excellent beer. Fry 6 tortillas in a little lard or shortening until crisp. Top each with a slice of ham. Mash 6 hard-boiled eggs with 2 canned peeled green chilies (or 2 teaspoons chili powder), a little salt, and enough tomato juice (or Mexican chili sauce) to moisten. Spread on the ham, put it in the oven for 1 to 2 minutes to heat, pour on a little more Mexican chili sauce, and serve with green olives.

■ **Another Version**—Scramble 6 eggs in 2 tablespoons butter with ¼ cup chopped ham and 2 chopped green chili peppers. Stir in 3 tablespoons heavy cream just as the eggs set. Divide the mixture among 6 fried tortillas. Makes 6 servings.

OEUFS COCOTTES AU JAMBON
(Eggs in Ramekins with Ham)

A favorite dish in France, not only at home but at the more elegant restaurants, are these little egg cocottes with ham. If you have no cocottes, small custard cups or ramekins do beautifully. Butter the cups well (allow 1 cocotte per serving); in the bottom of each put 1 tablespoon minced ham mixed with 1 teaspoon minced fresh parsley. Break 1 egg into each; sprinkle with salt and pepper and 1 tablespoon heavy cream. Put the cups in a pan of water, cover with a sheet of aluminum foil, and bake in preheated moderate oven (350°F.) for 10 minutes, or until the whites are set. This makes a nice dish for a ladies' luncheon. With it serve croissants; follow with a fresh strawberry salad.

EGGS PARMESAN

Butter a shallow baking dish well (a glass pie pan will do nicely) and break into it the required number of eggs. For each egg allow ½ ounce (2 tablespoons) slivered prosciutto or domestic ham, 2 teaspoons grated Parmesan cheese, and 2 teaspoons butter. Top eggs with ham, sprinkle with grated cheese, drizzle on the butter, and bake in preheated moderate oven (350°F.) until the whites are set.

■ **Another Version**—Put 2 cups cream sauce in the dish, sprinkle with ½ cup diced prosciutto, break 6 eggs onto this, sprinkle with 3 tablespoons grated Parmesan and 3 tablespoons melted butter, and bake as above. Either of these dishes, served with a simple green salad, makes an excellent lunch.

Note: This recipe uses prosciutto, but any other ham may be substituted.

TORTILLA CON JAMON
(Spanish Omelette with Ham)

Cook a small chopped onion in 3 tablespoons olive oil or butter until golden. Add ½ cup minced ham and ½ cup cooked peas and heat, mixing well. Beat 6 eggs slightly, season with pepper, pour over the hot vegetable mixture, and allow to set, shaking the pan so that it will not stick. When just set, but still moist on top, roll and slide onto a hot platter. Makes 4 servings.

■ **Another Version**—Fry small slices of ham and sliced potatoes until crisp, pouring the beaten eggs over them, and, when set on the bottom, turning by using a buttered plate. When both sides are cooked, slide onto a plate and cut into wedges.

HAM AND EGGS IN ASPIC

Here is another distinctive dish that is nice for lunch or to begin a summer dinner. There are two ways of preparing it, using poached eggs or eggs mollet (eggs cooked for 6 minutes in water just under the boil, then plunged into cold water and peeled).

For the first: Poach 6 very fresh eggs in water to which 1 tablespoon vinegar has been added. When set, lift with a slotted spatula and slide into cold water. In the meantime, cut fairly thin slices of ham into rounds and arrange on a flat pan. Trim eggs and place one carefully on each slice. Cool aspic until it is of the consistency of unbeaten egg white. Drizzle a little on each egg, and decorate with leaves of fresh tarragon, if available, or with tiny slivers of green pepper or pimiento. Chill for a few minutes, then pour the remaining aspic carefully around the eggs so that they are covered. Allow to set; then, using a round cutter (½ inch larger than the one used for the ham), cut each ham and egg from the aspic, lift with a spatula, and slide onto plates. Garnish with watercress.

For the second, with the eggs mollet: Pour ¼ inch of cooled aspic into cups, allow to set, decorate as above, top with the cooled egg, then with a slice of ham cut to fit the cup. Fill with aspic and allow to set before unmolding. To make the aspic, soften 1 envelope unflavored gelatin in ¼ cup water; dissolve in 1¼ cups (one 10½-ounce can) consommé that has been brought to the boil. Add 1 tablespoon Madeira or dry sherry, and use as above. Makes 6 servings.

HAM AND EGG SMØRREBRØD

Smørrebrød, those delectable open-faced sandwiches of the Danes, are never better than when made with ham and eggs. Here are two versions.

For the first *smørrebrød,* butter a whole slice of rye bread generously with sweet butter and cover with a good slice of Danish ham. Hard-scramble an egg, spread on a plate to cool, and cut into strips. Arrange 2 strips of egg on the sandwich, making three sections. Fill the middle one with chopped aspic and the two outer ones with sliced sautéed mushrooms. Garnish with a pickle slice. For the aspic, soften 1 teaspoon unflavored gelatin in 1 tablespoon cold water, and dissolve in 1¼ cups (one 10½-ounce can) consommé; add 1 teaspoon each of sherry and fresh lemon juice. Allow to set, then turn out and chop with a French knife.

For the second *smørrebrød,* cover half of a buttered slice of dark bread with chopped ham, the other half with chopped cooked chicken liver (or one half with sliced ham, the other with sliced liver pâté). Top with a medium-fried egg and garnish with a little fried onion. Serve while the egg is still hot.

QUICHE DE BOURBONNAISE
(Ham and Swiss-Cheese Pie)

Line a 9-inch pie pan with rich pastry, flute the edges prettily, and brush with slightly beaten egg white. Bake in preheated hot oven (450°F.) until the crust is set, but do not brown. Dice 6 ounces of cooked ham (1½ cups) and distribute on the bottom of the pastry shell. Sprinkle evenly with 1 cup grated Swiss cheese; then pour over a mixture of 1 cup scalded heavy cream, 2 beaten eggs, and 1 egg yolk; add grinding or two of black pepper, a little freshly grated nutmeg, and ¼ teaspoon salt. Bake in moderate oven (350°F.) until the mixture has set like a custard. Serve warm or cold, for lunch or supper, or for a wonderful picnic dsh. This, baked in a square pan and cut into squares, makes a delectable hors-d'oeuvre. Makes 6 servings.

HAM AND EGG PIE

Here's a simple dish that never fails to delight. Line a pie pan with pastry, sprinkle with slivers of cooked ham, break eggs on top, season with pepper and a very little salt (depending on the saltiness of your ham), and sprinkle with more ham slivers. Top with pastry and flute the edges; if you feel ambitious, decorate with pastry cutouts and glaze with slightly beaten egg. Bake in preheated hot oven (400°F.) until the crust is brown. Serve hot or cold. Makes about 4 servings.

HAM AND EGG TART

Here again we have a luncheon dish, or one that can begin a party dinner or make a family one. Line 12 small or 6 larger tart shells with pastry. Combine 1 cup minced cooked ham, 3 chopped hard-boiled eggs, 3 raw egg yolks, 1 cup heavy cream, and salt, pepper, and nutmeg to taste. Brush tart shells with egg white, allow to dry, and fill with the mixture. Bake in preheated moderate oven (375°F.) until nicely browned. Serve as is, or with a tomato or mushroom sauce.

ENGLISH HAM AND EGG CAKES

Chop 4 hard-cooked eggs, combine them with 1 cup chopped ham (¼ pound), ½ cup bread crumbs, 1 egg, 1 tablespoon minced parsley, and a little pepper. Taste; add salt if necessary. Form into flat cakes, dust lightly with flour, and sauté in butter or shortening until brown on both sides. Try these for breakfast with a broiled canned peach. Makes 4 servings.

CUSCINETTI FILANTI AL PROSCIUTTO
(Pillows with Italian Ham)

This is made in various ways, the one following being the simplest. Make sandwiches with sliced Mozzarella cheese and sliced prosciutto. For each 2 sandwiches allow ¼ cup milk, ¼ cup all-purpose flour, and 1 egg. Dip the sandwiches into the milk, then into the flour, and finally into the egg. Fry on both sides in olive oil; cut each sandwich into four triangles. Serve at once.

CROQUE MONSIEUR
(Fried Sandwich, French Style)

This glorified sandwich, well liked in France, is becoming popular in our own country. For each sandwich allow 2 slices of white bread, 1 slice of ham, and 1 of Swiss cheese, a little butter, 1 egg, and 1 tablespoon milk. Make a sandwich with the buttered bread, ham, and cheese. Beat the egg slightly with the milk; dip the sandwich into the mixture; turn so that all the egg is absorbed. Fry in butter or shortening until brown on both sides.

SPAGHETTI ALLA CARBONARA
(Spaghetti and Eggs on Ham)

A peasant recipe, this is made with the available foods in the more inaccessible parts of Italy. It is a delicious change from better known ways of preparing pasta.

    1 pound spaghetti
    1 garlic clove, crushed
    2 tablespoons olive oil
    2 cups diced ham (with some fat)
    4 eggs
    ¼ cup minced parsley (preferably Italian)
    ¾ cup grated Pecorino cheese

Cook spaghetti in salted water until just tender, not mushy. In the meantime, cook the garlic in the olive oil for 2 minutes; discard garlic. Add the ham to pan and cook until slightly crisp. Beat the eggs slightly, add the parsley and cheese, and mix with the well-drained spaghetti. Then pour over the very hot ham and the fat in the pan and mix well. If the mixture seems raw, cook over the burner for a minute or two, stirring well. Serve with more grated Pecorino cheese, if desired. Makes 6 servings.

HUEVOS ESCALFADOS FRITOS
(Poached Eggs and Ham, Fried)

Tricky to prepare, but worthwhile for anyone who likes to cook and eat. Poach 4 very fresh eggs in acidulated water, drain, and trim. (Don't let the eggs get too hard!) Make a thick white sauce with 3 tablespoons butter, ¼ cup all-purpose flour, and 1 cup milk. Add 1 tablespoon minced parsley and 1 cup ground ham. Add pepper and salt if needed and allow to cool. Dust each egg lightly with flour, then coat thickly with the ham mixture, using your hands. Dust again with flour; dip into egg that has been slightly beaten, then into crumbs. Allow to dry, then fry in deep fat (380°F. on a frying thermometer) until nicely browned. If these are properly done, they will be crisp outside, and the inside yolk still soft. One egg is sufficient for each serving, as it expands considerably. Makes 4 servings.

OEUFS SUR LE PLAT
À L'ANDALOUSE
(Andalusian Egg Platter)

For an individual serving, cook ½ cup shredded ham in 3 tablespoons butter, add ½ cup cooked peas, 2 diced pimientos, ½ cup diced fried potatoes (such as

Home-Fried Ham and Eggs

Spaghetti alla Carbonara ———————— *Eggs Carmen*

cut-up leftover French-fries), and a diced artichoke bottom. Heat all together; add ¼ cup tomato purée. Spread in a shallow ovenproof pan (a glass pie pan will do), make depressions in the mixture, and break egg into each. Pour ½ teaspoon butter over each; bake in preheated moderate oven (350°F.) until set.

HAM AND EGG PIROSHKI
(Little Russian Pies)
These little Russian pastries were originally served with soup, but they make delightful appetizers. Cook ½ cup chopped onions in 2 tablespoons butter until wilted. Add ½ cup chopped ham, 2 chopped hard-cooked eggs, 1 tablespoon chopped parsley, 1 teaspoon chopped dill or dillweed, and sour cream or stock to moisten. Roll pastry thin; cut into 2½- or 3-inch rounds. Put a spoonful of the

mixture in the middle of each, moisten edges, and pinch together firmly along the top, making little pointed canoe-shape pastries. Brush with beaten egg and bake in preheated hot oven (400°F.) until brown. Makes 24 piroshki.

PIZZA CON UOVA E PROSCIUTTO
(Ham and Egg Pizza)
Make hot-roll mix according to directions on the box. Divide dough into halves and roll each into a 10- to 12-inch circle. Put one on a cookie sheet generously brushed with garlic olive oil. Arrange halves of hard-boiled eggs on the dough, having rounded sides up. Sprinkle chopped prosciutto between the eggs, drizzle on a little more garlic-flavored olive oil, top with the other dough circle, and press edges together. Again paint with olive oil; bake in preheated hot oven (400°F.)

until brown. Makes 4 servings.

HAM AND EGG SALAD
For each head of romaine lettuce, heat ½ cup ham fat and in it cook ½ cup diced ham. Chop 3 hard-boiled eggs. Break lettuce into a bowl. Add eggs and 3 chopped green onions. To the ham and fat in the pan add 2 tablespoons wine vinegar and some pepper. When hot, pour over lettuce, mix thoroughly, and serve at once. Makes about 4 servings.

EGGS CARMEN
For each serving, put a slice of cooked ham on a lettuce leaf and spread with a mixture of 1 tablespoon each of shredded cooked carrots, shredded cooked beets, and shredded raw green pepper. Top with a cold poached egg; cover with a

dressing of half ketchup and half mayonnaise.

SWEDISH HAM CUSTARD

This is a favorite *smörgåsbord* dish. Mix 1½ cups diced cooked ham with 2 tablespoons all-purpose flour. Scald 3 cups milk, beat it gradually into 4 slightly beaten eggs, and add ¼ cup tomato ketchup and the ham. Pour into a greased 2-quart casserole and set in a pan of hot water. Bake in preheated moderate oven (350°F.) for 35 minutes, or until an inserted knife comes out clean. Makes 6 servings.

HAM TIMBALES

An old favorite with a new sauce. Cook ¾ cup milk and 1 cup bread crumbs together until they form a smooth paste. Add 1 cup chopped cooked ham, 2 egg yolks, and salt and pepper to taste. Beat 2 egg whites stiff and fold into the mixture. Fill custard cups two thirds full, put in a pan of hot water, cover with foil, and bake in preheated moderate oven (350°F.) until firm. Let rest for a moment before unmolding. Serve with a thin cream sauce (2 tablespoons each of flour and butter, 2 cups thin cream or rich milk) to which ¼ cup chopped ripe olives and 2 teaspoons chopped dill or dillweed have been added, along with salt and pepper. Makes 6 servings.

EGGS ZURLO

This classic dish may be made with leftover ham and leftover mashed potatoes. Chop the ham and add ½ cup of it (for each serving) along with 1 tablespoon chopped parsley and, if desired, 1 tablespoon chopped truffles, to 1 cup thin cream sauce. Make flat oval potato cakes with the mashed potato, dip into egg and crumbs, and fry brown on both sides. Top each cake with an egg mollet (eggs cooked for 6 minutes in water just under the boil, then plunged into cold water and peeled); pour sauce around them.

MOUSSE DE JAMBON
(Ham Mousse)

There are three kinds of mousses: the frozen, the hot, and the cold kind. This one is cold and mighty good eating. Soak 1 envelope unflavored gelatin in ¼ cup water. Heat ¾ cup milk. Beat milk into 3 egg yolks and cook over hot water until custardy. Add gelatin and stir until dissolved, then stir in 1 cup very finely ground ham. Cool. When almost set, fold in 3 egg whites, beaten stiff, ½ cup heavy cream, whipped, and ¼ cup mayonnaise. Taste; add salt if necessary. Pour into a mold and allow to set before unmolding. Makes about 6 servings.

HAM SOUFFLÉ

Cook together ¼ cup butter and ¼ cup all-purpose flour for 2 minutes. Add 1 cup milk and cook until thick; then stir in ¼ cup grated Cheddar cheese and 1 cup finely chopped ham. Beat 4 egg yolks until thick and combine with hot mixture. Taste for salt. Allow to cool; then beat 5 egg whites stiff and mix half of them thoroughly into the mixture. Fold in the remaining whites lightly, pour into a buttered soufflé dish, and bake in preheated moderate oven (350°F.) for 45 to 50 minutes. Serve with sautéed mushrooms or with parsley sauce. This is a white sauce made with part cream, a little prepared mustard, and a generous amount of freshly chopped parsley. Makes 4 to 6 servings.

HUEVOS EN TOLEDO
(Eggs in Toledo)

For each serving cook 1 cup minced ham and ¼ cup chopped mushrooms in 2 tablespoons olive oil. Add 1 cup hot cooked peas and spread on a platter. Top with fried eggs and garnish with stuffed green olives.

WIENER EIERKUCHEN
(Viennese Egg Cake)

Viennese, this, but more a casserole than a cake. Mix 2½ cups soft bread crumbs (about a fourth of 1-pound loaf) with 1½ cups milk, 6 well-beaten eggs, ½ cup chopped cooked ham, 1 tablespoon finely chopped onion, a little pepper, and salt to taste. Beat well together, pour into a greased casserole, and bake in preheated moderate oven (350°F.) for 45 minutes, or until set and nicely browned. Makes about 6 servings.

FRIED RICE WITH HAM

The Chinese add many different things to their fried rice, but none is better than when it's ham. Cook 1½ cups slivered ham in 2 tablespoons cooking oil for 3 minutes, along with 2 tablespoons chopped water chestnuts or mushrooms and 2 tablespoons chopped green onion. Stir in 3 cups cooked rice, brown lightly, then add 2 beaten eggs and 1 tablespoon soy sauce. Cook, stirring, until the eggs are cooked. Serve with more chopped green onion sprinkled on top. Makes about 4 servings.

EGGS FU YUNG

Combine ½ cup chopped water chestnuts, ¼ cup each of chopped green onions and chopped bamboo shoots (or celery), ½ cup bean sprouts, and ½ cup slivered cooked ham. Cook these for 2 minutes in 2 tablespoons cooking oil. Then combine with 6 slightly beaten eggs and salt or soy sauce to taste. Drop by the half-cupful onto a well-greased griddle, using a spatula to fold up the thin

part of the egg over the vegetables as soon as egg sets. When lightly brown on one side, turn and brown on the other. (Or make in one large cake, in a greased skillet, if preferred.) Serve with a sauce: Heat 1 cup chicken bouillon with 1 tablespoon soy sauce; cook until clear with 1½ tablespoons cornstarch dissolved in 2 tablespoons cold water. Makes about 6 servings.

VIENNESE HAM FLECKERL
(Ham and Noodle Casserole)

This recipe is a little complicated, but it's lots of fun to make and to eat. Make a noodle dough with 1 whole egg, 1 egg yolk, and ½ teaspoon salt, adding as much all-purpose flour as needed to make a stiff dough (about 1 cup). Knead until very smooth, then roll, but not too thin. Let dry slightly; then roll like a jelly roll and cut into ½-inch slices. Cut ribbons into ½-inch pieces, making squares. Allow to dry, then cook in boiling salted water for 5 minutes, or until tender. Drain thoroughly, then turn out on a clean cloth to drain some more. Sauté in ⅓ cup butter until lightly colored. Beat ¾ cup sour cream with 4 eggs; add 1 cup chopped ham and the noodles. Add salt if necessary, put in a buttered casserole, sprinkle with crumbs, and bake in preheated moderate oven (350°F.) for about 40 minutes, or until nicely browned. Makes 4 to 6 servings.

DEVONSHIRE FRIED EGGS

A strange combination, you may say, but try it for supper and change your mind. Fry slices of ham in butter, and in the same fat sauté fillets of sole, lightly dusted with flour. Then fry the eggs and serve all together on a sizzling hot platter.

QUICK HAM AND EGG DISHES

■ **Eggs Celestine**—Broiled ham on a toasted English muffin, with a poached egg on top. Cover with cheese sauce and brown under the broiler.

■ **Eggs à la Bayonne**—Fried eggs on a slice of fried ham, with a sauce made by combining equal parts of Béarnaise and tomato sauce.

■ **Eggs Italienne**—Broiled ham on a mound of rice or risotto, topped with an egg mollet, and covered with tomato sauce.

■ **Eggs Beauvilliers**—Put a fried egg on a slice of fried ham and cover with *sauce Madère* (Madeira sauce). To make the sauce, add 1 tablespoon butter, 1 teaspoon finely minced green onion, and a pinch of dried tarragon to the fat and juices in the skillet in which the ham was cooked. Stir in 1 tablespoon all-purpose flour. Gradually add ½ cup condensed consommé and ¼ cup dry Madeira wine and stir until sauce thickens.

POTTED HAM AND EGGS

You'll find this English dish is handy to spread on biscuits for tea or a snack. For each cup of finely ground leftover ham, chop 2 hard-cooked eggs equally fine and mix with 3 tablespoons soft butter and a dash of pepper or powdered mustard. Put in little pots or jars, cover tops with melted butter, and refrigerate until hungry time. Makes about 1⅓ cups.

HAM AND EGG BUTTER

This and the recipe above are kissin' kin. Mix 1 cup finely ground cooked ham with 3 sieved hard-cooked egg yolks, ½ cup butter, and 1 teaspoon paprika. Pound well together and serve on hot toasted crackers. Makes about 1½ cups.

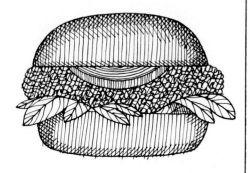

HAMBURGER—This term stands for ground beef prepared from the less tender cuts. After steak, hamburger is America's favorite meat, either in patties, or in meat loaves and countless other dishes.

The origin of the name hamburger for ground beef is open to speculation, although it was probably named for the German seaport of Hamburg. As one of the greatest ports in Europe, Hamburg had long engaged in trade with the Baltic provinces of Russia. The Balts of Estonia, Latvia, and Finland were fond of red meat, shredded with a dull knife and eaten raw. This dish, today a gourmet affair when made with fine steak, and called Beefsteak Tartare, may have pleased the Balts because of their origin, which connects them with the tribes of Tartary, or Mongolia, great riders, hunters, and meat-eaters all. After the people of Hamburg were introduced to this delightful novelty, their liking for it was great enough to immortalize the dish with their name. Or so the legend goes.

The reason for using ground meat, on the other hand, is not obscure at all: grinding tough cuts (and the meat of the past was infinitely tougher than ours) is a good way of tenderizing them. The ancient Egyptians ate ground meat, and

through the ages ground meat has been shaped into patties and eaten in all of Europe under different names; in France, it is called *bifteck*. Hamburger in a bun is a great American institution. It is said to have originated at the great St. Louis Exposition of 1904.

Hamburger, aside from being so popular a dish that the aroma of the meat sizzling on a grill should be captured like a perfume from home for American exiles abroad, has also become a symbol of modern, Americanized living. It is good; it is fast; it is inexpensive; it is easy to serve alone or in countless ways as a patty or in a ground-beef dish. Small wonder that hamburger stands have traveled from the United States to all parts of the globe.

Availability—Available in all stores selling meat, sold ready-ground by the pound or ground to order. It comes in various grades and prices determined by the cut of meat from which it is ground, and the amount of fat ground in with the meat. Also sold preshaped and frozen into hamburger patties. May be sold as a part of a ready-ground meat-loaf mixture which includes ground veal and pork.

Purchasing Guide—Price is determined by the amount of fat in the meat, which affects the degree to which the meat will shrink during cooking. The best all-round hamburger buy is ground chuck which has enough fat to make it juicy, but not enough to make it shrink excessively. Lean ground meat may be desirable when meat needs to be shaped and must be more compact; also good for low-calorie diets.

Meat should be a deep-red color with small flecks of white fat. Meat should be packaged in flat packages because a large round chunk of ground meat may spoil in the center since cold cannot penetrate the meat too quickly.

Have meat ground once for hamburgers and ground twice for meat loaf.

Storage—Wrap meat lightly and store in the coldest part of the refrigerator. When freezing meat, shape into patties or make into a large flat patty so that cold will penetrate meat quickly. Wrap well to keep air out and prevent meat from becoming gray and developing off-flavors. Place a double thickness of freezer paper or foil between each patty for easy separation.

☐ Refrigerator shelf, raw: 1 to 2 days
☐ Refrigerator shelf, cooked and covered: 3 to 4 days
☐ Refrigerator frozen-food compart-

ment, raw, prepared for freezing: 2 to 3 weeks
☐ Freezer, raw, prepared for freezing: 6 months to 1 year

Nutritive Food Values—Good source of protein and a variable source of fat, depending on the type of meat ground.

☐ Market ground, 3½ ounces, raw = 268 calories
☐ Ground lean, 3½ ounces, raw = 179 calories

Basic Preparation—Ground meat is generally shaped into a flat round patty and served in a round hamburger bun with relishes, ketchup, onion slices, etc. The patties may be broiled, panfried, or panbroiled. During cooking, they may be coated with slices of American cheese and broiled until cheese is melted. However, hamburger is very versatile and can be mixed and shaped to suit the need and occasion, and cooked with countless other ingredients to make a little meat go a long way.

☐ **To Broil**—Place meat on rack of broiler pan. Adjust rack and pan so that top of meat is approximately 2 inches below heat for a ¾-inch-thick patty. Broil about half of time indicated below. Season. Turn. Complete broiling; season and serve. For ground-beef patties, the time for total cooking is: rare 8 minutes, medium 12, and well done 14 minutes.

☐ **To Panfry**—Shape hamburgers, and cook in frying pan in a small amount of fat.

☐ **To Panbroil**—Preheat skillet. Do not add fat. When pan is very hot, put in meat; brown quickly on both sides. Do not cover pan. Reduce heat and cook slowly until done. If fat collects in pan, pour it off. Season meat before serving.

HAMBURGER COOK BOOK

A mealtime favorite of all families. From appetizers and soups to stews and casseroles, meat loaves and pizzas, the versatile hamburger is delicious, nutritious, and economical.

HAMBURGER PRINCESS

½ cup all-purpose flour
1 teaspoon sugar
  Salt
1 egg
¾ cup tomato juice
1 pound beef chuck, ground
  Butter or margarine (about 2 tablespoons)
6 slices of process American cheese

Mix flour, sugar, and ½ teaspoon salt. Beat egg with tomato juice and add to first mixture; beat until smooth. Mix meat and 1 teaspoon salt; shape into six 4-inch patties. Melt 1 teaspoon butter in 6-inch skillet. Pour in enough of tomato-juice mixture to cover pan thinly (one sixth of mixture). When done on bottom, turn and place a meat patty on cooked side. When underside is done, turn again. Sauté for about 4 minutes for medium to well done. Lift onto cookie sheet and roll up with meat on inside and edges underneath. Repeat until 6 rolls are made. Top each with a slice of cheese and put under broiler until cheese is just melted. (Loose beef can be browned, then rolled up in cooked pancakes.) Makes 6 servings.

HAMBURGER GUACAMOLE

1 pound beef chuck, ground
1 avocado
1 tomato, chopped
1 medium onion, chopped
¼ teaspoon hot pepper sauce
1 tablespoon fresh lemon juice
4 slices of toast

Shape meat into 4 good-size patties. Cook to desired doneness. Mash avocado and add next four ingredients. Put meat on toasted rounds of bread. Spoon some of mixture over each. Put under broiler or heat in oven for a few minutes. Serve with remaining sauce. Makes 4 servings.

HAMBURGER STEW

1 pound ground beef
1 tablespoon butter
1 onion, sliced
1½ teaspoons salt
¼ teaspoon pepper
1 tablespoon steak sauce
2⅓ cups (one 1-pound, 3-ounce can) tomatoes
3 medium potatoes, peeled and sliced
3 medium carrots, sliced
2 celery stalks, diced
  Split hot biscuits (optional)

Brown beef lightly in the butter, stirring with fork to break up meat. Add onion and cook for a few minutes longer. Add remaining ingredients except biscuits. Bring to boil and simmer, covered, for 30 minutes, or until vegetables are tender. Serve on biscuits if desired. Makes 4 to 6 servings.

LEMON PIE-PAN STEAK

1½ pounds beef chuck, ground
1 onion, sliced
6 lemon slices
1 cup ketchup
1 tablespoon Worcestershire
¼ cup water

Pat beef into deep 9- or 10-inch pie pan. Top with onion and lemon slices. Mix ketchup with remaining ingredients and pour over top of meat. Bake in preheated hot oven (400°F.) for about 30 minutes. Pour off some of the fat. Cut pie into wedges. Makes 4 to 6 servings.

SALISBURY STEAK WITH MUSHROOM SAUCE

1 pound beef chuck, ground
1 teaspoon salt
¼ teaspoon pepper
1 can (4 ounces) chopped mushrooms, drained
2 tablespoons butter or margarine
2 tablespoons flour
1 teaspoon curry powder
1 cup water
1 beef bouillon cube

Mix meat, salt, and pepper and shape into 4 patties. Panfry in lightly greased skillet until of desired doneness. Remove from skillet and keep hot. Cook mushrooms in butter for 2 or 3 minutes. Blend in flour and curry powder. Add water and bouillon cube; cook until smooth and thickened. Pour over meat patties and serve. Makes 4 servings.

SMOTHERED HAMBURGER STEAKS AND ONIONS

1 pound beef round or chuck, ground
½ cup water
1 teaspoon salt
¼ teaspoon pepper
¼ cup fine dry bread crumbs
4 medium onions, sliced
1 can (10¾ ounces) beef gravy

Mix first 5 ingredients. Shape into 4 large patties. Brown on one side, turn, add onion, and brown lightly. Add gravy, cover, and simmer for about 35 minutes. Makes 4 servings.

SWEET-AND-SOUR HAMBURGERS

1 pound ground beef
½ pound pork-sausage meat
1 teaspoon salt
⅛ teaspoon pepper
1 large onion, sliced
2 tablespoons soy sauce
½ cup water
¼ cup vinegar
⅓ cup firmly packed brown sugar

Mix first 4 ingredients and shape into 6 large patties. Brown on both sides in skillet. Add onion. Mix remaining ingredients and pour over patties. Cover, bring to boil, and simmer for 15 minutes. Makes 6 servings.

HAWAIIAN HAMBURGERS

1 pound beef round or chuck, ground
1 medium onion, minced
1 garlic clove, minced
½ cup soy sauce
¼ teaspoon ground ginger
  Sliced pineapple

Mix beef and onion and shape into 8 patties. Put in shallow dish. Mix next 4 ingredients and pour over patties. Let stand for 30 minutes, turning once. Drain; broil or panfry. Serve with sliced pineapple. Makes 4 servings.

PIZZA-BURGERS

1½ pounds chuck, ground
  Canned pizza sauce
  Sliced Muenster cheese
  Oregano
  Onion salt
  Anchovy fillets
  Grated Parmesan

Shape meat into 8 patties. Handle lightly; do not season. Panbroil slightly less done than desired and put on ovenproof platter. Pour a little pizza sauce over each, top with Muenster cheese, and sprinkle lightly with oregano and onion salt. Crisscross with anchovy fillets and sprinkle with grated Parmesan. Put in preheated moderate oven (375°F.) for 10 minutes. Or put under broiler until thoroughly heated. Makes 4 servings.

PEPPER-RING BURGERS

1 pound beef chuck, ground
¾ cup soft bread crumbs
1 teaspoon salt
⅛ teaspoon pepper
¼ cup milk
6 green-pepper rings, 2½ inches across, ½ inch thick
1 tablespoon fat
  Bottled barbecue sauce
6 split sandwich rolls, heated

Mix first 5 ingredients and shape into 6 patties. Press mixture into pepper rings, having meat cover cut edge of pepper on both sides. Brown patties on both sides in hot fat in skillet. Baste with sauce so both sides are covered. Cook to desired doneness and serve in rolls. Makes 6 servings.

HAMBURGERS, POLISH STYLE

1 onion, peeled
1 carrot, peeled
1 celery stalk
1 medium potato, peeled
  Few parsley sprigs
¾ pound beef chuck, ground
2 slices of bread, crumbled
1 egg
1½ teaspoons seasoned salt
¼ teaspoon seasoned pepper
2 tablespoons butter or margarine
1 cup dairy sour cream
⅔ cup canned French-fried onion rings

Force first 5 ingredients through medium blade of food chopper. Add to next 5 ingredients and mix lightly but thoroughly. Shape into 8 patties and brown on both sides in butter. Remove from skillet and blend sour cream into drippings. Put patties back in skillet. Cover and simmer for about 20 minutes. Top with onion rings. Makes 4 servings.

SAUERBRATEN HAMBURGERS

1½ pounds beef chuck, ground
1 tablespoon instant minced onion
1 egg
1½ teaspoons salt
¼ cup fine dry bread crumbs
⅓ cup milk
½ teaspoon grated lemon rind
1 tablespoon butter or margarine
1 can (10¾ ounces) beef gravy
2 tablespoons wine vinegar
½ teaspoon ground ginger
¼ cup firmly packed brown sugar
Dash of ground cloves
1 bay leaf

Mix first 7 ingredients lightly and shape in 6 large patties. Brown on both sides in butter in skillet. Remove patties and pour off fat. Mix remaining ingredients in skillet and bring to boil. Add patties, cover, and simmer for 30 minutes, turning once or twice and basting with the sauce. Makes 6 servings.

STUFFED HAMBURGER PATTIES

1 pound beef chuck, ground
1 medium onion, minced
1 teaspoon salt
¼ teaspoon pepper
1⅓ cups soft bread crumbs
¼ teaspoon poultry seasoning
¼ teaspoon seasoned salt
¼ cup margarine, melted
2 tablespoons fresh lemon juice

Mix beef, onion, salt, and ⅛ teaspoon pepper. Divide into 8 equal parts. With rolling pin flatten each between pieces of wax paper until about 5 inches in diameter. Leave on paper. Mix ⅛ teaspoon pepper and remaining ingredients. Spread on 4 patties and top with remaining 4 patties. Crimp edges with a fork. Remove from paper; broil until of desired doneness, turning once. Makes 4 servings.

PAPRIKA HAMBURGERS

1½ pounds beef chuck, ground
1 egg
1½ teaspoons salt
¼ teaspoon pepper
¼ cup fine dry bread crumbs
⅓ cup milk
¼ cup minced onion
1 tablespoon butter or margarine
1 teaspoon flour
½ cup vegetable-juice cocktail
1 tablespoon paprika
½ teaspoon steak sauce

1 can (10½ ounces) cream-of-vegetable soup
½ cup dairy sour cream
Hot cooked noodles (optional)

Mix lightly first 6 ingredients and 2 tablespoons onion. Shape into 8 patties. Brown on both sides in butter in skillet. Remove patties and pour off all but 1 teaspoon fat. Blend flour into fat in skillet. Add remaining onion, vegetable-juice cocktail, paprika, and steak sauce. Bring to boil and put patties back in skillet. Cover; simmer for 15 to 20 minutes. Remove patties and keep warm. Blend soup and sour cream into mixture in skillet and heat, stirring. Add patties and serve in skillet with noodles. (If preferred, put patties on a hot platter and pour sauce over the top.) Makes 4 servings.

BACON NUTBURGERS

6 slices of bacon
1½ pounds beef chuck, ground
1½ teaspoons salt
⅛ teaspoon pepper
6 tablespoons chopped nuts
3 tablespoons chopped parsley
2 tablespoons grated onion

Cook bacon until crisp; drain. Mix beef, salt, and pepper; divide into 12 equal portions and roll with rolling pin between 2 sheets of wax paper to form thin patties about 5 inches in diameter. Mix last 3 ingredients and spread on 6 patties. Top each with a bacon slice. Cover with remaining 6 patties and pinch edges together. Broil to desired doneness, turning once. Makes 6 servings.

BEEF CHEESEBURGERS DE LUXE

1½ pounds beef chuck, ground
2 cups shredded sharp Cheddar cheese
3 tablespoons grated onion
1½ tablespoons steak sauce
Pepper to taste
8 slices of bacon, partially cooked
Hot buttered French-bread slices
¼ cup soft butter or margarine
2 tablespoons minced stuffed olives

Mix first 5 ingredients and shape into 8 patties. Wrap a slice of bacon around each and secure with a wooden pick. Sauté for about 5 minutes on each side; serve on French bread. Mix butter and olives and top each patty with a dab of the mixture. Makes 8 servings.

HAMBURGERS WITH SHERRY-CHEESE SAUCE

½ pound process cheese, shredded
¼ cup milk
¼ cup sherry
1 pound beef round or chuck, ground
1 teaspoon salt
¼ teaspoon pepper
¼ cup sweet-pickle relish
4 slices of toast

Melt cheese in top part of double boiler over boiling water. Stir in milk and sherry; keep hot. Mix meat, salt, pepper, and relish; shape into 4 patties. Broil or panfry to desired doneness. Put on toast; top with cheese sauce. Makes 4 servings.

CHEESE-NUT BURGERS

Mix lightly 1 pound ground beef chuck, ¼ cup wheat germ, ¾ cup finely diced sharp Cheddar cheese, ½ teaspoon instant meat tenderizer, ½ cup chopped cashews or other nuts, and ¼ cup water. Shape into 4 to 6 thick patties and broil until of desired doneness. Makes 4 to 6 servings.

TENNESSEE HAMBURGER

1 pound beef round or chuck, ground
1 teaspoon salt
⅛ teaspoon pepper
1 garlic clove, minced
¼ cup prepared mustard
2 cups thinly sliced onions

Mix beef, salt, pepper, and garlic; shape into 2 large thin patties. Put one in a metal pie pan or layer-cake pan. Spread with mustard and cover with onions. Put second patty on top. Put under broiler until top browns lightly; turn and brown the other side of the double patty. Cover pan; bake in preheated moderate oven (350°F.) for about 50 minutes. Makes 4 servings.

BURGUNDY MEATBALLS WITH RAISIN SAUCE

1½ pounds beef chuck, ground
1 egg
1½ teaspoons salt
Dash of pepper
¼ cup fine dry bread crumbs
⅓ cup milk
2 tablespoons instant minced onion
1 tablespoon butter
1½ tablespoons flour
¼ teaspoon garlic powder
1 cup condensed beef bouillon or consommé
2 tablespoons tomato paste
½ cup seedless raisins
¼ cup dry red wine
Salt and pepper

Mix lightly first 6 ingredients and 1 tablespoon onion. Shape into 18 balls and brown on all sides in butter in skillet. Remove meatballs. Blend flour and garlic powder into drippings in skillet. Add remaining onion, next 3 ingredients, and meatballs. Cover and simmer for 10 minutes. Remove meatballs to a hot serving dish. Stir wine into sauce in skillet and season to taste. Pour over meatballs. Makes 4 to 6 servings.

MEATBALLS IN CURRIED TOMATO SAUCE

About 3½ cups (one 1-pound, 12-ounce can) tomatoes
¾ cup soft bread crumbs
1½ pounds ground beef
1 small onion, minced
1½ teaspoons seasoned salt
½ teaspoon salt
Pepper
3 tablespoons all-purpose flour
2 tablespoons margarine or other fat
½ teaspoon sugar
1 teaspoon curry powder
½ teaspoon monosodium glutamate
Hot cooked rice

Drain ½ cup juice from tomatoes and mix with bread. Add meat, onion, 1 teaspoon seasoned salt, the salt, and ⅛ teaspoon pepper. Mix lightly and shape into 24 balls. Dredge with the flour and brown on all sides in hot margarine. Remove meatballs and pour off fat. To skillet add remaining tomatoes and seasoned salt, ⅛ teaspoon pepper, the sugar, curry powder, monosodium glutamate, and meatballs. Bring to boil, cover, and simmer for 15 to 20 minutes, stirring occasionally. Serve hot with rice. Makes 6 servings.

CHILI MEATBALLS

1 pound ground beef
½ cup uncooked rice
1 small onion, chopped
1 teaspoon salt
¼ teaspoon pepper
2 tablespoons butter or margarine
2 cans (8 ounces each) tomato sauce or 1 can (15 ounces)
1 cup water
1 teaspoon chili powder
½ teaspoon ground cuminseed

Mix first 5 ingredients. Shape into 16 to 20 balls. Brown lightly on all sides in hot butter. Add remaining ingredients, bring to boil, cover, and simmer for about 45 minutes. Makes 4 servings.

KÖNIGSBERGER MEATBALLS

1 roll or 1 slice of firm bread
¾ pound beef chuck, ground
¼ pound ground pork
2 medium potatoes, cooked and mashed
2 anchovies, chopped
1 egg
About ½ cup all-purpose flour
Salt and pepper
Water
3 tablespoons butter
1 beef bouillon cube
1 tablespoon capers
Juice of ½ lemon

Moisten roll or bread with water and squeeze dry. Mix very thoroughly with meats, potatoes, anchovies, egg, 3 tablespoons flour, 1 teaspoon salt, and ⅛ teaspoon pepper. Shape into 16 balls, dredge with flour, and drop into simmering salted

water. Cover and simmer for about 15 minutes. Melt butter and blend in 2 tablespoons flour. Add 1 cup water and bouillon cube; cook, stirring, until thickened. Add capers, lemon juice, and pepper to taste. Add cooked meatballs and simmer for a few minutes. Makes 4 servings.

MEATBALLS WITH ALMOND-MUSHROOM NOODLES

1 can (10½ ounces) condensed tomato soup
1 cup dairy sour cream
1 pound beef chuck, ground
2 parsley sprigs, chopped
1 teaspoon salt
⅛ teaspoon pepper
⅓ cup fine dry bread crumbs
1 egg
3 tablespoons butter or margarine
1 medium onion, minced
1 garlic clove, minced
1 bay leaf
1 teaspoon fresh lemon juice
1 teaspoon paprika
2 cups wide noodles
¼ cup almonds, slivered
1 can (4 ounces) sliced mushrooms, drained

Mix soup and sour cream. Add ¼ cup of this mixture to beef, parsley, salt, pepper, crumbs, and egg; mix well. Shape into 16 small balls. Cook in 1 tablespoon butter until well browned. Remove meatballs. Cook onion and garlic in fat remaining in skillet until lightly browned. Drain off any remaining fat. Add meatballs, remaining soup mixture, bay leaf, lemon juice, and paprika. Bring to boil, cover, and simmer for 20 minutes. Uncover and cook for 10 minutes longer. Cook and drain noodles. Sauté almonds and mushrooms slowly in 2 tablespoons butter until almonds are golden brown, stirring frequently. Mix with noodles and arrange in a border on hot platter. Put meatballs and sauce in center. Makes 4 servings.

PEANUT HAMBURGER BALLS

¾ pound beef chuck, ground
¾ cup crunchy peanut butter
1 onion, minced
3 tablespoons chili sauce
1¼ teaspoons salt
⅛ teaspoon pepper
1 egg, beaten
2 tablespoons fat
2 cans (8 ounces each) tomato sauce

Mix first 7 ingredients and shape into 12 balls. Brown on all sides in hot fat. Remove meat and pour off fat. Put meat back in skillet with tomato sauce. Cover and simmer for about 30 minutes. Makes 4 servings.

BEEF, CARROT, AND OLIVE LOAF

2 pounds beef chuck, ground
1½ cups corn flakes

½ cup chopped parsley
½ cup shredded raw carrot
1 can (4½ ounces) chopped ripe olives
1 medium onion, chopped
2 garlic cloves, minced
2 tablespoons butter or margarine
2 teaspoons salt
½ teaspoon pepper
½ teaspoon each of ground sage and oregano
1½ cups milk
1 egg

Mix first 5 ingredients. Cook onion and garlic in the butter and add to first mixture with remaining ingredients. Mix well. Shape into a loaf in a baking pan. Bake in preheated moderate oven (350°F.) for about 1 hour. Makes 8 servings.

BEEF LOAF, FARMER STYLE

2 medium potatoes, peeled
1 large onion, peeled
1 small apple, peeled
2 canned pimientos
1¼ pounds beef chuck, ground
½ pound sausage meat
1¼ teaspoons salt
⅛ teaspoon pepper
⅔ cup undiluted evaporated milk

Force first 4 ingredients through medium blade of food chopper. Do not drain. Add remaining ingredients and mix thoroughly. Pack in loaf pan (9 x 5 x 3 inches) and cover top with a buttered piece of foil. Bake in preheated moderate oven (350°F.) for about 1¾ hours. Remove foil 15 minutes before loaf is done. Makes 6 servings.

BEEF-AND-TOMATO LOAF

2 pounds ground beef
⅓ cup milk
1¼ cups soft bread crumbs
1 medium onion, chopped
¼ cup chopped green pepper
2 teaspoons salt
¼ teaspoon pepper
1 teaspoon monosodium glutamate
1 tablespoon each of prepared horseradish and Worcestershire
2 eggs, beaten
3 firm tomatoes, peeled and cut into 1-inch pieces

Mix all ingredients except tomatoes lightly but thoroughly. Gently stir in tomatoes. Pack in loaf pan (9 x 5 x 3 inches). Bake in slow oven (300°F.) for about 1½ hours. Let stand for 10 minutes. Drain off liquid and turn loaf out on a hot platter. Makes 8 servings.

ORANGE-GLAZED MEAT LOAVES

6 tablespoons brown sugar
½ teaspoon powdered mustard
6 slices of small orange, unpeeled
1½ pounds beef, round or chuck, ground
2 cups soft bread crumbs
1 egg
1 medium onion, minced
1 medium green pepper, minced
¼ teaspoon pepper

Paprika Hamburgers

1 teaspoon salt
½ cup fresh orange juice
   Juice of 1 lemon

Put 1 tablespoon brown sugar in each of 6 greased small baking dishes. Sprinkle with mustard; put an orange slice in each dish. Mix remaining ingredients well. Press into baking dishes. Bake in preheated moderate oven (350°F.) for about 1 hour. Let stand for a few minutes before turning upside down on heated platter. Makes 4 to 6 servings.

CANADIAN HAMBURGER PIE
1 package (10 ounces) pastry mix
½ cup grated sharp Cheddar cheese
½ teaspoon paprika
   Dash of cayenne
1½ pounds beef chuck, ground
1 small onion, minced
1½ cups dry bread cubes
1 can (10½ ounces) beef bouillon or consommé
½ teaspoon salt
½ teaspoon pepper
¼ teaspoon each of ground thyme and marjoram
2 teaspoons Worcestershire

Prepare pastry mix as directed on the label, adding cheese, paprika, and cayenne before adding the liquid. Roll half of pastry on lightly floured board; fit into 9-inch pie pan. Cook beef and onion in skillet until meat loses its red color, breaking up meat with fork. Mix bread cubes and bouillon and let stand for a few minutes. Add beef mixture and remaining ingredients. Mix well and pour into pastry-lined pan. Roll remaining pastry and put over top, crimping edges. Bake in preheated moderate oven (375°F.) for about 45 minutes. Serve warm or cold. Makes 6 servings.

MEATBALL SHEPHERD'S PIE
1 pound ground beef
1 egg
2 cups soft bread crumbs
   Salt and pepper
3 tablespoons butter or margarine
1 large onion, minced
1 tablespoon flour
1 can (3 ounces) mushrooms, undrained
2 cups (one 1-pound can) tomatoes
1 package (10 ounces) frozen peas and carrots, thawed
⅛ teaspoon ground oregano
1 package (14 ounces) frozen whipped potatoes, thawed

Mix beef, egg, crumbs, 1 teaspoon salt, and ⅛ teaspoon pepper. Shape into 12 large balls. Brown on all sides in 2 tablespoons butter in Dutch oven or large skillet. Remove meatballs and brown onion in drippings remaining in pan. Blend in flour; add mushrooms and to-

matoes. Add meatballs and bring to boil. Cover and simmer for 30 minutes. Add peas and carrots and bring to boil. Add oregano, and season to taste. Pour into shallow 2-quart baking dish. Melt remaining butter in small saucepan, add potatoes, and heat. Spread on top of meat mixture. Put under broiler until lightly browned. Makes 4 to 6 servings.

HAMBURGER AND KIDNEY PIE
1 beef kidney
1 tablespoon fat
2 cups boiling water
1 pound beef chuck, ground
1 medium onion, chopped
2 tablespoons flour
¼ cup cold water
1½ teaspoons salt
¼ teaspoon pepper
1 teaspoon steak sauce
   Rich pastry (made with 1½ cups flour)

Cut kidney into crosswise slices; remove fat and gristle; then cut kidney into small pieces. Rinse in cold water and wipe dry. Brown on all sides in the fat. Add boiling water, cover, and simmer for 1 hour, or until tender. Meanwhile cook beef and onion, stirring with fork, until meat loses its red color. Add cooked kidney and liquid. Blend flour with cold water and stir into mixture. Cook until slightly thickened, stirring. Add seasonings and pour into 1-quart casserole. Roll pastry to ⅛-inch thickness and cut into strips. Arrange on mixture, lattice fashion. Brush with undiluted evaporated milk, top milk, or slightly beaten egg white, if desired. Bake in preheated hot oven (400°F.) for 20 minutes, or until pastry is brown. Makes 4 servings.

TEXAS SOMBREROS
1 pound beef chuck, ground
1 teaspoon monosodium glutamate
1 teaspoon salt
⅛ teaspoon pepper
½ teaspoon steak sauce
1 to 2 teaspoons chili powder
2 tablespoons butter
½ cup finely chopped celery
¼ cup finely chopped onion
¼ cup finely chopped green pepper
2 cups (one 1-pound can) tomatoes
1 can (8 ounces) tomato sauce
   Large corn chips
   Shredded lettuce

Sprinkle meat with monosodium glutamate, salt, pepper, steak sauce, and chili powder. Melt butter in skillet and add celery, onion, and green pepper; cook until almost tender. Add meat and cook, stirring with fork, until meat loses its red color. Add tomatoes and tomato sauce. Simmer, uncovered, for 30 minutes, or

until quite thick. Serve on corn chips and top with lettuce. Makes 4 servings.

BEEF AND NOODLE PLATTER
1 pound ground beef
1 tablespoon butter
   Salt and pepper to taste
1 can (10½ ounces) tomato soup
½ soup-can water
1 can (3 ounces) mushrooms, drained
6 ounces wide noodles
1 can (3 ounces) chow-mein noodles, heated in oven
   Green-pepper and pimiento strips

Brown meat lightly in butter, stirring with fork to break up meat. Season. Add soup, water, and mushrooms. Bring to boil and simmer, uncovered, for about 15 minutes. Cook and drain wide noodles. Put in center of hot platter. Pour meat mixture over noodles. Arrange chow-mein noodles around edge and garnish with strips of pepper and pimiento. Makes 4 servings.

CREAMED HAMBURGER AND CABBAGE
¾ pound beef chuck, ground
1 medium onion, minced
3 tablespoons butter or margarine
4 cups coarsely chopped cabbage
3 tablespoons all-purpose flour
2 teaspoons salt
¼ teaspoon pepper
¾ teaspoon paprika
½ teaspoon celery seeds
1½ cups milk

Brown meat and onion lightly in butter, breaking up meat with fork. Add cabbage and sauté lightly. Blend in flour and seasonings. Add milk, cover, and simmer for 15 to 20 minutes. Makes 4 to 6 servings.

BEEF AND RICE CASSEROLE
1 pound ground beef
1 cup uncooked rice
1 small onion, chopped
2 tablespoons butter or margarine
1 teaspoon seasoned salt
½ teaspoon pepper
½ teaspoon monosodium glutamate
1 teaspoon paprika
1 bottle (2 ounces) stuffed olives (⅓ cup), sliced
2½ cups (one 1-pound, 4-ounce can) tomato juice
1½ cups boiling water
½ cup grated sharp Cheddar or process American cheese

Cook first 3 ingredients in butter until lightly browned, breaking up meat with fork. Add remaining ingredients except cheese and bring to boil. Put in 2-quart casserole. Cover; bake in slow oven (300°F.) for 1 hour. Sprinkle with cheese and put back in oven, uncovered, for 5 minutes, or until cheese is melted. Makes 6 servings.

HAMBURGER-MACARONI CASSEROLE
4 ounces elbow macaroni
1 garlic clove, minced

1 pound beef chuck, ground
1 can (10½ ounces) condensed onion soup
¾ teaspoon salt
Dash of pepper
½ cup shredded sharp Cheddar cheese
3 slices of bread, crumbled
3 tablespoons butter or margarine, melted

Cook macaroni until tender; drain. Brown garlic and beef lightly in skillet, stirring with fork to break up meat. Add soup, salt, and pepper; mix well. Add macaroni and pour into 1-quart casserole or shallow baking dish. Sprinkle with cheese. Mix crumbs and butter and sprinkle on top. Bake in preheated moderate oven (350°F.) for 15 minutes. Makes 4 servings.

BEEF CASSEROLE WITH ALMONDS

1 pound ground beef
1 cup uncooked rice
2 small cans (10½ ounces each) or 2 envelopes chicken-noodle or beef-noodle soup mix
1 small onion, chopped
1 cup sliced celery
3 cups water
1 tablespoon soy sauce
½ cup slivered almonds

Cook beef until lightly browned, stirring with fork to break up meat. Put in 3-quart casserole. Mix remaining ingredients and pour over meat. Cover; bake in preheated moderate oven (350°F.) for 1 hour, or until rice is done, adding a little more water if necessary. Makes 6 servings.

BEEF, POTATO, AND BEAN CASSEROLE

1 pound ground beef
1 teaspoon monosodium glutamate
1 teaspoon salt
¼ teaspoon pepper
⅛ teaspoon ground oregano or thyme
2 cups thinly sliced peeled potatoes (2 large)
About 2 cups (one 1-pound can) red kidney beans, drained
2 medium onions, sliced
½ cup chili sauce

Mix first 5 ingredients lightly. Put in skillet and cook, stirring with fork to break up meat, until lightly browned. Put meat and remaining ingredients in layers in 2-quart casserole, beginning and ending with meat. Cover; bake in preheated moderate oven (375°F.) for 40 minutes. Uncover; bake for about 20 minutes longer. Makes 6 servings.

BEEF-STUFFED CABBAGE ROLLS

1 pound ground beef
½ cup uncooked rice
1 onion, minced
2 garlic cloves, minced
1 egg

Salt and pepper
1 white cabbage with tight leaves (about 4 pounds)
1 pound sauerkraut
3¼ cups (one 1-pound, 12-ounce can) tomatoes
¼ cup butter or margarine
1½ cups boiling water

Mix first 5 ingredients, 2 teaspoons salt, and dash of pepper. Cut core out of cabbage to depth of 3 inches. Put cabbage in a large kettle of boiling water over high heat. With tongs remove about 20 leaves as they wilt. Let leaves stand until cool enough to handle. Carefully cut out coarsest part of ribs. Cool remaining cabbage and cut coarsely or chop. Put half of chopped cabbage in a large kettle. Put a spoonful of meat mixture in center of each leaf; roll up, tucking ends under. Put on top of cabbage in kettle. Top with remaining cabbage, sauerkraut, tomatoes, and butter. Season with salt and pepper to taste. Add the boiling water. Bring to boil, cover, and simmer for 45 minutes. Makes 5 servings.

HAMBURGER-CORN SKILLET DINNER

1 pound beef chuck, ground
1 cup soft bread crumbs
1¾ teaspoons salt
⅛ teaspoon pepper
2 tablespoons margarine
About 1½ cups (one 12-ounce can) whole-kernel corn, drained
1 medium onion, sliced
2⅓ cups (one 1-pound, 3-ounce can) tomatoes, drained

Mix meat, crumbs, 1 teaspoon salt, and pepper. Melt margarine in covered skillet and cook meat mixture, stirring frequently, until well browned. Add corn and onion; sprinkle with ¾ teaspoon salt. Add tomatoes, cover, and simmer for about 25 minutes. Serve in skillet. Makes 4 to 6 servings.

HAMBURGER-ZUCCHINI SKILLET DINNER

1 pound ground beef
1 can (3 ounces) mushrooms, drained
2 tablespoons flour
1 teaspoon salt
¼ teaspoon pepper
1 teaspoon onion salt
¼ teaspoon garlic salt
½ teaspoon hot pepper sauce
½ teaspoon monosodium glutamate
2 medium zucchini, sliced thin
About 1¼ cups (one 10-ounce can) tomatoes
1 tablespoon vinegar
½ teaspoon seasoned salt

In skillet cook beef and mushrooms until meat loses its red color, breaking up meat with fork. Drain off most of fat.

Blend in flour and next 6 ingredients. Arrange zucchini on meat mixture and pour tomatoes over top. Add vinegar and sprinkle with seasoned salt. Cover and simmer for 30 minutes. Makes 4 servings.

FRENCH-FRIED HAMBURGER SANDWICHES

8 slices of very fresh bread
¾ pound beef round or chuck, ground
Salt and pepper to taste
2 eggs, beaten
¾ cup milk
Fat for deep frying

Remove crusts from bread. Shape meat into 4 patties and put one in center of each of 4 slices of bread, and season; top with remaining slices. Press the two together with hands. Seal edges with tines of fork dipped into hot water. Dip each sandwich into batter made by mixing eggs and milk. Put in wire basket and fry in hot deep fat (375°F. on a frying thermometer) until golden brown. The meat will be rare. (If you prefer the meat less rare, cook it first.) Makes 4 servings.

LASAGNE AL FORNO

2 tablespoons olive oil
1 medium onion, minced
1 garlic clove, minced
1 pound beef chuck, ground
1 teaspoon salt
½ teaspoon pepper
2 teaspoons grated lemon rind
¼ cup chopped parsley
2 cans (10¼ ounces each) meat sauce (about 2½ cups)
8 ounces lasagna, cooked and drained
1 pound Mozzarella cheese
1 pound ricotta (or creamed cottage cheese)
½ cup grated Parmesan cheese

Heat oil and cook onion and garlic in it until soft and transparent. Add beef, stirring with fork. Cook until lightly browned, stirring. Stir in salt, pepper, lemon rind, parsley, and meat sauce. Simmer over low heat for 15 minutes, stirring frequently. Spread about ¼ of sauce mixture on bottom and sides of a very large shallow baking dish. Top with a layer of lasagna placed lengthwise. Cover with a layer of half of Mozzarella and top this with half of ricotta. Sprinkle with ⅓ of grated Parmesan. Repeat procedure. Top with a third (and last) layer of lasagna, the remaining sauce, and Parmesan. Bake in preheated moderate oven (350°F.) for 30 minutes. To serve, cut into squares. Makes 6 servings.

Wild West Hamburger gains flavor from herbs and wine

Hail to the Hamburger

by Mary Hemingway

Whoever it was who first hit upon the idea of slicing meat thinly lengthwise and then chopping crosswise (a Chinese probably, and many years B.C.), deserves a curtsy, a salaam, and a salute. Not all together, please. To the doctors of Padua, Italy, who, in the eighth century, began prescribing chopped beef and onions fried together to cure their patients' colds, we owe at least a bow on a short winter afternoon.

At Aiguesmortes, the lovely golden-walled ancient town in the south of France from which King Louis IX, later Saint Louis, launched the Sixth and Seventh Crusades in 1248 and 1270, they say that it was the king's chef who invented the food grinder. A man in leather pedal pushers and a chef's apron, he is supposed to have been devoted both to his king and his vocation. He also knew the problems of cuisine aboard the ships which took the Christians through the Mediterranean to recover the Holy Land for Christendom. Each crusader had to bring his own fresh water for drinking. Even the king's chef had minimum space for preparing food and, come bad weather, minimum time over his fire to prepare something succulent and flavorsome for lunch. It was with these restrictions in mind, so they say, that the chef to King Louis IX invented the little wheel with its cutting edges and the small tunnel through which you push the food, and had the king's armorer make him the first meat grinder. (Fresh meat couldn't have lasted more than a day or two, but that was his problem.) My profound respects, herewith, to that cook and his invention, or to the legend.

Hoity-toity cooks may sneer, but approval and praise naturally follow to the public-service-minded man who decided, "Let us butchers do this job." And to all the other butchers who caught on, from Denmark to Costa Rica to Tasmania, saving housewives time and energy cutting away the muscle and the hard edges, pro-

viding the base for who knows how many hundreds of main-dish recipes. Here are some of Ernest's and my favorite ways of dealing with ground beef and some hamburger ideas, including the Wild West hamburger, which I invented to fortify us for tramping through sagebrush after pheasant, partridge, or ducks, or, after such hikes, to console us for not having shot our limits.

WILD-WEST HAMBURGER
(Papa's Favorite)

- 1 pound lean beef, ground
- 1 heaping teaspoon dried sage
- ½ teaspoon mixed-herb seasoning
- ½ teaspoon monosodium glutamate
- ½ teaspoon sugar
- Salt and pepper
- 2 spring onions, or shallots, finely chopped
- 2 garlic cloves, minced
- 1 heaping teaspoon India relish
- 2 tablespoons capers
- 1 tablespoon minced parsley, or 1 tablespoon dried parsley
- 1 egg, whipped in a cup
- ⅓ cup dry white wine
- 2 tablespoons oil for frying

What to do: Break up the meat with a fork and thoroughly mix into it first all of the dry ingredients (and afterwards all of the wet ingredients, including the wine), and let the bowl sit at room temperature for an hour, or at least for ½ hour. Make 4 fat, juicy patties which are soft but not runny.

There is only one correct way to fry a hamburger, I think, just as there is only one correct way to fry an egg. Have the oil in your skillet hot but not smoking when you drop in the patties, then turn the heat down, or take the pan off the stove for a minute. Fry the burgers for 4 minutes. Take the pan off the burner and turn the heat high again. Flip the burgers over, put the pan back on the high heat, and let them sizzle 1 minute. Lower the heat again and cook another 3 minutes. Both sides of the burgers should be crispy brown and the middle pink and juicy, and GOOD. Makes 2 servings.

COTTAGE PIE

The classic British treatment of ground beef, which you find properly done only in their homes. (The customary restaurant version is apt to taste like warm, wet blotting paper.) My jazzed-up variation:

- 2 tablespoons cooking oil
- 1 large garlic clove, chopped fine
- 1 large Spanish onion, chopped coarsely
- Salt and pepper to taste
- ¼ teaspoon sugar
- ½ teaspoon mixed-herb seasoning
- ½ teaspoon monosodium glutamate
- 1 pound lean beef, ground
- 2 large celery stalks, chopped horizontally

- 1 large carrot, coarsely grated
- ⅓ cup dry red wine
- Mashed potatoes

What to do: 1. Fry in the oil, the garlic, onion, salt, pepper, and other dry seasonings; stir until they are half-cooked, about 5 minutes. Add meat; stir until it is crumbled and mixed with the other things. Remove pan from the heat and add everything else, except potatoes, and let it sit, keeping warm, to blend the flavors.

2. Make a batch of smooth, creamy mashed potatoes with plenty of white pepper in them, using at least 4 fair-size potatoes.

3. Put the meat-and-vegetable mixture in a warmed casserole, spread the mashed potatoes on top (the potatoes should be 2 inches thick) and put the dish under the broiler to "tan" the potatoes. Enough for 3 to 5 people depending on appetites and the rest of the menu.

P.S. For a richer dish, mix ⅓ cup of grated Cheddar cheese with ⅓ cup of grated Parmesan cheese and spread it on top of the potatoes before putting the casserole under the broiler.

STIR-FRY GROUND BEEF
(As taught to me by the Chinese in Havana)

No self-respecting Chinese cook would use ground beef in a stir-fry dish, of which there are infinite varieties. They would buy their beef in a solid piece and thinly slice it. But the Chinese cooks have more time, or more patience, or they wield their knives more skillfully than I do, or they have all these sterling attributes together. Their end result is better food, but my cut-corner dish is good, too. You can order the fresh gingerroot from any Chinatown grocery. (No garlic, for once.)

- 1 large onion, coarsely chopped
- 3 tablespoons cooking oil
- 1½ cups Special Vegetable (see below)
- 1 pound lean beef, ground
- 1 heaping tablespoon fresh gingerroot, finely sliced
- 1 small can of water chestnuts, each chestnut sliced twice
- 2 tablespoons soy sauce
- 3 tablespoons dry white wine
- Pinch of pepper
- ½ teaspoon monosodium glutamate
- ¼ teaspoon sugar
- Rice or noodles

Special Vegetable: Now comes your freedom of selection. You need about 1½ cups of almost any fresh or frozen juicy vegetable, *finely sliced*. Pick out whatever you happen to have available that you fancy. It can be green pepper, green beans, wax beans, beets (good), cabbage, celery, broccoli, asparagus, fresh mushrooms (very good), green peas, or whatever.

What to do: You need three frying pans, one for the onions, one for the beef, one for your Special Vegetable.

1. Fry the onion slowly in a covered pan, to hold in its vapor and keep it warm. Use as little oil as possible.

2. Fry your Special Vegetable in as little oil as possible (this depends on the moisture in the vegetable) and add a little water, if necessary. Two minutes should do it, since you want your vegetable still fresh and in good form.

3. Fry the ground beef in a little oil, breaking it up and stirring it, three to four minutes. Then add to it the gingerroot, water chestnuts, soy sauce, wine, and seasonings (no salt), and cook two minutes more, until the new things are heated.

4. Into the meat pan, dump the onions, the Special Vegetable and its native juices. Stir a couple of times and serve with either white rice, wild rice, Chinese noodles, tagliatelli (big flat Italian noodles), macaroni, or spaghetti. Enough for 3 to 5 people, depending on appetites and what else you serve.

PICADILLO (pronounced "pee-kah-dee-yo")

This is what the Cubans do with ground beef instead of making hamburgers. There are many different versions of it but this one is the most authentic. (I leave out the tomatoes.)

    2 tablespoons cooking oil
    2 large garlic cloves, minced
    1 large onion, chopped coarsely
      Salt and pepper to taste
    ½ teaspoon monosodium glutamate
    1 pound lean beef, ground
    ⅓ cup dry white wine
    2 large ripe tomatoes, peeled and
      chopped
    ½ cup dark or light raisins, plumped
      up in hot water
    ⅓ cup pimiento-stuffed olives, sliced
      in thirds
    1 seeded green pepper, chopped in
      half-inch squares

What to do: In the oil, fry the garlic and onion for five minutes, stirring frequently. Add the seasonings, the meat, the wine, and stir again. Add the tomatoes, raisins, and olives, and stir. Add the green pepper and cook only long enough for it to get thoroughly hot; it should retain crispness and color.

One of *Picadillo's* charms is that all the chopping and slicing can be done in advance, the cooking requiring only a few (10) minutes' time. The Cubans serve this dish with plain white rice, either in a separate dish or with the *Picadillo* on top of the rice and its juices trickling down. (Enough for 3 to 5 people.)

HAMBURGER

A year ago and a month ago and a week ago, I saw served to helpless customers in various restaurants, rounds of gray, greasy, paper-thin agglomerations of meat and seasonings being presented as hamburger. A national disgrace! A hamburger worthy of the name should be at least 1 inch thick and 3 inches across; 4 inches is nobler. It can (why not?) contain all sorts of surprises besides salt, pepper, and ketchup. Here are some additions I have tried with success. Use ¼ pound of ground lean beef per hamburger. Never any bread or bread crumbs. Bind it with an egg, beaten up in a cup. For juiciness, in a pound of meat use a ¼, even ⅓ cup dry wine, red or white, depending on the other ingredients and seasonings. Take the ground beef out of the refrigerator an hour before you plan to cook it, mix in the extras, and let it rest comfortably at room temperature, the wine soaking into the meat. You'll see.

SURPRISE HAMBURGERS

With your 1 pound of lean ground beef, try mixing in one of the following:

1. A cup of grated Cheddar cheese, 1 clove of minced garlic, white wine, salt and pepper to taste.

2. A 5-ounce can of chopped water chestnuts, 2 chopped spring onions or shallots, 2 pinches of oregano, 2 tablespoons of soy sauce (no salt).

3. Three-quarters cup of finely chopped mushrooms, 3 pinches of marjoram, a big dollop of piccalilli, white wine, salt and pepper to taste.

4. Three-quarters cup of grated carrot, 1 minced garlic clove, 1 chopped onion, 3 pinches of thyme, red wine, salt and pepper to taste.

5. One-half of a 6-ounce can of tomato paste, diluted with ½ cup of tomato juice, ¼ teaspoon of sugar, 1 tablespoon of chopped dill pickle, salt and pepper to taste. (No wine.)

6. Three-quarters cup of finely chopped walnuts, 1 scant teaspoon of fresh, or a heaping teaspoon of dried dill seed, red wine, salt to taste.

7. One-half cup of grated tart apple, one chopped shallot, ⅓ cup of toasted, chopped almonds, red wine.

HARD COOKED—A term used to describe a method of cooking eggs in the shell to the stage where the egg white is firm yet tender and the egg yolk is firm but not rubbery. Eggs so cooked are often called "hard boiled." To achieve this result, it is necessary to cook eggs at a simmering, not hard-boiling, temperature during the entire cooking time. There are two ways to do this:

Cold-Water Method—Add cold water to eggs until 1 inch above eggs. Bring to a boil and simmer for 15 minutes. Place eggs in cold water to cool thoroughly. Roll egg to crack shell on its entire surface. Peel.

Boiling-Water Method—Carefully, with a spoon, lower room-temperature eggs into boiling water. Simmer for 12 minutes. Cool, and shell as above.

HARD SAUCE—This sauce is made by creaming butter with sugar, and flavoring it with brandy, rum, whisky, wine, or with extracts or spices. The sugar can be granulated, confectioners' sugar, or brown sugar. Cream is sometimes added to make the creaming easier. The sauce is chilled before use to stiffen it. It is served with a hot dessert such as a steamed pudding. It can also be served as an icing with fruit- or spicecakes.

Hard sauce is the traditional sauce for plum pudding. The combination of the brown, crumbly, hot pudding and the smooth, white, cold sauce is delicious. The sauce is of English origin, and in Great Britain it is called Brandy Butter, since it is flavored with brandy.

It takes time to make a good hard sauce. The sugar must be creamed into the softened, but not melted, butter slowly, and in small amounts. The sauce should be so thoroughly blended that no sugar crystals remain. The brandy or other flavoring should be added by pouring it over the last few tablespoons of sugar, thus blending it well into the mixture.

BASIC HARD SAUCE

Cream ⅓ cup butter, softened but not melted. To it add, a little at a time, 1 cup confectioners' sugar, beating after each addition. Beat in ½ teaspoon vanilla, a few drops at a time. Shape in balls or individual servings and chill, or put in serving dish to be spooned onto pudding. Makes 6 to 8 servings.

Sherry Hard Sauce

Make Basic Hard Sauce and beat in 1 to 3 tablespoons sherry.

Brandy Hard Sauce

Make Basic Hard Sauce and beat in 1 tablespoon brandy.

Creamy Hard Sauce

Make Basic Hard Sauce and beat in ¼ cup heavy cream.

Mocha Hard Sauce

Make Basic Hard Sauce and beat in 2 tablespoons strong coffee, 2 teaspoons cocoa, and ¼ cup heavy cream.

Lemon Hard Sauce

Make Basic Hard Sauce and beat in 1 teaspoon fresh lemon juice and 1 tablespoon lemon rind.

Orange Hard Sauce

Make Basic Hard Sauce and beat in 2 tablespoons fresh orange juice and 2 tablespoons orange rind.

Spicy Hard Sauce

Make Basic Hard Sauce and beat in ½ teaspoon ground cinnamon and ¼ teaspoon ground cloves.

Cherry-Nut Patties

Chop candied cherries and nuts. Make Basic Hard Sauce recipe, shape into a roll, and roll in cherries and nuts. Chill. At serving time, cut into serving-size slices.

FLUFFY HARD SAUCE

1 cup sugar
1 tablespoon soft butter
3 tablespoons heavy cream
3 egg whites, beaten until stiff
1 teaspoon vanilla extract

Mix sugar with butter and cream. Blend well. Gradually fold in egg whites and vanilla. Makes about 1½ cups.

BROWN-SUGAR HARD SAUCE

1½ cups firmly packed dark brown sugar
½ cup butter
⅓ cup light cream
1 teaspoon vanilla extract or 2 tablespoons rum

Mash brown sugar to remove all lumps. Cream butter until soft and gradually beat in brown sugar. Gradually beat in cream and vanilla. Blend well. Chill. Makes about 1⅔ cups.

HARDTACK—A large, hard biscuit made of unsalted dough and dried after baking to make it easy to store and preserve. Hardtack is also called "ship biscuit" or "pilot bread" because of the custom of serving it on shipboard during the prolonged sea voyages of the past when it was impossible to store fresh bread.

Hardtack is used in army and navy commissaries and is also available in food stores. It is often served with chowders, soups, and stews, sometimes broken into pieces and added to the dish.

Hardtack is an excellent biscuit for those who like dry, light biscuits.

HARE—Hare is a cousin of the rabbit and belongs to the *Leporidae* family of rodents. Generally speaking, hares are European and rabbits are American. There are many varieties of each.

Although the names are often used interchangeably, genuine hares are not found in the United States and the two animals are quite different. Rabbits are born naked and blind; hares are born furred with eyes opened. After a month's suckling, hares are able to look after themselves. They are generally bigger than rabbits and have longer ears and feet. Their coats are beautiful, often silky. There are blue-gray hares in the far north of Europe, with black-tipped ears which turn white in the winter. In Ireland, russet-colored hares never show a trace of white in their furs. Some French hares have coats the color of ripe corn. Some hares grow huge, like Belgian hares, reaching thirteen pounds.

The meat of a hare differs greatly in taste depending on its age. A tender leveret, as young hares are called, has white meat that tastes like chicken. It can be cooked as chicken is cooked. Older hares have strong-flavored, tougher meat. They are treated like game and cooked slowly, often after being marinated to make the meat more tender. Hare is seldom available in the United States.

HARICOT—A French word meaning "bean." *Haricots blancs* are "white beans," *haricots verts* are "green beans."

In French culinary language, a *haricot* can also be a mutton or lamb stew made with potatoes and onions. A *"haricot"* does not contain beans; the name is a corruption of the French *halicot*, meaning "chopped very fine."

HASENPFEFFER—The literal translation of this German word is "hare pepper." In practice it stands for a highly seasoned stew of rabbit or hare, which has been marinated to make the meat more tender. The marinade can be wine, or equal parts of vinegar and water, seasoned with onion slices, bay leaf, salt and pepper, juniper berries, or any other marinade seasonings. The meat rests in the marinade for one or several days (depending on its age). It is then browned in fat and braised in the marinade. Sweet or sour cream is added to the final gravy.

Hasenpfeffer is a hunter's dish that has been adopted for family use. It is an excellent way of serving rabbit or hare. Any venison or game can be cooked in the same manner.

HASENPFEFFER

1 cup each of water and vinegar
1 clove
1 bay leaf
1 teaspoon salt
6 peppercorns
1 onion, sliced
1 rabbit or hare, cut into serving pieces
¼ cup butter or margarine
¼ cup all-purpose flour

Cook water, vinegar, spices, and onion together for 5 minutes. Pour over rabbit pieces and let stand in refrigerator for 2 days. Remove rabbit from marinade, and pat dry. Fry in the butter until brown. Reserve marinade. Add flour and let it brown lightly. Add 1 cup strained marinade and simmer gently for 1½ hours, until rabbit is tender. Add more marinade if necessary. If desired, add ½ cup dairy sour cream to sauce when meat is cooked and removed from heat. Makes 4 servings.

HASH—A mixture of foods chopped into small pieces and mixed. The word is most commonly applied to a mixture of meat or poultry, potatoes, and seasonings. Other vegetables may be added. For that matter, hash may be made of almost any other ingredients: there is even a marshmallow dessert which bears the name "Heavenly Hash."

Corned-beef hash and roast-beef hash are available canned and frozen.

HASH COOK BOOK

HASH PREPARED WITH FRESH INGREDIENTS

HASH WITH MUSHROOMS

¼ cup butter or margarine
½ pound sliced fresh mushrooms
2 cups diced cooked beef, lamb, chicken, or turkey
1½ cups brown gravy
Salt and pepper
Crumbled dried thyme, basil, or rosemary
Hot toast
1 tablespoon chopped parsley

Heat butter and sauté mushrooms until tender. Add meat and gravy, and heat until piping hot. Season to taste with salt and pepper and crumbled dried thyme. Serve on hot toast garnished with chopped parsley. Makes 4 servings.

VEAL HASH

3 cups diced cooked veal
1 onion, minced
3 tablespoons butter or margarine
1 cup diced cooked potatoes
1 cup veal broth
1 pimiento, diced
1 cup heavy cream or undiluted evaporated milk, scalded
2 egg yolks, slightly beaten
Salt and pepper

Use leftover meat or simmer a knuckle of veal in well-seasoned water until tender. Cut meat into very small even cubes. Cook onion in butter for 2 or 3 minutes. Add potatoes and broth; heat to boiling. Add meat and pimiento; simmer for 2 or 3 minutes. Pour hot cream slowly over egg yolks. Add to meat mixture. Heat gently until thickened, stirring carefully. Add more salt and pepper if necessary. Serve at once. Makes 4 servings.

FRANKFURTER HASH

4 cups finely diced cold boiled potatoes
1 medium onion, chopped
3 tablespoons all-purpose flour
Salt and pepper
¼ cup milk
½ pound frankfurters, thinly sliced
3 tablespoons butter or margarine
½ cup shredded sharp Cheddar cheese

Combine potatoes and onion. Sprinkle with flour and season to taste. Add milk and frankfurters. Put in shallow baking dish or pie pan. Dot with butter. Bake in preheated hot oven (425°F.) for 30 minutes. Top with cheese. Bake for 5 minutes longer, or until cheese is melted. Makes 4 servings.

MAINE CORNED-BEEF HASH

4 cups cold cubed cooked corned beef
3 cups cubed boiled potatoes
¼ cup butter or margarine
¾ cup boiling water
Salt and pepper

Trim meat free from gristle and fat. Place with potatoes in chopping bowl. Chop until meat and potatoes are in shreds. Melt butter in heavy skillet. Add boiling water and meat and potato mixture. Season with salt and pepper to taste. Cook over lowest possible heat for about 15 minutes, or until a thin brown crust has been formed on the bottom of the hash. Fold over as for an omelet. Slide onto heated serving dish. Makes 4 to 6 servings.

CHICKEN HASH À LA RITZ

4 large chicken breasts or 3 to 4 cups cooked chicken, white meat only
Chicken bouillon
2 tablespoons butter
1 cup mushrooms, sliced
½ cup minced green pepper
¼ cup minced pimiento
⅔ cup light dry sherry
1 cup heavy cream
1½ cups medium white sauce made with light cream instead of milk
1 teaspoon salt
White pepper

Simmer chicken breasts in chicken bouillon to cover for 30 to 45 minutes, or until tender. Remove skin, bones, and tendons. Cut chicken into ¼-inch or smaller dices. In heavy skillet heat butter until golden, but do not let brown. Cook mushrooms, pepper, and pimiento in butter for 5 minutes. Add chicken, ⅓ cup of the sherry, and the heavy cream. Simmer over low heat, stirring frequently, for 10 minutes, or until sauce has cooked down to about half the initial quantity. Add white sauce and blend thoroughly. Season with salt, and pepper to taste. Just before serving, stir in remaining sherry and a little more heavy cream if sauce looks too thick. Serve on buttered toast, or with asparagus and wild rice. Makes 2 or 3 servings.

TURKEY HASH

¼ cup butter
2 tablespoons flour
½ cup heavy cream
¾ cup chicken bouillon
Grated rind of 1 lemon
¼ teaspoon white pepper
⅛ teaspoon ground mace
½ pound mushrooms, sliced, or 3- to 4-ounce can sliced mushrooms
3 cups diced turkey
1 cup oysters (optional)

Melt 2 tablespoons butter and stir in flour. Cook, stirring constantly, until smooth and golden. Combine cream and bouillon. Stir gradually into flour mixture. Cook, stirring constantly, until thickened and smooth. Stir in lemon rind, pepper, and mace. Cook mushrooms in remaining butter for 3 minutes. Add mushrooms and turkey to sauce. Cook over lowest possible heat, stirring frequently, until thoroughly heated through. Just before serving, add oysters. Serve with plain or wild rice, or with corn pudding. Makes 3 servings.

POTATOES HASHED IN CREAM

1 medium onion, minced
2 tablespoons butter or margarine
About 2 cups (1-pound can) potatoes, drained and chopped
½ cup light cream
Salt and pepper
Chopped parsley
Paprika

Cook onion in butter in skillet until lightly browned. Add potatoes and cream; simmer for 5 minutes. Season with salt and pepper to taste. Put in serving dish and sprinkle with parsley and paprika. Makes 4 servings.

PEPPER HASH

12 sweet red peppers
12 sweet green peppers
12 medium onions
6 cups white or cider vinegar
2 cups sugar
¼ cup salt

Remove stems and seeds from peppers and peel onions. Put vegetables through food grinder, using medium blade. Cover with boiling water and let stand for 15 minutes. Drain and repeat. Drain again. Add vinegar, sugar, and salt. Cook gently for 30 minutes. Pour into hot sterilized jars, and seal. Makes about 4 pints.

HEAVENLY HASH

25 marshmallows
25 candied cherries
2 cups heavy cream
1 cup blanched almonds, chopped
½ teaspoon each of vanilla and almond extracts

Cut marshmallows into 4 pieces each; use scissors for easier working. Slice all but 6 cherries. Combine marshmallows and heavy cream. Refrigerate for 1 hour. With rotary beater, whip mixture until stiff. Fold in other ingredients. Chill for 2 to 4 hours; dessert must be very cold. Cut remaining cherries into halves. At serving time, decorate hash with halved cherries. Makes 6 servings.

CANNED HASH

BAKED CORNED-BEEF HASH AND TOMATOES

1-pound can corned-beef hash
2 tomatoes, halved

Heavenly Hash

Chicken Hash à La Ritz

Prepared mustard
Salt and pepper
Onion salt
Worcestershire
Sugar
Butter
Fine dry bread crumbs

Put hash in small shallow baking dish or pie pan. Press tomato halves into hash and spread with mustard. Sprinkle with salt, pepper, onion salt, Worcestershire, and sugar to taste. Dot with butter and sprinkle with crumbs. Bake in preheated hot oven (400°F.) for 25 minutes. Makes 2 servings.

BROILED CORNED-BEEF-HASH MOUNDS

4 thin slices of bread
1- pound can corned-beef hash
¼ cup chili sauce
⅓ cup shredded sharp Cheddar cheese
1 medium onion, cut into rings
1 tablespoon melted butter

Toast bread in broiler on one side. Mix hash and chili sauce and heap on untoasted sides of bread, taking care to cover edges. Broil under medium heat for 15 minutes, or until slightly browned. Sprinkle with cheese and top with onion rings. Brush rings with butter; broil only until cheese is melted. Makes 2 servings.

CORNED-BEEF HASH WITH CREAMED EGGS

1- pound can corned-beef hash
1 tablespoon margarine
½ can cream-of-mushroom soup
¼ teaspoon Worcestershire
¼ cup heavy cream
2 hard-cooked eggs, quartered
1 pimiento, cut into strips

Open both ends of can and push out hash. Cut across into 4 slices. Brown slowly in margarine in skillet, turning to brown both sides. Meanwhile, combine soup, Worcestershire, and cream in top part of double boiler; heat over boiling water. Add eggs and pimiento; heat. Serve as sauce on hash. Makes 2 servings.

CORNED-BEEF HASH WITH MUSTARD SAUCE

1- pound can corned-beef hash
1 tablespoon bacon fat
Hot Mustard Sauce

Heat hash thoroughly in fat in skillet. Serve in mounds with hot Mustard Sauce. Makes 2 servings.

Mustard Sauce

1 medium onion, minced
2 tablespoons margarine
1 tablespoon all-purpose flour
½ teaspoon salt
Dash of pepper
¾ cup milk
1 tablespoon prepared mustard

Cook onion in margarine in heavy saucepan until yellow. Stir in flour, salt, pepper, and milk. Cook slowly until slightly thickened. Add mustard. Makes 1 cup.

CORNED-BEEF HASH LYONNAISE

1 tablespoon margarine
2 medium onions, sliced
2 cans (1 pound each) corned-beef hash

Melt margarine in skillet; add onions and cook for a few minutes. Add hash, mix well, and cook until brown. Makes 4 servings.

CORNED-BEEF HASH O'BRIEN

1 small onion, minced
½ medium green pepper, chopped
1 tablespoon margarine
1 pimiento, chopped
1- pound can corned-beef hash

Cook onion and green pepper in margarine until onion is lightly browned. Add pimiento and hash; cook, stirring occasionally, until hash is browned. Makes 2 servings.

HASH-STUFFED CABBAGE ROLLS

6 large cabbage leaves
1 small onion, minced
1 tablespoon margarine
1- pound can corned-beef hash
2⅓ cups (one 1-pound, 3-ounce can) tomatoes, drained
1 garlic clove, minced
¼ teaspoon ground oregano
½ teaspoon salt
⅛ teaspoon pepper
½ cup grated Parmesan cheese

Cook cabbage leaves in boiling water for 3 minutes. Drain and dry on absorbent paper. Cook onion in margarine until lightly browned. Add to hash. Divide mixture among cabbage leaves. Roll leaves; tuck ends under and arrange in shallow baking dish. Mix tomato pulp and remaining ingredients except cheese. Pour over cabbage rolls. Bake in preheated hot oven (400°F.) for 35 minutes. Sprinkle with cheese; bake for 10 minutes longer. Makes 2 servings.

ROAST-BEEF HASH CASSEROLE

1 can (12 ounces) roast-beef hash
¼ cup butter or margarine
1 cup sharp Cheddar cheese
Dash of Worcestershire
1 egg white, stiffly beaten

Spread roast-beef hash in shallow casserole. Cream butter; mix in cheese and Worcestershire, and then the egg white. Spoon over hash in casserole. Bake in preheated hot oven (425°F.) for 15 minutes, or until puffy. Makes 4 servings.

BARBECUED BEEF HASH

1½ tablespoons onion, chopped
1 teaspoon butter
1 can (12 ounces) roast-beef hash
⅓ cup ketchup
1½ tablespoons vinegar
1 tablespoon Worcestershire
⅓ teaspoon salt
Pepper to taste
4 hamburger rolls, toasted

Brown onion in butter. Add next 6 ingredients and mix well. Heat slowly and serve on toasted rolls. Makes 4 servings.

HAZELNUT—This grape-size, smooth-shelled nut grows on shrubs and trees belonging to the genus *Corylus*. The nuts grow in clusters and each is wrapped in a fuzzy outer husk that opens as the nut ripens. The hazelnut is also known as a cobnut or filbert.

Hazelnuts are an essential nut in European dessert cookery and baking. The nuts are often toasted for a browner color and a better flavor; they are never blanched.

Whole hazelnuts can be salted, or sugared, or eaten as is. Chopped hazelnuts can be used in candies, baked goods, and desserts. Sliced hazelnuts can be added to salads and to main dishes for texture.

Availability and Purchasing Guide—Hazelnuts are sold in the shell, in bulk or by the pound. Look for nuts with clean shells that are free from scars, cracks, or holes. The shells should be well filled so that the kernel does not rattle.

Shelled salted hazelnuts are sold in bulk and packaged in film bags. Fresh-shelled kernels should be plump, meaty, crisp, and brittle.

☐ 2¼ pounds in-shell = 1 pound shelled = 3½ cups

Storage—Keep tightly covered and away from light.
☐ Kitchen shelf: 1 month
☐ Refrigerator shelf: 3 to 4 months
☐ Refrigerator frozen-food compartment, prepared for freezing: 6 months
☐ Freezer, prepared for freezing: 1 year

Nutritive Food Values—Hazelnuts provide protein, fat, iron, and thiamine.
☐ 3½ ounces = 634 calories

Basic Preparation—To shell hazelnuts, use

a nutcracker as the shell is brittle. Remove the kernel intact. To slice or chop nuts, use a long sharp knife and a cutting board.

☐ **To Toast**—Place nuts on a cookie sheet in preheated moderate oven (350° F.) for 5 to 6 minutes, stirring once. Turn them out on a rough cloth and rub them briskly in the cloth. This will remove fine skin fibers. The nuts must then be picked over. They can be ground in a blender or a nut mill, and used like other nuts.

☐ **To Roast in Oven**—Spread nutmeats in a shallow pan and place in preheated hot oven (400°F.) for about 7 minutes, or in preheated slow oven (275°F.) for 20 minutes. Stir nuts frequently to prevent scorching. For salted nuts, add 1 teaspoon salt per cup of nutmeats. If desired, while nutmeats are warm, rub off skins with cloth or between fingers.

☐ **To Skillet-Roast**—Heat 2 teaspoons cooking oil in a skillet over low heat. Add nutmeats and 1 teaspoon salt per cup of nuts. Stir constantly until thoroughly heated. Drain well on paper towels.

☐ **To Grind**—Use a special nut grinder or an electric blender; when butter or paste is desired, use a meat grinder. Hazelnuts are excellent when ground, with a dry grain that is not oily.

HAZELNUT AND MUSHROOM SAUCE
½ cup sliced hazelnuts
½ onion, minced
¼ cup sliced mushrooms
¼ cup butter or margarine
2 tablespoons all-purpose flour
1 teaspoon salt
¼ teaspoon pepper
2 chicken bouillon cubes
2 cups hot water

Brown hazelnuts, onion, and mushrooms in butter; remove from skillet. To fat, add flour and seasonings, mixing well. Add bouillon cubes which have been dissolved in the hot water; cook until thickened. Return hazelnuts, onion, and mushrooms to sauce; serve hot over rice. Makes about 2½ cups.

HAZELNUT CREAM
½ cup shelled hazelnuts
1 cup milk or light cream
2 egg yolks
¼ cup sugar
1 teaspoon vanilla extract
1½ teaspoons unflavored gelatin
1 tablespoon water
½ cup heavy cream, whipped

Spread hazelnuts in pie pan and toast in moderate oven (350°F,) until skins are coming loose. Place in towel and rub to remove skins. Grind in nut grinder or blender. Combine with milk, egg yolks, and sugar. Cook over lowest possible heat, stirring constantly, until *almost* boiling. Remove from heat. Add vanilla.

Soften gelatin in water. Stir into hot custard until completely dissolved. Cool; fold in whipped cream. Pour into glass serving dish and chill until set. Makes 3 large servings.

CHOCOLATE DIAMONDS WITH HAZELNUTS
2 ounces (2 squares) unsweetened chocolate
½ cup butter
1 cup sugar
2 eggs
½ cup sifted all-purpose flour
¼ teaspoon salt
½ teaspoon vanilla extract
⅔ cup chopped hazelnuts

Melt chocolate and butter over hot water. Add remaining ingredients except nuts and mix well. Spread in greased pan (1 x 10 x 15 inches). Sprinkle with nuts. Bake in preheated hot oven (400° F.) for about 12 minutes. Cool slightly and cut into 1½-inch diamonds in pans. Makes about 4 dozen.

HAZELNUT TARTS
Pastry (2-cups flour recipe)
½ cup firmly packed brown sugar
1 tablespoon all-purpose flour
⅛ teaspoon salt
1 cup dark corn syrup
2 eggs, well beaten
2 tablespoons melted butter or margarine
1 teaspoon vanilla extract
1 cup chopped hazelnuts
Evaporated milk

Line tart shells with pastry. Mix sugar, flour, and salt; add syrup, eggs, butter, and vanilla; pour into pastry. Sprinkle nuts over top and brush edges of tarts with evaporated milk. Bake in preheated moderate oven (350°F.) for 10 minutes; reduce heat to slow (325°F.) and bake for 25 minutes longer. Makes 8 tarts.

HAZELNUT CINNAMON BUNS
2 cups sifted all-purpose flour
2 teaspoons baking powder
½ teaspoon salt
5 tablespoons shortening
⅔ cup milk
¼ cup butter or margarine
¼ cup firmly packed brown sugar
1 teaspoon ground cinnamon
½ cup sliced hazelnuts
¾ cup light corn syrup

Sift dry ingredients together; cut in shortening. Add milk and knead for 1 minute. Roll out on floured board into a sheet 12 x 6 inches. Spread with butter, brown sugar, cinnamon, and nuts. Roll as for jelly roll. Cut into 1-inch slices. Pour 1 tablespoon syrup into each greased muffin pan; put slice of dough in each. Bake in preheated very hot oven (450° F.) for 12 minutes. Makes 1 dozen.

HEAD CHEESE—Head cheese is a well-seasoned cold cut made of the edible parts of a calf's or a pig's head such as

the cheeks, snouts, and underlips, to which sometimes brains, hearts, tongues, and feet are added. The meat is boiled, stripped from the bones, skinned, cut into pieces, and seasoned with onions, herbs, and spices. Then it is put into a mold and pressed into a firm, jellied mass.

Head cheese is named so misleadingly because, at one time, cheese was added to the meat. It is available in food stores, as are other cold cuts, but it can also be made at home.

Head cheese is used in Scandinavian *smörgåsbord,* in French hors-d'oeuvre, and in German, Swiss, and Austrian sandwiches. Every country where farm people butcher meat has its own version of head cheese.

HEAD CHEESE
1 calf's or pig's head
Water
White wine
1 onion, studded with 4 cloves
6 celery stalks with leaves
4 parsley sprigs
1 carrot, sliced
1 bay leaf
12 peppercorns
2 teaspoons salt
Cayenne, ground nutmeg, and ground sage

Have butcher clean the head and remove the snout. Reserve tongue and brains. Wash head well and place in a kettle large enough to cover the head with equal parts of water and wine. Add tongue and onion studded with cloves. Tie celery, parsley, carrot, bay leaf, and peppercorns in a cheesecloth bag. Add. Bring water to a boil and simmer for about 4 hours, skimming the surface as it cooks. Remove tongue from water after 1½ hours. Skin tongue and cut into 1-inch cubes. Remove head from water and reserve cooking liquid. Remove meat from head and cut into 1-inch cubes. Drop brains into cooking liquid and simmer for 15 minutes. Cut brains, after removing the membrane, into 1-inch cubes. Toss with tongue and meat from head, and season to taste with salt, cayenne, nutmeg, and sage. Spoon mixture into a loaf pan or mold, pressing firmly. Pour ½ cup of the cooking liquid into the pan. Cover pan and weight to keep meats under the liquid. Cool, and then chill for 48 hours. Serve chilled and cut into slices. Makes 8 servings.

HEART—The hearts of beef, veal, lamb, and pork are used in cookery, especially in Scandinavia and in central Europe. Poultry hearts are usually used as giblets.

Hearts are tasty meat when properly cooked. Since they are one of the less tender cuts, they must be cooked slowly in moist heat, by braising and stewing. Stuffing adds to the interest of the dish.

Hearts are nutritious and inexpensive; and when seasoned with thyme, marjoram, or other herbs, and cooked in a good sauce, make a good family dish.

Hearts can be used in any recipe calling for sliced, diced, or ground meat.

Availability and Purchasing Guide—Beef heart is the largest and averages 3 to 3½ pounds; it may weigh as much as 5 pounds. One heart makes about 8 servings. Veal (calf's heart) is smaller and more tender. It weighs ¾ to 1 pound and makes 2 or 3 servings. Pork heart averages ½ pound and makes 1 or 2 servings. Lamb heart is the smallest and weighs ¼ to ½ pound. Usually one heart is allowed per serving. Occasionally two very small lamb hearts are served as a single portion.

Storage—Keep in refrigerator loosely wrapped. Maximum storage time is 3 to 4 days as heart spoils rapidly. Quality is best when used within 24 hours.

☐ Refrigerator shelf, raw: 3 to 4 days
☐ Refrigerator shelf, cooked: 5 to 6 days
☐ Refrigerator frozen-food compartment, prepared for freezing: 2 to 3 weeks
☐ Freezer, prepared for freezing: 6 months to 1 year

Nutritive Food Values—Heart is high in protein, iron, riboflavin, and niacin, and has fair amounts of thiamine.

☐ Beef, 3½ ounces, raw = 108 calories
☐ Veal, 3½ ounces, raw = 124 calories
☐ Pork, 3½ ounces, raw = 113 calories
☐ Lamb, 3½ ounces, raw = 162 calories

Basic Preparation—Wash heart. Cut out fat, veins, and arteries. Use whole, sliced, or ground. Braise or cook in liquid.

☐ **To Braise**—If desired, stuff heart before braising. Brown the heart on all sides in a small amount of shortening. Add about ½ cup of liquid. Season with salt and pepper. Simmer, covered, over low heat on top of the range or in preheated slow oven (300° to 325°F.). Check occasionally for moisture; if necessary, add a little more hot liquid to prevent scorching.

☐ **To Cook in Liquid**—Add 1 teaspoon

●● TIMETABLE FOR COOKING HEARTS ●●

	BRAISED (After Browning) (Hours)	COOKED IN LIQUID (Hours)
Beef		
Whole	3 to 4	3 to 4
Sliced	1½ to 2	
Veal (calf)		
Whole	2½ to 3	2½ to 3
Pork	2½ to 3	2½ to 3
Lamb	2½ to 3	2½ to 3

Cooking times are based on top of the range or cooking in a slow oven (300°F. to 325°F.).
A pressure cooker shortens the cooking time to about 1 hour. Follow manufacturer's directions for accurate cooking times.

salt for each quart of water to be used. Place heart in deep heavy saucepan. Add water to cover and any desired seasonings. Simmer, covered, until tender.

SAVORY STUFFED HEART

1¼ cups rice, cooked
    Few celery leaves, chopped
3 onions, chopped
1 teaspoon poultry seasoning or
    ½ teaspoon each of ground thyme and sage
    Salt and pepper
1 beef heart
2 tablespoons fat
2 cups beef bouillon or water

Mix rice and next 3 ingredients; season to taste with salt and pepper. Trim heart and remove large tubes, excess fat, and blood vessels. Season well inside and out with salt and pepper. Fill with some of rice mixture and sew edges together. Brown well in hot fat in heavy kettle. Cover; cook slowly without added water for 2 hours. Remove meat and pour off all fat. Put remaining rice mixture in kettle; add bouillon and season to taste. Put heart on top, cover, and simmer for 1 hour longer, or until meat is tender. Makes 8 servings.

BEEF HEART WITH VEGETABLES

1 beef heart
2 teaspoons salt
¼ teaspoon pepper
1 teaspoon mixed pickling spice
1 celery stalk
4 carrots, sliced
4 onions, sliced
4 potatoes, sliced
    Bottled gravy sauce

Trim heart; remove large tubes, excess fat, and blood vessels. Cover with water. Add salt, pepper, pickling spice, and celery. Cover and simmer for 2 hours, or until tender. Remove heart, reserving stock, and slice. Put vegetables in bottom of casserole and cover with sliced heart. Add strained stock and a little gravy sauce. Cover, bake in preheated moderate oven (375°F.) for 1 hour. Makes 4 servings.

SCOTCH HEART PATTIES

1¼ pounds beef heart
1 medium onion
½ cup quick-cooking rolled oats
1½ teaspoons salt
⅛ teaspoon pepper
    All-purpose flour
2 tablespoons fat
1½ cups water

Wash and trim heart and remove large tubes, excess fat, and blood vessels. Force heart and onion through food grinder, using fine blade. Add oats, salt, and pepper. Let stand for at least 30 minutes. Then, with well-floured hands, shape mixture into 8 thin patties, coating each patty with flour. Brown slowly on both sides in hot fat. Remove patties and keep hot. Blend 1½ tablespoons flour into drippings remaining in skillet. Add

water and cook until thickened. Season with additional salt and pepper if necessary. Serve as a sauce with the patties. Makes 4 servings.

HEART STEW

1½ pounds beef or veal heart
2 tablespoons all-purpose flour
1 teaspoon salt
    Dash of pepper
2 tablespoons cooking oil
2 onions, sliced
1½ cups water
    Hot mashed potatoes

Trim heart; remove large tubes, excess fat, and blood vessels. Cut meat into thin slices. Dredge with flour, salt, and pepper. Brown lightly in hot oil. Add onion and water. Cover and simmer for 45 minutes. Serve with potatoes. Makes 4 servings.

DANISH VEAL HEARTS

2 veal hearts (about 1½ pounds)
6 parsley sprigs, chopped
2 onions, sliced thin
1 tablespoon fat
½ bay leaf
4 peppercorns
1 teaspoon salt
    Dash of pepper
2 small carrots, diced
1 celery stalk, diced
1 cup water
¼ cup heavy cream

Trim hearts and split lengthwise. Remove large tubes, excess fat, and blood vessels. Stuff hearts with parsley and half of onion; close with skewers or sew with string. Brown on all sides in fat in heavy kettle. Add remaining onion, the seasonings, carrots, celery, and water. Cover; simmer for 2 hours, or until hearts are very tender. Remove to hot serving platter. Strain broth, add cream, and pour over hearts. Makes 4 servings.

Note: Pork or lamb hearts may be substituted for the veal.

FRIED HEART SLICES

2 veal hearts (about 1½ pounds)
3 tablespoons cooking oil
1 garlic clove, halved
    Salt and pepper
    Fresh lemon juice
1 tablespoon chopped scallion tops or parsley

Trim hearts; remove large tubes, excess fat, and blood vessels. Slice very thin. Heat oil and garlic slowly for 3 minutes; remove garlic. Add heart slices; brown quickly on both sides. Remove to platter; sprinkle with salt and pepper to taste. Squeeze a little lemon juice over all. Sprinkle scallions on top. Makes 4 servings.

Note: Pork, beef, or lamb hearts may be substituted for the veal.

VEAL HEARTS WITH FRUIT STUFFING

2 veal hearts (about 1½ pounds)
    Salt and pepper to taste
8 pitted dried prunes
2 tart apples, peeled and sliced

3 tablespoons butter or margarine
1 cup water
¾ cup light cream

Trim hearts and split lengthwise. Remove large tubes, excess fat, and blood vessels. Sprinkle hearts inside and out with salt and pepper. Stuff hearts with prunes and apple slices. Skewer or sew opening together. Brown hearts on all sides in butter. Gradually add water and 1 teaspoon salt. Bring to a boil, cover, and simmer for 1½ hours, or until hearts are tender. Remove hearts and slice. Stir cream into pan juices. Reheat but do not boil. Serve over heart slices. Makes 6 servings.

HERB—An aromatic plant used to add flavor to food. These plants usually owe their flavoring qualities to essential oils which are readily soluble or easily volatized by heat and quickly permeate the foods with which they are mixed. For culinary use the seeds of some of these plants are the seasoning agent, in others it is the foliage. The herbs most used in American kitchens are parsley, sage, thyme, marjoram, dill, fennel, tarragon, basil, chives, oregano, and savory.

Strictly speaking, only seed plants which do not develop woody persistent tissue can be considered herbs, but certain plants which do not qualify botanically have long histories of use in cooking as flavoring agents. These include such flowers as the rose, marigold, violet, and scented geranium.

From the earliest times herbs have been used in cooking and medicine and for their sweet scent. They have played a large part in folklore and all sorts of magical properties have been accredited to them. The Assyrians, shapers of one of the earliest of recorded civilizations, who settled along the Tigris in what now is Iraq about 3000 B.C., used herbs. Among the 200 plants they were familiar with were dill, fennel, origanum, and thyme. The Egyptians sprinkled parsley on the graves of their dead, and both Greeks and Romans put sweet marjoram in funeral wreaths.

The Greeks and Romans also believed in love potions made from various herbs, including anise, basil, fennel, and garlic. It was thought that anise made one's face young, that basil attracted scorpions (especially if pounded together with crabs), and that thyme could not grow unless it was blown upon by sea winds. Herbs were also used for all sorts of medical cures, and of course, in cookery.

The Middle Ages continued the use of culinary herbs and the herb gardens of monasteries and castles were lovely to behold. Anise, mint, and parsley were favorites for gravies, sauces, and relishes. Dill added flavor to vegetables. Puddings, tarts, pastries, cakes, and conserves were made with the addition of sweet marjoram, thyme, savory, and anise. Some more unusual culinary preparations included marigolds for soup and drinks (as well as for "angry words"), and cumin for roasted peacock. Borage flowers were used as a garnish, and rue was much more popular than it is now. Basil was "for potage," and also to "make a woman shall not eat of anything that is set on the table." This feat was accomplished by serving the food on a hidden bed of basil, because "men say that she will eat none of that which is on the dish whereunder the basil lieth."

Herbs have always been used for beverages, both alcoholic and nonalcoholic. Today, country people and herbalists are still fervent supporters of herb teas and wines. Woodruff is a traditional and continuing ingredient in the *Maibowle* of the Germans, while wormwood is used for absinthe.

Many herbs, including geranium leaves and mint, were said to have healing powers for wounds, and various common and unpleasant ailments have been thought to be curable by herbs. Present-day herbalists continue the tradition, and modern pharmacists use herbs in preparation of some medicines. The type of herb for the type of ailment has differed in different times and different countries. Baldness, a problem throughout the ages, has been thought to be stopped by onions, parsley, and southernwood.

Queen Victoria's mother, a demanding woman, recommended a violet drink to "soothe the system" in case of bronchitis, fevers, and catarrhs.

Herbs have long been used for a cosmetic effect. Sir Hugh Platt, an Englishman writing in 1609, claims they "relieue," or relieve, for ladies, "The wrongs that Nature on their person wrought/Or parching sun with his hot firie rayes." Sir Hugh recommends sorrel "to take staines out of ones hands presently." "To take away the freckles in the face," according to Sir Hugh, you must "wash your face in the wane of the moone with a spunge, morninge and euening with the distilled water of Elder Leaues, letting the same drie into the skinne. Your water must be distilled in Maie."

The careful instructions as to the time of day and year which are necessary for this herbal remedy to be efficient are not uncommon in herb lore. Herbs have always been connected with magic and superstition, and have sometimes been explained in terms of astrology. From earliest times the influence of the moon upon plants has been considered important. The 17th-century astrologers had complicated charts where they reckoned that each disease was caused by a planet. The illness could be cured either by use of herbs belonging to an opposite sign, or by sympathy, with the herb of the same sign.

Garlic has been worn in an amulet or carried in the pocket or eaten, to ward off all sorts of evil, including vampires, the evil eye, and witches. The plant is used in many spells and charms, and was thought, because of its humanlike form, to screech when it was uprooted. There was also a belief that whoever pulled up the root would himself die. Its juice acted as an anesthetic, as a love potion, to help abscesses, and to soften ivory, as well as "for devil sickness or insanity," "sterility," or "heavy mischief in the home." In fact, it was claimed that it "cures every infirmity except only death where there is no help."

The smell of the aromatic leaves of the herbs, as well as the flowers of some of them, contributes to their flavor and probably accounts for some of the magical properties given to them. But they have long been used for their smell alone. Today the essential oils from roses and sweet calamus are used commercially in perfume, scented soaps, and other sweet-smelling preparations. The early burning of aromatics for the gods was to unleash their smell. In medieval days lavender and sweet flag were often strewn on the floor. Sweet woodruff, which smells like new-mown hay, lent its fragrance to floors and was put among clothes in chests. Costmary and bay scented the medieval version of finger bowls at tables. Potpurris, a mixture of dried flower leaves, are improved with the addition of herbs now, as they have been for years.

Considering the wide uses of herbs, it is not surprising that rulers throughout the ages have been interested in information about them. The Roman Emperors had botanists all over the empire sending back herbs to the capital. Physicians in the later Middle Ages and Renaissance constantly checked herbal experiments in an attempt to keep them up-to-date and free from error. Partly because of the great financial value of herbs and spices in the Middle Ages, when they were used extensively by the rich to flavor and preserve food in those days of nonrefrigeration, Columbus was allowed to set forth on his famous voyage to the New World by Ferdinand and Isabella, who hoped he would discover the spice islands of the East.

Our colonial ancestors set great store

by herbs and used them much as they had in the old country. All gardens had their corner where herbs were grown, if not an herb garden proper. Many of these herb gardens of the old colonial mansions were ravishingly planted in formal designs in the English fashion. We can still see them in colonial Williamsburg, for instance, filling the air with their sweet scent. The Indians of America used many of the weeds growing in the fields and forests for herb teas and medicines. The colonial housewife often had to consult her Indian squaw neighbor to find out if an interesting-looking and smelling plant was poisonous.

Today, herbs have become once more part of daily living. They are easy to cultivate, in a backyard garden or in pots or a box on a kitchen window sill. They prefer light, moderately rich, well drained soil, and a sunny exposure. The great majority of culinary herb plants are annuals which are replaced each spring with new fresh plants. The perennials such as sage and tarragon are propagated by stem cuttings. Few gardening efforts are less troublesome or more rewarding than growing herbs of one's own, for nothing adds such zest and flavor to one's cooking as a pinch of a favorite herb.

When cooking with herbs, here is a word of caution: Be selective about the kinds of herbs used and conservative about the amounts. Use preferably only one herb to flavor a dish if the herb has a pronounced flavor, and don't use too many different herbs in the course of a meal, or the palate will be confused. How little or how much of an herb to use is essentially a question of personal taste, arrived at by experimentation. But remember that a little goes a long way when it comes to herbs, and that not everybody likes the same herbs.

Use ⅓ to ½ teaspoon dried herbs for every tablespoon fresh herbs. This proportion depends on the age of the dried herbs as the flavor of dried herbs deteriorates on standing. Crumble herbs before using to release flavor.

The leaves and/or roots of some herbs, called "potherbs," are themselves cooked and served as vegetables. These include the leaves of borage, chervil, chicory, Good-King-Henry, lovage, orach, rampion, and sorrel; the leaves and roots of sweet cicely and rampion; the roots of skirret. When cooking potherbs, boil leaves as you would spinach, roots as you would turnips.

A CHART OF THE BEST-KNOWN HERBS AND THEIR CULINARY USES

NAME	ORIGIN AND DESCRIPTION	PART USED— FORM AND FLAVOR	CULINARY USES	
			Appetizers & Soups	Meat & Poultry
ANGELICA (Angelica archangelica)	Grows in northern Europe, western Asia, but is not grown in this country now except in a few private gardens. Usually biennial, with care is a weak perennial. It grows about 7 ft. high on hollow stems. The leaves are large, yellow-green, and serrated; roots are long and fleshy; small flowers are greenish-white.	Leaves, leafstalks, and stems, dried or fresh roots, and dried seeds are used. The stems are imported from France. The leaves are not available here. The flavor is bitter and aromatic, resembling juniper berries.	Use chopped fresh leaves as garnish for fish canapés. Flavor vegetable or bean soup with cut-up root and seeds.	Use whole leaves as garnish for meat dishes, stews.
ANISE (Pimpinella Anisum)	Grows in Europe, Asia Minor, India, Mexico, South America, and other temperate and hot countries. An annual, it reaches up to 2 ft. high with light-green leaves, notched 3 times, and yellowish-white flowers. The seeds are downy and ridged, brown with tan stripes when dried.	Fresh and dried leaves, and powdered flowers are used. All have sweetish licorice flavor.	Refreshing flavor for lobster or shrimp cocktail, for cream-of-cabbage or cauliflower soup.	Add to beef or veal stew for a subtly sweet taste and aroma.
BASIL, SWEET (Ocimum Basilicum) **BASIL, DWARF** (O. minimum) **BASIL, ITALIAN** (O. crispum) Also called Curly Basil **BASIL, LEMON** (O. citriodora)	Native to Near East; grown throughout the world. Sweet basil is an annual plant growing 1 to 2 ft. tall. The leaves are large (up to 2 in.), glossy, dark green. Dwarf basil comes with purple or green leaves and is smaller and more bushy than sweet basil. The bush grows up to 10 in. with leaves a maximum of ½ in., or in truly dwarf size with leaves ¼ in. or less. Italian basil has large wrinkled, light-green leaves. Lemon basil grows about 18 in. tall. Its leaves are not so shiny as those of sweet basil.	Leaves with leaf stems, fresh, dried, or ground, are used. The flavor of the standard sweet basil is like spicy cloves. The smaller varieties have much the same taste, while the lemon basil has a more fruity flavor. Italian basil has a stronger odor and taste and must be used with care.	A pinch gives variety to seafood cocktails and dips; or to bean, pea, beef, tomato, or turtle soups.	Sweetly fragrant with hamburger, sausage, veal, beef, pork, duck, and lamb or beef stews. Rub hare or venison lightly with basil before roasting.
BAY LEAF (Laurus nobilis) Also called Laurel Leaf	Mediterranean, Asia Minor, Portugal, Central America, southern United States. Leaf of a small evergreen tree with spreading branches. The leaves are smooth, waxy, and from 1 to 3 in. long and 1 in. or more wide. When fresh, only the underside is pale yellowish-green but the brittle dried leaf is yellowish-green all over, shiny on top and dull underneath.	The dried leaf, whole or ground, is used in cooking. Its bitter pungent flavor is even stronger when the leaf is crushed.	A tempting seasoning in tomato juice, chowders, and beef, lamb, mutton, or game soups, either alone or in an herb bouquet.	Add it to game, pot roasts, stews, tripe, or shish kabobs. Try with chicken or duck, roasted or in pies.
BORAGE (Borago officinalis)	Grows widely throughout the world, including Europe, Asia, and eastern United States. An annual, it is over 2 ft. tall, and is covered with grayish hairs which make it look grayish-green and fuzzy. Some of the oval leaves are as long as 6 in. The bright blue flowers are star-shape.	Leaves and flowers, dried or fresh, can be used. The foliage has the flavor and aroma of cucumber.	Dried or fresh leaves add a pleasant flavor to soups. May take the place of parsley.	
BURNET (Sanguisorba minor)	Asia, North America. Leaflets are very long and deeply toothed. This gives them a fernlike effect. There are 10 varieties of this herb, but this is the one used in cooking.	Fresh or dried leaves have delicate odor and flavor like cucumber. Seeds, dried and pounded, have limited use for vinegar.	Place fresh or dried leaves in soups at beginning of cooking. Goes well in asparagus, celery, Lima-bean, or mushroom soups.	Use in stews.

Fish & Seafood	Cheese & Eggs	Breads & Stuffings	Sauces & Gravies	Vegetables & Salads	Desserts & Beverages
Add fresh or dried leaves to water in which fish is poached. Use fresh whole leaves as garnish for baked and broiled fish.		Use chopped dried leaves sparingly in poultry stuffing.		The blanched stalk may be eaten like celery, cooked as a vegetable, or prepared with sugar and eaten like rhubarb. The stems may be cooked with sugar, rhubarb, and a little lemon. Add leaves, whole or chopped, to green salads. Cook fresh leaf shoots like spinach, although they have a somewhat bitter flavor. Roast or boil roots.	Leaflets and stems are good candied in sugar syrup with lemon or lime added, and, if desired, green food coloring. Use as decoration for cakes, confections. Sprinkle chopped fresh leaves on fruit salad; add whole leaves as garnish to cold drinks. Dried roots and fruits flavor cakes and candy; cooked stems flavor rhubarb jam.
A sprinkling in fish stuffings gives subtle flavor.	Add a little to cottage cheese as a lunch salad.	Gives an unusual taste to rolls, scones, or to stuffing for fish.	Use a little to give an elusive, licoricelike flavor to pudding sauce.	Add to beets, carrots, pickles, sauerkraut; to apple, beet, cucumber salad.	Sprinkle seeds over a coffeecake; mix into cookies, fruit compote, preserved fruit.
Try it with crab, lobster, mackerel, shrimps, swordfish, eel, or in fish dressings and butters.	A pungent addition to rarebits, omelets, scrambled eggs, soufflés.	Its clovelike flavor is delectable stirred into corn bread or muffins. Try adding to other herbs or alone in stuffing for duck.	Add to herb butters, in stuffings, marinades, tomato sauce.	Use it with eggplant, onions, rutabaga, squash, tomatoes, for sure, and in green, or seafood, carrot, cauliflower, cucumber, or tomato salads. Sprinkle over boiled potatoes or peas.	Its sweet, warm quality adds to the deliciousness of fruit compotes.
Gives fine flavor to fish stews, pickled fish, or to steamed lobster, shrimps.		Tasty in poultry stuffings.	Pleasant bitter taste to spark meat or tomato sauce, marinades, or gravies.	Cook with artichokes, beets, carrots, tomatoes, or crumble into fish or potato salad. Delicious in salad dressing for tomato salad or in jellied seafood.	Consider using a bit when making custards.
				The young leaves are similar to spinach and may be cooked with other greens or used alone as a vegetable. Add a few fresh leaves to water in which green peas, beans, or salsify (oyster plant) are cooked. In salads, leaves may be combined with cabbage, cucumber, lettuce, or mixed greens.	The beautiful star-shape borage flowers may be candied and used to decorate cakes and cookies. Sprigs of flowers and leafy tips give fragrance and elegance to iced tea, fruit and wine drinks, and to lemonades.
		Use chopped leaves like parsley in stuffings.	Leaves or dried and pounded seeds used as flavoring for salad dressings and vinegar.	Toss fresh young leaves in beet, cabbage, carrot, celery, lettuce, mixed-green, or tomato salad; or mix dry herb with dressing. Fresh or dried leaves may be added to mayonnaise dressing before serving. Boil fresh young leaves like spinach, or place leaves in water in which vegetables are cooking.	Use leaves for tea, and fresh sprigs to garnish iced drinks.

A CHART OF THE BEST-KNOWN HERBS AND THEIR CULINARY USES

NAME	ORIGIN AND DESCRIPTION	PART USED— FORM AND FLAVOR	CULINARY USES Appetizers & Soups	Meat & Poultry
CAPER (Capparis spinosa)	A native of the Mediterranean, now cultivated in southern Europe and North Africa as well as in southern United States. The caper plant is a low (about 3 ft.) trailing bush, with pinkish flowers and oval green leaves.	Capers are small unopened flower buds, gathered in the early morning before they have opened. They are usually pickled in brine, but are also available dried in bulk.	Add capers to canapés in place of olives.	Use as a garnish for leftovers, especially cold roasts.
CARAWAY (Carum Carvi)	Grows in Europe, temperate Asia, Japan, and parts of United States and Canada. Usually a biennial, it grows over 2 ft., with feathery bright-green leaves like a carrot and with small flowers, usually white, growing like Queen Anne's Lace in umbrellalike clusters.	The dried fruit, caraway seed, is often used whole or ground, as are the fresh young leaves, leaf stems, and roots. Seeds have a sharp flavor like a mixture of anise and dill; leaves are milder in taste. The sweet root has a much more delicate flavor than parsnips.	Chopped leaves and young shoots, as well as seeds, give a distinctive flavor to bean or cabbage soups or to clam chowder.	Adds subtly pungent quality to beef à la mode, goulash, or sauerbraten. Place sprigs in bottom of pan for roast goose or pork. Use leaves as garnish for meat.
CELERY, CULTIVATED (Apium graveolens, var. dulce) **CELERY, WILD** (A. graveolens) Sometimes called Smallage	Celery grows in temperate zones throughout the world. Usually biennial, although sometimes annual, it has wrinkled pale-green leaves and tiny white flowers which grow in large umbrella-shape clusters. Golden Heart celery has bleached white stalk; Pascal, a green stalk. The seeds which form on the flower stalks are less than ¼₆ in. long. Wild celery is a lower plant that resembles lovage, with which it has sometimes been confused.	All parts: root, stalk, leaves (fresh and dried), and seeds (dried, whole, or ground) can be used in cooking. All parts have a somewhat sweet flavor. The root is considerably sweeter than the stalk, which has a mildly sweet aromatic flavor. The leaves are more sharp and pungent. The seeds have the flavor of the fresh celery, but the seed covering provides a somewhat bitter taste.	Canapés, cheese, fish, shellfish may be sprinkled lightly with seed just before serving. Or add chopped celery to ingredients and garnish with stalk and leaves. Fresh leaves especially good in soups.	Add to meat loaves, stews, and pot roasts.
CHERVIL (Anthriscus Cerefolium)	Native of Europe; naturalized in northeast United States. An annual growing up to 2 ft., it has delicate, fernlike bright-green leaves, much like parsley. The flowers are small and white and grow in clusters.	Leaves, fresh or dried, as well as whole sprigs, are used in cooking and as a garnish. The root of the tuberous variety may be cooked and eaten like a carrot. The leaves and stalk have a mild parsley flavor, sometimes with a whiff of licorice or tarragon. A curly-leafed variety has a definite anise-like flavor and smell.	The tender leaves garnish a dish, or season asparagus, chicken, spinach, or sorrel soups.	Is friendly with beef, game, lamb, pork, veal, poultry. Good in meat loaf.
CHIVES (Allium Schoenoprasum)	Grows in Europe and temperate Asia, as well as extensively in United States. A relative of the onion, chives grow in clumps, with a tiny bulb under the ground and tubular green leaves rising above to a height of 10 in. The thin flowers are lavender.	The tiny bulb and the freshly picked flowers can be used as well as the fresh, frozen, freeze-dried, or dried leaves. The green leaves and the bulb have a mild onion flavor.	Garnish for dips, soups, or appetizers; happy addition to seafood cocktails or to Vichyssoise.	Chop the slender leaves over beef, game, lamb, pork, veal, or poultry dishes. The bulbs are used in sausage.
CLARY SAGE (Salvia Sclarea)	Native to southern Europe and Mediterranean countries. This 3- to 4-ft. biennial has unusually large leaves (about 9 in.) at its base. They are gray-green and quite broad. The leaves at the top are smaller. Although a member of the sage family, it is commonly referred to as Clary.	Leaves, fresh or dried, ground or whole, have a lavenderlike odor, and taste, naturally enough, like sage.	Try a teaspoon of chopped dried leaves in meat soups.	A fresh or dried leaf in the roasting pan; use dried powdered leaf in sausage.
COSTMARY (Chrysanthemum Balsamita) Also called Bible Leaf or Alecost	A native of western Asia, it grows wild in some parts of North America. A perennial, it grows over 3 ft., with shrubby stems, and light-green, slightly downy leaves. The flowers are like small daisies, although sometimes there are no white petals.	Leaves, fresh and dried, are used and have a lemony mint odor.		Crushed fresh leaves or dried leaves flavor beef and hamburgers. Place a costmary leaf in the bottom of the roasting pan for chicken, wild duck, or venison.

Fish & Seafood	Cheese & Eggs	Breads & Stuffings	Sauces & Gravies	Vegetables & Salads	Desserts & Beverages
			Most fish and meat sauces are enhanced by the addition of capers. Use with oily sauces or dressings.	Always use in antipasto. Use as a garnish for other green and vegetable salads.	
	A pleasant smooth taste in cheese spreads, cream or cottage cheese, creamed eggs.	Seeds, of course, in rye bread. Also widely used in muffins, rolls, and scones.	Add a little to give zest to sour-cream dressing for salads.	Add sprigs of leaves to water in which cabbage, cauliflower, potatoes, or turnips are boiled. Combine seeds with beets, sauerkraut, potatoes, noodles, creamed onions, turnips, or cabbage. Use fresh herb in cabbage, cucumber, lettuce, potato, and tomato salads. Cook leaves like spinach or use as salad green; boil roots as vegetable and eat plain or with cream sauce.	Use seeds in baked pears, baked apples, applesauce, spice cake, poundcake, sugar cookies, and pumpkin pie, or sugar-coated as candy.
Shredded codfish and salmon croquettes are good flavored with seed. Use in chowders and stews. Add a stalk to water in which fish is poached.	Scrambled eggs, cream and cottage cheese pep up with seed. Add chopped celery to creamed or deviled eggs or omelets.	Biscuits and salty bread are enhanced by celery seed.		Put seed in cauliflower, cabbage, and stewed tomatoes. Mix chopped celery with carrots, onions, peas, tomatoes, green peppers. Use with fish, potato, and vegetable salads; seeds especially good with cabbage salad. For fruit salads add seed to your favorite dressing and serve; or mix chopped celery in with ingredients. Serve cooked celery plain or with sauce.	
Goes well with all kinds of fish.	Stir some into cream or cottage cheese, omelets, or scrambled eggs.		Mild parsleylike flavor for Béarnaise and butter sauces and French dressing.	Try a little chopped leaf with asparagus, beets, carrots, eggplant, or spinach. Green or potato salads are sparked by this parsleylike herb. Cook the herbage as a potherb, or use as salad green.	
Less pungent than the onion, this is a happy seasoning for any fish.	Chop the leaves fine and mix with cottage or cream cheese or into omelets. Use dried leaves in fondues.		Chop them into sour-cream dressing or try some in vinaigrette sauce.	Chopped leaves are good in creamed vegetables, with potatoes, green salads. For an exotic touch, add some of the flowers to a green or cucumber salad. Try pickling the tiny bulbs like onions.	
	Chopped fresh leaves are good in omelets and for flavoring bland cheeses.	May be used like sage in stuffings.	Use leaves in salad dressing and in spice-hot sauce for barbecue.	Add a touch to the water in which yellow vegetables are cooking.	
					Place a leaf in the bottom of the baking pan when baking poundcake. The flavor is very dominant, so take care to use only 1 leaf. It is an ingredient in herb teas. Use in eggnog, or to garnish strawberry shrub.

A CHART OF THE BEST-KNOWN HERBS AND THEIR CULINARY USES

NAME	ORIGIN AND DESCRIPTION	PART USED— FORM AND FLAVOR	CULINARY USES	
			Appetizers & Soups	Meat & Poultry
DILL (Anethum graveolens)	Native to Europe; naturalized in North America. This 2- or 3-ft. high plant, grown as an annual, has fine wispy bluish-green leaves and a hollow gummy stem. The yellow flowers are in large umbrella-shape clusters. The seeds are very tiny.	The leaves and stems, fresh and dried (the fresh are better), as well as the seed of this herb are used. Leaves are quite pungent and stems are bitter; both should be finely chopped for use. The aromatic seeds are available whole or ground; have a sharp taste.	Sprinkle in avocado or fish cocktails, or into bean, borscht, split-pea or tomato soup.	Fresh pungent flavor for lamb chops, stew, or a bowl of rich creamed chicken. Sprinkle over broiled steak or cook with corned beef.
FENNEL, WILD (Foeniculum vulgare) **FENNEL, SWEET** (F. vulgare, var. dulce) Also called Finocchio or Florence Fennel **CAROSELLA** (F. vulgare, var. piperitum)	Wild fennel and the form cultivated in gardens (sweet) are known primarily for their wispy bright-green leaves. Both are erect perennials, the wild variety growing over 4 ft. high. The stems are smooth and glossy and thin in comparison to those of the Carosella, a variety of the garden-grown fennel. It has thickened stalks like celery and grows to the height of about 2 ft. Finocchio is considerably shorter than the wild, and the base of the stems is very thick, overlapping like celery.	Seeds, fresh, as well as dried whole or ground; leaves; stems; bulbous bases and roots of finocchio and carosella are all edible and used in cooking. Flavor is sweet, like anise. Finocchio is especially sweet.	Try this to give a faint sweet quality to fish or seafood cocktails; or try in cabbage or fish soup.	Liver, pork, lamb stew, duck, or goose gain new flavor from this herb.
FENUGREEK (Trigonella Foenum-Graecum)	Grows in Europe and the Orient as well as in United States. An annual, it grows, usually not branching, to about 2 ft. The leaves are as long as 1 in. and the plant has white flowers, growing alone or in pairs.	Dried seeds, available whole, suggest a burnt-sugar or maple taste. The fresh leaves and stems are also used.	Use in meat and vegetable soups.	Good in moderation with beef, lamb, pork, and veal dishes.
HORSERADISH (Armoracial apathifolia or Radicula armoracia)	Although there is no agreement on the botanical name for this perennial, native to southeastern Europe, it is widely known for its long thick branching wrinkled white root, which grows deep into the ground. The flowering stem above the ground is as high as 3 ft.; the leaves are of 2 kinds: the first look like combs, about 9 ft. long and 4 in. across; the next are long (14 in.) oblong leaves, shiny and green, with scalloped edges.	Root and leaves are used. Whole fresh root has no odor; the sharp familiar horseradish aroma is only unloosed when it is grated or ground. It is available fresh or preserved in vinegar. The early leaves taste of bitter herbs, with a biting aftertaste.	Use ground root with cream cheese and sour cream for a pleasing dip for fresh vegetables.	Good to accompany roast or boiled beef, lamb, or mutton.
HYSSOP (Hyssopus officinalis)	This perennial, 1 to 2 ft. tall, has long stems with narrow pointed stalkless dark-green leaves, 1 to 2 in. long. Variations of hyssops have different leaf formations, and other than the blue flowers of this type.	Leaves, flowers, stems, and young shoots, fresh or dried, have a bitter aromatic flavor.	Crush 1 or 2 tender young leaves in bottom of bowl for fruit cocktail; particularly good with cranberries. Add a little freshly minced or dried leaves to sweet vegetable soups while cooking.	Minced herb cuts grease on all fatty meats. Sprinkle duck or pheasant lightly with minced herb before roasting. Fresh or dried leaves give additional flavor to game, kidney, or lamb stews.
LEMON BALM (Melissa officinalis)	Native to southern Europe; now in all temperate climates, including eastern United States. It is a very leafy perennial which grows higher than 2 ft. tall. The leaves, which are up to 3 in. long, are almost round, dark green, and slightly hairy. The flowers are pale yellow and grow in clusters.	Leaves, fresh or dried, are used for their lemon-minty smell and flavor.	Cream soups may be sprinkled lightly with minced leaves just before serving.	Rub roast lamb lightly with crushed fresh or dried leaves before you place it in the oven.

Fish & Seafood	Cheese & Eggs	Breads & Stuffings	Sauces & Gravies	Vegetables & Salads	Desserts & Beverages
An unusual flavoring for your favorite fish dish; or add a few seeds to water in which fish is boiled.	Both leaves and seeds excellent for cheese spreads, cottage or cream cheese.	Sprinkle a few seeds in rye or other dark-bread dough to give carawaylike flavor.	Warm, sharp taste to liven drawn butter or sour-cream dressings; good in vinegars. Beef gravy peps up with addition of a few chopped leaves of dill.	A few seeds improve beets, cabbage, carrots, cauliflower, peas, snap beans, potato salad. Leaves flavor cabbage, cauliflower, or turnips. Seeds, with some stems and leaves, used, of course, to pickle cucumbers.	Slightly sharp flavor of seeds adds savor to apple dumplings or stewed pears, and is tasty in cake.
A delicious sweet flavor to add to fish puddings.	It adds importance to omelets or to scrambled eggs.	Italian bakers stud bread and rolls with it. It is good in muffins, too.	Try it in egg or fish sauces.	Delightful seasoning for beets, celery, lentils; mixed in rice or squash; added to sweet pickles. Use leaves in salad, or boil them as potherb. Eat raw stems like celery. Try seeds to spice beets, or put them in sauerkraut.	Adds unusually good flavor to apple dishes, to coffeecakes, and to sugar cookies. Flavor wine with base of finocchio.
				Try with blackeye peas.	Cookies, gingerbread, and rice puddings are flavored with this herb.
Freshly ground root good with most seafoods, a classic with oysters.			Cream sauces for beef, fish, ham, and other meats are livened with ground root. Gives dash to cocktail sauces for fish and shellfish. Good in salad dressings and flavored mayonnaise.	Fresh young leaves, finely chopped, may be added to green salads.	
Garnish any fatty fish sparingly with minced fresh leaves.				Toss freshly minced herb in vegetable salads.	Use with sweet fruit in pies such as apricot or peach.
		Crushed dried leaves may be added to traditional stuffings; especially good for pork or turkey.	Delicious in cream sauces and those served with fish. Add chopped fresh leaves just before serving.	Chopped fresh leaves may be added to fruit, mixed, or tossed green salad. Or try cooking leaves with chard.	This herb is a welcome addition to tea, fruit drinks, lemonades, or wine cups. If the drink is cold, garnish with a sprig of balm; if the drink is hot, crush 1 or 2 leaves in the bottom of the cup.

A CHART OF THE BEST-KNOWN HERBS AND THEIR CULINARY USES

NAME	ORIGIN AND DESCRIPTION	PART USED— FORM AND FLAVOR	CULINARY USES	
			Appetizers & Soups	Meat & Poultry
LEMON VERBENA (Lippia citriodora)	Originally from Argentina and Chile; now is found in many mild climates. A perennial shrub which grows from 10 ft. in warm climates and to 10 in. in pots. The yellow-green leaves are long, narrow, and pointed at the end and grow in whorls of 3 or 4 woody branches.	Dried or fresh leaves of this plant are used; they have a delicate lemony flavor and smell.	Garnish fruit cups with a tiny leaf.	
LOVAGE (Levisticum officinale)	Native of southern Europe; United States' North Atlantic seaboard also grows wild Scotch Lovage, used for medicinal purposes. True lovage is a tall (5 to 7 ft.) plant, with large heavy light-green leaves like celery, and with clusters of yellowish flowers.	Fresh and dried leaves, stem bases, leafstalks, root, and seeds are used. Greens have celerylike flavor; root tastes and smells strong.	Add a few leaves to tomato-juice cocktail. Leaves give celery flavor to soups.	Cook beef, lamb, mutton, veal, rabbit, or venison stews with seeds in cheesecloth bag. Leaves give celery flavor to stews.
MARIGOLD (Calendula officinalis) Also called Pot Marigold	Native to southern Europe and eastern Asia. A hardy annual, growing from 1 to 2 ft. tall, it has curling green pinnate leaves and bright golden flowers. Flowers, which can be as large as small sunflowers, have oval golden-yellow and orange petals around circular heads.	Dried heads and petals pulverized into powder are used as well as fresh ones. They have a somewhat bitter taste, but lend a subtle flavor and golden color to foods if they are added in moderation. A very little goes a long way.	Try adding 2 or 3 petals to your favorite fish-chowder recipe. A very little powder may be added in cooking chicken broth. Flowers added to vegetable soup is a good idea, too.	Add ½ teaspoon powder to venison stew. Try flavoring braised beef or pot roast with ½ teaspoon powder.
MARJORAM (Majorana hortensis) More exactly, Sweet or Knotted Marjoram	Native to Mediterranean area as a perennial, but usually grown as an annual in cooler regions such as northern United States. It grows over 1 ft. tall and the leaves are downy light-green ovals of up to 1 in. The minute flowers sometimes are pinkish or lilac. The herb has a fragrant odor and a spicy taste. It resembles sage in flavor although it is considerably less strong. A smaller variety, M. onites, resembles M. hortensis, except it has milder flavor. Pot marjoram is usually only sweet marjoram under another name.	Although flowering tips are used in medicine and industry, the leaves are the only part employed in cooking. They have a fragrant aroma and a spicy taste, somewhat resembling sage although considerably less strong.	Add a pinch to avocados, mushrooms, pâtés, to clam chowder or onion soup.	Delightful seasoning for beef, pork, veal, pot roasts, and savory stews.
MINT (Mentha)	There are over 30 varieties of mint, and about a dozen cultivated in the United States. The varieties listed below, the most useful for culinary purposes, are found in temperate zones throughout the world. Other mints, not listed here because their use is limited, include Corn Mint and Water Mint. The mints differ somewhat in appearance, but all have square red-tinged stems and purple flowers, in whorls or spikes.	The fresh leaves of all the mints listed can be used for flavoring. Tastes vary slightly, but all mints have aromatic refreshing aroma. The oil from leaves is used commercially. Spearmint is widely available dried and powdered as "mint." Uses for "mint," fresh or dried, follow. Some experimentation with substitution of different types is possible, for most members of the mint family mix well.	Aromatic addition to cranberry juice, fruit cup, or to soups such as pea.	Delicate flavoring for lamb, ham, veal, ragouts.
MINT, AMERICAN APPLE (M. gentilis)	The only one of 2 varieties of apple mint used for cooking (the other has woolly leaves). A hardy perennial with smooth grayish-green leaves with yellow streaks. Shorter than some mints, as it is low growing with a tendency to spread. Its purple flowers blossom in whorls and there are almost square stems.	Leaves have a delicate fruit aroma and taste, refreshing and with a trace of apple.		
MINT, BERGAMOT (M. citrata) Also called Orange and Lemon Mint	Smooth oval leaves, edged with purple, up to 2 in. long. The leaves are broader than those of the more familiar peppermint.	The leaves have a fragrance mixed with lavender, although orange predominates after they have been smelled for a while.		

Fish & Seafood	Cheese & Eggs	Breads & Stuffings	Sauces & Gravies	Vegetables & Salads	Desserts & Beverages
				Fresh or canned fruit salads may be garnished with a small leaf.	A crushed leaf may be placed at the bottom of the cup or glass before pouring drink. Delicious for making jellies. Lemon Verbena tea is one of the most popular of the herb teas.
				Blanched root can be served like celery. Boil leaves as a potherb. Add a few seeds to salad dressing and serve over mixed fruit. To give a celery flavor to salads rub inside of bowl with a few leaves.	Candy the root, or, for an even more adventurous sweet, candy the leaf stalks and stem bases. Use lovage seeds as a garnish or ingredient as you would caraway seeds.
Add a few petals to other vegetables in a seafood stew.	A little powder will give color to butter and cheese.	Color buns with a dash of powder.		Cook rice with ¼ teaspoon marigold powder instead of saffron.	Add a few crushed petals to baked or boiled custard or to custard sauce. Color cakes with a dash of powder. Try making marigold cordial.
Sprinkle it over fish before baking or into a cream sauce for fish.	Gives subtle variety of flavor to omelets, scrambled eggs, soufflés.	Delicious in poultry stuffing, or added to biscuit dough or herb breads.	Delicate flavoring for spaghetti sauce or your favorite gravy.	Adds interest to corn, beans, carrots, eggplant, Lima beans, peas, spinach, beans, or to a crisp green salad.	
Refreshing change when cooked with any fish.	Tantalizing flavor for cream or cottage cheese.		Make it into mint sauce to serve with roast lamb. Add to French dressing for green salads. Make flavored vinegar.	Add to cabbage, carrots, celery, potatoes, snap beans, or to jellied salads.	Sweet and tangy in custards, fruit compotes, ice cream, in fruit punch, juleps, mint tea. Make a sugar syrup to add flavor to beverages. Make your own mint jelly or add to currant jelly.
				Preferred with cabbage to spearmint because it is more delicate.	Especially recommended in applesauce and pie.
				Used with chopped cabbage instead of spearmint, as Bergamot is more delicate.	Especially recommended for jelly.

NAME	ORIGIN AND DESCRIPTION	PART USED— FORM AND FLAVOR	CULINARY USES	
			Appetizers & Soups	Meat & Poultry
CURLEY MINT (M. spicata, var. crispa)	The mint has dull-green crinkly wide leaves and grows 2 ft. at its tallest. As it has long weak stems and many slender branches, it has tendency to sprawl during summer. The spikes are tipped with violet flowers.	Leaves have piny-resinous odor.		
PEPPERMINT (M. piperita)	There are 2 varieties: Black (var. vulgaris) and White (var. officinalis). Both have pointed leaves 1 to 2 in. long and ½ in. wide, with toothed edges. The flower spikes are thick and blunt. Black has dark-green leaves tinged with purple, and purple flowers tinged with red. It is taller than white variety. The white has light-green leaves.	One of the most popular mints. The oil from white mint is considered of best quality, as the black's is stronger. Largely used commercially, but fresh leaves can be employed by the home cook for an aromatic pungent flavor.		
SPEARMINT (M. spicata, var. viridis)	The most popular of the culinary mints, it resembles peppermint, but the lance-shape leaves are stemless and longer. The flower spikes are long and narrow and pointed. Pale-purple flowers.	Fresh leaves, as well as dried and powdered ones, are used. Recommended for all uses of mint. Very sweet aromatic, one of best mints for flavorings.	See Mint.	See Mint.
MUSTARD, BLACK (Brassica nigra) **MUSTARD, WHITE** (B. alba or B. hirta)	Native to Europe and western Asia and cultivated in western United States, this mustard grows wild throughout country. Black mustard is a hardy annual, growing up to 4 ft., with yellowish-green smooth leaves and the bright yellow flowers characteristic of mustard. The white mustard is a small 18-in. plant, with tender green leaves that spread very quickly.	Both mustards are grown for their seed, which is commercially prepared as mustard flour, the basis of prepared mustard; available also as powdered mustard. Whole seeds of both varieties can be used, but only the leaves of the white are eaten. The black seeds are smaller and considerably more pungent than those of the white.	Tender young white-mustard leaves may be used sparingly in sorrel or lettuce soup.	Season roasts lightly with powdered mustard. Use a bit to flavor creamed chicken or turkey.
NASTURTIUM (Tropaeolum majus or minus)	These annuals, one tall and climbing (T. majus) and one low and bushy (T. minus), have flowers and leaves used in cooking. The small plant, native to Peru, has more flowers and in brighter hues. The leaves are almost circular; the flowers all shades of yellow, orange, and dark red. The light-green seeds turn light brown, and are ridged and wrinkled.	Young stems, leaves, and flowers have peppery taste. Pickled seeds and pods used in place of capers.		
OREGANO (Origanum vulgare) Often called Wild Marjoram	Native to Eurasia, also grows widely in northeast United States and Canada. There are many varieties of this plant, differing in appearance. In general, an erect perennial, growing up to 3 ft., with branching hairy stems (sometimes purplish) and dark-green leaves shaped like a roundish egg.	Fresh or dried leaves and tops are used, and have sweet aromatic flavor like sweet marjoram or thyme. Oregano is stronger than these two and should be used with care.	Try a pinch in vegetable-juice cocktails, in bean, beef, game, or tomato soup.	It's pungent, so use with care to season beef, lamb, pork, veal, sausages, Swiss steak, or any poultry.
PARSLEY (Petroselinum crispum)	there are more than 30 forms of this carrot-type plant. The main varieties include double-curled, moss-leaved, fern-leaved, and turnip-rooted, whose names describe their leaves or roots. A small green plant, its leaves and flowers vary according to kind.	Leaves have familiar refreshing taste and aroma.	Use it as a garnish, as an ingredient in soup bouquets.	A nutritious flavorful addition to beef, lamb, pork, veal, poultry.

Fish & Seafood	Cheese & Eggs	Breads & Stuffings	Sauces & Gravies	Vegetables & Salads	Desserts & Beverages
			CULINARY USES		
					Especially recommended in juleps and punches.
					Try making your own peppermint wafers instead of buying them. Or boil leaves and add marmalade for an unusual dessert sauce.
See Mint.	See Mint.	See Mint.	Best kind for traditional mint sauce, chopped leaves in sweetened vinegar.	Adds strong sweet flavor to cabbage, carrots, potatoes, snap beans, or to jellied salads.	Add to sugar syrup to flavor iced beverages.
Add powdered mustard to other ingredients in making deviled crab.	Use powdered mustard in deviled eggs. Flavor cottage cheese and cream cheese with a pinch of powdered mustard.			Cook greens as potherb. Use 1 teaspoon chopped fresh leaves in salad or add ½ to 1 teaspoon seed with mixed green-vegetable salad. A bit of seeds peps up coleslaw. Sprinkle a few seeds onto hot boiled beets, or boil cabbage with a few seeds. White seeds are used in preparing pickles.	
	Chopped fresh leaves and stems are good, like watercress, with cream- or cottage-cheese spreads.		Use pickled seeds in sauces in place of capers. Especially good with brown sauce for mutton.	Toss chopped young stems and leaves or whole leaves into mixed-green or vegetable salads. Use flowers as edible garnish.	For an exotic and pretty touch, float flowers in tea.
Adds intriguing taste to any fish, but it's pungent, so take care.	Aromatic flavor to give distinction to cheese spreads or omelets.	A favorite with Mexican and Italian cooks. Good in pizzas, rolls, stuffings.	Sprinkle it in fish butter sauce; in cream, meat, spaghetti, or tomato sauces. Add to marinades for game.	Use a little with broccoli, beans, carrots, Lima beans, mushrooms, onions, peas, potatoes, tomatoes. Add to aspics or potato salad. On its own can be boiled as potherb.	
Exciting flavor for fish stuffings, creamed seafood, or for salmon.	Add a pinch to cheese sauces, deviled or scrambled eggs, or to omelets.	Mild and good in biscuits, herb breads, muffins, stuffings, or added to butter for toast.	Seasoning for butters, marinades.	Seasoning and garnish for most vegetables and salads.	

A CHART OF THE BEST-KNOWN HERBS AND THEIR CULINARY USES

NAME	ORIGIN AND DESCRIPTION	PART USED— FORM AND FLAVOR	CULINARY USES	
			Appetizers & Soups	Meat & Poultry
ROSE (Rosa, various species)	There are countless varieties of the rose. Some of the most well known include the Damask rose, the Cabbage rose, and the China rose. The beautiful petaled flowers growing from thorny stems are known to gardeners throughout the world.	Petals, preferably fresh with the base cut off, and hips, fresh or dried, are used. (Hips are the small berries left after the flowers dry, and are the rosebush's fruit.) Rosewater is available commercially, although it may be made at home. The heavily perfumed rose varieties used in cooking have a honeyed scent.	Crush a rose petal into fruit cups. Try making rose-hip soup.	For an exotic delight, glaze baked chicken with rosewater and honey. Rub deer and venison with dried hips, mashed and blended with seasonings and marjoram, before baking. Add hips to rabbit stews.
ROSEMARY (Rosmarinus officinalis)	Grows wild in southern Europe, cultivated in Europe and United States. It grows slowly, but reaches height of 4 or 5 ft. Not hardy in the north. An evergreen shrub, has branching stems which bear long (up to 1½ in.) thin dark-green leaves, curving a bit like pine needles. The undersides are grayish and slightly hairy. The flowers are bluish.	Leaves, fresh and dried, and the fresh tops are used in cooking and garnishing. They have a pungent spicy flavor.	Fresh or dried, it gives exciting flavor to fruit cups, chicken, pea, spinach, and turtle soups.	Its affinity for hearty foods fits it well to blend with beef, game, lamb, pork, veal, poultry.
RUE (Ruta graveolens)	Southern Europe was its home. The little perennial, growing up to 2 ft., has evergreen deeply cut grayish-green leaves, which are thick and covered with a nonhairy bloom which rubs off when touched. The pretty four-petaled flowers are yellow.	Leaves, fresh and dried, are used but are very bitter and should be used sparingly.	Blend into chicken broth. Gives a delightfully different flavor to minced chicken or mushroom canapés. Try a few minced (or if you're feeling adventurous, whole) leaves between buttered brown bread for different sandwiches.	Add a few leaves to beef, lamb, chicken, or kidney stews, during or before cooking.
SAGE (Salvia officinalis)	Native to northern Mediterranean countries, but grows now in all temperate zones. Yugoslavia raises one of the best varieties of sage, Dalmatian sage, which is imported by United States. There are over 500 varieties of this popular herb. Besides the imported Dalmatian sage and the Garden sage (Salvia officinalis), there are White sage, Cyprus sage, a garden variety known as S. horminum, Meadow sage, Pineapple sage (with pineapple fragrance), and Clary sage (see Clary). Most are perennial shrubs with grayish leaves. Garden sage grows 1 to 2 ft. high and has bluish or purplish flowers.	Leaves, fresh and dried, chopped or powdered, are used. The flavor is aromatically bitter; the Pineapple and Dalmatian sages are milder.	A pinch adds extra flavor to cheese dips, pâté, chowders, consommé, and bland cream soups.	It's vital for sausage, and a happy thought in stews, with poultry, or to season rabbit. Rub on a little ground sage before roasting beef, lamb, pork, mutton, or veal.
SAVORY, SUMMER (Satureia hortensis) **SAVORY, WINTER** (S. montana)	Summer savory is native to Mediterranean; now cultivated throughout Europe and United States. Bushy, with many branches, this annual grows up to 18 in. on its weak stems, but falls down easily. The leaves are dark green, and the bush has a great mass of pinkish, bluish, or purplish flowers. Winter savory is similar, but is an annual, somewhat shorter and woodier and falling down and spreading. Its leaves are stiffer than those of summer savory.	Leaves, fresh and dried, are used and have a somewhat resinous aroma. Winter savory has a stronger flavor, but can be used with discretion where summer savory is used.	A piquant touch for pâté, vegetable juices, consommés, chowders, bean or lentil soups.	Adds a deliciousness to a chicken loaf, hamburger, lamb, veal, to stews and poultry stuffing.

Fish & Seafood	Cheese & Eggs	Breads & Stuffings	Sauces & Gravies	Vegetables & Salads	Desserts & Beverages
Try poaching fish in milk with a little rosewater sprinkled over fish.	Add a few chopped fresh petals to scrambled eggs.	Coffeecakes flavored with rosewater or syrup are good.	Rose petals in sauces and gravies for game help remove "gamy" taste.	Fresh or canned fruit salads may be spiced with 1 or 2 fresh petals.	Rose-petal syrup, made with petals and sugar, or rosewater, deliciously flavors custards, puddings, cookies, cakes, chiffon pies, fruit jello, dessert pancakes, and ice creams. Blend crushed rose leaves with orange-blossom honey, or add to fruit and mint jellies and jams.
Exciting flavor for fish stuffings, creamed seafood, or for salmon.	Add a pinch to cheese sauces, deviled or scrambled eggs, or to omelets.	Sweet fresh-tasting herb to crumble into herb breads, stuffings.	Sweet fresh-tasting herb to add to cheese, cream, jelly, or game sauces, or to use in marinades.	Tonic addition to lentils, mushrooms, peas, potatoes, spinach, squash, fruit salads.	
	Mix finely minced leaf with cottage or cream cheese for a delicious spread.			Sprinkle a little minced rue over boiled potatoes. Or add to dressing for chicken, veal, tuna-fish, or vegetable salad.	
Belongs in fish stuffings, where it adds appetizing flavor, a faint fragrance. Put a sage leaf inside mild-flavored fish when baking or add to the water in which you boil fish.	Warm astringent taste to give variety to Cheddar cheese, or to your cheese spreads.	Especially good in cheese bread, and, of course, in stuffings.	Appetizing seasoning for brown sauce, French dressing, or for meat gravies.	Try with Brussels sprouts, carrots, eggplant, Lima beans, onions, peas, or tomatoes.	
Happy with baked or broiled fish.	Its aromatic flavor will improve cream cheese. Try it with scrambled eggs.	Fragrant flavorful addition to herb bread and to meat or poultry stuffings.	Aromatic flavoring for barbecue, fish, seafood, or poultry sauces and gravies.	Add a bit when cooking artichokes, beets, cabbage, peas, rice, sauerkraut. Classic with green beans. Fresh leaves are good tossed into salad.	Tastes good in stewed pears, or used with quinces.

A CHART OF THE BEST-KNOWN HERBS AND THEIR CULINARY USES

NAME	ORIGIN AND DESCRIPTION	PART USED— FORM AND FLAVOR	CULINARY USES Appetizers & Soups	Meat & Poultry
SWEET CICELY (Myrrhis odorata) Also called Sweet Chervil and Myrrh	Native to Europe, this perennial's hairy stems grow 2 to 3 ft. high. The leaves are fernlike, the flowers small and whitish. The long seed (up to 1 in.) is narrow and ribbed.	Fresh leaves and seeds are used. Seeds should be sliced and eaten with other herbs. All have an aniselike flavor, although the leaves are weak in taste.	Chopped leaves flavor cream soups with faint anise flavor.	Good in stews.
SWEET FLAG (Acorus Calamus) Often called Calamus	Grows in North Temperate Zone throughout world. The plant has yellow-green sword-shape leaves rising from base up to 3 ft. The flower is a dry spike. It grows from a large underground rhizome into a smaller underground stem. Not to be confused with the poisonous blue flag, which has dark-green leaves with no smell.	Leaves, stem, roots, and rhizome, fresh and dried, have strong spicy ginger-like aroma. Rhizome is apt to be tough and requires long boiling.	Young leaves are good addition to chicken soup. Or for winter, use dried and ground leaves or root.	Add to chicken stew young leaves dried and ground or fresh.
TARRAGON (Artemisia dracunculus) Often called French Tarragon	Native to western and southern Asia, now grows in temperate and cold United States and southern Europe. A perennial, it grows somewhat like a shrub to a height of above 18 in. The dark-green leaves are long, narrow, and pointed, and occur along the woody stems at intervals.	Leaves, fresh and dried, are used in cooking. Their flavor is somewhat like anise.	Piquant addition to chicken livers, vegetable juices, chowders, consommés.	Highly valued for use with pheasant, sweetbreads, tongue, veal, chicken, or turkey dishes.
THYME, GARDEN (Thymus vulgaris) Also called English Thyme **THYME, WILD** (T. Serpyllum) Also called Creeping Thyme	Garden thyme grows widely in Europe, United States, and Canada; wild thyme, a native to Europe, temperate Asia, and North Africa, grows in North America from southeastern Canada to North Carolina. Garden thyme is a bushy little perennial, about 1 ft. tall, with gray-green leaves, ½ to 1 in. long. English thyme is a variety with broad leaves. There are many varieties of the wild thyme, which, as its name implies, creeps along the ground, rising to varying heights. It becomes firmly matted and its leaves are of many colors as well as green, according to the variety. Some are striped white, some greenish-yellow; flowers may be bluish, purplish, white, or red.	Leaves and the leafy and flowering tops, fresh or dried, of both thymes are used. Both wild and garden thyme have pungent flavor and a sweet fragrance. Leaves and flowers of certain varieties of thyme have particular aromas which are distinctive. Of the creeping thymes, Lemon thyme (T. citriodorus) has lemony scent; Caraway thyme (T. Herbabarona) smells and tastes as name implies; Thymus azoricus has fruity citrus aroma. The chart indicates where a certain variety is especially recommended for use.	Sprinkle a little in seafood or vegetable-juice cocktails; in a gumbo or fish chowder.	Use with restraint with beef, game, lamb, pork, veal, or in meat loaf. Rub caraway thyme over meat to preserve it and flavor it.
WATERCRESS (Nasturtium officinale)	Native to temperate Europe. Naturalized in North America in brooks and ponds. A short perennial, it has very small round shiny dark-green leaves, paler green stems, and small white flowers.	The fresh leaves and stems have a slightly peppery flavor and are crisp.	Garnish canapés and seafood appetizers with chopped leaves. Or mix into fruit and vegetable-juice cocktails. Try minced watercress in cheese, fish, and meat sandwich fillings. Add a half bunch of minced sprigs to fish chowders, and creamed potato or vegetable soups. Or use as sorrel.	A pretty garnish for broiled, boiled, or roasted meats and poultry.

CULINARY USES

Fish & Seafood	Cheese & Eggs	Breads & Stuffings	Sauces & Gravies	Vegetables & Salads	Desserts & Beverages
				Root, raw or boiled, can be eaten with oil and vinegar alone or in salads. Fresh leaves add to salads.	Use seeds like cloves or caraway in dessert flavoring.
Use dried root as substitute for ginger in a fish dish.			Young leaves flavor fish sauce.	Slice tiny unborn leaves in center of the young stalk into green salads.	Candied root makes a delicious confection alone or to flavor cream, custard, or rice pudding.
Delicious seasoning for baked or broiled fish, especially for lobster.	Sprinkle it over scrambled eggs or omelets.		Best known in tarragon vinegar; good, too, in butters, marinades, and added to mustards and flavored mayonnaise. A must for Sauce Béarnaise.	Has an almost spicy taste which adds to asparagus, beans, beets, broccoli, cabbage; tossed green, tomato, fish, or jellied salads.	
Pungent warm addition to any type of fish.	Mix it with cream or cottage cheeses, sprinkle on shirred or creamed eggs.	Important in poultry and vegetable stuffings; adds taste to biscuits, herb breads, or waffles.	Delightful addition to an herb bouquet or to seafood sauce.	Try with beans, beets, carrots, onions, potatoes, or in aspics.	Use T. azoricus in creams and custards. Lemon thyme especially good in jellies.
Minced or whole, garnishes whole fish.	Blend into cottage or cream-cheese spread or into omelets and scrambled eggs.	Minced cress added to biscuit dough or piecrust is delicious and nutritious.		Use as sorrel in your favorite recipe. Sprinkle minced leaves over carrots, cauliflower, potatoes, green beans, and sweet vegetables. Or boil as potherb and serve with your favorite sauce.	

HOW TO BUILD AND PLANT THIS HERB GARDEN IN YOUR OWN BACKYARD

When you discover how easy herbs are to grow, you will collect them avidly and tuck them into odd places about your yard. To start you on your way with herbs, here is a collection of 18 different culinary kinds growing in clay-colored flue tiles and arranged in a group to be viewed from all four sides; a perfect feature for a sunny terrace or patio. And you may adapt the idea to your site by regrouping the tiles any way you wish; they might even be set into a slope. Flue tiles are obtained in various shapes and heights from building supply dealers. Tiles may be cut into halves; let a mason show you how. When you decide on an arrangement that pleases you, sink the tiles two inches or more into the ground and fill them with good garden soil after first loosening the earth beneath the tiles with a spade to insure drainage. You may grow your herbs from seed sown in the soil-filled tiles when the weather warms in spring. But with the exception of the parsley and sweet woodruff you need only two or three plants of a kind so it may be more practical to buy them from a garden center or an herb specialist.

1 Sweet woodruff	10 Rue
2 Chives	11 Lemon Balm
3 Mint	12 Burnet
4 Sweet Marjoram	13 Oregano
5 Dill	14 Catnip
6 Thyme	15 Sage
7 Winter savory	16 Fennel
8 Summer savory	17 Parsley
9 Basil	18 Nasturtium

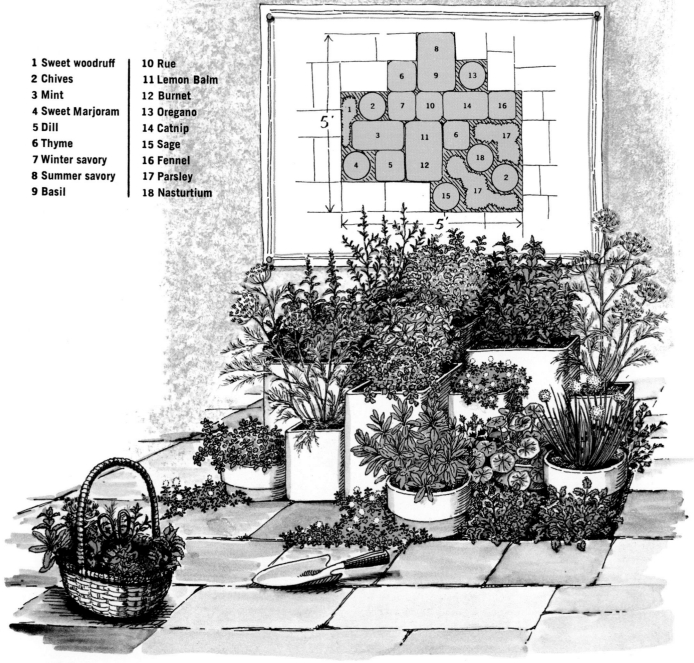

HERMIT—A dark, spicy cookie filled with fruits and nuts. The dark color comes from molasses or brown sugar and ground spices. Hermits may be served plain or with a glaze.

Hermits are early American cookies that originated in New England. They are also found in the South and other parts of the country. Their origin is as obscure as their name. They belong to the group of spicy cookies of the clipper-ship and the spice-trade days. They bear enchanting names like Snickerdoodles, Kinkawoodles, Brambles, Tangled Britches and they all resemble each other; the difference is that one may contain cinnamon, but not other spices, the other raisins and no citron, etc.

BROWN-SUGAR HERMITS

½ cup soft butter
1 cup firmly packed brown sugar
2 eggs
2 cups sifted cake flour
1 teaspoon baking powder
½ teaspoon salt
1 teaspoon ground cinnamon
¼ teaspoon each of ground cloves and nutmeg
2 cups seeded raisins, chopped
½ cup chopped nuts

Cream butter and sugar. Add eggs, one at a time, beating until light after each addition. Add sifted dry ingredients, raisins, and nuts; mix well. Drop by teaspoonfuls onto greased cookie sheets. Bake in preheated moderate oven (350° F.) for about 10 minutes. Makes about 4 dozen.

MOLASSES HERMITS

¾ cup soft butter or margarine
1½ cups light brown sugar, packed
½ cup molasses
3 eggs
4 cups sifted cake flour
1 teaspoon each of salt, cinnamon, and ground nutmeg
½ teaspoon each of cloves, allspice, and mace
¼ cup strong coffee
1 cup chopped nuts
1 cup each of raisins and currants
Confectioners' sugar

Cream butter and sugar until light. Beat in molasses. Add eggs, one at a time, beating thoroughly after each addition. Sift flour, salt, and spices and add to first mixture alternately with coffee, beating until smooth. Fold in nuts and fruit. Pour into pan (15 x 10 x 1 inches) lined with wax paper. Bake in preheated moderate oven (350°F.) for about 20 minutes. Turn out on rack and peel off paper. Slip onto cutting board and cut in 35 bars about 3 inches x 1½ inches. Sprinkle with confectioners' sugar.
Note: These will stay moist a long time.

MINCEMEAT HERMITS

1 cup sifted all-purpose flour
¼ teaspoon each of salt, baking soda,
and ground nutmeg
½ teaspoon ground cinnamon
⅓ cup butter
⅓ cup firmly packed light brown sugar
1 egg
½ cup mincemeat
1 tablespoon dairy sour cream
Vanilla Glaze

Sift first 5 ingredients and set aside. Cream butter and sugar. Add egg, and combine mixtures. Then add mincemeat and cream, mixing by hand. Drop by heaping teaspoonfuls in mounds onto ungreased cookie sheet, leaving 2 inches between mounds. Bake in preheated hot oven (400°F.) for 10 to 12 minutes. Remove from oven and frost with Vanilla Glaze while hot. Makes 20.

Vanilla Glaze
Mix 1½ cups sifted confectioners' sugar, dash of salt, 1 teaspoon vanilla extract, 2 tablespoons melted butter, and about 2 tablespoons heavy cream.

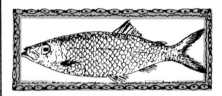

HERRING—These small, salt-water fish belong to the family *Clupeidae,* and the shad, alewife, and sardine are related to them. Also related to this family is a fresh-water variety, lake herring, sometimes called "cisco." Herring is an important food fish, both for human consumption and as the basic diet of other food fishes.

Herring have small heads; they are streamlined and covered with silvery, iridescent scales. Mature herrings measure around ten inches, but they can be larger. They are migratory fish, and appear to spend most of their lives in the deep waters offshore. In the spring they come to the beaches in enormous numbers in order to spawn. The sight of schools of herring, several miles wide, shimmering in the moonlight like an iridescent tapestry as they progress to the shore, is an unforgettable one. Their migrations are uncertain, and no one knows why sometimes they stay away from some shores for years.

Herring females lay an average of 10,000 to 60,000 eggs at each spawning. At spawning time, the female rubs herself against rocks, sand, or seaweed, on which she drops her eggs. These can be seen floating on top of the sea, resembling sawdust. Both eggs and herring are preyed upon by other fish and gulls, porpoises, and sharks.

The economics of many nations were based upon herring. The spawning ground influenced the location of cities, and the capricious habits of the herring often brought disaster, for when the fish did not come, there was no food. Herring have always been fished commercially on a vast scale. Holland's great foreign trade was built upon her successful herring fisheries. One of the reasons why Charles I of England (1600-1649) was overthrown by his subjects (and eventually lost his head) was because he interfered with their free fishing rights. He wanted to tax the fishing rights to get money to fight the Dutch herring trade of the time.

In Europe, especially in Great Britain and in the countries that border on the North Sea, fresh herring is greatly appreciated.

Preserved herring in many varieties is a staple food of Holland and the Scandinavian countries. The herring is salted, pickled, or smoked and dressed with sauces. Many of these herring delicacies are imported into the United States and, along with our own preserved herring, can add considerable variety to a budget diet.

Kippers and bloaters are two herring specialties of England. The fish are cured by salting and smoking. They are baked or broiled just long enough to heat them through. Kippers (a contraction of "kippered herring" referring to the method and ingredients used in the process of curing them) and bloaters (the latter are larger herring) are tasty English breakfast food and are served also at high teas and suppers.

Rollmops, the favorite German herring dish, is a rolled-up pickled herring. Like other pickled herring, it can be bought in food stores.

Availability and Purchasing Guide — All year round, although the supply fluctuates depending upon the catch.

Herring is sold fresh, salted in brine, mild-smoked, hard-smoked, pickled in wine sauce or other seasoned sauces or with sour cream, and kippered.

Canned herring is available pickled in tomato or wine sauce, as grilled fillets, and rolled with anchovies. Pickled herring in wine sauce or with sour cream is available in jars.

Storage

☐ Fresh and mild-smoked, refrigerator shelf: 1 to 2 days
☐ Fresh and mild-smoked, refrigerator frozen-food compartment, prepared for freezing: 2 to 3 weeks
☐ Fresh and mild-smoked, freezer, prepared for freezing: 1 year
☐ Salted in brine, refrigerator shelf: 1 week
☐ Hard-smoked, pickled, and kippered,

Rollmops

refrigerator shelf: 2 to 3 months
- [ ] Canned, kitchen shelf, unopened: 6 months to 1 year
- [ ] Canned, kitchen shelf, opened and covered: 3 to 4 days

Nutritive Food Values—Good source of protein and fat. Fresh herring is high in phosphorus. The caloric value of 3½ ounces of fresh salt-water herring can vary from 98 to 176 calories depending on the variety. The value of 3½ ounces of smoked herring varies from 196 to 300 calories depending on variety and method of smoking.
- [ ] Fresh-water herring (cisco), 3½ ounces, raw=96 calories
- [ ] Salad in brine, 3½ ounces=218 calories
- [ ] Kippered, 3½ ounces=211 calories

Basic Preparation—*Fresh herring* is prepared as is any other fresh fish.

Herring in brine should be soaked in fresh water for 24 hours. Water should be changed several times. After soaking, remove head, split, fillet, and skin fish. Prepare as desired.

Smoked herring should be soaked in water or in half milk and half water for several hours. The longer it is soaked the less smoky it will taste.

Kippers and bloaters, if heavily salted, may have to be soaked as other smoked herring is. They should be just heated through or they will be dry. Serve as a breakfast dish with eggs and toast.

Pickled herring is eaten as is and can be chopped and mixed with other foods, with salads, sandwich spreads, etc.

GRILLED ENGLISH HERRING

Cut heads, tails, and fins off washed and gutted herrings. Split open along the backbone; draw out the backbone with as many fine bones as possible. Wipe fish and sprinkle with pepper and salt. Dip fish into fine oatmeal, coating it both inside and out. Place fish on broiler rack. Dot each with 1 teaspoon bacon fat. Broil for 10 minutes on each side, or until crisp and golden brown. Serve immediately with mustard sauce or with lemon.

PICKLED HERRING

6 herring in brine
1 onion, sliced
½ lemon, sliced
1½ cups cider vinegar
3 bay leaves
⅛ teaspoon crushed red pepper
1½ teaspoons mustard seeds
½ teaspoon sugar

Clean herring and soak in cold water for 24 hours, changing water several times. Remove head and bones; rinse and drain. Arrange in covered refrigerator dish in layers with onion and lemon. Combine vinegar with remaining ingredients. Bring to boil; cool; pour over herring. Store, covered, in refrigerator for 3 to 4 days before serving. Makes 6 servings.

ROLLMOPS

6 herring in brine
Prepared mustard
2 small sour pickles, sliced
2 onions, thinly sliced
1 tablespoon capers
1 red pepper, cut up
6 peppercorns
2 bay leaves
1½ cups cider vinegar
1 cup water

Clean herring and soak in cold water for 24 hours, changing water several times. Remove head and bones. Rinse and drain. Spread herring with prepared mustard, pickle slices, onion slices, and capers. Roll up each herring and secure with toothpicks. Place in small container with red pepper, peppercorns, and bay leaves. Do not use a metal container. Boil together vinegar and water. Cool; pour over herring. Cover and let stand for 3 to 6 days. Drain before serving. Serve with sour cream, if desired. Makes 6 servings.

HERRING IN SOUR CREAM

5 herring in brine
1 cup dairy sour cream
2 tablespoons cider vinegar
1 teaspoon Worcestershire
½ teaspoon powdered mustard
2 onions, sliced
Dash of cayenne
Chopped parsley

Clean herring and soak in cold water for 24 hours, changing water several times. Remove head, skin, and bones. Rinse and drain. Cut into 1-inch pieces. Combine remaining ingredients; add herring and mix lightly. Place in glass jar; cover. Let stand in refrigerator for about 12 hours before serving. Makes 6 servings.

BROILED CISCO

Preheat broiler. Wash fish and dry quickly with damp cloth. Lightly dust with flour. Put fish on broiler pan, brush with butter, margarine, or oil. Broil fillets, 2 inches from heat, for 5 to 7 minutes; do not turn, but baste once during broiling. Broil whole fish 6 inches from heat; broil for 4 minutes, then turn and broil for 5 minutes on second side.

BROILED KIPPERED HERRING

8 mild kippers
¼ cup melted butter
Juice of 1 lemon
Paprika
3 teaspoons chopped scallions

Without breaking the skin along the back, split kippers and spread butterfly-style, skin-side down in shallow baking dish. Brush with butter and lemon juice, sprinkle with paprika, and bake in preheated moderate oven (350°F.) for 10 minutes. Garnish with scallions. Makes 4 servings.

FRIED SMOKED HERRING

8 smoked herring
Pepper
1 cup cornmeal
Fat for cooking

Wash herring and soak in cold water for 24 hours, changing water twice. Rinse and dry. Sprinkle with pepper and roll in cornmeal. Fry in shallow fat (⅛ to ¼ inch) in skillet for about 12 to 15 minutes or until brown and crisp, turning once. Makes 4 servings.

HERRING BUTTER

Mix ¼ cup creamed butter, 2 teaspoons ground smoked herring or herring paste, and a few drops of fresh lemon juice. May be spread on bread for canapés, alone, or as a base for another food.

HICKORY—A large family of American trees of the genus *Carya,* all of which have hard wood suitable for timber. Many have rich green leaves in summer which turn a brilliant yellow in fall. Some hickory varieties are raised commercially.

The extremely hard wood of the tree has made hickory a synonym for firmness. Andrew Jackson, who was elected president of the United States in 1828, was known as Old Hickory to point up his toughness in war or peace.

Pecan and pignut trees are both members of the hickory family. The thin-shelled nuts of these trees are known as pecans and pignuts. The "hickory" nuts available commercially come from the shagbark or shellbark hickories and have a hard shell.

The hickory nut was eaten by the Indians before the first American colonists arrived in the new country. The name pohickery, mentioned as early as 1653, is a shortened form of the word used by the Virginians to describe an Indian food of water and pounded nuts.

The Indians in Florida used hickory nuts to make a milky liquor which they called "milk of nuts." A contemporary observer, writing in 1775, reported that "this milk they are fond of and eat it with sweet potatoes in it."

Modern cooks find hickory nuts more useful in cakes, cookies, sweet breads, and candies. They can also be used in any recipe calling for pecans.

The shells of hickory nuts are so hard that it is usually necessary to use a hammer to crack them in order to remove the nutmeats.

Availability and Purchasing Guide—Hickory nuts are available only in certain localities. They are sold by the pound in bulk, unshelled; they are rarely available shelled.
- [ ] 3 pounds hickory nuts = 1 pound shelled meats

Storage—Store, in a covered container, in a cool dry place, refrigerate or freeze.
- [ ] In shell, kitchen shelf, covered: 1 year
- [ ] Shelled, kitchen shelf, covered: 2 to 3 months.
- [ ] Shelled, refrigerator shelf: 4 months
- [ ] Shelled, refrigerator frozen-food compartment: 6 months
- [ ] Shelled, freezer: 6 months to 1 year

Nutritive Food Values—Hickory nuts are high in fat.
- [ ] 3½ ounces = 673 calories

HICKORY NUT CAKE
- 1 cup butter or margarine
- 2 cups sugar
- 3 cups sifted all-purpose flour
- 1 tablespoon baking powder
- 1 cup milk
- ½ teaspoon each of vanilla and orange extracts
- 1 tablespoon grated lemon rind
- 7 egg whites, beaten until very stiff
- 1 cup hickory nuts, chopped

Cream butter until soft. Gradually beat in sugar, a little at a time. Beat until fluffy. Sift together flour and baking powder. Add flour and milk alternately with butter mixture, beginning and ending with flour. Stir in vanilla and orange extracts and grated lemon rind. Fold in beaten egg whites. Pour into greased 9-inch angel-food pan. Scatter hickory nuts on top of batter. Bake in preheated moderate oven (350°F.) for about 1 hour. Cool in pan. Makes one 9-inch cake.

HICKORY NUT CREAMS
- 3 cups firmly packed light brown sugar or maple sugar
- 1 cup light cream or evaporated milk
- ½ teaspoon vanilla extract
- 1 tablespoon butter
- 2 cups hickory nuts

Mix sugar with cream until sugar is dissolved. Bring to a boil and boil to 234° F. on a candy thermometer, or until a small amount dropped into cold water forms a soft ball. Cool mixture to 110° F., or lukewarm. Add vanilla, butter, and nuts. Beat with a spoon until creamy. Drop by teaspoons onto wax paper. Makes about 36 creams.

NUT BREAD
- 3 cups sifted all-purpose flour
- 1 cup sugar
- 1½ teaspoons salt
- 4 teaspoons baking powder
- ¼ cup shortening
- 1 egg, well beaten
- 1¼ cups milk
- 1 cup coarsely chopped hickory nuts

Sift flour with sugar, salt, and baking powder. Cut in shortening until mixture resembles coarse cornmeal. Beat egg with milk and add liquid all at once to dry ingredients. Stir until just blended. Stir in nuts. Pour mixture into a well-greased pan (9 x 5 x 3 inches). After baking, cool on a rack and slice while warm.

HICKORY CRESCENTS
- 1 cup ground hickory nuts
- 1 cup butter
- ¾ cup sugar
- 2½ cups sifted all-purpose flour
- 1½ teaspoons vanilla extract
- Vanilla Sugar

Combine nuts, butter, sugar, flour, and vanilla. Knead to a smooth dough and shape about 1 teaspoon of dough at a time into a small crescent about 1½ inches long. Bake on ungreased cookie sheets in preheated moderate oven (350° F.) until slightly browned, about 15 to 17 minutes. Cool for 1 minute. While still warm, roll cookies in Vanilla Sugar. Cool completely, and roll again in Vanilla Sugar. Makes about 6 dozen.

Vanilla Sugar
Cut 2 or 3 vanilla beans into 1-inch pieces. Put in jar with 1 pound sifted confectioners' sugar. Let stand for 3 days. The longer the sugar stands, the more fragrant it becomes.

HIGHBALL—An American drink made from whisky or other hard liquor, mixed with water, soda water, or ginger ale and served with ice in a tall glass.

HOECAKE—This is the cornmeal cake of the early American settlers, which often served as bread. The cooking facilities of colonial households were generally primitive, and ovens, even when existing, could not be heated easily. The inventive settlers baked a cornmeal and water mix-

ture on the blades of their hoes on hot coals in front of a wood fire and called them "hoecakes."

Today's hoecakes are baked in a frying pan or on a griddle like any other hot cake.

OLD-FASHIONED HOECAKE
- 1 cup white cornmeal
- ½ teaspoon salt
- Boiling water

Mix the meal and salt and add enough boiling water to make a dough that is soft, but not thin enough to be a batter. Heat a well-greased 6- or 8-inch frying pan, and spread the dough on it in one cake, flattening with a spoon or spatula. Cook until very brown on one side, then turn with a pancake turner and let brown as long as can be done without burning.

HOLLANDAISE—A rich sauce of French origin made with egg yolks and butter. It is served with eggs, fish, vegetables, and, occasionally, meat. The origin of the name is obscure; there is no historical evidence that it originated in Holland. There may be a slight clue in the old French culinary language where we find that fish served with melted butter was called *à la hollandaise*, since the sauce we know today as hollandaise is so rich in butter.

How to Cook Superbly: Hollandaise

by Helen Evans Brown

Hollandaise sauce is not only a classic accompaniment for asparagus, broccoli, and other vegetables, it is the base of other famous sauces: Béarnaise, mousseline, maltaise, and choron. It is also a chef's way of obtaining a beautiful brown glaze on many entrées and a necessary ingredient for many famous dishes including eggs Benedict. It is really no great feat to make hollandaise perfectly for, unlike an omelet, it requires no practice. There is just one simple thing to remember, and that is not to let it cook over too high heat. If you do, it will break or separate. But even that catastrophe can usually be remedied.

There are three ways to make hollandaise. The one usually found in most cook books I will skip, because I consider the other two better, each for a different reason. The first of these, the method used by most European-trained chefs, has the advantage of perfect flavor and consistency and is easy to make. The second, or blender method, is even easier, although the resulting sauce has two small faults, probably recognized only by experts: the egg yolks have a slightly raw taste and the consistency is a bit too fluffy.

FIRST METHOD

EQUIPMENT

You will need a kitchen bowl, preferably a heavy crockery one (not metal) that will heat slowly and hold the heat. Select a size that will fit over a saucepan or the bottom part of a double boiler without touching the hot water beneath. A 3-cup bowl is usually right as it allows room for beating. You will also need a wire whisk. The French type (called a *fouet* in France) is perfect but there are American whips that do very well. One is a spoon-shape device edged with a coil of wire; the other is also spoon-shape, but crisscrossed with wire. A split or slotted spoon, or a bundle of twigs such as those used in Sweden, can also be used, as can a spoon or plastic scraper if you work fast. A fork doesn't reach the curves of the bowl; therefore some of the mixture may overcook. You will also need a knife for cutting the butter or a small pan for melting it, if you prefer that method.

INGREDIENTS

    3 egg yolks
    ¼ cup hot water
    1 tablespoon fresh lemon juice (or to
       taste)
       White pepper or cayenne to taste
       Ground nutmeg to taste (optional)
    ½ cup (¼ pound) soft butter, cut into
       slices, or melted butter

HERE'S HOW

1. Put the bowl over the pan of warm water, making sure that the bottom is at least ½ inch from the top of the water. Place over low heat.

2. Put the egg yolks in the bowl and, while whisking or stirring vigorously, drizzle in the hot water. Add lemon juice and pepper or cayenne, continuing to beat. Add nutmeg if you wish (early French recipes called for it, but it is rarely used today). Don't let the water boil or you'll have scrambled eggs. If it approaches that point, remove from heat. If it does boil, put bowl in cold water for a minute to cool it slightly. The egg-and-water mixture will become fluffy and thickened, the whisk coated, and the yolks will lose their raw taste.

3. When the egg mixture reaches that point, add a slice of the butter and stir until it melts. The sauce should begin thickening. Add more butter, whisking the while, until all is added and the sauce is so thick that the bottom of the bowl will show for a split second when you stir. If it doesn't thicken properly, give it more heat but not too much. A quicker method is to melt the butter and drizzle it in with one hand while beating with the other. This works very well if you are careful to pour very slowly, at least at first until the mixture starts to thicken. It has an added advantage in that you can leave the milky residue in the melting pan, thus improving the flavor of the sauce.

4. Your sauce is now done and can be held over warm (never hot) water until you're ready to serve (up to 1 hour or more). Remember that hollandaise is a warm, not hot, sauce. Makes about 1½ cups.

SECOND METHOD

EQUIPMENT

All you need is an electric blender.

INGREDIENTS

Cut egg yolks to 2 and hot water to 1 tablespoon. All of the other ingredients remain the same. Melt butter until it is very hot, almost boiling.

HERE'S HOW

1. Rinse container of blender with hot water; put in place, add egg yolks, hot water, lemon juice, and seasonings, and whirl at high speed for 3 seconds.

2. Remove top (just the small opening if your blender is so provided, otherwise just lift lid enough to add butter). Pour the foaming butter in very slowly, keeping the blender turned on. (You may get splattered if you stand too close, so watch it!) As soon as all the butter (but not the milky residue) is added, your hollandaise is ready to serve. Makes about ⅔ cup.

HINTS

■ **Separation**—If your hollandaise should separate from overheating, try adding a few drops of boiling water or thick cream while beating vigorously.

■ **Thinness**—If it is too thin, it means you haven't cooked it enough or have added the butter too fast. If you suspect the first, just return the bowl to water that is under the boil and beat until thickened. If you think you may have added the butter too quickly, warm a bowl in hot water, then put about 1 teaspoon of heavy cream and 1 tablespoon of the sauce in it and whisk vigorously. Gradually add the remaining sauce, 1 spoonful at a time, until all is added and the sauce is thick.

■ **Reheating**—Hollandaise can be kept in the refrigerator for 2 or 3 days or frozen for weeks. (Remember that egg yolk is a perfect culture for bacteria, so don't let it stand around in a warm place.) When reheating, put a bowl over warm water, as above, and add 1 spoonful of the sauce at a time, beating after each addition. If it should separate, treat as above. Or put it over warm water all at once and beat hard until smooth and warm.

VARIATIONS

■ **Béarnaise Sauce**—Follow Hollandaise recipe but omit lemon juice. Instead soak 1 teaspoon dried tarragon in 2 tablespoons tarragon vinegar and cook with 2 teaspoons chopped shallots or green onions until the vinegar is absorbed. Add to the hot water and continue as above. Omit nutmeg but add a pinch of powdered mustard, if desired. Strain if you wish. Serve with steaks, lamb, meat loaf, fish, and vegetables.

■ **Choron Sauce**—Add 2 tablespoons tomato paste to 1 recipe of Béarnaise Sauce. Serve with fish, eggs, steaks, meat-

Frankfurter, Hominy, and Green-Pea Casserole

balls, or meat loaf.

■ **Mousseline Sauce**—Combine 1 recipe of Hollandaise Sauce with ½ cup heavy cream, whipped. Serve with soufflés, vegetables.

■ **Maltaise Sauce**—Follow Hollandaise recipe but substitute ¼ cup fresh orange juice for the hot water, in either method; in the blender method use 3 egg yolks. Also add 1 teaspoon grated orange peel. Serve with boiled vegetables or fish.

SPECIAL USES

■ Add 2 or 3 tablespoons hollandaise to 1 cup Béchamel or cream sauce.

■ Or add ¼ cup hollandaise to 1 cup whipped cream (or ½ cup each of whipped cream and cream sauce) and use for masking foods that are to be glazed or browned under the broiler.

HOMESTYLE—The word describes a home-kitchen way of cooking food or a home-cooked meal. When food is cooked for hotels, restaurants, institutions, and factories, the dishes taste differently from those prepared at home. The difference in flavor and texture is due to the fact that the food is cooked in large amounts at one time, that many of the ingredients are prepared in advance rather than just at cooking time, and that the food is kept hot on steam tables and other equipment instead of being cooked just before serving.

To cook homestyle is to try to approximate the methods used in home cooking: small quantities, good seasonings, and cooked to order, which means cooked fresh for the meal.

HOMINY—Kernels of hulled dried corn from which the germ has been removed. It is also known as "samp." Ground hominy is called grits. Hominy is apparently a word of Algonquian Indian origin, implying small particles. It is a truly American food, unknown anywhere else.

Hominy is cooked in water or milk, and may then be fried, baked, or served with a sauce. It is a popular staple in the South and Southwest.

Availability and Purchasing Guide—Sold by the pound as pearl, hominy (hull removed mechanically), and lye hominy (hull removed chemically). Hominy grits are available in three grinds: fine, medium, and coarse.

Canned hominy is also available.

Storage

☐ Kitchen shelf: stores indefinitely
☐ Refrigerator shelf, cooked and covered: 4 to 5 days

Nutritive Food Values—Good source of carbohydrate.

☐ Hominy and hominy grits, 3½ ounces, cooked = 51 calories

Basic Preparation

☐ **To Cook Hominy**—Soak overnight in water to cover. Pour hominy into salted boiling water (1 part hominy to 4 parts water). Cook over low heat. Cover and simmer for 4 to 5 hours, or until hominy is tender. Stir often during cooking. Use as is or beat butter into the hominy before serving. Beating whitens hominy. Milk or cream (½ cup for each 1 cup raw hominy) may be beaten into the hominy before serving.

☐ **To Cook Hominy Grits**—Soak 1 cup grits in water to cover for 1 hour. Drain. Add 3 cups boiling water and 1 teaspoon salt, and cook in double boiler up to 1 hour, or until tender. Length of cooking time will depend on whether grits are fine, medium, or coarse.

SALT PORK, BEANS, AND HOMINY

½ pound navy beans
½ pound hominy
½ pound salt pork
Salt and pepper
Crumbled dried marjoram

Soak beans and hominy overnight. Drain and cover with fresh water. Cut salt pork into strips and mix with beans and hominy. Season to taste with salt, pepper, and marjoram. Simmer, covered, for at least 5 hours, or until beans and hominy are tender. Makes 6 to 8 servings.

FRANKFURTER, HOMINY, AND GREEN-PEA CASSEROLE

In a greased 2-quart casserole, arrange in 3 pie-shape portions the following: 1 pound frankfurters, brushed with melted margarine and scored with sharp knife; 3½ cups cooked hominy (one 1-pound, 13-ounce can), drained; 2 cups (one 1-pound can) peas, drained. Pour ¼ cup margarine over hominy and peas. Sprinkle with 4 slices of cooked bacon, chopped. Bake for 25 minutes in preheated moderate oven (350°F.). Makes 4 servings.

HOMINY AU GRATIN

3½ cups (one 1-pound, 13-ounce can) hominy
1 cup water
1 teaspoon salt
½ cup grated sharp cheese
¼ cup butter or margarine
1 cup warm milk

In a skillet combine all ingredients except milk. Simmer over low heat for 10 minutes, or until butter and cheese are melted. Stir occasionally. Gradually stir in milk and cook, stirring occasionally, over low heat until thick and bubbly. Put under broiler and cook until top is golden-brown. Makes 8 servings.

MEXICAN HOMINY

1 medium onion, minced
1 medium green pepper, chopped
¼ cup butter or bacon fat
3½ cups (one 1-pound, 13-ounce can) cooled hominy, drained
1 teaspoon chili powder
½ teaspoon salt
⅛ teaspoon pepper

Cook onion and green pepper in the butter in top pan of chafing dish over direct heat for about 10 minutes. Add remaining ingredients, and heat. Makes 4 servings.

HOMINY AND CHEESE

3½ cups (one 1-pound, 13-ounce can) cooked hominy, drained
¾ pound sharp Cheddar cheese, cut into pieces
¾ cup milk
½ teaspoon salt
2 eggs, beaten
⅛ teaspoon pepper
⅛ teaspoon celery seed

Put all ingredients in skillet. Cook over low heat, stirring frequently, until cheese is melted. Makes 4 servings.

BUTTERY GARLIC GRITS

1 cup fine hominy grits
4 cups boiling water
Salt
½ cup butter
¼ pound garlic-smoked cheese, shredded
2 eggs, beaten, and water to make 1 cup
½ cup crumbled corn flakes

Cook grits in boiling salted water for 7 to 10 minutes. Remove from heat. Stir in butter, shredded cheese, eggs and water. Pour into ungreased 1½-quart baking dish. Sprinkle corn flakes on top and cook in preheated moderate oven (350°F.) for about 45 minutes. Serve in casserole hot from the oven. Makes 4 servings.

FRIED SALT PORK AND MILK GRAVY ON HOMINY GRITS

Boil ⅓ cup fine hominy grits with 1¾ cups water and ¼ teaspoon salt for 10 minutes. Cut rind from 3 ounces of salt pork and slice pork thin. Cover with boiling water and let stand for 5 minutes, then drain and dip into flour. Fry slowly until brown and crisp. Remove salt pork and pour off all but 1 tablespoon fat drippings. Stir in 1 tablespoon flour and 1 cup skim milk. Bring to boil; cook until slightly thickened, stirring constantly. Season to taste with salt and pepper. Serve pork and gravy on grits. Makes 2 servings.

BAKED HOMINY GRITS

2 cups cooked hominy grits
⅔ cup milk
3 tablespoons melted butter or margarine
2 eggs, beaten

Combine all ingredients and pour mixture into a buttered shallow 1-quart baking dish. Place pan in a pan of hot water. Bake in preheated moderate oven (375° F.) for 1 hour. Makes 6 servings.

GRITS BATTER BREAD

1 egg, beaten
½ cup cooked hominy grits
1 cup white or yellow cornmeal
1 teaspoon salt
Boiling water
1 tablespoon shortening

Combine egg, grits, cornmeal, and salt. Pour enough boiling water over mixture to make a batter of the consistency of light cream, about 1½ cups. Melt shortening in 8-inch square pan. Pour batter into pan. Bake in preheated moderate oven (350°F.) for 40 minutes. Bread will not brown. Makes 4 servings.

FRIED HOMINY GRITS

2 cups cooked hominy grits
2 eggs, beaten
2 tablespoons milk
¼ cup fine cracker crumbs
½ cup shortening
Bacon

Press hominy into a small loaf pan (7⅜ x 5⅜ x 2¼ inches). Chill for several hours. Unmold. Cut into ½-inch slices. Beat eggs with milk and dip slices into mixture. Roll slices in cracker crumbs and coat well. Heat shortening; fry slices to a golden brown on both sides. Serve with slices of crisp bacon. Makes 4 to 6 servings.

HOMINY PUFFS

2 cups cooked hominy grits
2 eggs, separated
¼ cup all-purpose flour
1½ teaspoons baking powder
½ teaspoon salt
Fat or lard for deep frying

Mix hominy with egg yolks. Stir in flour sifted with baking powder and salt. Beat egg whites until stiff but not dry, and fold them into the hominy mixture. Drop by tablespoonfuls into hot deep fat (360° F. on a frying thermometer). Fry until deep brown. Makes about 18 puffs.

HOMOGENIZE—This is a word of Greek origin, composed of *homos,* meaning "the same," and *"genos,"* kin or kind. In culinary language, "to homogenize" is to reduce an emulsion to particles of the same size and to distribute them evenly. The word is most frequently used for milk, but also for salad dressings and mayonnaise.

The homogenized milk we drink is pasteurized milk that has been processed mechanically to break up the fat globules into a tiny size so that they will stay in the liquid part of the milk rather than rise to the top. In other words, the cream is incorporated into the milk so that the milk is uniform rather than consisting of thin milk topped by cream.

The origin of homogenized milk lies in patents granted to two Frenchmen in 1892. They wanted to make margarine and invented machines that were the first homogenizing machines. These machines blended fats and water into a smooth whole. Their use for milk came later, in 1899, when another French inventor, Auguste Gaulin, noticed the fat globules in milk and decided to make a smooth, homogenous milk emulsion, which he did, adapting the principles of the homogenizing machines and taking out his own patents. This new milk appeared for the first time at the World's Fair in Paris in 1900, where it stirred up great curiosity. The milk was called Gaulin's Milk or *lait homogénéisé*, and from this developed our name.

The first time American readers heard about homogenized milk was in April 1904, when it was described to them in *The Scientific American*. The first introduction, in Quebec, Canada, in 1904, was not successful. The new milk was reintroduced in Ottawa in 1927, and by 1932 it could be found in many large Canadian cities.

In the United States, the first homogenized milk was introduced experimentally at the University of Illinois in 1921, but it did not become popular until the early thirties. Studies made at the Children's Hospital in Philadelphia, which proved that homogenized milk was more digestible for babies than ordinary milk, led to its acceptance in American homes. Today, over two thirds of all American milk is homogenized.

HONEY

HONEY—A sweet sticky liquid made by honeybees from the nectar of plants. The bees suck the nectar from the flowers and store it in their honey sacs where it undergoes certain changes. Later the bees deposit the liquid in honeycombs where, with other changes, it becomes honey.

Honey is the oldest sweetener known to man, and was just about the only one until sugar cane was discovered in the New World and cultivated on a large scale to produce sugar.

All ancient literature mentions honey and honeybees with much feeling and gratitude for their bounty. The Bible perhaps expressed this best, speaking of a land "flowing with milk and honey."

In the early days, honey was gathered from the hives of wild bees in rocks, crevices, and trees. Later on, tame bees and their hives were part of every monastery, castle, or farm garden. As honey was the principal sweetener until the 18th century, almost every small rural household kept its bees. We read in old English manor account books how the tenants often paid their rent in honey, and in old cook books how hams were originally cured in honey, and fruits preserved in honey solutions. The rinsings of the combs were used to make mead, the ancient honey drink that was known to all the people of antiquity, from the Druids in Britain to the Persians.

Throughout the world honey was used not only in cooking, but also for medicinal purposes, in ceremonials, and in worship. The wax from the combs was equally part and parcel of daily life. Strips of clean linen dipped into melted wax were used to bind up wounds. The wax was used to waterproof leather, smooth sewing yarn, and even to make a kind of primitive chewing gum.

Reading the literature of the past, we may marvel at the enormous amounts of honey consumed. But we must remember that in those days there were many more flowered meadows and wild lands, and that beekeeping was not a hobby as it is now, nor was honey a special food product, but part of the household's economy.

Honey is served plain on bread, muffins, biscuits, waffles, or pancakes. It blends well with butter or peanut butter for sandwiches. Honey is used in cooking in cakes, cookies, breads, and sauces. It may be used as a sweetener for milk, fruit drinks, or hot beverages and is popular on hot or cold cereal, ice cream, and fruits. Honey is also used as a glaze for baked ham. It can be used to glaze carrots and sausage links, to drizzle warm over ice cream or on broiled grapefruit, to sweeten lemonade or iced tea, to mix with cream cheese for salad, to sweeten baked apples, and to sweeten raw cranberry relish.

Availability and Purchasing Guide—Honey is available year round in jars, cans, pails, and cardboard containers. The flowers from which bees gather nectar largely determine the color, flavor, and aroma of honey. When there is no designation of the flower source on the container, the honey is a blend of different floral types. Sweet clover, clover, and alfalfa honey constitute well over half of the honey produced in this country.

Color—The color varies from the water-white of sage honey through the golden color of clover honey to the reddish brown of buckwheat honey. Usually the lighter the color of honey, the milder the flavor.

Style—Honey is available in three styles: extracted, comb, and chunk. About three fourths of the yearly crop is sold as extracted honey.

☐ Extracted honey—This is the liquid honey separated from the comb. Some processors filter it to make it clear. It is the type most used in honey cookery.

The crystallized or granulated form of extracted honey with its fine creamy texture makes a smooth spread for breads. This is labeled granulated, creamed, fondant, spread, or spun. Whipped honey is crystallized honey which has been whipped to make it light and fluffy. Also available is honey butter, a blend of honey and butter.

☐ Comb honey—Sections of the waxen comb, filled with honey just as the bees stored it. Section-comb is sold from the hive in wooden frames usually weighing about 1 pound. Cut-comb honey has been taken from the frames and cut into small squares. Both of these are fragile and hard to handle so few stores stock them but they are available at farm markets and roadside stands.

☐ Chunk honey—Consists of parts of the comb in a container with extracted honey filled in around the chunks.

Storage—Honey should be stored in a tightly covered container at room temperature in a dry place. If container is left open, the honey will absorb moisture and may ferment. If tightly covered, honey may be kept for several months at room temperature (about 70°F.) at a low relative humidity. Do not store in refrigerator for the cold temperature hastens crystallization of the sugar. Crystallization will occur if kept too long but this does not harm the honey. To reliquefy, place the container in a pan of warm water until the crystals disappear. The water should not be hotter than the hand can stand.

Nutritive Food Values—Honey is almost pure carbohydrate. It is a predigested sweetener, and as such is valuable in certain special diets.

☐ 3½ ounces, extracted = 304 calories

Basic Preparation—Use low to moderate oven temperatures for baking, for honey caramelizes at a low temperature and will brown quickly. Honey cakes and cookies will remain moist longer than those made with sugar and are generally leavened with baking soda.

Honey should be measured accurately. Thick honey rounds up over the top of a measuring spoon or cup, so cut off with a spatula. Be sure to scrape all the honey from the measuring container; heated honey will pour more easily than cold honey and heating makes it easier to measure. Honey becomes darker and thicker with age and is not desirable for baking. It can be used as a spread or syrup.

When honey is substituted for sugar it is necessary to adjust the amount of liquid in the recipe. To substitute honey for sugar: 1 cup honey contains about ¼ cup water, therefore deduct ¼ cup liquid from the amount in the recipe for each cup of honey used. One cup honey is as sweet as 1 cup sugar so no adjustment is necessary for taste. Honey's tendency to absorb moisture presents problems when it is substituted for sugar in frostings, confections, and crisp cookies. Since the amount of moisture absorbed tends to make baked products temperamental, the amount of flour used in any recipe in which honey is substituted for sugar may have to be changed from what the recipe specifies. This has to be done by experimentation, adding flour a little at a time until the desired consistency of dough is achieved.

HONEY BUTTER
Blend ½ cup each of soft butter and honey. Store in refrigerator. If a thinner butter is desired, use ¾ to 1 cup honey to ½ cup butter. Serve with hot biscuits or on hot waffles or pancakes. Good, too, in making cinnamon toast.

Honey-Fruit Butter
To recipe for Honey Butter, add a little grated orange or lemon rind; chopped nuts, dates, or dried apricots. Serve on raisin bread.

HONEY GLAZES
■ For Baked Ham—Mix 1 cup honey with ½ cup orange juice, cranberry sauce, or cider. About 45 minutes before ham is baked, remove rind. Score fat and insert whole cloves in center of squares. Cover with glaze and finish baking, basting frequently.

■ For Carrots or Onions—In saucepan melt ¼ cup butter or margarine. Add ¼ cup honey, and blend. Add hot cooked whole carrots or white onions and cook until glazed, turning frequently.

HONEYED BEETS
  3 cups cooked beets, diced
  2 tablespoons butter
  1 tablespoon grated orange rind
  ¼ cup fresh orange juice
  ½ cup honey
  ½ teaspoon salt
  ½ teaspoon pepper

Place beets in heavy saucepan. Add all other ingredients. Cook over low heat, stirring constantly, until liquid has evaporated and honey forms a glaze over beets. Do not brown. Makes 4 servings.

STRAWBERRY-HONEY BAVARIAN
  1 package strawberry-flavored gelatin
  1 cup undiluted evaporated milk
    Juice and grated rind of 1 lemon
  ¼ cup honey

Honey: Extracted, Chunk, and Comb

18 ladyfingers, split
1 package (12 ounces) frozen strawberries

Dissolve gelatin in 1 cup hot water. Chill until partially set. Pour milk into refrigerator tray and freeze until mushy. Turn into chilled bowl and whip until stiff. Add lemon juice and rind and honey. Beat until well blended. Fold in gelatin; chill until set. Just before serving, arrange 6 ladyfinger halves around edge of each sherbet glass. Spoon Bavarian into glasses; top with partially thawed strawberries. Makes 6 servings.

HONEY MOUSSE

3 egg yolks
¾ cup strained honey
1 cup heavy cream, whipped
2 egg whites, stiffly beaten

Beat together egg yolks and honey until light. Fold in whipped cream first, then beaten egg whites. Pack into 1½-quart mold, and freeze. Makes 6 to 8 servings. **Note:** A fragrant flower honey, such as orange or rose honey, would be excellent for this French recipe.

PENNIES FROM HEAVEN

½ cup water
1 cup honey

Combine water and honey and bring to a boil. Cook until it reaches the soft-ball stage, or 240°F. on candy thermometer. Drop hot mixture, 1 teaspoon at a time, into a dish filled with firmly packed crushed ice. The ice must be as firm as the ice in snow cones.

HONEY-GLAZED APPLES

Peel and core 4 cooking apples. Bring 1 cup each of water and honey to boil in deep saucepan. Slowly cook 2 apples at a time in syrup until tender, turning apples occasionally. Remove to serving dishes. Boil syrup until thick. Cool slightly and pour on apples. Serve warm or cold, topped with dairy sour cream and a grating of nutmeg. Makes 4 servings.

HONEYED PEARS

7 pounds ripe but firm pears
1 cinnamon stick
1 teaspoon ground ginger
Grated rind of 1 lemon
2 cups cider vinegar
3 pounds honey

Peel and core pears, but leave whole. Combine all other ingredients and bring to a boil. Cook pears in syrup over medium heat until tender; test with cake tester. Cook only a few pears at one time. Remove pears with slotted spoon and place in sterilized jars. Remove cinnamon stick from syrup. Cook syrup until reduced by half. Pour over pears. Seal jars.

Makes about 3 quarts.
Note: Use firm pears, such as Seckel pears, and serve as a relish with roast meats and poultry.

HONEY-NUT-APPLE PIE

3 tablespoons all-purpose flour
¼ teaspoon salt
1 teaspoon ground cinnamon
½ teaspoon ground nutmeg
½ cup dairy sour cream
¾ cup honey
½ cup chopped pecans
6 medium tart apples
Pastry for 2-crust 9-inch pie, unbaked

Mix first 4 ingredients; then add sour cream, honey, and pecans. Peel and slice apples and stir into first mixture. Line pie pan with half of pastry, add filling, and adjust top crust. Bake in preheated hot oven (425°F.) for 30 minutes. Reduce heat to moderate (350°F.) and bake for about 15 minutes longer. Makes 6 to 8 servings.

HONEY-ORANGE-ALMOND CAKE

½ cup shortening
½ cup sugar
½ cup honey
Grated rind of 1 orange
5 egg yolks
2 cups sifted cake flour
2 teaspoons baking powder
½ teaspoon salt
½ cup milk

Honey-Orange-Almond Cake   Strawberry-Honey Bavarian

¼ cup ground blanched almonds
Confectioners' sugar
Slivered almonds

Cream shortening; add sugar gradually, beating until light and fluffy. Add honey and orange rind and mix well. Then add egg yolks, one at a time, beating thoroughly after each addition. Add sifted dry ingredients alternately with milk, beating until smooth. Add nuts. Line greased pan (9 x 9 x 2 inches) with unglazed brown paper, then grease again. Pour mixture into pan. Bake in preheated moderate oven (350°F.) for 50 minutes, or until done. Sprinkle with confectioners' sugar and garnish with slivered almonds.

DUTCH HONEY CAKE
½ cup firmly packed dark brown sugar
1 egg
½ cup honey
3 tablespoons dark molasses
1 teaspoon baking soda
½ teaspoon baking powder
¼ teaspoon pepper
¼ teaspoon each of ground allspice, cinnamon, nutmeg, and mace
3 tablespoons butter, melted
1½ cups sifted all-purpose flour

Beat together sugar and egg. Beat in honey and molasses. Soften baking soda in 2 teaspoons water and stir into mixture. Combine baking powder, spices, and melted butter. Beat into mixture. Gradually beat in flour, a little at a time. Thoroughly grease and flour a loaf pan (9¼ x 5¼ x 2¾ inches). Pour mixture into it. Bake in preheated moderate oven (350° F.) for 30 to 45 minutes, or until knife blade inserted in center comes out clean. Cool in pan for 5 minutes. Remove, and cool on wire rack.

HONEY-DATE BARS
1 cup honey
3 eggs, well beaten
1 teaspoon vanilla extract
1⅓ cups sifted all-purpose flour
1 teaspoon baking powder
¼ teaspoon salt
2 packages (6½ ounces each) pitted dates, cut up
1 cup chopped nuts
Fine granulated sugar

Mix honey, eggs, and vanilla; beat well. Add sifted dry ingredients, dates, and nuts. Spread in greased pan (13 x 9 x 2 inches). Bake in preheated moderate oven (350°F.) for about 45 minutes. Cool in pan. Cut into bars 1 x 3 inches; roll in sugar. Makes 39.

BUTTERED HONEY NUTS
6 ounces shelled unsalted nuts
1 tablespoon melted butter
1 tablespoon honey

Spread nuts on a cookie sheet. Bake in preheated slow oven (300°F.) for 15 minutes. Mix butter and honey and pour over nuts. Stir until nuts are completely coated with the honey mixture. Store in airtight container until ready to serve. Makes 1⅓ cups.

HONEY-CREAM SAUCE
Mix ½ cup honey, ½ cup light cream, and 2 tablespoons butter; cook over low heat for 10 minutes. Add a little rum flavoring if desired. Makes about 1 cup.

LEMON-HONEY SPREAD
2½ cups honey
Grated rind of 1 lemon
¾ cup strained fresh lemon juice
⅓ cup liquid pectin or ½ bottle

Combine honey, lemon rind, and lemon juice in saucepan. Bring to a rolling boil, stirring constantly. Stir in pectin. Bring again to a full boil. Boil for exactly 1 minute. Remove from heat when jelly sheets from spoon. Skim; pour into hot sterilized jelly glasses. Seal with paraffin. Makes 1 quart.

Note: This is delicious on hot toast, pancakes, waffles, or with cold meats.

HONEY TOPPING
½ cup sweet butter
¼ cup honey
¼ teaspoon ground cinnamon, nutmeg, mace, ginger, or any combination of these spices to taste
½ cup heavy cream, whipped

Cream butter until soft and fluffy. Beat in honey and spices. Gradually beat in whipped cream, beating until mixture is smooth and fluffy. Chill until serving time. Use as a quick topping for cakes, pancakes, waffles, or French toast. Makes about 1 cup.

HONEYDEW MELON—These melons
belong to the muskmelon family, whose varieties include cantaloupes, honeydews, casaba, and Persian melons. Honeydews have a smooth yellowish-white rind, and their flesh is sweet and green.

Honeydews were enjoyed by the Egyptians as early as 2400 B.C. The Persians knew them before that, since muskmelons had been grown in Persia since antiquity. So fragrant were the melons that they reminded the Persians of a favorite perfume, musk. There is a tale of a jeweled Persian prince who had himself wakened at night to eat a melon that had reached the peak of perfection at that particular moment.

Honeydews were brought to the United States about sixty years ago. At first, they were grown under climatic and soil conditions similar to those of their Asiatic ancestors, in low hot river valleys and deltas, but now they flourish in all the irrigated parts of the Southwest, and in California.

Honeydew, cut into wedges, is served with lemon or lime slices. It is a fine accompaniment for meat, seafood, sliced cheese, and, served as melon balls, combines well with other fruits in salads and desserts. Wedges of honeydew are good garnished with other fruits, especially berries.

Availability—Honeydews are available from May to October, with August and September the most plentiful months. A combination of honeydew and cantaloupe balls is available frozen, in sugar pack.

Purchasing Guide—These oblong melons average 4 to 6 pounds and are 7 to 10 inches long. Select melons with creamy yellow rinds that feel velvety. Ripeness is also indicated by a softening at the blossom end.

Storage—Allow underripe melons to ripen at room temperature. Rinse ripe melons, dry well, and wrap in wax paper, foil, or plastic bag. Chill in refrigerator. The tissues of melons held too long at low temperatures break down rapidly at room temperature. Cut melon should be wrapped well and kept in the refrigerator.

Nutritive Food Values—Honeydew contains vitamin C.

☐ Fresh, 3½ ounces = 33 calories
☐ Frozen melon balls, syrup pack, 3½ ounces = 62 calories

HONEYDEW RINGS WITH SHRIMP SALAD
1 medium-size ripe honeydew melon
Head lettuce
Shrimp Salad
Fresh parsley
Mayonnaise

Wash honeydew and cut into 6 rings. Save end pieces to add to fruit cup or fruit salad. Remove seeds from rings, peel, and cut into 1-inch wedges. Shred lettuce and place in each of 6 individual salad plates, over which arrange honeydew wedges in circles. Fill center of each with Shrimp Salad. Garnish with fresh parsley and serve with mayonnaise as a main-dish salad. Makes 6 servings.

Shrimp Salad
3 cups diced cold cooked shrimps
1½ cups diced celery
½ teaspoon finely chopped onion
½ teaspoon salt, or to taste
⅛ teaspoon pepper
2 tablespoons fresh lemon juice
⅓ cup mayonnaise

Combine all ingredients. Toss lightly, and chill. Makes 4½ cups.

AVOCADO-MELON SALAD
Halve avocados and remove seeds. Scoop out pulp carefully. Reserve shells. Cube avocado pulp. Lightly toss avocado cubes with watermelon and honeydew balls. Pile in scooped-out avocado shells. Sprinkle with lemon juice.

HONEYDEW AND ORANGE DESSERT
Place 3 cups fresh honeydew melon balls and 2 cups fresh orange sections in a bowl. Combine 6 tablespoons fresh lemon juice, 2 tablespoons fresh lime juice, and ¼ cup sugar and pour over fruit. Chill, and serve in sherbet glasses. Makes 6 servings.

HOREHOUND (Marrubium vulgare)—
Horehound is a member of the mint family, a large family of plants including herbs such as thyme, marjoram, and basil. It shares an aromatic odor with its better-known relatives, but is very bitter in taste. Horehound also refers to the extract or candy made from the plant and used for coughs and colds.

Horehound is native to the Old World countries of southern Europe, northern Asia, and the Orient, but it is now found in most parts of the world except the tropics. Although it is used mainly for horehound candy, it was known to the ancient Egyptians, whose priests referred dramatically to it as "Seed of Horus," "Bull's Blood," and "The Eye of the Star." As early as the 1st century Pliny the Elder, the famous Roman scholar and historian, recommended it as a medicinal plant of great value. His contemporary, Columella, added that it had great use in killing flies. A dish of milk with horehound should be put in the place bothered by the pests. The 13th-century German philosopher and theologian, Albertus Magnus, mentions it as a cough medicine and Michael Drayton, the English poet (1563-1631) gives other explicit uses: "For comforting the spleen and liver—get for juice, Pale Horehound."

Now, after a long history as a popular medicine and cough remedy, horehound is most often used to make horehound candy, a brittle sugar candy made with brown sugar and leaves or stems of horehound. But the adventurous cook can also use a leaf to flavor braised beef or beef stew and cakes and cookies.

HORS-D'OEUVRE—The literal translation of these French words is "outside of the main work." Hors-d'oeuvre are small appetizers that are not part of the menu, but serve as an introduction to a meal.

In American culinary language the terms hors-d'oeuvre, appetizer, and canapé are often used interchangeably for foods served with drinks or as a first course. To be literal about the matter: while it is true that both hors-d'oeuvre and canapés are appetizers, canapés are morsels of food with a base of bread or crackers and are eaten with the fingers; hors-d'oeuvre, which can be hot or cold, are eaten at the table with a knife and fork.

An endless variety of foods lend themselves to hors-d'oeuvre: oysters, shrimps, canned fish, meat, crisp vegetables, cold cuts, and cheeses. All the foods served on a Scandinavian smörgåsbord or an Italian antipasto table are perfect hors-d'oeuvre foods. Many hors-d'oeuvre can be prepared beforehand, frozen, and reheated at serving time.

MUSHROOM PASTRIES

- 1 can (3 ounces) chopped mushrooms
- 2 tablespoons butter or margarine
- 2 tablespoons all-purpose flour
- ⅔ cup heavy cream and mushroom liquid
- ½ teaspoon instant bouillon
- ½ teaspoon paprika
- ¼ teaspoon pepper
  Dash of garlic salt
- 1 teaspoon instant minced onion
- ½ teaspoon bottled thick meat sauce
- 1 egg yolk, slightly beaten
  Potato Pastry Shells

Cook mushrooms lightly in butter; blend in flour. Stir in cream and liquid, bouillon, and seasonings. Cook until thickened, stirring. Stir small amount of mixture into egg yolk. Add to remainder of filling and cook for a few minutes longer. Fill Potato Pastry Shells. Bake in preheated very hot oven (450°F.) for 10 to 15 minutes. Serve warm or cool. Makes 30 tiny pastries.
Note: Make these shortly before serving.

Potato Pastry Shells

- ½ cup shortening
- 1 cup sifted all-purpose flour
- ½ teaspoon salt
- ½ cup cold riced potato

Cut shortening into flour and salt. With fork, stir in potato. Put a rounded meas-uring teaspoon of the mixture into each of 30 tiny tart pans. Press with finger firmly on bottom and sides of pans, leaving center hollow.

DEVILED EGGS

- 3 hard-cooked eggs
- 1½ teaspoons mayonnaise
- ½ teaspoon prepared mustard
- ½ teaspoon pickled-onion juice
- ¼ teaspoon celery salt
  Salt, pepper, and paprika
  Pickled onions, halved

Cut eggs into halves lengthwise. Remove yolks and mash with mayonnaise, mustard, onion juice, and celery salt. Add salt and pepper to taste. Fill whites with seasoned yolks. Sprinkle with paprika and top each egg half with half a pickled onion. Makes 3 servings.

ANCHOVY EGGS

Shell hard-cooked eggs and cut into halves lengthwise. Spread each half with mayonnaise and top with a drained rolled anchovy fillet.

WILTED CUCUMBERS AND ONIONS

- 2 large cucumbers
- 1 large onion, sliced thin
- 1 cup cider vinegar
- 1 teaspoon celery seed
- 1 teaspoon sugar
- ½ teaspoon salt
- ¼ teaspoon pepper

Peel cucumbers; slice thin. Add remaining ingredients. Let stand in refrigerator for at least 2 hours before serving. Makes about 2 pints.

CURRY PUFFS

- 2 garlic cloves, mashed
- 1 slice of green gingerroot, mashed
- 1½ tablespoons minced onion
- 1 tablespoon curry powder (or more to taste)
- 2 tablespoons butter
- ½ pound ground beef
- 1 tablespoon fresh lime juice
- ½ teaspoon salt
- 1 recipe plain pastry (2½ cups flour recipe) made with half butter, half lard

Sauté garlic, gingerroot, onion, and curry powder together in butter for 5 minutes. Add meat and stir constantly until meat loses red color. Add lime juice and salt, and mix well. Cool. Roll pastry and cut into 2-inch rounds. Place a bit of meat mixture on one round. Moisten edges of round with water and cover with another pastry round, pinching edges well to hold them together. Bake on ungreased cookie sheet in preheated very hot oven (450° F.) for 15 minutes, or until nicely browned. Makes about 2 dozen.

CLAM PASTRIES

- Potato Pastry Shells (at left)
- 1 can (10½ ounces) minced clams, drained
- 1 tablespoon instant minced onion
- ¼ cup minced green pepper
- 1 egg
- ½ cup heavy cream
- 2 tablespoons minced celery and leaves

½ cup fine dry bread crumbs
1 tablespoon melted margarine
Dash of cayenne
¾ teaspoon salt
¼ teaspoon pepper

Prepare Potato Pastry. Put 1 rounded teaspoon of pastry into each of 2 dozen 1¾-inch muffin-pan sections, pressing firmly with finger onto bottom and sides of pans; leave centers hollow. Bake in preheated very hot oven (450°F.) for about 12 minutes. Mix remaining ingredients and fill baked shells. Put under broiler until golden-brown. Serve hot. Makes 2 dozen.

FRENCHED HAM AND SWISS

Cut the crusts off thin-sliced bread and spread each slice with a mixture of grated Swiss cheese and cream, mixed well to make a paste. Place a thin slice of ham between each two slices of bread. Dip into beaten egg; then fry in butter. Cut into bite-size pieces. Serve hot.

CHEESE OLIVE PUFFS

2 cups grated sharp Cheddar cheese
1 cup all-purpose flour
½ teaspoon paprika
¼ pound (½ cup) butter or margarine
3 to 4 dozen small stuffed olives

Combine all ingredients except olives; mix very well; chill. For each puff, use a generous teaspoonful and shape into a ball. Push finger into center to make a deep depression, put olive in and shape dough around to fully cover olive. Bake in preheated hot oven (400°F.) for about 15 minutes, or until baked but not browned. Serve hot. Makes 3 to 4 dozen.

CRABMEAT STUFFED MUSHROOMS

¼ teaspoon powdered mustard
Salt and cayenne
1 teaspoon Worcestershire
½ cup hot water
½ cup soft bread crumbs
1 tablespoon cream
1 tablespoon butter
1 cup crabmeat
15 to 20 medium-large mushroom caps
Melted butter
Buttered crumbs

Combine all ingredients except last 4 in saucepan and simmer for about 5 minutes. Add crabmeat. Meanwhile sauté mushroom caps in melted butter. Fill with crab mixture, top with buttered crumbs, and broil just enough to brown crumbs.

CUCUMBER CUPS

1 medium cucumber, diced
¼ cup ketchup
¼ cup chili sauce
2 tablespoons fresh lemon juice
1 teaspoon Worcestershire
1 teaspoon prepared horseradish
Dash of hot pepper sauce
1 head bibb lettuce

Combine all ingredients except lettuce and toss to mix. Serve on lettuce leaves. Makes 8 to 10 servings.

SAVORY APPLE SLICES

Apples
Fresh lemon juice
Shredded sharp Cheddar cheese
Deviled ham or chicken

Slice apples in rings ¼ inch thick. Remove core and dip in lemon juice. Spread some with cheese, and the rest with ham. Broil just enough to heat.

HERRING SALAD

2 herring in brine
2 cups diced cooked potato
1½ cups diced pickled beets
¼ cup diced sweet pickles
1 large apple, diced
1 small onion, minced
1 cup diced cooked veal
¼ cup vinegar
2 tablespoons water
2 tablespoons sugar
¼ teaspoon pepper
2 hard-cooked eggs, quartered

Clean and soak herring in cold water for 24 hours, changing water several times. Remove head, skin, and bones. Rinse, and drain; cut in cubes. Mix with potato, beets, pickles, apple, onion, and veal. Toss lightly. Combine vinegar, water, sugar, and pepper; pour over salad ingredients; toss lightly until all is well seasoned. Chill. Garnish with eggs. Makes 6 to 7 cups.

TOMATO-AVOCADO HORS-D'OEUVRE

1 avocado
1 teaspoon grated onion
½ teaspoon Worcestershire
Dash of cayenne
½ teaspoon salt
2 tablespoons salad oil
1 tablespoon vinegar or fresh lemon juice
½ pound tomatoes
Watercress

Peel and mash avocado with fork; add seasonings, oil, and vinegar, and chill. Peel and cut tomatoes into 6 thick slices; chill. Top each tomato slice with a spoonful of avocado, and garnish with watercress. Makes 6 servings.

AVOCADO HORS-D'OEUVRE

Peel avocado, cut in two, and remove seed. Slice and marinate in highly seasoned French dressing for 30 minutes. Sprinkle with chopped stuffed olives.

INDIAN BROILED SHRIMPS

1 pound raw shrimps, shelled and deveined
1 cup boiling water
1 teaspoon salt
1 teaspoon ground coriander
½ small onion, minced
8 peppercorns
¼ cup cooking oil
1 teaspoon salt
½ teaspoon ground cuminseed
1 teaspoon ground turmeric
1 tablespoon fresh lemon juice or lime juice
1 large lemon or lime, cut into wedges

Combine shrimps, boiling water, salt, coriander, onion, and peppercorns in saucepan. Bring to a boil; cook for 2 to

3 minutes, or until shrimps just begin to turn pink. Remove from water; reserve. Heat oil in skillet; remove from heat. Stir in salt, cuminseed, turmeric, and lemon juice. Add shrimps and toss to coat shrimps with mixture. Place shrimps in shallow baking pan. Broil under medium heat for about 5 minutes, or until shrimps are pink and slightly browned on the edges. Serve with lemon or lime wedges. Makes 4 to 6 servings.

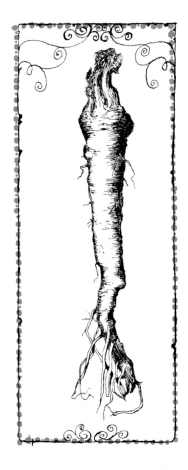

HORSERADISH (Armoracia lapathifolia)—This tall, hardy plant with glossy green, toothed leaves and large amounts of small white flowers is grown for its pungent roots. These are large, fleshy, white, and cylindrical. When grated they have a sharp flavor and a pungent odor. The roots are usually dug in the fall. Peeled and grated, served as is or in vinegar, they are used as a condiment for fish, seafood, meats, game, and in sauces.

Horseradish is a native of southeastern Europe. It has been used since antiquity, long before Christian times. It is one of the five bitter herbs of the Jewish Passover festival, when it is served symbolically during the Seder services.

Horseradish is sold fresh as a root or commercially prepared as preserved white or red horseradish, which is the grated root mixed with vinegar or beet juice and bottled.

Fresh horseradish should be grated as soon as possible after purchase.

Dried horseradish root is also available. To reconstitute, add 2 tablespoons water to each tablespoon dried horseradish. Do this 30 minutes before serving to develop full flavor. Add ½ cup heavy cream for additional flavor. The flavor of dried horseradish is not as strong as that of fresh-grated horseradish.

Horseradish is also sold blended into various seafood sauces.

HORSERADISH SAUCE

1 small onion, minced
2 tablespoons butter or margarine
1 cup light cream
2 egg yolks
¼ cup freshly grated or prepared horseradish, well drained
Salt and cayenne

Brown onion lightly in butter. Add cream and bring to boil. Pour over slightly beaten egg yolks. Add horseradish and return to heat. Cook gently until slightly thickened, stirring. Season with salt and cayenne to taste, and serve hot on boiled beef, fish, or tongue. Makes about 1 cup.

HORSERADISH WHIPPED-CREAM SAUCE

½ cup heavy cream
¼ cup prepared horseradish, well drained
¼ teaspoon salt
1 teaspoon sugar
Paprika

Whip cream until thick. Fold in horseradish, salt, and sugar. Pile lightly in serving dish, and sprinkle with paprika. Serve on cold roast beef, fish, or vegetables. Makes about 1 cup.

TUNA SALAD WITH SOUR-CREAM HORSERADISH SAUCE

Shredded lettuce or other greens
2 cans (7 ounces each) tuna, flaked
1 cup dairy sour cream
1 teaspoon fresh lemon juice
2 teaspoons sugar
½ teaspoon salt
½ teaspoon powdered mustard
2 teaspoons prepared horseradish
2 eggs, hard-cooked
Paprika
Dill pickles
Cherry tomatoes

Arrange lettuce on serving dish. Arrange tuna in center. Mix sour cream, lemon juice, sugar, salt, mustard, horseradish, and finely chopped egg whites. Pour over fish. Sprinkle top with finely chopped egg yolks, and paprika. Garnish with dill pickle wedges and tomatoes. Makes 6 servings.

GREEN BEANS WITH HORSERADISH SAUCE

1 tablespoon butter
2 tablespoons all-purpose flour
Salt and pepper to taste
1 cup milk
3 tablespoons prepared horseradish

2½ cups (one 1-pound, 4-ounce can) cut green beans, drained

Melt butter in a saucepan. Stir in flour, salt, and pepper; blend. Gradually stir in milk; cook over low heat, stirring constantly, until thickened. Add horseradish and drained beans. Heat quickly. Serve with beef, lamb, or veal. Makes 4 servings.

HOT CAKE—This is another term for a griddle cake, pancake, flannel cake, or flapjack. It is a thin, golden-brown cake, always served hot and with butter, syrup, corn syrup, jelly, jam, or honey.

HUBBARD SQUASH—A large winter squash, with a thick, hard, and warty skin. The plant is a long running vine with compound tendrils and large round leaves. There are several varieties, such as the Green, Blue, or Golden Hubbard. Some of them, like the Blue Hubbard, grow so large that they are sold in pieces or sections.

Squash, and its first cousin the pumpkin, are vegetables of American origin.

Availability and Purchasing Guide—Fresh squash is available from late August to March. It is also available canned and frozen.

Look for fresh squash with hard warted rind free from blemishes. Avoid squash with watery spots.

Storage—Will keep well for months in a dry cool place at temperature of about 50°F. For long storage, select squash which are unbruised and have stem attached.

☐ Refrigerator shelf, uncut: 4 to 6 months

☐ Refrigerator shelf, cooked: 4 to 5 days

☐ Refrigerator frozen-food compart-

ment, cooked and prepared for freezing: 2 to 3 months

☐ Freezer, cooked and prepared for freezing: 1 year

Nutritive Food Values—Excellent source of vitamin A, ½ cup providing more than a day's quota. Contains a fair amount of iron and riboflavin.

☐ 3½ ounces, raw = 39 calories

Basic Preparation—Wash thoroughly. Cut into serving pieces or pieces small enough to handle. A large knife and a mallet are useful. Remove seeds and stringy portion. Peel if desired.

☐ **To Cook**—Use 1 inch of boiling salted water and cook, covered, for 25 to 30 minutes. Remove from rind with a spoon and mash, adding seasonings and butter, or serve in individual pieces with rind.

☐ **To Bake**—Season with salt and pepper. Put a small piece of butter in each piece of squash; add a little honey, if desired. Bake, covered, in preheated moderate oven (375°F.) for 45 to 60 minutes.

☐ **To Freeze**—Use firm squash. Wash, cut into pieces, and remove seeds. Cover with water and cook until tender. Remove rind and press pulp through a sieve. Cool. Pack in containers, leaving ½-inch headspace. Seal.

SQUASH CASSEROLE

2 cups mashed cooked Hubbard squash
4 tablespoons butter or margarine
3 tablespoons brown sugar
1 tablespoon prepared mustard
1 egg, slightly beaten
Salt and pepper to taste
½ cup crushed corn flakes or cornflake crumbs

Mix squash with 2 tablespoons each butter and brown sugar, the mustard, egg, and salt and pepper. Put in shallow 1-quart baking dish or 9-inch pie pan. Mix corn flakes with remaining butter and brown sugar and sprinkle on top. Bake in preheated moderate oven (350°F.) for 20 minutes, or until thoroughly heated. Makes 4 to 6 servings.

SQUASH BAKED IN SHELLS

3 pounds Hubbard squash
Butter or margarine
2 tablespoons minced onion
2 slices of bread
1 egg
1 teaspoon salt
⅛ teaspoon pepper
Fine cracker crumbs

Remove seeds and stringy portion, and cut squash in 2- to 3-inch pieces. Put in baking pan, and top each piece with a little butter. Bake in preheated moderate oven (350°F.) for 1 hour, or until tender. Scoop out squash, keeping shells intact. Mash squash. Cook onion lightly in 2 tablespoons butter. Add squash. Dip bread in water, squeeze dry, and add to squash. Cook over low heat, stirring frequently, for 15 minutes. Stir in egg and seasonings. Pile lightly in reserved shells and sprinkle with crumbs. Dot with butter and bake in preheated moderate oven (350°F.) for 15 minutes, or until golden-brown. Makes 6 servings.

SQUASH PATTIES

Use cold leftover mashed Hubbard squash. Shape in flat cakes, dip in slightly beaten egg, and roll in fine dry bread crumbs. Sauté in hot margarine until browned on both sides.

SQUASH MUFFINS

    2 cups sifted all-purpose flour
    2 teaspoons baking powder
    2 tablespoons sugar
    ¾ teaspoon salt
    1 egg, beaten
    ⅔ cup milk
    1 tablespoon cooking oil
    1 cup strained cooked Hubbard squash

Sift dry ingredients into bowl. Mix egg and remaining ingredients, and add all at once to first mixture. Stir only enough to dampen dry ingredients. Fill greased muffin cups half full with the mixture, and bake in preheated very hot oven (450°F.) for 15 to 20 minutes. Makes 16 medium-size muffins.

COMPANY SQUASH PIE

    1 cup strained cooked Hubbard squash
    1 cup heavy cream
    1 cup sugar
    3 eggs, slightly beaten
    2 tablespoons brandy
    1 teaspoon each cinnamon and nutmeg
    ½ teaspoon ginger
    ½ teaspoon salt
      Unbaked 9-inch pie shell

Mix all ingredients, except pie shell. Pour into shell and bake in preheated moderate oven (375°F.) for about 45 minutes, or until firm. Cool before serving.

HUCKLEBERRY—An edible berry of the
species *Gaylussacia,* and the shrub of the same name. The huckleberry is dark blue to black in color and is found growing from the tropics to the arctic. There are a number of varieties, growing on low or high bushes and in an acid soil. The bushes are very prolific, and they can take over a neglected field.

In many parts of the United States the term huckleberry is also applied indiscriminately to blueberries, which belong to the genus Vaccinium, but a huckleberry is more acid than a blueberry, and each huckleberry contains ten hard little seeds, whereas a blueberry has a larger number of seeds so minute they are hardly noticeable.

Availability—June, July, and August, usually sold locally since they do not ship well.

Purchasing Guide—Select clean, plump, and dry berries with a deep-black or dark-blue color. Berries may have a light bloom; this varies with the species.
    □ 1 pint = about 2 cups berries

Storage—Sort first if necessary, but do not wash until ready to use.
    □ Kitchen shelf: 1 to 2 days
    □ Refrigerator shelf: 1 to 2 weeks
    □ Refrigerator frozen-food compartment, prepared for freezing: 2 to 3 months
    □ Freezer, prepared for freezing: 1 year

Caloric Value
    □ 3½ ounces = 62 calories
Basic Preparation—Wash berries gently just before using. Do not allow berries to soak in water. Remove any stems. Serve huckleberries with cream or milk. Use to make jam, in tarts, puddings, and pies, and in any recipe calling for blueberries.
    □ **To Freeze**—Wash berries in cold water. Drain. Dip berries into boiling water for 20 to 30 seconds. Chill quickly in cold water.
    □ **To Freeze, Loose Pack**—Spread berries in a single layer on a shallow pan with sides or tray. Freeze until firm. Pour into freezer container, leaving no headspace.
    □ **To Freeze, Sugar Pack**—Mix 4 cups berries with ½ cup sugar. Stir gently until sugar dissolves. Pack in containers, leaving ½-inch headspace. Seal.

HUCKLEBERRY GRIDDLE CAKES

    2 cups unsifted all-purpose flour
    2 teaspoons baking powder
    ½ teaspoon salt
    3 tablespoons sugar
    1 egg, well beaten
    2 cups milk
    2 cups washed and well-drained huckleberries, coated lightly with flour

Sift flour with baking powder, salt, and sugar. Beat egg with milk and add all at once to the flour. Beat until smooth. Fold in huckleberries. Bake pancakes on a lightly greased hot griddle. Serve with whipped butter and honey, if desired. Makes 4 to 6 servings.

HUCKLEBERRY SHORTCAKE

    4 cups sifted all-purpose flour
    4 teaspoons baking powder
    1 teaspoon salt
    ½ cup butter or margarine
    2 eggs
    1¼ cups milk
    4 cups washed and well-drained huckleberries
      Sugar
      Grated orange rind

Sift flour with baking powder and salt. Cut in butter until mixture resembles coarse cornmeal. Beat egg with milk and add all at once to the flour mixture. Stir only until just blended. Place dough on a lightly floured board and knead a few times to form dough into a smooth ball. Cut dough into halves and roll each half into a rectangle 12 x 8 inches. Place one oblong on a well-greased cookie sheet.

Mix huckleberries with sugar and orange rind and spread on dough, making a layer of berries about ¾ inch thick. Moisten outside edges of rectangle with water. Top with second rectangle and pinch edges to seal. Bake in preheated moderate oven (350°F.) for 30 to 40 minutes, or until top is deeply browned. Cut into squares and serve with thick cream. Makes 10 to 12 servings.

HUCKLEBERRY COTTAGE PUDDING

    ¼ cup butter or margarine
    ⅔ cup sugar
    1 egg, slightly beaten
    2 cups all-purpose flour
    3 teaspoons baking powder
    ¼ teaspoon salt
    1 cup huckleberries, washed
    1 cup milk
      Lemon Hard Sauce, see page 878

Cream butter until light and fluffy. Add sugar and beat until light. Add egg and beat well. Sift dry ingredients; sprinkle ¼ cup of mixture on berries. Add remainder alternately with milk to first mixture, beating until smooth. Fold in berries. Bake in greased pan (8 x 8 x 2 inches) in preheated moderate oven (350°F.) for about 35 minutes. Serve hot with Lemon Hard Sauce. Makes 6 large or 9 small servings.

HUCKLEBERRY CREAM-CHEESE PIE

    1½ cups fresh huckleberries
    12 ounces cream cheese
    1 tablespoon all-purpose flour
    3 egg yolks
    2 egg whites
    3 tablespoons sugar
    ½ teaspoon salt
    ¾ cup dairy sour cream
      Pastry for 1-crust 8-inch pie, unbaked

Rinse huckleberries in colander and let drain thoroughly, or dry on paper towels. With fork stir softened cream cheese until smooth. Add flour and mix thoroughly. Lightly beat egg yolks with 1 egg white; add sugar, salt, and sour cream. Combine egg mixture with cream-cheese mixture, stirring well. Line 8-inch pie pan with pastry and brush lightly with remaining egg white. Dust huckleberries lightly with flour and place in thick layer in pastry-lined pan. Smooth cream-cheese mixture evenly over huckleberries and bake in preheated moderate oven (350°F.) for 30 minutes, or until set. Makes 6 servings.

HUNGARIAN COOKERY

The incomparable cuisine
of Hungary,
from goulash to apple strudel,
is an expression of
people who care greatly
for excellent food.

by Nika Hazelton

Hungary is a country blessed with an original and delicious cookery of her own, developed and refined by a people who care greatly for excellent food.

Hungary lies at the crossroads of West and East. Through the centuries, many people crossed, fought, and settled in the lands of the Magyars, which is the name the Hungarians use for themselves. The Magyars came from the distant slopes of the eastern part of the Ural Mountains, in what is now Russia, as long ago as 896 A.D., and founded their state on the banks of the Danube. Turks, Slovaks, Serbs, Croats, Poles, Slovenes, Russians, Germans, and Austrians mingled in Hungary in the centuries that followed and contributed to the Hungarian kitchen and to the country's food habits and traditions.

The Turkish conquest of Hungary in the 16th and 17th centuries left a lasting influence, for the Turks introduced coffee, melons, spices, nuts, and, above all, the use of paprika.

But strains from even farther away can be found in Hungarian cooking. Through the centuries, the cooks brought by the princes and princesses who married Hungary's royalty introduced new ways of cooking and seasoning. The influence of the courts of France and Austria was especially marked since the Hungarians adopted their ways with enthusiasm, as we see in the old Hungarian cook books which are full of French cooking terms. In their turn, these foreign recipes were translated into dishes that are still part and parcel of present-day Hungarian cooking, such as the meats and fish dishes cooked with wine, the use of fruit, etc. To Austrian influences goes some of the credit for Hungary's excellent dumplings and superlative cakes, to which the Hungarians added their own twist, such as filling strudel dough with ground poppy seed.

Another factor that contributed to the excellence of Hungarian food was the resources of the country. In the warm yet temperate climate, fruits and vegetables grow to rare lusciousness. The plains yielded tender beef and lamb, the farmyards fattened pigs into famous hams and pork products, and fattened geese and ducks as well. Hungarian goose liver is comparable to the renowned goose liver of Alsace. The deep forests abounded in game, including wild boar, and hunting was a favorite sport. Hungary has no access to the sea, but the trout of her mountain streams and, above all, the unrivaled *fogas,* a very white and extremely delicate kind of perch-pike found in beautiful Lake Balaton, is famous throughout Europe. And finally,

the wheat of the great Hungarian plains was considered the finest for baking. In the old days, European cook books specified that fine baking required Hungarian flour.

The most typical ingredients of Hungarian cooking are paprika powder, onions, green peppers, tomatoes, sour cream, lard or goose fat, instead of other shortenings, noodles and other pastas.

The Hungarian housewife does not use paprika as a garnish the way we do, but by the tea- or tablespoonfuls as an integral part of a meat, soup, or vegetable dish, to give it flavor and a rosy color.

The color of paprika is a fiery-red, but the spice itself need not be any hotter than pepper, if as hot. This spice with the exquisite aroma and mildly pungent taste is made from the capsicum pepper, which grows especially well on Hungarian soil. The ground spice is produced from special pepper varieties which are grown for the purpose and widely exported. There are many degrees of pungency in the spice, ranging from the hottest to the mildest, and they are graded according to government specifications. It is important that paprika, whatever its degree of pungency, be used as freshly ground as possible, when fragrance is most enticing. In fact, Hungarian paprika, called "noble and sweet" by the people, has a fragrance unmatched by the paprika of any other country. In cooking, it should not be added to the sizzling fat, but rather to the dish, one school of cooks says. And of course, hot or mild paprika, and the grades in between, are a matter of individual preference, in Hungary as well as anywhere else.

Other Hungarian food specialties whose fame has spread are the sausages, Herz salami, quite possibly the best dry salami ever made, and *tarhonya,* a kneaded dough of flour and eggs which is broken into pieces the size of small peas. The paste is then dried quite hard, so that it will keep for a long time. *Tarhonya* can be cooked in water or broth like noodles and served like them as an accompaniment with gravy dishes, or browned first in lard with minced onions and paprika and then simmered in as much liquid as it will absorb.

When it comes to noodles, the Hungarians use them often in an original manner combined with cottage cheese, nuts, or poppy seeds. Some noodle dishes are sugared and used as desserts.

The most famous Hungarian desserts are dumplings filled with fresh fruit, pancakes, and strudels. Every kind of fruit and nuts is used for strudel fillings, and there are also nonsweet ones, such as cabbage and cheese.

Among the many delicious fruits grown in Hungary which are liberally used by all of the population fresh, as compotes, or in jams, special mention must be made of the apricots. They are exquisite in flavor and either as fruit or distilled into brandy, they are delicious.

SOUPS

GULYÁSLEVES
(Goulash Soup)

    3 medium onions, chopped
    2 tablespoons butter or margarine
 1½ pounds beef chuck, cut into ½-inch
      cubes
    2 tablespoons paprika
  ½ teaspoon caraway seeds
    1 garlic clove, crushed
  ½ teaspoon grated lemon rind
    4 cups beef bouillon
      Salt to taste
    2 medium potatoes, peeled and cut
      into ½-inch cubes

Cook onions in butter until golden. Add beef and paprika and cook, stirring constantly, until slightly browned. Add caraway, garlic, lemon rind, and bouillon. Season to taste. Simmer, covered, for 1½ hours. Add potato and cook for 30 minutes longer. Makes 4 to 6 servings.

SÓSKA LEVES
(Sorrel Soup)

  ½ pound sorrel
    4 cups chicken consommé
    2 egg yolks
    2 tablespoons heavy cream
      Salt and white pepper
    1 cup dairy sour cream

Clean sorrel and chop into fine pieces. Cook for 10 minutes in consommé. Mix egg yolks and cream and add slowly to soup, beating constantly with wire whisk. Season to taste. Cool, then chill in refrigerator. Just before serving, beat in sour cream, and top with a spoonful of the sour cream. Makes 4 servings.

Note: To serve hot, beat in sour cream and heat gently.

KÖMÉNY LEVES
(Caraway Soup)

    6 cups water
    1 teaspoon salt
    2 tablespoons caraway seeds
    3 tablespoons bacon fat or butter
  ¼ cup all-purpose flour
    1 egg yolk
  ½ cup dairy sour cream
    6 slices of roll, toasted

Bring water to boil. Add salt and caraway and simmer for 20 minutes. Strain soup through fine sieve. Blend fat or butter with flour. Blend with some of the soup, return to soup, and bring to boil. Beat egg yolk with sour cream;

add a little of the soup to it. Remove soup from heat and beat mixture into it. Serve with a slice of toasted roll in each soup plate. Makes 6 servings.

MEAT, FISH, AND POULTRY

MAGYAR GULYÁS
(Hungarian Goulash)

2 pounds lean beef chuck, cut into 1½-inch squares
Salt and pepper to taste
¼ pound lard or sweet butter
1 to 1½ pounds onions, sliced
2 tablespoons sweet paprika or 1 tablespoon hot paprika
1 tablespoon flour
Hot water or dry white wine
2 cups dairy sour cream

Season meat with salt and pepper. Heat lard almost to smoking point in heavy saucepan. Brown meat in it on all sides. Add onions. Stir in paprika; there should be enough paprika to color meat and onions a reddish brown. Over low heat cook, stirring, until all the pan juices have been absorbed. Sprinkle with flour and cook for 1 minute. Add hot water or wine to cover meat. Simmer, covered, over low heat for 1 to 1½ hours, until meat is tender and the onions have cooked down to a pulp. Check occasionally for liquid; if necessary, add a little more. Stir in sour cream and heat through but do not boil. Serve with buttered noodles sprinkled with caraway seeds. Makes 4 to 6 servings.

MAJORANNÁS TOKÁNY
(Beef Stew with Marjoram)

2 pounds beef chuck or round, in one piece
2 tablespoons lard
1 pound (3 medium) onions, coarsely chopped
2 teaspoons ground marjoram
Salt
Pepper (there should be quite a lot of pepper)
2 cups water
1½ cups dry white wine
½ pound lean bacon
1 cup dairy sour cream

Cut beef into strips 1 x 3 inches. Heat lard in Dutch oven to smoking point. Cook onion in hot lard until soft and golden. Add meat. Sprinkle with marjoram and season to taste with salt and pepper. Add water and wine. Simmer, covered, over lowest possible heat for 45 minutes, or until half done. While meat is cooking, cut bacon into strips the same size as the meat. Cook bacon partially until limp and until most of the grease has cooked out. Drain bacon and add to meat. Continue to simmer, covered, for 45 minutes longer, or until meat is tender. Remove from heat and stir in sour

cream. Return to heat; heat through but do not boil again. Serve with rice or noodles. Makes 4 to 6 servings.

SAVANYU ÖKÖRFAROK
(Sour Oxtail Ragout)

2 oxtails, disjointed
½ cup cider vinegar
1 onion
1 carrot
1 garlic clove
Grated rind of 1 lemon
2 bay leaves
2 whole cloves
6 peppercorns
½ teaspoon salt
Boiling water
2 tablespoons fat
2 tablespoons all-purpose flour
¼ cup dairy sour cream
Paprika

In a large saucepan combine oxtails with vinegar, onion, carrot, and seasonings. Cover with boiling water and cook, covered, over low heat until meat is tender. Drain, and reserve 1 cup liquid. Melt fat and stir in flour. Gradually stir in liquid from meat. Cook over low heat, stirring constantly, until smooth and thickened. Add oxtail pieces. Just before serving, stir in sour cream and sprinkle with paprika. Makes 6 servings.

BORJÚ PÖRKÖLT
(Veal Paprika)

2 pounds veal cutlet, sliced thin
2 tablespoons butter or margarine
1 garlic clove, minced
1 tablespoon sweet paprika
1 cup water
1 cup heavy cream
½ teaspoon salt

Pound veal well. Pat dry with absorbent paper. Melt butter. Brown veal quickly with garlic and paprika. Add water, cover, and simmer for 1 hour. Add cream and salt. Heat through, and serve. Makes 4 to 6 servings.

DISZNÓKARAJ MAGYAROSAN
(Hungarian Pork Chops)

6 pork chops, about ½ inch thick
Salt and pepper
1 medium onion, chopped
1 garlic clove, minced
3 tablespoons lard or butter
1 bay leaf
¾ cup chicken bouillon
1 cup dairy sour cream
2 teaspoons paprika

Trim excess fat from pork chops and sprinkle chops with salt and pepper. Sauté onion and garlic in lard until soft and golden. Push aside or remove from skillet. Add pork chops and brown on all sides. Pour off fat. Lower heat and add bay leaf and bouillon. Cook, covered, over low heat for about 1 hour. Transfer chops to hot serving plate and keep hot. Reduce pan juices to half by cooking over high heat. Add sour cream and paprika and blend thoroughly with pan juices. Heat through, but do not boil. Pour sauce over chops. Makes 4 to 6 servings.

BÁRÁNY PÖRKÖLT ÁRPAKÁSÁVAL
(Lamb and Barley Stew)

2 pounds lamb shoulder, cut up and trimmed of excess fat
Flour
Salt and pepper to taste
2 tablespoons cooking oil
1 cup chopped onions
4 medium tomatoes, quartered
2 bay leaves
2 tablespoons pearl barley
6 dried prunes, pitted
1 garlic clove, minced
1 teaspoon sweet paprika
1 cup water or bouillon
2 tablespoons sweet or dairy sour cream (optional)

Coat lamb pieces evenly with flour mixed with salt and pepper. Brown on all sides in oil in heavy skillet or Dutch oven. Add onions and cook until onions are soft but not brown. Add all other ingredients except cream. Cover and simmer over low heat for 1½ to 2 hours; or bake in very slow oven (250°F.) for 3 to 4 hours. (This stew should cook as slowly as possible.) Check for moisture; if too dry, add a little more water or bouillon, 1 tablespoon at a time. Remove from heat and stir in cream. Do not cook again. Makes 4 to 6 servings.

HÉT VEZÉR TOKÁNY
(Seven Chieftains' Tokany)

2 tablespoons lard
4 slices of bacon
½ pound onions, sliced
1 tablespoon paprika
1 pound lean boneless pork, cut into strips 3 x 1 inch
1 pound beef chuck or round cut into strips 3 x 1 inch
1 pound boneless veal cut into strips 3 x 1 inch
1 cup water
2 green peppers cut into strips
2 small tomatoes, peeled, seeded, and chopped
Salt and pepper
½ cup dairy sour cream
1 tablespoon flour

Heat lard in Dutch oven. Cook bacon until limp. Remove bacon and cut into strips; reserve. Cook onions in hot fat until soft and golden-brown. Stir in paprika. Cook for 2 minutes. Add pork. Simmer, covered, over low heat for 30 minutes. Add beef and veal and simmer for 45 minutes. Add a little hot water, about 1 cup, to prevent sticking. Add green peppers, tomatoes, salt and pepper to taste, and bacon. Simmer, covered, for 20 minutes, or until peppers are tender, stirring occasionally. Combine sour cream and flour to a smooth paste. Stir into stew. Simmer over low heat for 4 minutes, stirring constantly. Serve with steamed rice or noodles. Makes 6 to 8 servings.

Note: Hungarians often combine different meats in their stews for a tastier effect. The seven chieftains are national heroes who led the Magyars to the present country in the 9th century.

SZÉKELY GULYÁS
(Szekely Sauerkraut Goulash)

1 pound boneless beef chuck
1 pound boneless veal shoulder
½ pound lean pork
2 small onions, sliced
2 teaspoons butter
1 pound sauerkraut
   A few peppercorns
2 teaspoons paprika
1 teaspoon caraway seeds
1 cup bouillon
2 cups dairy sour cream

Cut the meat into cubes as you would for any stew. Cook the onions in butter to golden-yellow. Add meat, sauerkraut, peppercorns, paprika, caraway seeds, and bouillon. Cook, covered, for about 1 hour in an ordinary pan, or in a pressure cooker for about 15 minutes at 15-pound pressure. Very slowly pour the juice from the cooking pan into a dish with the sour cream, stirring all the while so it will not curdle. Thicken with a little flour, if necessary. Pour the mixture back into the pan and let it stand on an asbestos pad over low heat until used. It improves with waiting and can be reheated. The use of salt depends on taste and on the saltiness of the sauerkraut. If the kraut is too salty, wash it. Makes 5 or 6 servings.

SONKÁS PALACSINTA
(Pancakes Layered with Minced Ham)

1 cup cold milk
1 cup cold water
4 eggs
1 teaspoon salt
2 cups sifted all-purpose flour
¼ cup melted butter or margarine
   Ham Filling
¼ cup buttered bread crumbs

Beat together milk, water, eggs, and salt. Add flour gradually, beating constantly until smooth. Add melted butter. The consistency should be that of heavy cream. Refrigerate for at least 1 hour before baking pancakes. Lightly grease a 7-inch crêpe pan or skillet, heat to smoking, and pour in just enough of the batter to coat the bottom lightly. Tilt pan to be sure that all is covered. Brown lightly on one side. Turn and brown on the other. Put one pancake in a baking dish, spread some of the Ham Filling on it, then top with another pancake. Keep warm in slow oven (300°F.). Continue layering in this manner until all pancakes (about 12) and Ham Filling are used. Sprinkle top with buttered bread crumbs. Bake in preheated moderate oven (350° F.) for 20 minutes, until filling is set. Cut into wedges to serve. Makes 8 servings.

Ham Filling

1 pound cooked ham, minced
4 eggs, separated
1 cup dairy sour cream
   Salt

Mix ham, egg yolks, and sour cream.

Beat egg whites until stiff. Fold into mixture. Season to taste.

CSIRKE PAPRIKÁS
(Chicken Paprika with Sour Cream)

1 frying chicken (about 3 pounds),
   cut into pieces
2 medium onions, chopped fine
2 tablespoons sweet paprika
3 tablespoons butter or margarine
½ cup chicken bouillon
1 cup dairy sour cream
   Salt and pepper

Brown chicken, onions, and paprika in the butter. Add bouillon. Simmer, covered, over low heat for 30 minutes, or until tender. Stir in sour cream and heat through. Season to taste. Makes 4 servings.

SZEGEDI CSIRKE PAPRIKÁS
(Chicken Stew)

3 tablespoons lard
4 large onions, sliced
1 tablespoon sweet paprika
1 teaspoon caraway seeds, crushed
2 frying chickens (about 3 pounds
   each), cut into pieces
   Salt
3 cups water
1 pound potatoes, peeled and quartered
3 medium carrots, thickly sliced
3 cups canned tomatoes
   Pepper

Heat lard in Dutch oven. When smoking hot, add onions. Cook until soft and golden-brown. Add paprika, caraway seeds, and chicken pieces. Toss and cook over medium heat for 5 to 10 minutes, or until chickens are golden-brown. Sprinkle with salt. Add water. Simmer, covered, over lowest possible heat for 30 minutes, or until chicken is half done. Add potatoes, carrots, and canned tomatoes. Season to taste with salt and pepper. Continue to simmer, covered, for 30 minutes longer, or until chicken and vegetables are tender. Serve with buttered *tarhonya* or buttered noodles and a green salad. Makes 6 servings.

TEJFELES SÜLT PONTY
(Pike Baked in Cream)

2 pounds pike fillets
1 teaspoon caraway seeds
½ teaspoon salt
½ cup fine dried bread crumbs
1 cup dairy sour cream

Place ⅓ of fish in greased baking dish. Sprinkle with ⅓ of caraway seeds, salt, bread crumbs, and sour cream. Repeat until all ingredients are used. Bake in preheated slow oven (325°F.) for 20 to 30 minutes, or until fish is flaky. Makes 4 servings.

VEGETABLES, PASTAS, AND SALADS

RAKOTT KRUMPLI
(Potato and Egg Casserole)

6 slices of bacon, chopped

1 tablespoon butter
6 medium potatoes, boiled and sliced
6 hard-cooked eggs, sliced
   Salt and pepper
2 tablespoons chopped parsley
½ to ⅔ cup dairy sour cream

Cook bacon in hot butter until crisp. Drain; reserve fat. Place alternate layers of potatoes, hard-cooked eggs, and bacon in greased 2-quart baking dish. Season each layer with salt and pepper to taste, but remember that bacon may be very salty. Sprinkle with parsley. Stir reserved bacon fat into sour cream. Pour over potato mixture. Bake, covered, in preheated moderate oven (350°F.) for 15 to 20 minutes, or until golden. Makes 4 servings.

TEJFELES BAFFŐZELÉK
(Dried Beans in Sour Cream)

½ pound dried white beans, washed
   Salt
1 medium onion, chopped fine
2 tablespoons butter or margarine
2 tablespoons flour
1 tablespoon vinegar
1 cup water
½ cup dairy sour cream

Soak beans in water overnight. Drain. Cover with fresh water, add 1 teaspoon salt, and simmer for 2 to 3 hours, or until tender. Brown onion in butter; blend in flour. Add vinegar and water, and stir until thickened. Drain beans when done and mix into sauce. Stir in sour cream and allow to heat through but do not boil. Season to taste. Makes 4 to 6 servings.

ZELLER SALÁTA
(Celery-Root Salad)

3 celery roots
   Boiling salted water
   Salt, pepper, and mayonnaise

Peel celery root and cut into julienne strips. Drop into boiling salted water and cook for 15 to 20 minutes, until tender. Cool. Season with salt, pepper, and mayonnaise to taste. Chill for 2 hours. Makes 6 servings.

ZÖLD PAPRIKA SALÁTA
(Green-Pepper Salad)

4 large green peppers
½ cup olive oil
2 to 4 tablespoons vinegar, depending
   on strength (dressing should be mild)
   Salt and pepper to taste
½ teaspoon sugar

Remove seeds and inside ribs of peppers. Cut into ½-inch slices. Drop for 1 minute into boiling water. Drain. Place in glass serving dish. Make a French dressing with remaining ingredients. Pour over peppers. Marinate at room temperature for 1 hour. Serve as is or chilled. Makes 4 servings.

TARHONYA
(Egg Barley)

4 cups all-purpose flour
5 eggs
1 teaspoon salt

Sift flour. Make a well in the center. Break eggs into well and mix together with the flour. Add salt. Knead dough until it is perfectly smooth. Allow to dry a little. Chop with a knife until pieces resemble barley in size. Or press through a special sieve which will make pieces of the same size. Spread pieces out and allow to dry for 24 hours. Store in jars with tight lids. To cook, brown *tarhonya* lightly in butter; then add water to cover and simmer for 15 minutes. Or, if it is to be served in a soup, it can be cooked in that without browning.

DIÓS TÉSZTA
(Boiled Noodles with Walnuts)

8 ounces fine noodles
½ cup chopped walnuts
2 tablespoons butter or margarine

Cook noodles in salted water according to package directions. Drain. Meantime, sauté walnuts in butter until lightly browned. Add to drained noodles. Place in top part of double boiler over hot water for 30 minutes before serving to meld the flavors. Makes 4 servings.

Makos Tészta
(Boiled Noodles with Poppy Seeds)

Cook noodles as above. Drain. Toss with ¼ cup butter and 2 tablespoons ground poppy seeds. Omit nuts. Or, substitute 1 tablespoon caraway seeds for the poppy seeds. Omit nuts.

DESSERTS

SZILVÁS GOMBÓC
(Plum Dumplings)

12 plums
   Almond extract
12 small lumps of sugar
⅓ cup butter
2 cups sifted all-purpose flour
2 cups cooked potatoes, riced and chilled
1 teaspoon salt
2 eggs
2 tablespoons butter

¾ cup fine dry bread crumbs

Cut plums just enough to remove pits. Keep fruit as intact as possible. Sprinkle a drop of almond extract on each lump of sugar. Push 1 sugar lump into cavity of each fruit. With pastry cutter or two knives, cut butter into flour until it resembles coarse meal. Stir in potatoes and salt. Add eggs and mix thoroughly. With hands work dough until smooth. On slightly floured board roll out dough to ¼-inch thickness. Cut into 3- or 4-inch squares, depending on size of fruit. Place a plum on each square. Moisten edges of dough and fold dough over fruit. Pinch edges together. With floured hands roll dumplings into round balls. Cook a few at a time in kettle of gently boiling water. The water must continue to boil. Cook for 10 to 15 minutes, depending on size. Carefully lift out with slotted spoon and keep warm. Heat butter and brown crumbs in it. Roll dumplings in buttered crumbs. Serve hot. Makes 6 servings.

Savanyu Ökörfarok   *Diós Tészta*

■ **Variation** — Use apricots instead of plums.

CSERESZNYE KISÜTVE
(Deep-Fried Cherries)

1 cup sifted all-purpose flour
¼ cup sugar
½ teaspoon ground cinnamon
⅓ cup milk
½ cup dry white wine
3 eggs, lightly beaten
1 pound ripe firm sweet cherries, with stems
  Shortening for deep frying
  Confectioners' sugar

Combine flour, sugar, and cinnamon. Stir in milk and wine to make a smooth paste. Beat in eggs. Let batter rest for 30 minutes. Tie 4 or 5 cherries into clusters with thread. Dip each cluster into batter, making sure cherries are well coated. Carefully lower clusters into hot deep fat (370°F. on frying thermometer). When browned, remove with slotted spoon. Cook only a few clusters at one time. Drain on absorbent paper and sprinkle with confectioners' sugar. Serve immediately. Serve 1 or 2 clusters for each individual helping.

ALMÁSRÉTES
(Apple Strudel)

Strudel Dough:

1 egg, slightly beaten
½ teaspoon salt
  Cooking oil
1 cup unsifted all-purpose flour
  Butter
  Sugar

Apple Filling:

¼ cup seedless raisins
  Water
6 to 8 medium apples
  Sugar
¾ cup fine soft bread crumbs
⅓ cup butter
½ cup chopped blanched almonds
1 tablespoon ground cinnamon

Mix egg, salt, 2 tablespoons oil, and the flour. Add 1 tablespoon warm water and mix to form soft dough. On lightly floured board knead for 10 to 15 minutes, or until dough is very smooth and very elastic. Brush top with oil and cover with a warm bowl. Let stand for 30 minutes. Soak raisins in 2 tablespoons water. Peel apples, slice thin, and sprinkle with ½ cup sugar. Brown crumbs in ⅓ cup butter. Roll strudel dough as thin as possible on a large lightly floured cloth, (about 36 inches square). Melt ½ cup butter and brush some on top of dough. With palms up, slip hands underneath dough and stretch dough carefully to paper thinness, working from the center out. If edges remain thick, cut them off. Dough should almost cover the cloth. Brush with more melted butter to keep pliable. Pile apples in a row about 2 inches from one end of dough. Combine undrained raisins, bread crumbs, almonds, cinnamon, and ½ cup sugar; spread over remaining dough. Fold over the dough about 1 inch along the edges of dough at the top and bottom of the row of apples. Lift edges of cloth nearest the apples so that the dough falls

Sóska Leves   Sonkás Palacsinta   Cseresznye Kisütve

over apples; continue to roll dough over and over with the help of cloth. Put roll on cookie sheet in a U shape. Bake in preheated hot oven (400°F.) for 30 minutes. Brush 2 or 3 times with melted butter. Five minutes before strudel is done, sprinkle thickly with more sugar. Makes 12 3-inch pieces.

Cheese Strudel
Strudel Dough (see recipe page 921)
1 tablespoon butter
¼ cup sugar
4 eggs
1 pound cottage cheese, sieved
3 tablespoons dairy sour cream
⅓ cup seedless raisins
2 tablespoons melted butter

Prepare dough as for Apple Strudel. Cream butter with sugar. Beat in eggs. Mix in cottage cheese, sour cream, and raisins. Spread mixture evenly over the dough which has been brushed with melted butter. Bake as for Apple Strudel.

Nut Strudel
Strudel Dough (see recipe page 921)
1 cup ground nuts
1 cup sugar
½ cup milk
Grated rind of 1 lemon
½ cup yellow raisins
2 tablespoons melted butter

Prepare dough as for Apple Strudel. Mix nuts with sugar and milk. Cook over low heat until mixture is slightly thickened. Add lemon rind and raisins. Spread filling on strudel dough which has been brushed with melted butter. Bake as for Apple Strudel.

Cherry Strudel
Strudel Dough (see recipe page 921)
2 tablespoons melted butter
½ cup dry bread crumbs
½ cup ground blanched almonds
1½ cups dark sweet cherries, pitted
1 cup sugar
¼ cup dairy sour cream

Prepare dough as for Apple Strudel. Brush with melted butter and sprinkle with bread crumbs and almonds. Scatter cherries over the dough and sprinkle with sugar. Roll up and brush with sour cream. Bake as for Apple Strudel.

Cabbage Strudel
3½ cups grated cabbage
1 tablespoon salt
1½ tablespoons sugar
2 tablespoons fat
½ teaspoon white pepper
Strudel Dough (see page 921)
2 tablespoons melted butter

Mix cabbage with salt. Let stand for 30 minutes. Squeeze out liquid. Add sugar and cabbage to hot fat and cook until lightly browned and tender. Stir in pepper. Prepare dough as for Apple Strudel. Spread cooled cabbage mixture over the dough which has been brushed with melted butter. Bake as for Apple Strudel.

Poppy-Seed Strudel
Strudel Dough (see page 921)

1 pound freshly ground poppy seeds
½ cup sugar
Grated rind of 1 lemon
½ cup milk
⅓ cup raisins
2 tablespoons melted butter

Prepare dough as for Apple Strudel. Mix poppy seeds with sugar, lemon rind, and milk. Cook over low heat until thickened. Add raisins and blend well. Cool, and then spread on strudel dough which has been brushed with melted butter. Bake as for Apple Strudel.

DIÓS TEKERCS
(Hungarian Walnut Roll)
1 package active dry yeast or 1 cake compressed
½ cup lukewarm water*
4 cups sifted all-purpose flour
½ teaspoon salt
6 egg yolks
¾ cup warm milk
Filling
1 cup chopped walnuts
⅓ cup milk, scalded
2 tablespoons sugar
1 small vanilla bean, grated

Sprinkle dry yeast or crumble cake yeast into warm water. *Use very warm water (105°F. to 115°F.) for dry yeast; use lukewarm water (80°F. to 90°F.) for compressed. Let stand for a few minutes, then stir until dissolved. Place sifted flour and salt in a large mixing bowl; form a well in the center and place in it the yeast, egg yolks, and milk. Gradually incorporate the flour into the other ingredients; knead in bowl until mixture is smooth. Cover and let rest while preparing the Filling. Roll out dough to a rectangle ½ inch thick; spread with Filling and sprinkle with 1 cup chopped walnuts. Roll as for jelly roll. Cut into 1½-inch pieces and place, cut side up, in a buttered ring mold or tube pan. It may be necessary to make 2 layers. Let rise in a warm place until doubled in bulk. Bake in preheated moderate oven (350°F.) for 25 minutes. Remove from oven and pour over ⅓ cup scalded milk mixed with 2 tablespoons sugar and 1 small vanilla bean, grated. Return to oven for 15 minutes longer. Remove from oven and cool on a rack.

Filling
Cream together ¾ cup sugar and ¾ cup sweet butter; add a 1½-inch piece of vanilla bean, grated.

HUSZÁRCSÓK
(Hussar's Kisses)
⅔ cup sweet butter (must be butter and sweet is the best)
⅓ cup sugar
1 egg yolk
2 eggs
1⅓ cups sifted all-purpose flour
⅓ cup finely chopped nuts
⅓ cup raspberry jam

Cream butter with sugar. Add egg yolk

and 1 egg. Blend in flour. Chill. Pinch off walnut-size pieces of dough and shape into balls with floured hands. Put on ungreased cookie sheet. With pencil or finger make a deep depression in center of each ball. Beat remaining egg and brush cookies with it. Sprinkle with nuts. Bake in preheated moderate oven (350°F.) for 15 minutes, or until golden. Cool. Fill depressions with jam. Makes about 32.

HYDROGENATE—Hydrogenation is a process which converts liquid oils into semisolid, malleable fats. Further processing incorporates air or an inert gas, resulting in a solid bland fat (hydrogenated fat) which is soft and creamy in consistency and creamy-white in color. When melted, it has the same keeping quality for successive fryings and the same high smoking point as the original oil. It will not acquire food flavors if foods are properly cooked in it. This hydrogenated fat is sold under many trade names and is excellent both for frying and baking. Corn, cottonseed, and soybean are the oils most frequently used to make hydrogenated vegetable fats. The process of hydrogenation is also employed to better the consistency of animal fats such as lard, in the manufacture of some margarine, and for industrial purposes such as soapmaking.

The importance of the hydrogenation of fats cannot be overemphasized. It is done on an enormous scale, and has made possible the use of vegetable-seed oils as substitutes for the more expensive animal (hog and beef) fats and for butter in cooking and baking.

The first research in hydrogenation was done by French chemists between 1897 and 1905. It was carried on in England, where a process was patented by W. Norman in 1903. An English firm is said to have hydrogenated whale oil in 1906 or earlier.

Today, practically every American producer of shortening oils and margarine uses the hydrogenation process and so do comparable manufacturers throughout the world. Processors of nonedible oils and fats use it, too.

ICE—When water solidifies, it is called ice. Water, like all liquids, when sufficiently cooled becomes solid. The freezing point of water is 32°F. or 0°C. Ice is transparent in color; it is also lighter than water, which accounts for the familiar sight of ice floating on water. Ice is greater in bulk than the corresponding amount of water. It expands almost ten per cent in mass upon freezing.

The verb "to ice" means to cover or to chill or cool with ice. It is also applied to coating, as, a cake, with an icing, although the more common term for this is frosting.

For most household purposes, ice is frozen in the refrigerator frozen-food compartment or freezer in a variety of shapes, generally as ice cubes. Ice for household purposes can also be bought commercially in blocks varying from twelve and a half to 300 pounds, as snow, marbles, cubes, etc.

Today, anyone with a refrigerator can cool drinks with ice. This was not always so; ice has a history as a luxury product. Cooled wines, drunk by Solomon, are mentioned in the Bible. Hippocrates, the early Greek physician, thought cold drinks to be unhealthy. He wrote that "it is dangerous to heat, cool, or make a commotion all of a sudden in the body—let it be done which way it may—because anything that is excessive is an enemy to nature. But for all this, people will not take warning, and most men would rather run the hazard of their lives or health than be deprived the pleasure of drinking out of ice."

In the 1st century A.D., the Roman Emperor Nero sent slaves to the nearby mountains to gather ice for chilling. Pliny the Elder, the famous Roman naturalist, shared Hippocrates' distrust of iced drinks, but for sanitary reasons. He put his drinks in jars in the ice and snow, to prevent contamination.

Another disapproving statement on the practice of chilling by ice was made by Seneca, a Roman philosopher of the same time. His objection was not only on sanitary grounds, but also because of the great trouble and expense. He tells how the snow carried from the mountains was used to pack perishable foods. Snow, packed in chaff or straw pits, solidified into ice and was used to ice drinks. So many slaves had to be sent out to the mountains to gather snow, that it was an expensive practice that only the rich could afford.

A refinement on the packing of snow into pits to turn it to ice was the discovery that boiled water in a container packed in the middle of the snow would turn to ice. In mid-16th century, the Italians, who were the primary drinkers of iced drinks, discovered that saltpeter added to the packing around the container hastened the cooling process.

Experiments in ice-making were common during the 17th century. Francis Bacon, one of the first great English experimental scientists, died in 1626 as a direct result of a cold caught while stuffing a fowl with snow to try to preserve it.

Ice was used and stored in America from early colonial days in the North, where it could be gathered from frozen ponds and streams. The ice business in America started in 1799 when a shipload was sent from New York to South Carolina. Five years later a Boston entrepreneur shipped ice to the West Indies, and shortly afterward another Boston firm introduced ice to the English.

In the 19th century every southern plantation had its own icehouse, and all industrial centers built ice storage houses. The supply of natural ice was limited, however, and it seemed as if ice would end its history as it had begun it, by being a luxury item.

But, from 1755 when Dr. William Cullen of Scotland had attempted to make ice by mechanical means, experimenters had been working on the problem. The 19th-century experimenters who worked on means of mechanical freezing were justifiably proud of their work. One inventor, the Englishman Thomas Masters, wrote in 1844 about the age as an "age of invention." He continued: "Art has, however, not rested content with providing the luxuries and preparing the necessaries of humanity; it has dared to imitate nature in the production of its most wonderful phenomena, and *ice,* once the sole produce of her mighty laboratory, has been made by the skill and enterprise of her subject; man."

By 1870 there were four commercial ice-making plants in the United States. At the end of the century, pressed by the need for ice, the industry expanded rapidly. In 1944, 6,800 plants were producing almost fifty million tons. Today the great growth in mechanical refrigerators and freezers, electric or gas, has turned almost every American home into its own ice-making plant, and coin-operated ice-cube dispensers are found in convenient public locations.

The Uses of Ice in Cookery

■ Ice Cubes—The most popular ice form used is the ice cube which can be frozen in special ice-cube trays at home. Ice cubes may be plain water, water mixed with fruit juices or punches, and double-strength coffee or tea. They can be frozen plain or for decorative use by placing cherries, mint leaves, gumdrops, small pieces of lemon and lime, strawberries and pineapple into the water before freezing.

■ Ice Rings and Blocks—Water, plain or colored with vegetable coloring, may be frozen in ring molds or pans and used to chill large bowls of punch. Flowers, leaves, fruits may be placed on top of the ice or may be frozen into the ice.

To keep ice clear, use boiled cooled water or distilled water for freezing. Freeze ice quickly; when ready to unmold, keep ice mold in the refrigerator for thirty minutes and then remove to room temperature until ice melts slightly. Unmold and place into chilled punch. If ice is subjected to too rapid temperature changes, it will crack.

■ Ice Bowls—An ice bowl may be made by filling a large bowl with water and pressing a smaller bowl into the water. Hold in place with a weight. Tape the bowls together so they will not move during freezing. Freeze until firm. Dip bowls into lukewarm water for a few seconds to loosen ice bowl. Leave the ice bowl in the freezer until ready to fill. Fill with ice cream or chilled fruits or chilled seafood or sherbet. Be sure to use a serving dish under it which can accommodate a certain amount of melting.

■ Shaved Ice—The ice is shaved or crushed finely and used in preparing mint juleps and daiquiris; to chill melon, grapefruit, relishes, shrimp cocktail, vichyssoise, jellied consommé, oysters, clams on the half shell, and other dishes which must be served and eaten icy cold.

Shaved ice is also shaped into cones. Sweet flavored syrup is spooned over it and it is eaten much as one would eat ices.

■ Ice Sculpture—Many restaurants and hotel chefs specialize in ice sculpture of great beauty. However, this is an art in itself which requires years of skill and a cold room in which to work. Simple ice molds can be made using the various metal molds usually used for molding gelatin desserts. Handle and unmold as directed in Ice Rings and Blocks above. Dry ice underneath the mold can prevent its melting during the meal.

DRY ICE

Dry Ice is the trademarked name of a product made of solidified carbon dioxide. It can burn if touched, and dissipates when it melts. Any room in which Dry Ice is being used should be ventilated. It serves as a refrigerant and is usually available at ice supply houses or from distributors who supply it to manufacturers. Any home owner who stores an appreciable amount of food in a freezer should know who the local suppliers are since, in the event of a power shutdown lasting more than a day or two, dry ice

obtained quickly can be used to prevent the deterioration or spoilage of frozen food.

ICE—The word ice is used to describe a frozen mixture of a fruit juice or purée, a sweetener, and water. Occasionally ices are made with coffee or wine instead of fruit juice. Such mixtures are often called "water ices" to distinguish them from the sherbets, ice creams, and other frozen desserts to which eggs, milk, cream, etc., are added.

Most ices are stirred often during the freezing process so that the finished product has a smooth texture, and they are frozen firm. Frappés are ices frozen only to a mushy consistency and granités are ices which, although frozen firm, are stirred very little so that their texture is rough and icy.

Ices are usually one part sugar to four parts liquid. Ices may be frozen in a refrigerator or freezer, or, for best results, churned in a crank freezer. When ices are not frozen in a crank freezer, they must be stirred every thirty minutes to break up ice crystals and make them smaller. They may also be frozen halfway, then whipped with a beater, and frozen until firm. Ices can be frozen in any kind of container or mold or even in individual molds.

Ices are sold commercially in a variety of flavors, both in bulk and prepackaged containers.

The bright fresh flavor of ices allows them to be served very simply or in elegant style. Place scoops into fruit juices or punches, in fruit cups, on melon wedges, any fresh or canned fruit; ices can be used to fill hollowed-out apples, oranges, grapefruit, drizzled with liqueurs, or topped with candied fruits and nuts.

Flavored ices have been a delicacy from the earliest days. It is thought that the Chinese were the first to perfect this art and that they taught it to the Indians, Persians, and Arabs. It might also be a development of the early Greek and Roman practice of putting ice and snow in their beverages.

Marco Polo, the famous 13th-century Italian voyager to China, brought back reports, if not recipes, of the oriental custom of eating water ices. They became popular, first in Venice and then throughout Italy, from the 14th century on. It is said that Bernard Buontalenti, a 16th-century Italian architect, was the first to manufacture frozen drinks and desserts.

Catherine de Medici helped spread the custom of eating ices. When she came to France in 1533 as a fourteen-year-old bride to marry the future Henry II, she brought with her Italian cooks who knew the secret of ices. The frozen desserts became so popular that Catherine's son, Henry III, is said to have eaten ices every day.

Until 1660, when an Italian cook who was to Gallicize his name into Procope arrived in Paris from Italy, ices were the province solely of the court. When the Café Procope was founded as a place serving ices, the eager Parisians ate the ices to such an extent that soon other restaurateurs were following the lead of the clever Italian. By 1676 there were so many shops that they had to incorporate and the members of the corporation had to be officially authorized to sell their popular products.

In the 18th century the development of ices was rapid. Ices, frozen into fantastic shapes and equally fabulously decorated, were popular desserts at elegant banquets. The late 18th century and the first French Empire set up ices as the height of fashionable elegance.

Some modern versions of ices provide a striking contrast to their royal history. It was in America in 1926 that a California fair concessionaire named Epperson came to New Jersey to visit friends. He left his glass of lemonade, with a spoon in it, on his windowsill one cold day. When he returned he found the lemonade frozen, with the spoon rigid in the middle. Carrying the glass to the bathroom he ran water on it, and the ice came out in a single piece with the spoon frozen in, acting as a handle. He was quick to see the possibilities of his discovery and christened it the "epsicle." Later this was changed to the now famous "popsicle."

APPLE AND GRAPE-JUICE ICE
2 cups apple juice
1 cup grape juice
½ cup light corn syrup
Few grains of salt

Combine ingredients and pour into chilled freezing can of ice-cream freezer; cover. Surround with mixture of 4 parts crushed ice and 1 part rock salt. Turn crank slowly and steadily until turning becomes difficult. Remove dasher; repack in ice and salt. Let stand for at least 1 hour. Makes 1½ quarts.

APRICOT ICE
1 cup sugar
2 cups water
2 cups apricot nectar
¼ cup fresh lemon juice

Combine sugar and water, and cook for 5 minutes. Cool. Stir in apricot nectar and lemon juice. Pour into freezer trays and freeze until almost firm. Remove to bowl, and beat until smooth. Return to

trays and freeze until firm. Makes 4 to 6 servings.

Note: Any nectar can be substituted for the apricot.

CANTALOUPE ICE
4 cups peeled, seeded, ripe cantaloupe, cut into pieces
Juice of 2 lemons
½ cup sugar

Strain cantaloupe through a sieve or whirl in blender. Add lemon juice and sugar. Place in freezing trays and freeze until almost firm. Place in bowl and beat until smooth. Return to trays and freeze until firm. Makes 4 to 6 servings.

FRESH COCONUT ICE
2 large coconuts to yield 6 cups grated coconut and 4¼ cups extracted coconut milk
3½ cups boiling water
½ teaspoon vanilla extract
1 cup coconut water
1 cup sugar
Grated coconut

Crack coconuts and reserve coconut water. Grate; there should be 6 cups grated coconut meat. Pour boiling water over grated coconut. Let stand for 15 minutes. Strain through a triple layer of cheesecloth, squeezing out as much of the milk as possible. Add vanilla, coconut water, and sugar, and stir until sugar is dissolved. Freeze in refrigerator trays or in ice-cream freezer as usual. Serve with additional grated coconut sprinkled on top. Makes 6 to 8 servings.

COFFEE ICE WITH WHIPPED CREAM
1½ cups ground Italian-style coffee
⅓ cup sugar
5 cups boiling water
Whipped cream, sweetened to taste

Combine coffee, sugar, and water in top part of double boiler. Steep over simmering water for 30 minutes. Cool. Strain through a strainer lined with a triple thickness of cheesecloth. Freeze in ice-cube tray until almost firm. Remove to bowl and beat until smooth. Return to trays and freeze until almost firm; the ice should be a little on the mushy side. Spoon into glasses and top with whipped cream. Makes 6 servings.

CURRANT-JELLY AND RASPBERRY ICE
12 sprigs of fresh mint
1 cup currant jelly
1¼ cups boiling water
1 cup fresh raspberries

Cut mint fine, using scissors. Combine with jelly and boiling water; simmer for 5 minutes. Cover and let stand until cold. Strain. Add raspberries. Pour into chilled freezing can of ice-cream freezer. Cover; surround with mixture of 4 parts crushed ice and 1 part rock salt. Turn crank slowly and steadily until turning becomes difficult. Remove dasher; repack in ice and salt. Let stand for at least 1 hour before serving. Makes 5 to 6 servings.

FRUIT-JUICE ICE
4 cups water
1½ cups sugar
2 cups orange, pineapple, apple, cranberry, etc., juice, or ¾ cup fresh lemon juice

Cook water with sugar until it boils, and boil for 5 minutes. Cool, and add fruit juice. (Use one fruit juice or a blending of many fruit juices.) Pour mixture into freezer container and freeze until very firm, stirring mixture every 30 minutes if frozen in a freezer tray. Makes 8 to 10 servings.

INSTANT BLENDER LEMON ICE
6 or 8 ice cubes
⅓ to ½ cup sugar
1 lemon, cut into small pieces, peel and pulp

Put all ingredients into a blender. Whirl until well combined. Serve at once. Makes about 4 servings.

LEMON FRAPPÉ
1 cup fresh lemon juice, or more, depending on tartness desired
Grated rind of 1 large lemon
3 cups water
1 cup sugar

Combine lemon juice and lemon rind. Boil water and sugar together for 5 minutes. Cool; stir in juice and rind. Freeze in refrigerator trays at coldest temperature. Stir twice during freezing, the second time stirring to a firm mush just before serving. Makes 4 servings.

MUSCATEL ICE
1 can (29 ounces) canned apricot halves
1½ cups sugar
2 cups boiling water
1 cup cold water
Juice of 2 lemons
1 cup Muscatel wine (or Tokay or Malaga)
¼ teaspoon salt

Drain apricots and reserve juice. Purée in a blender or food mill. Return fruit to fruit juice. Dissolve sugar in the boiling water; cool. Add apricots with juice and remaining ingredients. Pour into container of ice-cream freezer. Pack ice around with rock salt, and churn. Makes about 2 quarts.

ORANGE ICE
4 cups freshly squeezed orange juice
1 can (6 ounces) frozen orange-juice concentrate, undiluted
1 tablespoon grated lemon rind
Juice of 1 lemon
¼ cup light corn syrup or honey

Combine all ingredients. Freeze in refrigerator trays until mushy. Beat and freeze again. Serve with a dash of orange liqueur or on fruit salad, if desired. Makes 6 to 8 servings.

Note: This may be frozen in cubes to flavor drinks.

PEACH ICE

1 package (12 ounces) sweetened
  frozen peaches
⅛ teaspoon almond extract
1 egg white
  Few grains of salt

Thaw peaches and put through ricer or coarse sieve. Add almond extract. Pour into freezing tray and freeze until thick and mushy. Remove to well-chilled bowl; beat with rotary beater until mixture is fluffy. Fold in stiffly beaten egg white and salt. Beat again with rotary beater; return to freezing tray until ready to serve. Makes 4 to 6 servings.

FRESH PINEAPPLE ICE

1 large ripe fresh pineapple
½ cup honey
4 cups water
  Grated rind of 1 lemon
  Juice of 1 lemon

Pare pineapple, removing all dark eyes. Grate on cheese grater or force through food chopper. Combine with honey, water, and lemon rind. Simmer, covered, for 10 minutes. Strain and cool. Stir in lemon juice. Freeze in freezer trays until mushy. Beat until smooth and freeze again. Serve frozen mushy with additional fresh pineapple. Makes 4 to 6 servings.

PLUM ICE

12 to 20 (one 1-pound, 14-ounce can)
  plums or prunes
½ cup fresh orange juice
  Juice of 2 lemons
⅓ cup honey

Pit fruit, and force pulp with juice through ricer or sieve. Add remaining ingredients; mix thoroughly. Pour into refrigerator tray. Put tray in lowest compartment of freezing unit. With temperature control at coldest point, freeze until partly frozen. Remove to ice-cold bowl; beat with chilled rotary beater or electric mixer until light. Return to tray and freeze until firm. Makes 6 servings.

RHUBARB ICE

1½ teaspoons unflavored gelatin
¼ cup cold water
4 cups diced pink rhubarb
  Grated rind of 1 orange
1⅓ cups light corn syrup
  Few grains of salt

Soften gelatin in cold water. Cook rhubarb, orange rind, and corn syrup for about 20 minutes. Add softened gelatin and salt, stirring until gelatin dissolves. Pour into freezing tray; freeze until thick and mushy. Remove to well-chilled bowl and beat with rotary beater until the mixture is fluffy. Return to tray and freeze until firm. Makes 6 servings.

STRAWBERRY ICE

2 quarts fresh strawberries
1½ cups sugar
1 cup water
  Juice of 1 lemon

Wash and hull strawberries. Combine with all other ingredients. Rub through a fine sieve or whirl in blender. Pour into freezing trays. Freeze until almost firm. Place in bowl and beat until smooth. Return to trays and freeze until firm. Makes 6 servings.

STRAWBERRY, APRICOT, RASPBERRY, OR PEACH FRAPPÉ

2 cups fruit purée made from fresh or
  canned fruit
  Fresh lemon juice
4 cups water
1½ cups sugar

Purée fruit, which has been cooked if fresh and firm. If fruits are soft, purée them as they are and do not cook. Add lemon juice to taste. Cook water with sugar and let boil for 5 minutes. Cool, and add to puréed fruit. Pour mixture into freezer tray or into an ice-cream freezer. If using a freezer tray, stir ice every 30 minutes to keep ice crystals small, or freeze until half frozen and beat with a rotary beater until smooth. Freeze again to a thick mush just before serving. Makes 8 to 10 servings.

TANGERINE ICE IN ORANGE SHELLS

2 cans (6 ounces each) frozen
  tangerine juice
1 envelope unflavored gelatin
½ cup sugar
6 large thick-skinned oranges

Set refrigerator control for fast freezing. Blend tangerine juice with 3 juice-cans water. Soften gelatin in ½ cup juice. Put over low heat and stir until dissolved. Add gelatin and sugar to remaining juice. Pour into refrigerator trays and freeze until firm, stirring occasionally. Remove to cold bowl and beat until fluffy. Return to trays and freeze until firm. Cut tops from oranges about one third of way down. Scoop out pulp; reserve for later use. Cut edges of shells sawtooth fashion. Fill with ice and put in freezing section until ready to serve. Makes 6 servings.

THREE-FRUIT ICE

½ cup sugar
1 cup water
2 bananas
  Juice of 2 lemons
1 cup bottled grape juice

Cook sugar and water together for 5 minutes. Add mashed bananas, lemon juice, and grape juice. Cool; pour into refrigerator tray. Put tray in lowest compartment of freezing unit. With temperature control at coldest point, freeze until partly frozen. Remove to ice-cold bowl; beat with chilled rotary beater or electric mixer until light. Return to refrigerator tray and freeze until firm. Makes 5 to 6 servings.

WATERMELON GRANITÉ

4 cups ripe watermelon meat, seeds
  removed
2 tablespoons fresh lemon juice
½ cup sugar

Purée watermelon in blender or food mill; add lemon juice and sugar and stir until dissolved. Pour into refrigerator tray and freeze for 30 minutes to 1 hour. It is better not to let it get too solid. Makes 4 to 6 servings.

ICE CREAM—America's favorite dessert is a frozen food made from milk products, sweetening, flavoring, and other ingredients, depending on whether it is homemade or made commercially. By far the largest amount of ice cream consumed in the United States is commercial ice cream. Homemade ice cream has become a delicacy, made only for special occasions.

Ice cream may contain cream, fresh or evaporated milk, a sweetener such as sugar or honey or an artificial sweetener. Fruits, nuts, and flavorings are added to suit the fancy. The choice of flavorings is varied: from vanilla to liqueurs.

Commercially made ice cream also contains milk fat (also called butterfat), stabilizers added to improve the body of the ice cream, to make the ice cream smooth by keeping the ice crystals small, and to give it more resistance to melting. It may contain some nonfat milk solids.

It is impossible to say who invented ice cream. Marco Polo, who traveled extensively through China in the late 13th century, reported the oriental practice of making water and milk ices. Water ices were popular in Venice and Italy from the 14th century on. In 1660 an Italian confectioner set up in Paris a café serving ices, which was soon copied throughout Paris. It is possible that some of these early water ices may have contained milk and cream.

The first recorded occasion of the appearance of ice cream was at an elaborate banquet given by the English king, Charles I, around 1640. The frozen "cream ice" was such a surprise and such a success that Charles called in the cook and ordered him to keep the recipe a secret forever. To prove that he was serious, the king pensioned off this cook for a generous sum. But the cook did not keep his word and ice cream became a popular, if at first strictly luxurious, specialty.

Later in the century, across the channel in France, Louis XIV's guests at a state dinner were surprised to see, as one of them has reported, "in silver gilt cups, what apparently was a freshly laid egg colored like those of Easter, but before the company had time to recover from their surprise at such a novelty for dessert, they discovered that the supposed eggs were delicious sweet-meats, cold and compact as marble."

The American colonists were not far behind their European neighbors. A guest of Governor Bladen of Maryland describes a dinner of 1744: "We had a dessert no less curious; among the rarities of which it was compos'd was some fine Ice Cream which, with the Strawberries and Milk, eat Most Deliciously."

In 1774 there was a public announcement of the delicacy. Philip Lenzi of London would prepare special orders of ice cream, declared an advertisement in a New York paper. Three years later an ice-cream advertisement read: "Ice cream of what sort they will please to order."

Many leaders in American government were connected with the rise in popularity of ice cream in this country. The first President, George Washington, had two "pewter ice cream pots," presumably for making ice cream at Mount Vernon. He was introduced to ice cream by Mrs. Alexander Hamilton, the wife of the Secretary of the Treasury, in 1789. Thomas Jefferson, the third president, was an enthusiastic gastronome and had learned recipes for ice-cream dishes while in France. Guests at his state dinners were sometimes served such luxuries as meringue glacée and baked Alaska.

Perhaps the most famous American patroness of ice cream was Dolly Madison, who served as hostess for the wifeless Jefferson as well as for her own husband, James Madison, the fourth president. A contemporary speaks of the great moment of one of Dolly's parties: "Mrs. Madison always entertains with grace and charm, but last night there was a sparkle in her eye that set astir an air of expectancy among her guests. When finally the brilliant assemblage—America's best—entered the dining room, they beheld a table set with French china and English silver, laden with good things to eat, and in the center, high on a silver platter, a large shining dome of pink ice cream." She served strawberry ice cream at the second Inaugural Ball of 1812.

Ice cream's rich flavor and taste was so soothing and popular that Emerson, the famous Concord writer, complained about the lack of conversation in homes in 1841: "We dare not trust our wit for making our house pleasant to our friends and so we buy ice cream."

As early as 1893, only forty-two years after the making of the first American commercial ice cream in 1851 by Jacob Fussel, an American magazine called ice-cream sodas "the national beverage." Ice-cream cones first appeared at the St. Louis Fair in 1904. Credit for their dis-

covery goes to Mr. E. Hamwi, a Syrian waffle vendor. Ice cream was sold in little dishes at the Fair. One day, an ice cream vendor located next to Mr. Hamwi's stand ran out of dishes. Mr. Hamwi, observing the predicament, helped out by rolling one of his thin, wafer-like waffles into the shape of a cone. This hardened as it cooled. The ice cream was put into it to the customer's delight, and a great new American institution was born.

Ice cream is, without doubt, along with pie, America's most beloved dessert. The consumption of it has risen greatly during the last thirty years; between 1935 and 1939 Americans consumed an average of 8.4 quarts a year. In 1963 they ate 15.4 quarts each. In fact, it often appears that ice cream has transcended its role as dessert and become a staple food, eaten at all times. Vanilla ice cream outsells all other flavors, with chocolate second and strawberry third in popularity.

Making Ice Cream at Home

Homemade ice cream is made by either the stirred or the still-frozen method. The *stirred method* uses a crank freezer surrounded by ice and salt and turned by hand or by an electric motor. It is important to be sure that the lid, can, and dasher (scraper) are sterilized in boiling water, that the lid fits properly, and that melted ice does not seep into the can. For freezing ice cream, a mixture of one part salt to six parts ice by weight, or one part salt to twelve parts ice by measure, is frequently used. Coarse ice-cream salt must be used, as table salt dissolves too rapidly. The dasher is turned slowly until it begins to be difficult to turn so that the warm mixture will not be churned, then the dasher is turned more quickly to whip air into the ice cream. A hardening period of about 1 hour is necessary to complete freezing.

The *still-frozen method* (refrigerator ice cream) requires some means other than continuous stirring to keep the ice crystals small and to incorporate air. Rapid freezing and the use of a variety of materials that interfere with crystal formation are relied on to keep the crystals small. Rapid freezing is aided by setting the controls of the refrigerator at the lowest setting. The mixture can also be removed from the refrigerator occasionally and stirred to remove it from the sides of the container. Air can be incorporated by folding in a fluffy beaten product such as whipped cream, or by taking the ice cream from the refrigerator and beating before freezing is completed.

Even when a good recipe is skillfully used, the texture of refrigerator ice cream is usually less smooth than that of ice cream made in a crank freezer and

becomes coarser on storage because the ice crystals grow. Refrigerator ice cream is best eaten soon after freezing.

Commercial Ice Cream

Commercial ice-cream mixtures are pasteurized, homogenized, aged, frozen, and hardened. By federal or state standards ice cream must contain per gallon a minimum of 10 per cent milk fat, minimum 20 per cent total milk solids, stabilizer maximum .5 per cent (not more than .2 per cent emulsifier permitted), as well as a weight of minimum 4.5 pounds per gallon and minimum 1.6 pounds food solids per gallon.

There are some diet ice creams available in which noncaloric sweeteners are used.

Milk sherbet or fruit sherbet is a frozen dessert made of a milk product such as milk, or milk and cream, fruit or fruit juice, and sweetening. Water, flavorings, and stabilizers may be added. The number of calories supplied are slightly less than those from plain ice cream.

Frozen custard, French ice cream, or *French custard ice cream* are all frozen products in which eggs or egg yolks are added to the usual ice cream ingredients.

Ice milk is a frozen dessert similar to ice cream but contains less milk fat and total milk solids. Ice milk is often served from the freezer in the soft state at refreshment stands, under various trade names.

Imitation ice cream or *mellorine* is a frozen dessert in which fats other than butterfat are used. It may resemble ice cream or ice milk depending on its fat content, as the other ingredients are similar. The fat most commonly used is a blend of hydrogenated vegetable oils. Its sale is regulated by state laws and is permitted in fourteen states.

Storage—Refrigerate in refrigerator frozen-food compartment with temperature control at coldest setting.
- ☐ Refrigerator frozen-food compartment, in ice-cream carton: 2 to 3 days
- ☐ Freezer, in ice-cream carton: 8 months

Nutritive Food Values—Small amounts of protein and calcium, depending on the amount of milk solids used in making the ice cream. High in fat content, especially when made with cream.

The caloric value of 3½ ounces of ice cream product varies with the ingredients used and the amount of fat content, from about 193 to 222 calories. The diet ice creams contain about 150 calories in 3½ ounces. For 3½ ounces of ice milk the caloric value is 152.

Everybody's favorite dessert.
It's delicious plain: it's a great mixer.
From the informality of a cone
to an impressive party cake, a pleasure
that people never outgrow.

STILL-FROZEN ICE CREAMS

VANILLA ICE CREAM

4 cups milk
1 box (3 ounces) vanilla pudding mix
1 cup light corn syrup
1 teaspoon vanilla extract
1 teaspoon almond extract
1 cup heavy cream or chilled evaporated milk

Add milk gradually to pudding powder; add corn syrup; mix until smooth. Cook over low heat until thickened, stirring constantly. When cool, freeze in refrigerator trays. When frozen around the edges, remove to chilled bowl and beat well with rotary beater. Add vanilla and almond extracts. Whip cream; fold into partially frozen pudding mixture. Freeze until firm. If desired, serve with fruit sweetened with honey. Makes about 1½ quarts.

CHOCOLATE ICE CREAM

4 cups milk
3 ounces (3 squares) unsweetened chocolate
1 cup sugar
1 tablespoon flour
¼ teaspoon salt
2 eggs
1 envelope unflavored gelatin
¼ cup cold water
2 teaspoons vanilla extract
1 cup heavy cream

Pour half of milk into top part of a double boiler; add chocolate; heat until melted. Combine half of sugar with flour and salt; add hot milk slowly, stirring well. Return to double boiler; cook for 10 minutes, stirring frequently. Combine remaining ½ cup sugar and 2 cups milk with beaten eggs; add to hot mixture; add gelatin soaked in water. Cook until custard coats a silver spoon. When cool, freeze in refrigerator trays. When partially frozen, beat well; add vanilla. Whip cream or chilled evaporated milk until stiff; fold into mixture; freeze. Makes about 1½ quarts.

PINEAPPLE ICE CREAM

½ cup sugar
1 cup water
Dash of salt
About 1 to 1¼ cups (one 9-ounce can) crushed pineapple
1 cup heavy cream, whipped

Bring first 3 ingredients to boil and boil for 5 minutes. Cool. Add pineapple; pour into tray. Freeze in freezing compartment of refrigerator or in freezer until mushy. Fold in cream; freeze until firm. Makes 1 quart.

RUM-RAISIN ICE CREAM

2 egg yolks
½ cup sugar
Few grains of salt
1 cup light cream
1 cup heavy cream
1½ teaspoons vanilla extract
½ cup seeded raisins, slivered or ground, soaked for several hours in 2 to 3 tablespoons Jamaica rum

Beat yolks until light, add sugar, then salt and light cream; blend well. Fold in whipped heavy cream and vanilla. Partially freeze. Stir once, and when it is of frappé consistency add the raisins. Continue freezing. Makes 6 servings.

ALMOND ICE CREAM

3 eggs
¾ cup sugar
¼ cup water
¼ cup fresh milk
1¾ cups heavy cream or 1 can (14½ ounces) undiluted evaporated milk, partially frozen
¾ teaspoon almond extract

Beat eggs and sugar until light in top part of double boiler; stir in water and fresh milk. Cook, stirring constantly, over hot, not boiling, water until thick enough to coat a metal spoon. Chill. Whip partially frozen cream until stiff. Fold in egg mixture and almond extract. Freeze in refrigerator tray at coldest temperature until frozen 1 inch in from edge of tray. Turn into chilled bowl and beat with a rotary beater until creamy. Return to tray and chill until firm. Makes 6 servings.

ICE 'N CREAM

1 cup grape juice
1 cup apple juice
¼ cup lime juice
¾ cup superfine sugar
1½ cups heavy cream
1 teaspoon vanilla extract
⅔ cup chopped nuts

Combine fruit juices and ½ cup sugar. Pour into refrigerator tray, and freeze. Whip cream with remaining ¼ cup sugar; add vanilla and half of nuts. Pour over frozen fruit juices, and freeze. Serve garnished with remaining nuts. Makes 8 servings.

STIRRED ICE CREAMS

FRENCH VANILLA ICE CREAM

6 egg yolks
2 cups milk
1 cup sugar
¼ teaspoon salt
2 cups heavy cream
1 tablespoon vanilla extract

In top part of double boiler beat egg yolks and milk with rotary beater. Add sugar and salt; cook, stirring constantly, over hot, not boiling, water until thick enough to coat a metal spoon. Let cool, then add cream and vanilla. Freeze in a crank-type freezer, using 8 parts cracked ice to 1 part rock salt. Makes about 1½ quarts.

Banana Ice Cream

Use recipe above, omitting all but 1 tea-spoon vanilla. Force 3 large ripe bananas through sieve and add pulp to ice-cream mixture. Freeze.

Peach Ice Cream

Use recipe for French Vanilla Ice Cream, substituting 1 teaspoon almond extract for vanilla. Partially freeze. Add 2 cups sweetened crushed fresh peaches, or use thawed frozen peaches. Finish freezing. Makes 8 to 10 servings.

Strawberry Ice Cream

Use recipe for French Vanilla Ice Cream, omitting vanilla. Partially freeze. Add 2 cups sweetened crushed fresh strawberries, or use thawed frozen strawberries. Finish freezing. Makes 8 to 10 servings.

Raspberry Ice Cream

Use recipe for French Vanilla Ice Cream, omitting vanilla. Partially freeze. Add 2 cups sweetened strained fresh raspberries, or use thawed frozen raspberries. Finish freezing. Makes 8 to 10 servings.

CHOCOLATE FREEZER ICE CREAM

4 cups milk
2 ounces (2 squares) unsweetened chocolate
1 cup sugar
1 tablespoon flour
¼ teaspoon salt
2 eggs
2 cups light cream
1 tablespoon vanilla extract

Pour half of milk into top part of a double boiler; add chocolate; heat until chocolate melts. Combine half of sugar with flour and salt, add hot milk slowly and stir until well mixed. Return to double boiler; cook for 10 minutes, stirring frequently. Combine remaining sugar with eggs; add to hot-milk mixture; cook until custard coats a silver spoon. Add remaining milk, cool, and strain into freezer can of ice-cream freezer. Add unbeaten cream and vanilla. Pack in ice and salt, using 8 parts chopped ice to 1 part rock salt. Freeze as usual. Makes about 1½ quarts.

BLUEBERRY ICE CREAM

4 cups fresh blueberries
¼ cup water
1 cup sugar
¼ teaspoon salt
Juice of 1 lemon
2 cups light cream

Put berries in saucepan with water. Cover and simmer for 10 minutes, or until berries are soft. Mash; put through a sieve. Add sugar, salt, and lemon juice; cool. Mix with cream and freeze in a crank freezer. Makes 1½ quarts.

FRESH STRAWBERRY ICE CREAM

2 quarts strawberries
2 cups sugar
3 quarts heavy cream
Pinch of salt

Clean and hull berries and sprinkle them

with sugar. Cover and let stand for 1½ to 2 hours. Mash them lightly. Mix cream with salt and pour into freezer; freeze until mushy. Remove cover of freezer and stir in strawberries. Re-cover and continue freezing until solid. Makes about 1½ gallons.

ICE CREAM PARFAITS

CINNAMON CHOCOLATE PARFAIT

To softened chocolate ice cream add ground cinnamon to taste. Pour some Chocolate Fudge Sauce (page 931) into parfait or other tall glass (fruit-juice glass can be used). Fill with alternating layers of cinnamon-chocolate ice cream and Chocolate Fudge Sauce. Top with whipped topping. Sprinkle with ground cinnamon.

TWO-TONE CHERRY PARFAIT

Flavor softened vanilla ice cream with a little maraschino-cherry juice and some chopped cherries. Fill parfait or other tall glass (fruit-juice glass can be used) alternately with the cherry-ice cream mix-

ture and pistachio ice cream. Top with whipped cream and a whole maraschino cherry or chopped pistachio nuts. Put in freezer for a short time before serving.

MOCHA PARFAIT

Fill parfait or other tall glass (fruit-juice glass can be used) with alternate layers of Chocolate Fudge Sauce (pg. 931) and coffee ice cream. Top with whipped cream or other whipped topping. Decorate with Chocolate-Covered Coffee Beans (right). Serve at once or store in freezer.

STRAWBERRY PARFAIT

Alternate layers of thawed frozen strawberries and vanilla ice cream in a parfait glass. Top with whipped ice cream and a maraschino cherry.

BLUEBERRY PARFAIT

Spoon a little Blueberry Sauce (right) into bottom of a parfait or other tall glass (fruit-juice glass can be used). Alternate layers of vanilla ice cream and Blueberry Sauce. Top with whipped cream or whipped topping and whole blueberries.

SAUCES FOR ICE CREAM

■ **Apricot Cherry Sauce**—Combine 2 cups (one 1-pound jar) apricot jam and ½ cup coarsely chopped red maraschino cherries. Makes about 2 cups.

■ **Blueberry Sauce**—In saucepan blend 2 teaspoons cornstarch and 1 tablespoon water. Add ¼ cup sugar, ⅓ cup water (or syrup from canned blueberries), and ⅛ teaspoon salt. Cook until clear and slightly thickened, stirring. Add 2 cups washed fresh blueberries, or drained canned or frozen. Boil for 2 or 3 minutes. Makes 2 cups.

■ **Butterscotch Sauce**—Combine in saucepan 2 cups firmly packed brown sugar, ½ cup undiluted evaporated milk, ¼ teaspoon salt, ⅓ cup light corn syrup, and ⅓ cup butter. Bring to boil and cook rapidly for 3 minutes (to 220°F. on a candy thermometer). Makes 2 cups.

■ **Chocolate-Covered Coffee Beans**— Melt semisweet chocolate over hot water. Put each bean on tip of teaspoon and dip into chocolate until coated. Place on wax

paper. Allow to harden in refrigerator.

■ **Chocolate Fudge Sauce**—Melt 3 ounces (3 squares) unsweetened chocolate in ¾ cup milk over low heat, stirring constantly. Beat until smooth. Add ¼ teaspoon salt, 1½ cups sugar, and 3 tablespoons light corn syrup; cook, stirring, for 5 minutes. Add 1 tablespoon butter or margarine and ¾ teaspoon vanilla extract. Serve warm or cold. Makes about 2 cups.

■ **Pineapple Mint Topping**—Drain well 1 to 1¼ cups (one 9-ounce can) crushed pineapple. Combine pineapple with 2 tablespoons crème de menthe or melted mint jelly. Makes 1 cup.

■ **Raspberry Sauce**—Thaw 1 package (12 ounces) frozen raspberries. Press through fine sieve or whirl in blender; strain. Add 3 tablespoons sugar; dissolve in saucepan over medium heat. Cook rapidly for 3 minutes. Cool. Makes about 1 cup.

■ **Flavored Whipped Cream**—Before whipping, try adding one of the following to flavor heavy cream:
1. Instant coffee powder
2. Instant cocoa mix
3. Quick strawberry-flavored beverage mix
4. Brown sugar instead of granulated sugar
5. Your favorite flavoring extract

Or, fold one of these into the whipped cream:
1. Chopped nuts
2. Macaroon crumbs
3. Chocolate sprinkles
4. Chopped raisins
5. Grenadine instead of sugar

TOPPINGS FOR ICE CREAM SUNDAES

ORANGE AND BLUE SUNDAE
Top peach ice cream with equal parts of orange segments, sliced bananas, blueberries.

STOP-AND-GO SUNDAE
Mix chopped green and red maraschino cherries; add a little light corn syrup.

HOT CARAMEL SUNDAE
Melt ½ pound caramels with 2 tablespoons water over hot water.

ORIENTAL SUNDAE
Cut up undrained preserved kumquats. Good on chocolate ice cream.

MARSHMALLOW SUNDAE
Top ice cream with bought marshmallow cream. Best on peach, pineapple, chocolate.

NUTMEG SUNDAE
Grate fresh nutmeg generously over vanilla or peach ice cream.

GINGER SUNDAE
Top ice cream with ginger marmalade or chopped preserved gingerroot in syrup.

PEACH SUNDAE
Top vanilla ice cream with frozen or sweetened sliced fresh peaches.

MAPLE-RUM SUNDAE
Top coffee ice cream with hot maple syrup flavored with rum or rum extract.

BRITTLE SUNDAE
Sprinkle crushed nut brittle over coffee, vanilla, chocolate, or caramel ice cream.

CHOCOLATE-MINT SUNDAE
Melt thin chocolate mints over hot water; serve on vanilla, chocolate, pistachio.

Two-Tone Cherry Parfait
Orange and Blue Sundae
Cherry Ice Cream Soda
Ice 'n Cream
Harlequin Crinkle Cups

BRANDIED FRUIT SUNDAE

Serve cut-up brandied fruit on coffee, pineapple, coconut, banana, or vanilla.

MOLASSES CHIP SUNDAE

Top vanilla, banana, or chocolate ice cream with crushed molasses chips.

PINEAPPLE SUNDAE

Serve canned pineapple pie filling on vanilla or banana ice cream.

CRANBERRY-ORANGE SUNDAE

Add orange segments to cranberry sauce. Or use raw-cranberry relish to top vanilla.

ARABIAN SUNDAE

Moisten chopped dates with honey. Serve on butter-pecan or burnt-almond ice cream.

CANDIED FRUIT SUNDAE

Serve moist mixed candied fruits on vanilla or pistachio ice cream.

TROPICAL SUNDAE

Add chopped coconut, white raisins, and nuts to Butterscotch Sauce.

JUNIOR SUNDAE

Pour junior apricot-and-applesauce over vanilla ice cream. Top with raisins.

CEREAL SUNDAE

Top vanilla, coffee, chocolate, or banana ice cream with sugar-coated cereal.

CHOCOLATE-RUM SUNDAE

Melt chocolate rum wafers over hot water; serve on vanilla or chocolate ice cream.

JAM OR PRESERVES SUNDAE

Serve cherry, plum, apricot, or berry jam or preserves on choice of ice cream.

COOKIE SUNDAE

Top choice of ice cream with crushed fig cookies, coconut bars, or macaroons.

ZIPPY SUNDAE

Top choice of ice cream with Cointreau, crème de menthe, or any cordial.

MOCHA SUNDAE

Flavor bought chocolate syrup with powdered coffee for chocolate ice cream.

MINCEMEAT SUNDAE

Spike warm mincemeat with rum or brandy—best on vanilla ice cream.

COCONUT SUNDAE

Roll balls of strawberry or other ice cream in coconut. Serve with any sauce.

ORANGE SUNDAE

Top chocolate or vanilla ice cream with frozen orange juice concentrate.

PINEAPPLE-GINGER SUNDAE

Add a small amount chopped candied gingerroot to pineapple jam; serve on vanilla.

PARTY PINK SUNDAE

Top vanilla ice cream with 1 or 2 tablespoons grenadine.

ICE-CREAM SODAS

Each recipe makes one serving.

■ *Black-and-White*—Follow the directions for Chocolate Soda (below), substituting vanilla for chocolate ice cream.

■ *Chocolate*—Put 2 to 3 tablespoons chocolate syrup in a large glass. Add ¼ cup milk and a large scoop of chocolate ice cream. Almost fill with chilled soda water. Stir.

■ *Cherry*—Put 2 tablespoons bought cherry-sundae topping in tall glass. Add ¼ cup milk and vanilla ice cream. Fill with chilled soda water; stir; top with cherries.

■ *Coffee*—Several hours before making sodas, mix in a saucepan ½ cup sugar, ½ cup light corn syrup, ¾ cup water, and a dash of salt. Bring to boil, stirring constantly. Remove from heat and stir in 2 tablespoons instant coffee. Cool. Add ½ teaspoon vanilla extract. Refrigerate. For each soda, put 2 to 3 tablespoons syrup in large glass; add ¼ cup milk and large scoop of vanilla or coffee ice cream; almost fill with chilled soda water; stir.

■ *Cola, Root-Beer, Sarsaparilla, or Ginger-Ale*—Put a scoop of vanilla ice cream in a large glass. Almost fill with chilled beverage desired. Stir.

■ *Lemon*—Put 2 tablespoons frozen, concentrated lemonade in tall glass. Add a scoop of vanilla ice cream. Almost fill with chilled soda water. Stir.

■ *Peach or Apricot*—Put ⅓ cup mashed frozen, canned, or sweetened ripe fresh peaches or apricots in a large glass. Add ¼ cup milk, a large scoop of peach or vanilla ice cream, and almost fill with chilled soda water. Stir.

■ *Pineapple*—Put ⅓ cup sweetened, drained, canned crushed, or fresh shredded pineapple in large glass. Add ¼ cup milk and a large scoop of vanilla or pineapple ice cream. Almost fill with chilled soda water. Stir.

■ *Strawberry or Raspberry*—Put ⅓ cup frozen or crushed, sweetened, fresh berries in a large glass. Add 3 tablespoons milk and a large scoop of vanilla ice cream. Almost fill with chilled soda water. Stir.

ICE-CREAM CAKES AND DESSERTS

ICE-CREAM SHADOW CAKE

1 large angel-food cake ring

2 pints chocolate ice cream
2 cups heavy cream, whipped and sweetened
Chocolate sauce

Cut angel cake into three layers. Spread 1 pint ice cream (softened) between each two layers. Spread whipped cream on top and sides of cake; freeze. When ready to serve, remove from freezer and dribble chocolate sauce over top and sides of cake. Cut into wedges to serve. Makes 12 servings.

Note: If freezer isn't available, chill cake and have cream whipped before filling cake. Fill with ice cream; spread with cream. Dribble sauce over top and sides and serve at once.

LADYFINGER ICE-CREAM CAKE

Line a 2-quart mold or mixing bowl with about 2 dozen ladyfingers, split. Pack with 3 pints peppermint-stick ice cream. Cover with foil; freeze for several hours or overnight. Unmold and garnish with a wreath of whipped cream; sprinkle with "shot" candies; arrange candy fruit slices around the cake base. Makes about 8 to 10 servings.

ICE-CREAM CAKE

Cover bottom and sides of three 8-inch layer-cake pans with one piece of wax paper or foil; spread 1 pint softened ice cream in each. Strawberry, coffee, or any desired flavor or combination of flavors may be used. Put in freezer until firm. Split two 8-inch sponge layers into halves, making 4 layers. Cover with foil a circle of cardboard cut to fit the cake. On it assemble cake by placing ice-cream layers between sponge layers; remove wax paper or foil from ice cream. Press slightly so layers will stay together. Put in freezer until ice cream is hard. Whip 1½ cups heavy cream, ¼ cup confectioners' sugar, and 1 teaspoon vanilla extract until stiff; spread on top and sides of cake. Reserve some of cream and use in pastry tube to decorate cake. Return cake to freezer; let stand until cream is frozen. Package, and keep in freezer until ready to serve. Cut and serve while it is frozen. Makes 12 to 16 slices.

CHOCOLATE ICE-CREAM ROLL

    4 eggs
      Sugar (about ¾ cup)
    ½ cup sifted cake flour
    ½ teaspoon baking powder
    ¼ teaspoon salt
    1 teaspoon ground cinnamon
    ¼ teaspoon baking soda
    3 tablespoons cold water
    2½ ounces (2½ squares) unsweetened chocolate, melted
      Ice cream (French Vanilla or Banana, page 929)

Beat eggs slightly. Gradually add ⅔ cup sugar and beat until thick and lemon-colored. Sift flour, baking powder, salt, and cinnamon. Add to egg mixture and

Strawberry Parfait   *Blueberry Parfait*   *Ladyfinger Ice-Cream Cake*   *Melon à la Mode*

blend well. Add 3 tablespoons sugar, the soda, and water to chocolate; mix. Fold into batter. Grease a jelly-roll pan (15½ x 10½ x 1 inch), line with wax paper, and grease again. Pour in batter. Bake in preheated moderate oven (375°F.) for about 15 minutes. Turn out on damp towel; remove paper carefully. Roll lengthwise with towel; cool. Unroll, and spread with softened ice cream; re-roll. Freeze until firm. Cut into slices to serve. Makes 8 servings.

HARLEQUIN CRINKLE CUPS

Melt separately 6 ounces each of semi-sweet chocolate and butterscotch pieces in top part of double boiler over hot water. Place 10 to 12 paper baking cups (3 to 4 inches in diameter) in muffin-pan sections. With spatula, line half the inside and bottom with melted chocolate and the other half with melted butterscotch. Put muffin pan in refrigerator until ready to use. Then quickly peel off paper cups. Fill crinkle cups with butter-pecan ice cream. Decorate with pecan half.

JELLY-ROLL SANDWICHES

For each serving use two ½-inch slices of jelly roll or poundcake; put together with a slice of ice cream. Serve at once, or package airtight in foil and freeze. Top with sundae topping or strawberry jam, if desired.

COFFEE-CHOCOLATE PIE

½ cup fine chocolate-cookie crumbs
1 quart coffee ice cream
¼ cup chocolate syrup

Butter a 9-inch pie pan and sprinkle with cookie crumbs, reserving 2 tablespoons for top of pie. Carefully spread softened ice cream over crumbs. Sprinkle remaining crumbs on top around edge of pie. Place in freezer until hard. Run tines of fork deeply over pie; pour chocolate syrup into hollows thus formed. Freeze uncovered; then cover with foil; keep in freezer until ready to serve. Cut into 6 or 8 pieces.

APRICOT ICE-CREAM PIE

9- inch pastry shell, baked
¼ pound marshmallows
  Apricot preserves
2 egg whites
⅛ teaspoon salt
¼ cup sugar
2 pints vanilla ice cream

Chill pastry shell. Heat marshmallows and 2 tablespoons preserves in top part of double boiler over boiling water until marshmallows are half melted. Remove from heat and beat until smooth. Beat egg whites with salt until foamy; gradually add sugar and beat until stiff. Fold in marshmallow mixture. Press ice cream quickly into chilled shell. Spread with ½ cup preserves. Cover with marshmallow meringue, spreading to cover ice cream

completely. Put under preheated broiler for 1 or 2 minutes, or until lightly browned. (This meringue browns very quickly.) Cut into wedges and garnish each with spoonful of preserves. Makes 6 to 8 servings.

SUMMER SNOWBALLS

Scoop vanilla ice cream onto cookie sheets; cover with transparent plastic wrap; freeze firm, package in plastic bags, and store in freezer until ready to use.

If preferred, cut bulk ice cream into cubes. Roll in one of the following coatings and serve with sauce:
• Plain or toasted coconut coating with butterscotch or chocolate sauce
• Chocolate "shot" candy or chopped candied-fruit coating with soft custard or nesselrode sauce
• Crushed peppermint candy or chopped nut coating with chocolate or marshmallow sauce
• Crushed peanut-brittle coating with chopped peaches or soft custard sauce

STRAWBERRIES À LA MODE

Stud a large bowl of vanilla ice cream with whole fresh strawberries dipped into sugar. When ice cream has softened slightly, spoon into individual dishes. Also good with fresh raspberries or sliced peaches.

MERINGUES GLACÉES

⅛ teaspoon salt
½ teaspoon cream of tartar
2 egg whites
½ cup sugar
½ teaspoon vanilla extract
1 pint strawberry ice cream
1 package (10 ounces) frozen
  strawberries, thawed

Add salt and cream of tartar to egg whites and beat with rotary beater until foamy; gradually add sugar and continue beating until very stiff. Add vanilla. Spoon some onto lightly buttered brown paper on cookie sheet and flatten to make 4 thin bases about 1½ inches in diameter. With a pastry tube or spoon, surround bases with remaining meringue to height of 2 inches, leaving center unfilled. Bake in preheated very slow oven (250°F.) for 1¼ hours. Transfer paper to a damp board and remove meringues with a spatula. When cold, fill with ice cream and top with strawberries. Makes 4 servings.

FROZEN CRÊPES

■ **To make crêpes:** Beat until smooth 2 egg yolks, ¾ teaspoon salt, 2 teaspoons each of melted butter and sugar, ½ cup all-purpose flour, and 1 cup milk. Beat 2 egg whites until they form soft peaks. Fold into batter and let mixture stand for about 1 hour. Brush a 5- or 6-inch skillet with oil. Heat until very hot. Pour on batter by scant ¼ cupfuls. Tilt until

pan is completely covered. Turn crêpe after about 15 seconds. Makes 16.
■ **To fill:** Place narrow roll of ice cream in center of each crêpe. Bring edges to center. Store in freezer as each is made. Serve with hot Chocolate Fudge Sauce (page 942). Top with chopped nuts.

MELON À LA MODE

For each serving, fill a chilled cantaloupe or honeydew half with two or more contrasting flavors of ice cream, or ice cream and sherbet or berries.

ICE-CREAM BONBONS

1 quart ice cream
2 cups chopped pecans or other nuts
12 ounces (1 large package) semisweet
  chocolate pieces
½ cup margarine
1 tablespoon instant coffee powder

Make ice-cream balls with large melon-ball scoop. Immediately roll each ball in nuts. Put in freezer until thoroughly frozen, at least 1 hour. Melt chocolate and margarine in top part of double boiler. Add coffee, and mix. Remove from heat, but keep warm over hot water. Use a fork to dip ice-cream balls into chocolate, working as quickly as possible. When you've dipped 10 or 12, place them in freezer and continue. When chocolate is thoroughly firm, set bonbons in paper cups, 3 or 4 to each individual serving. Cover or wrap with foil or plastic wrap; store in freezer. Makes 30 to 36.

BANANA SPLIT

1 ripe banana
1 scoop each of vanilla, chocolate,
  and strawberry ice cream
2 tablespoons strawberry preserves
2 tablespoons pineapple preserves
2 tablespoons chocolate sauce
  Whipped cream
2 tablespoons chopped nuts
1 maraschino cherry

Cut banana into halves lengthwise. Put on plate, cut side up. Arrange ice cream scoops in row between banana halves. Spoon strawberry preserves over one scoop, pineapple over another, and chocolate sauce over the last. Top with cream and garnish with nuts and cherry. Makes 1 serving.

ICE CREAM AS A DESSERT SAUCE

Serve softened vanilla ice cream over:
• Fresh strawberries with Cointreau
• Toasted angel-food cake wedges
• Chocolate cake or gingerbread
• Brownies with chocolate sauce
• Sliced bananas and oranges
• Peach or apple crisp, oven-warm
• Strawberry or peach shortcake
• Fruited or plain gelatin dessert
• Waffles with fruit or berry sauce

INDIA'S COOKERY

By William Clifford

The subtle cuisine of the vast land of India is a culinary tour
of a fascinating country whose civilization, including the art of
good eating, began thousands of years before our own.

India is a world apart, a land unto itself. From the Vale of Kashmir to Cape Comorin, from Gujarat to Assam, it spans nearly as much of the globe as all of western Europe from Scandinavia to Greece. The sacred earth of Mother India nurtures even more human beings (not to mention cows, buffaloes, monkeys, insects, and cobras) than there are Europeans. So many people, living in such a vast expanse of land, tropical and temperate, lush and arid, mountainous and flat, naturally enough, enjoy all sorts of food.

The foods of India and the Indian ways of serving them have evolved over thousands of years. By contrast, classical French cooking dates only from the 18th century. Age alone is no proof of greatness, but anything that survives so long a test of time is certainly worth close scrutiny. What one finds, on looking closely at India, is a national cuisine of such variety and subtlety that it is rivaled only by the Chinese and the French. This will come as a great surprise to most westerners, who tend to think of Indian cooking as beginning and ending with curry. While it is true that a simple curry does not exemplify all the treasures stored away in the many chambers of the house of Indian cuisine, it is also true that an understanding of curry opens the door to that house.

One sometimes hears that curry is not really Indian or that Indians do not use ready-mixed curry powders. The first claim is not true. The word curry appears in languages of both north and south India, and to Indians it means a dish of vegetables or meat with a spicy sauce, not a dry dish. The claim that Indians never use prepared curry powder has more truth, but an Indian wife who grinds and mixes fresh spices every day ends up with powders and pastes much like the ones you can buy prepackaged. She changes the quantities and combinations according to the food she is cooking, family preferences and traditions, or her mood. You can do the same by adding individual spices to commercial curry powders.

Curry powders vary greatly in strength and taste, and you might like to make a taste test of several of them. Include both American and Indian-made ones, together with curry pastes, which are made of the same spices as the powders, mixed with oil and vinegar. Generally the Indian powders and pastes are hotter. All of them, domestic and foreign, contain the same basic six ingredients: coriander, turmeric, cuminseed, fenugreek, black pepper, and cayenne or chili pepper. The proportions vary from brand to brand, or from home to home in India. Although more coriander than anything else is generally used, I have seen formulas where it was used in equal measure with turmeric or with both turmeric and cuminseed.

After these basic six there are at least twenty other ingredients that turn up in curry powders in smaller amounts. These include mustard, anise, poppy, celery, and caraway seeds; various dried green leaves including bay; dried peas, onion, and garlic; ginger, dill, nutmeg, mace, cardamom, cloves, cinnamon, orange peel, sugar, and salt. The sweeter spices such as cardamom, cloves, and cinnamon are less often found in Indian curry mixtures than in American ones. Indians tend to reserve them for puddings and other sweets, elaborate rice dishes, and other special preparations.

The reason Indians began to prepare food with all these spices and seasonings is not positively known. One theory holds that curry was invented to cover up the taste of food that was of inferior quality or that had gone bad in the tropical climate. The trouble with this idea is that a good blend of curry brings out the fundamental flavor rather than kills it. Spices will help to preserve good food, but they do not make bad food palatable.

Another possibility is that the eating of highly spiced, hot foods is done instinctively in tropical lands because this causes perspiration, opening the pores and offering relief from the heat. A third and most reasonable explanation holds that the spices came to be used because they were there. If you live in a land where cloves stud the trees and tempt you with their aroma as you walk by, you are likely to use more of them than if they must be shipped thousands of miles and sold by the ounce in a store.

To taste and compare curry powders, I recommend first frying the powder in a couple of tablespoons of oil or butter, then adding chopped onions and more butter, and finally whatever principal ingredient you want to flavor with the sauce. This can be meat or chicken, or for a shorter cooking time something precooked like hard-cooked eggs or fish balls. Add water if necessary, simmer for a few minutes to blend flavors, add salt, and taste. This gives you a much more authentically Indian sauce than the cream sauce into which curry powder is so often blended in western cooking.

While properly blended spices enhance the flavor of the food you put them with, too much hot pepper can scorch your tongue and kill your taste temporarily. If you get accidentally burned in your curry experiments, be reassured that the fire will die away in half an hour or less and leave no scars, and the knowledge you gain is worth the risk. Until you taste eggplant in curry, you do not know the full taste of eggplant. A delicate fish that gives up the ghost when deep fried and served with tartare sauce will reveal hidden depths of taste in the right spices.

After tasting your curry powders, try out the basic six ingredients individually in the same way. Black and cayenne peppers you already know. Coriander, the plant that dominates curry powder, is a member of the parsley family. It grows in every Indian garden, and its fresh green leaves look something like our big-leaved Italian parsley, which is another carrot cousin. It has a strong pungent flavor, one you may have encountered in both Mexican and Chinese cooking, where fresh coriander leaves are used extensively. The ground seeds of the coriander that go into curry powder are much milder than the leaf, and a dish seasoned with ground coriander alone may remind you faintly of a mild chile con carne or a curry. It has no hot peppery quality.

Cuminseed used alone has a pleasant taste, one that might again call to mind a mild chile con carne. Turmeric has a bright yellow color; a pinch of it will color a whole dish, like saffron. Indians use saffron too, but it is very expensive and its assertive flavor is considered most suitable for sweets and fancy rice dishes. The yellow color in most meat and vegetable dishes comes from turmeric. Turmeric alone has a somewhat bitter taste, but it can be combined very effectively with mustard seed and hot pepper in seasoning a fish. Fenugreek alone is generally too rank, although it serves brilliantly to season a dish of creamed spinach, the way the French do it with mace. This illustrates the exciting principle of combining spices, that an ingredient which fails to please on its own may make an invaluable contribution in a mixture.

My own introduction to food in India, twenty years ago, was not so scientific as this.

Ashore in Bombay after a three-week voyage from Liverpool in 1945, I tasted my first food on Indian soil at the venerable Taj Mahal Hotel. A table-d'hôte lunch at the Taj in those days began with an hors-d'oeuvre that was basically European but included an Indian taste or two. It is instinctive with an Indian cook to put a bit of coriander leaf into the ravigote, minced hot green chili to pep up anything calling for chopped onion, and a pinch of curry powder in the mayonnaise. Then followed an important main dish, a choice of something European or a curry. And finally a macédoine of tropical fruits or ice cream of an indigenous flavor such as mango, coconut, pomegranate, or pistachio.

By a stroke of luck my first curry at the Taj was the most unusual: a curry of quail. I have since been told that in the refined Moghul cooking of Lucknow chicken is served only in the winter and quail only in the summer. It was August, the monsoon season in Bombay, and the tiny birds had been brought in from the nearby marshes. The quail curry of the Taj was rich with butter, coconut, and poppy seeds, included tomatoes and yogurt, and was finished in the Moghul style, with cream, saffron, lime juice, and cashew nuts. Cashews are the chief nuts of southern India. Almonds and pistachios predominate in the North, and peanuts are found everywhere. Any nuts, ground, help to enrich and thicken a curry, as do yogurt and cream, and such minced vegetables as onions, tomatoes, squashes, and cucumbers. Indians do not thicken sauces with flour or cornstarch or meat gelatin.

The Taj curry was positively paraded to the table by a trio of bearers. Number One filled oversize dinner plates with mountains of rice, not ordinary boiled rice, but extra-quality (India is said to have 200 varieties) rice pilaf, rich with onions and spices, butter and stock, saffron and edible silver leaf. Number Two heaped on the curry. Number Three offered an enormous silver tray of condiments. These included thin crisp wafers made of split-pea flour, usually seasoned with crushed black pepper and cumin-seeds in north India but plain in the South, called *popadam* or *papar;* deep-fried bits of dried fish with the saltiness of bacon, called Bombay duck; a mango chutney (sweet) and a mango pickle (sour); coconut scrapings with minced hot chilies and coriander leaves; and a mixture of sliced onions, tomatoes, and fresh lime with minced chilies and coriander. There were no raisins or sieved hard-cooked eggs.

This service was what certain colonials would have called a three-boy curry. A six-boy or ten-boy curry meant that many bearers and more dishes to sample and combine. Actually even the third bearer, the one with the condiments, was superfluous with two such nobly seasoned dishes as a Moghul curry and rich pilaf.

When I had gone through the Taj repertory of curries I began to look around Bombay for other types of food. There were several places popular with the British army, but they seemed to serve everything fried: fried mutton or fish cutlets with Indian seasonings, fried steak with fried eggs, fried tomatoes and onions, fried chips, even fried bread. About the only thing not fried was the Sergeant Major's tea, made with condensed milk, strong and sweet. Then I found the India Coffee House, where snacks were available, including small meat or vegetable fritters, together with fine strong south India coffee.

South India grows some of the world's choice coffee, but there isn't enough for export. You can't even get a good cup of it in north India, except at the India Coffee Houses in the few big cities. Young intellectuals use these coffeehouses as people do everywhere in the world, for meeting friends and seeing a bit of life and having long hours of conversation. They and the coffee-loving populace of southern India mostly drink their coffee mixed with hot milk and sugar, and aerated—poured back and forth from metal tumbler to bowl in flashing streams that contribute to the scene at coffee stalls and on railway platforms in the south. The aeration introduces oxygen, which improves the coffee's flavor. Cashew nuts, either salted or spiced, go well with an after-dinner coffee enriched with cream.

What coffee is to the south, tea is to northern India. It grows in excellent quality on the slopes around Darjeeling and extensively in Assam. It is drunk in the morning, often twice, and in the afternoon at teatime. Some people enjoy it throughout the day. All Indian tea is black, that is to say fermented, and virtually everyone takes it with milk and sugar. It should be brewed in a clean pot, for at least six minutes to get full flavor, and any that is left in the pot should be thrown away after fifteen minutes, when the undesirable tannin starts to come out. The thing that affects the flavor of tea most, after the quality of the leaf itself, is the quality of the water. If you don't get good tea with your city water supply, you can try bottled or well water.

One day while searching for new eating places in Bombay I came upon Joshi's Bangle Shop. "Genuine Bombay Bangles," the sign said, "S. Joshi, Prop." The walls of the small open-front shop were solidly lined with racks of bangles—glass bracelets, mostly, encrusted with tiny mirrors, gilt wires, beads, imitation pearls and stones. They were dazzling, full of life, as colorful as the tropical birds of India. S. Joshi was hopping about in the shop like a bird, chattering to himself the glib phrases of the pitch-

man, like a pianist practicing scales. We became friends, and I went back many times.

When one of Joshi's important customers arrived in her curtained automobile or carriage, he would pull a large flowered curtain across the whole front of his shop. If I came to call during one of these visits (the curtain gave me the feeling that a seance must be going on inside), I waited for Joshi at the India Coffee House or at a small vegetarian restaurant that sold a safe glass of ice water for a penny. This restaurant also made good ice cream and sold dishes of spicy vegetables for about ten cents each.

Most people of India are vegetarians, most of all in the West and the South. This may be largely on account of poverty or tradition, but in Joshi's case it was conviction. He pointed out to me that man is the only animal that appears to eat both meat and vegetables by nature, and that can make a choice. He was throwing in his lot with the peaceful vegetarian cow rather than the destructive carnivorous tiger. He and other Indian vegetarians get their protein mainly from dried peas and beans and from milk products. Here, in fact, are two of the basic four or five items in the diet of the ordinary Indian villager, who is nearly always a vegetarian out of poverty. Dried peas and beans are cooked with a little salt and hot pepper or spice into a soup, which may be thick or thin, called *dal*. Milk is drunk mainly with tea or coffee, or is turned into curds or yogurt or buttermilk.

Then every Indian eats grain, mainly rice in the East and South, wheat in the North and West. Whole wheat is ground and made into thin rounds of unleavened bread called *chapati*. Variations include mixing whole wheat and white flours or wheat and rice, rolling and folding the bread into many thin layers with butter in between, and deep-frying rather than frying on a dry griddle, then on the coals, as *chapati* are cooked. In northwest India a popular bread called *nan* is made of white flour, lightly leavened, and baked in a clay oven. There are other breads thin as paper, some baked in ovens, some made of fermented dough, some made with milk. But the poor man's bread is the *chapati* of whole-wheat flour and plain water, cooked without fat.

In the South rice is ground to a paste with lentils and water, fermented, and made into a light steamed cake called *idli*, or into a thin pancake called *dosa*. *Masala dosas* are these pancakes stuffed with a spiced vegetable such as potatoes.

The only remaining item in the ordinary villager's diet is tea or coffee, drunk with milk and sugar. As he moves up the economic ladder he is likely to add more milk and sugar for making sweets, and more fat for cooking or dribbling on cooked food. Except in certain richly endowed regions he isn't likely to take to high-quality animal protein or fruits or even a wide range of vegetables.

One of the exceptional regions is the Punjab, in northwest India, where the climate permits the richest farms and best diet of the whole land. Here live the tall bearded Sikhs, who love to eat. Another exception to the ordinary village diet is found along the seacoast and in riverine areas such as Bengal. There fish are eaten by a good part of the people. Lobsters are transported a thousand miles from Bombay and Calcutta to Delhi, largely for the delectation of the Bengali community in the capital.

I was very pleased when Joshi felt that he could invite me to his home for lunch. We had been talking about the curries served at the Taj and other European-style eating places in Bombay. None of them, he said, represented the way people ate at home in Bombay or anywhere in India. They were adaptations of north Indian dishes, made for the British taste. Why wasn't more authentic Indian food available to visitors, in public hotels and restaurants, I wanted to know. Because the British didn't care, Joshi explained, and neither did the Indians.

The important day came, and Joshi took me to his house in the Bombay suburbs. We sat on the veranda, and when lunch was ready we washed our hands there, pouring the water from a brass pot and letting it fall on the flowerbeds. At the dining table our metal trays had been filled with *chapati*. We each received a small metal cup of thin *dal* with tomatoes, hot pickles, and a couple of milk sweets. It is a regional peculiarity of Gujarat to eat both wheat and rice at the same meal, and to have sweets at the beginning, with the bread. When our *chapati* were gone, we got a mound of plain rice, together with more *dal* and curds. Several dishes of spiced vegetables were passed, including a delicious okra with buttermilk. There was one dish of curried minced lamb, called *keema,* that had been made because the family feared I couldn't be satisfied unless I had some meat. Feeling rather like a tiger, I ate it, but tried to explain that with so many other wonderful dishes it wasn't necessary.

Joshi's luncheon party was a success, and his brother's children entertained their schoolmates for days afterward with accounts of the American sahib who ate with his fingers. Joshi and I met many more times and made several excursions into the neighboring countryside, where we took along picnic lunches. On a trip to the Elephanta Caves in Bombay Harbor there was cold rice with buttermilk, hot chilies, and coriander leaves for my vegetarian friend, and for the carnivorous American delicious little chicken sandwiches with Indian seasonings, wrapped in fresh cool green leaves to keep them moist.

One had to travel only a few miles outside Bombay to see villages with the primitive qualities of Biblical times, and to realize that India is living in many different centuries, in many stages of development, simultaneously. One thing that ties the modern cities and the primitive villages together is the common celebration of festivals. Religious festivals, harvest festivals, fertility festivals, patriotic festivals—India celebrates some thirty of them as national holidays, more than one every two weeks. Maharajas and schoolchildren, shopkeepers and housewives, officials and laborers, all of them love holidays.

No month of the year is without its celebrations, beginning in January with the rice-harvest festival of the South, Pongal. The newly gathered grain is ceremoniously cooked and shared by the whole family, including the beloved cows and bullocks, whose horns are painted bright orange and blue and festooned with tinsel for the occasion. The liveliest and most colorful festival, Holi, is enjoyed all over north India in March. Grateful for the warming sunshine and riotously colored flowers of spring, people throw colored powders or colored water on their friends and even on strangers in the street. If you have old clothes, that's the day to remember to wear them. Indians who have nothing but old clothes, and no change of them, may go around for weeks afterward looking like harlequins. Formal greetings and sweetmeats are given at Holi.

In September comes Ram Lila in the North (called Durga Puja in Bengal) and the great spectacle of Dasara in the South. In Mysore the former Maharaja parades his palace elephants, which have charming flower designs painted around their ears and down their trunks. Their toenails are also decorated. Here are shown the royal howdahs and ceremonial mahouts, leftovers of colonial and princely India. October brings Diwali, the night when the whole country becomes a fairyland of flickering oil lamps. Diwali honors the goddess Lakshmi, or Kali in Bengal. This holiday has recently become the chief annual occasion for exchange of gifts, and stores in all the big cities advise you to "Do Your Diwali Shopping Early."

Nationally or locally India honors the holidays of every major religion. In December, Christmas is celebrated by Christians, in Kerala and scattered throughout the land. Hindus and Moslems in big cities may also mark December 25, especially if their children go to English schools and if they have foreign friends.

Soon after independence in 1947, India was divided into a series of large states, some old, some new, some familiar names with reduced territory, some familiar territory with altered names. Bengal in the East and the Punjab in the West—each lost a large part of its land to Pakistan. The United Provinces in north-central India kept the same initials while changing the name to Uttar Pradesh. Travancore and Cochin on the southwest coast became Kerala. Madras remained Madras but lost its northern part to Andhra, which took in most of Hyderabad. The division was made along linguistic lines. Except for Hindi, a different major language is spoken by almost all the people in each state. While the boundaries between cooking styles are not so sharp or easy to define as between the languages, I think it is clear that there are major regional differences.

Just as France can be divided into areas where food is cooked principally in butter, olive oil, or lard, India has cooking fats that predominate in certain areas sufficiently so that at least one authority has said the country could be divided up according to oils rather than languages. In Madras the common oils are sesame and peanut; in Kerala, coconut; in Bombay, sesame; in Bengal, mustard; in the Punjab, butter oil or ghee. Ghee is clarified butter, with the solids and water removed. Clarified butter, unlike butter with impurities, apparently keeps forever. Some of it was found in the ruins of Mohenjo-Daro, more than 3,000 years old, and it hadn't turned rancid yet.

In the last analysis, just about every food known to man is eaten by at least a few of the diverse people in some corner of India's climatic and geographic spectrum. The variety of fruits is staggering: a dozen kinds of bananas in one city market at one season, many different mangoes, papayas, sweet limes, pineapples, custard apples, sour limes or lemons, pomegranates, guavas, tangerines, apples, pears, grapes. I have eaten large yellow raspberries in Kashmir, where all the familiar temperate-climate fruits and vegetables are grown. The Indian Ocean and certain rivers teem with fish. Nonvegetarian Hindus normally eat only chicken, mutton, and goat, but Moslems eat beef as well, when they can get it. Only Christians and aborigines eat pork, and a scattering of hunters eat game birds and animals.

Despite her great variety, India's countryside is still impoverished, communications are poor, and a traveler stopping at a rural *dak* bungalow may be offered nothing better than brown soup and mutton cutlets or Country Captain, a dish named for colonial officers who dropped in unannounced and were given hash. And just as fine cooking has largely been home cooking in India, the influence of Indian food in the West has been so slight that it almost escapes detection. A pinch of curry powder in soup or mayonnaise; a curry-flavored white sauce with shrimps, chicken, or lamb; Major Grey's chutney; Indian tonic or quinine water—these are about all most of us have ever been offered from the cuisine of this vast and varied subcontinent. For us the best of Indian cooking is still a world apart, a land unto itself, waiting to be discovered.

NOTE
Estimated servings are based on using a single meat or fish dish as a main course. If many dishes are offered on a buffet table, more servings are possible from each dish.

PACHADI
(Yogurt Salad)
Here is a thin soupy salad in the style of Madras, cool and nourishing, delicious on a hot day. You can drink it or eat it with a spoon, have it as a first course, or serve it with a hot curry.

    1 pint plain yogurt
    1 medium tomato, peeled and diced
    1 teaspoon minced hot green chili
      pepper
    1 small onion, minced
    ¼ cup chopped fresh coriander leaves
      or parsley
    1 teaspoon mustard seed
    ½ teaspoon cuminseed
      Salt to taste

Stir all ingredients together until well mixed. (Juice from the tomato will thin out the yogurt.) If fresh hot green peppers are unavailable, use canned Mexican or Italian ones, adjusting quantity to taste. Makes 4 servings.

MURGHA KARI
(Chicken Curry with Tomatoes)
This dish from the Punjab takes only 30 minutes to prepare. In India, fresh

tomatoes would be used in this dish.

    4 medium onions, chopped
    2 tablespoons curry powder
    ½ cup butter or cooking oil
    1 cup or 1 can (8 ounces) tomato
      sauce
    2 teaspoons salt
    1 frying chicken (2 to 3 pounds)
    ¾ cup hot water

Use a casserole or large skillet with lid. Cook onions and curry powder in butter for 10 to 15 minutes. Add tomato sauce and salt. Disjoint and skin chicken, and place in sauce. Cook, uncovered, over medium heat, turning frequently until sauce becomes quite dry and chicken tests done with fork, about 15 minutes. Add hot water, cover pot, and cook over low heat for 5 minutes. Makes 4 servings.

KEEMA MATAR
(Chopped Meat with Peas)
A simple north Indian dish (the one prepared especially for me at Joshi's lunch), this is one of the best ways to dress up chopped meat.

    1½ pounds lamb or beef, ground
    1 tablespoon minced garlic
    2 tablespoons curry powder
    1 cinnamon stick
    1 teaspoon minced fresh gingerroot
      or ½ teaspoon ground ginger
    1 teaspoon salt
    1 package (10 ounces) frozen peas

Sauté meat in skillet, chopping and turning to break it up. As soon as pan becomes moist, add all other ingredients except peas. Stir and cook until meat is done, keeping it crumbly, not caked. Add peas and cook and stir until just thawed and heated through. Serves 4.

CHAPATIS
(Whole-wheat Pancakes)
    1¾ cups whole-wheat flour
    ½ teaspoon salt
      About 1 cup water

Mix flour and salt. Gradually stir in water, mixing to form a firm dough. Knead lightly 2 to 3 minutes. Break off pieces the size of a small walnut, and roll paper thin on floured board. Cook quickly on both sides on ungreased griddle. Put on baking sheet, and put under broiler until puffed and lightly browned and crisp, turning once. Serve hot with butter. Makes about 2½ dozen.

PALAK GOSHT
(Lamb with Spinach)
This Punjab dish is relatively dry.

    1½ pounds lamb cut into 1-inch cubes
    1 cup plain yogurt
    1 medium onion, chopped
    1 tablespoon ground coriander
    1 teaspoon each of ground turmeric
      and cuminseed
    ⅛ teaspoon cayenne
    2 teaspoons salt

    ¼ cup butter or margarine
    1 pound spinach, washed and chopped

Place lamb in yogurt to marinate for at least 2 hours, preferably overnight. Sauté onions and all spices in butter. Add lamb with yogurt, and mix together. Sauté for another 5 minutes. Place spinach on top of meat, cover, and cook over low heat for 40 minutes, or until meat is done. Stir as necessary to prevent sticking; in the end, meat and spinach will be mixed together. Makes 6 servings.

SOOWAR KA GOSHT VINDALOO
(Sour Pork Curry)
This is the sour curry popular in Bombay. In this recipe it is made with pork, but it can be made with any meat, with poultry, or even with shrimps.

    2 pounds lean pork, cut into ¾-inch
      cubes
    ½ cup vinegar
    4 medium onions, chopped
    1 teaspoon minced garlic
    1 tablespoon minced gingerroot or
      1½ teaspoons powdered ginger
    1 tablespoon mustard seed
    1 teaspoon ground turmeric
    ½ teaspoon cayenne
    ¼ cup cooking oil
    1 cup chicken bouillon
    6 medium potatoes, peeled and
      quartered

Marinate meat in vinegar, onions, garlic, and seasonings for 2 hours or more. Place in top-stove casserole with oil and bouillon. (Sesame oil is used in western India, but any cooking oil will do.) Cook over medium heat for 20 minutes. Add potatoes and cook slowly, covered, for about 40 minutes, or until they are tender. Add more bouillon if necessary. Makes 6 servings.

ROGAN GOSHT
(Lamb Curry)
An exceptionally rich dish of the Punjab, this type of lamb curry needs plain rice or *chapati* to go with it. It may also be made with beef.

    2 medium onions, chopped
    1 cup butter or margarine
    1 pound small white turnips, peeled
      and halved
    2 pounds lamb in large cubes
    1 tablespoon sugar
    1 cup plain yogurt
    1 tablespoon ground coriander
    ¼ to ½ teaspoon cayenne
    2 teaspoons salt
      Hot water
    ½ teaspoon each of ground cardamom,
      cloves, and saffron

Brown onions in the butter. Add all other ingredients except saffron, and cook for 25 minutes, or until meat is browned. Add 1 cup hot water. Reduce heat and simmer, covered, for 45 minutes, or until meat is tender. Dissolve saffron in 1 tablespoon hot water and add just before serving. Makes 6 servings.

Chapati

Rogan Gosht

Pachadi

Gajar Halwa

Bhaji Malida Machli

SARSON BHARA KEKDA
(Shrimps with Mustard)

Here is the Bengali specialty that features the taste of turmeric, without the other curry-powder spices.

    2 tablespoons mustard seed, ground
    1 teaspoon ground turmeric
    ¼ cup mustard oil or any cooking oil
    1 large onion, ground
    1½ pounds shrimps, peeled and deveined
    1 tablespoon minced hot green chili peppers
    1 teaspoon salt

Make a paste of the mustard seed and turmeric with a little water. Add all other ingredients, cover, and cook at the gentlest simmer until shrimps are fully pink, 5 to 10 minutes, depending on size of shrimps. Makes 4 servings.

KEKDA BENGALI
(Bengali Crab)

This recipe may also be made with fresh lobster meat, scallops, or shrimps. As a matter of fact, the word *kekda* means either crab or shrimp.

    2 packages (6 ounces each) frozen King crabmeat
    2 medium onions, chopped
    6 tablespoons mustard oil or cooking oil
    1 tablespoon minced gingerroot or 1 teaspoon powdered ginger
    1 cup plain yogurt
    1 teaspoon each of ground coriander, turmeric, cuminseed, and salt
    1 teaspoon minced hot green chili pepper

Allow crabmeat to thaw partially. Cook onions in the oil until brown, add all other ingredients except crabmeat, and simmer for 5 minutes. Add crabmeat and simmer until thoroughly thawed, then simmer for another 5 minutes. Makes 4 servings.

BHAJI MALIDA MACHLI
(Stuffed Fish with Greens)

    1 whole striped bass or haddock (3 to 4 pounds)
    ½ cup chopped fresh coriander or parsley
    ½ cup chopped green onions, including tops
    2 tablespoons hot green chili pepper
    2 tablespoons minced gingerroot or 1 teaspoon powdered ginger
    2 teaspoons salt
    ¼ cup cooking oil
    2 tablespoons fresh lime juice

Wash fish and wipe dry. Combine all other ingredients and place as much in cavity of fish as it will hold. Brush remainder over outside of fish and place on rack in fish steamer or boiler. Steam with small amount of water until flesh tests done with fork. If no steamer is available, fish may be wrapped in foil and baked in preheated moderate oven (350°F.) for 45 to 50 minutes. Makes 4 servings.

CHANNA KARI
(Chick-Pea Curry)

This provides the vegetable protein required by the many Indians who eat no meat. If you use canned rather than dried chick-peas, it is quick to prepare.

    1 tablespoon curry powder
    1 tablespoon minced garlic
    ½ cup chopped sweet green pepper
    ¼ cup cooking oil
    2 cans (each 1-pound, 4 ounces) chick-peas
    1 teaspoon salt
    ¼ cup chopped fresh coriander or parsley

Sauté curry powder, garlic, and green pepper in oil. Add chick-peas and salt, stir, and heat through. Simmer for 5 minutes and serve sprinkled with coriander. Makes 6 servings.

MOONG KI DAL
(Mung Beans)

Another of India's best-known foods, rich in protein, this *dal* is made with either mung beans, the dark-green beans used for bean sprouts, or green split peas.

    1 cup mung beans or split peas
    2 tablespoons curry powder
    1 teaspoon salt
    2 whole hot green chili peppers
    2 medium onions, sliced
    ¼ cup cooking oil

Soak beans in water to cover for several hours. Bring to boil, add curry powder, salt, and peppers, and cook for 1 to 2 hours, depending on desired texture of finished dish. Peppers will have lost most of their heat and may be given to anybody who wants them. Amount of water used will determine whether the result is a thick soup or a mush. Fry onions in the oil until very brown and place on top of *dal* with any unabsorbed oil when serving. Makes 6 servings. ings.

DAHI BHATH
(Rice with Buttermilk)

This is Joshi's cold rice, as it was made for our picnics. Carry it in foil or eat it at home in hot weather.

    1½ cups cold cooked rice
    1 cup buttermilk
    1 teaspoon each of minced garlic and hot green chili pepper
    ¼ cup chopped fresh coriander
    Salt to taste

Combine all ingredients. If rice does not hold together, add more buttermilk until desired stickiness is reached. Makes 4 servings.

PONGAL

This rice dish has the same name as the January harvest festival in South India. It can be made either hot or (as follows) sweet.

    ½ cup mung beans or green split peas
    ½ cup butter or margarine
    Water

    ¾ cup uncooked rice
    ⅔ cup sugar
    ½ cup cashew nuts
    ¼ cup raisins
    Pinch each of ground cloves and cardamom

Fry beans in 1 tablespoon of the butter until lightly browned. Bring to boil 3½ cups water, add beans and rice, and cook until very soft. Add 2 tablespoons water to sugar and boil to a syrup, about 10 minutes. Add cooked rice and beans to syrup and stir, adding remaining butter, nuts, and raisins. Serve hot, sprinkled with cloves and cardamom. Makes 6 servings.

GAJAR HALWA
(Carrot Dessert)

One of India's most delicious and nutritious desserts.

    Water
    1 can (14 ounces) sweetened condensed milk
    2 cups grated carrot
    1 cup cooking oil, butter, or margarine
    2 tablespoons each of chopped blanched almonds and raisins
    ¼ teaspoon ground saffron
    1 tablespoon fresh lime juice, heated

Add 1 can of water to condensed milk and bring to boil. Add carrot and cook over low heat for about 45 minutes, stirring occasionally. Add oil gradually. Cook until fat begins to separate. Then add almonds and raisins, and the saffron dissolved in lime juice. May be eaten hot or cold. Makes 6 servings.

INVERT SUGAR—A mixture that results from the process used in making jelly, jam, candy, and frosting. With the use of heat and an acid, sugar is changed from sucrose to a mixture of glucose and fructose. Invert sugar keeps the sugar crystals small; therefore, the resulting product is creamier and smoother. The acid used may be vinegar, lemon juice, or cream of tartar. Heat alone can cause inversion of sugar but it occurs more quickly when an acid is added.

Acid in fruit juice also stops jellies and jams from recrystallizing; therefore, it keeps them clear and smooth.

IRISH COOKERY

BY MAURA LAVERTY □ Cead mile failte, *a hundred thousand welcomes,*
this is the flavoring we offer with every dish in Ireland.
Not, indeed, that Irish food needs sauce or embellishment.
Thanks to our soft, mild climate, the lush grazing of our pasturelands
gives us prime meat and dairy products, and the richness of
our soil gives us the best of vegetables and fruits.
To serve a plump Irish chicken other than plain boiled or roast
would be a sin against its tender goodness
and an insult to the skilled woman who reared it.

Plain boiled in its jacket is how we prefer our potato, the vegetable which is a "must" at least once a day in every home. It may be that there are four hundred ways of preparing potatoes, but I have yet to sample one which equals the flavor of the boiled Irish potato. Of course, we serve our potatoes in many other ways. Potato cakes dripping with butter may not be a weight reducer, but they are certainly a delight to the eye and to the palate. Boxty, the traditional dish eaten on Shrove Tuesday, is composed of grated raw potatoes and mashed cooked potatoes with a binding of flour. You may have your boxty baked on the griddle or fried in the pan, but whichever method you choose, you must never forget to stir into the mixture that all-important ring wrapped in paper which foretells an early marriage for the lucky finder.

Although the potato blight of Black '47 which decimated our population taught us not to place too much reliance on the "spud," we in Ireland still believe that a day without potatoes is a day without nourishment. In the West, no one uses the cold term "potato field"; with affection they speak of "the potato garden." The very names of Irish potatoes are gastronomic poetry: Ulster Chieftain, Golden Wonder, Aran Banner, May Queen, Skerry Champion, etc.

According to the World Health Organization, we Irish rank high on the list of well-fed peoples. I have often wondered if this is not due mainly to the fact that forty-nine per cent of our population is agricultural, and that most of our farms are small holdings of from thirty to forty acres. Because of this, our farmers produce enough food for themselves and for town dwellers. And the short distances between towns and farms make us independent of processed and frozen food. "Plastic food," as we call it, and no one will ever convince us that it can be as flavorsome and nutritious as the food which comes straight from the good earth.

Long, long ago a poet sang, "A plenteous place is Ireland of hospitable cheer." Part of that cheer is the bread made in our own kitchens with our own grain and buttermilk. White bread, griddle bread, brown bread, potato bread, buns, scones, and potato cakes—the making of these is a daily ritual in most Irish homes. The eating of them is a thrice-daily delight whether served plain with golden butter or with our heather-scented honey or with the homemade jams of which we are proud. Sometimes, but not often enough, our bread is accompanied by cheese, for cheese making

on an industrial scale is comparatively new in this pastoral land of ours.

Being gemmed with lakes and rivers, it is natural that Ireland should abound in fish. The lazy Suir, the tree-fringed Blackwater, the broad Boyne, and the lovely lakes of the Shannon—these are the principal sources of that noblest of fish, the gleaming salmon. I have stood on Galway Bridge and watched those arcs of silver take the leap with an indolence which bespoke their fatness.

Every lake and river in Ireland offers a wealth of trout, both brown and speckled. From the Liffey to the smallest lake in Connemara, you will find trout galore. So well stocked are our rivers and lakes with salmon and trout that these are among our chief exports to France and Britain where, no doubt, cooks have their own ways of preparing them. Here, at home, we like our salmon poached and served whole with melted butter and lemon; or cut into thick slices and simmered golden in butter. And I know of no better way with a good-size trout than to split it, remove the backbone, dip it into seasoned rolled oats, and fry it in butter. Some people like to add a little vinegar and mustard to the butter in which the trout has been fried.

As in so many other countries, Christmas is the great Irish feast. It commences on Christmas Eve with the lighting of the Christmas candle which is placed in the window of every house in the country as a sign to any homeless strangers who may be abroad that we are eager and willing to try to compensate for the cold welcome offered to Mary and Joseph on the first Christmas Eve. When midnight ends the Christmas Eve fast, there is a meal of spiced beef, corned brisket rich in spices, simmered to tenderness and served cold. For dinner on Christmas Day there is the special fattened fowl, a goose stuffed with sage-and-onion dressing, or a roast turkey ringed with golden sausages and bursting with parsley-and-thyme dressing. In either case, a boiled ham accompanies the fowl. The time-honored pudding on Christmas Day is, of course, a flaming plum pudding which may have been made for as long as six months in advance, since its brandied, fruity spiciness improves with keeping. The same is true of the cake of the year: every cook worth her salt makes a rich fruitcake well in advance. Layered with marzipan and coated with snowy icing, it is decorated to taste. In our house, for many years the choice has been a miniature crib.

BREADS

BASIC RECIPE FOR SODA BREAD
2 cups unsifted all-purpose flour
1½ teaspoons baking powder
¾ teaspoon salt
¼ teaspoon baking soda
1 cup buttermilk

Mix dry ingredients. Add buttermilk and stir to make a soft dough. Turn out on lightly floured board and knead for about 1 minute. Shape the dough into a round loaf about 8 inches in diameter. Put in a greased round pan or on a greased cookie sheet. With a sharp knife, cut a cross on the top. Bake in preheated moderate oven (350°F.) for 40 minutes, or until done. Bread is done if it sounds hollow when tapped with the knuckles. Cool on its side before cutting. For a soft crust, wrap loaf in a tea towel and stand on its side to cool.

BOXTY-ON-THE-GRIDDLE
For this recipe I am indebted to Grannie Doyle of Lennox Street, Dublin, who told me, "Now I'll tell you how our boxty bread was baked. My mother took a couple of grated raw potatoes and a skillet of hot mashed potatoes, 3 or 4 handfuls of flour with a bit of butter rubbed in and a generous grain of salt—all mixed well and rolled out on the board, cut into squares, and baked on a well-greased griddle to the tune of the children singing:

Three pans of boxty, baking all the day, What use is boxty without a cup of tay?

The children in those days got very little 'tay.' Each one got a nice tin porringer of m'lk and sat up to the table and ate hot buttered boxty to the fill—and we lived."

BOXTY-ON-THE-PAN
1 cup each of grated raw potatoes, all-purpose flour, and mashed potatoes
2 teaspoons each of baking powder and salt
2 eggs
Milk to mix (about ¼ cup)

Squeeze the grated raw potatoes in a cloth to remove as much moisture as possible. Sift the flour with baking powder and salt. Mix all potatoes and dry ingredients well together with beaten eggs; add sufficient milk to make a dropping batter. Drop by tablespoonfuls onto a hot buttered frying pan and cook over moderate heat, allowing about 4 minutes on each side. Serve hot and well buttered, with or without sugar. Makes 4 to 6 servings.

SOUPS

COCK-A-LEEKIE SOUP

When the Scottish planters came over the border and took over the rich Ulster farms, ordering their rightful owners "to Hell or to Connaught," they brought with them just one good thing: their cock-a-leekie soup.

1 elderly fowl (stewing chicken, about 4 pounds)
4 pounds boneless shin of beef
3 dozen leeks
3 quarts cold water
1 tablespoon salt
1 teaspoon pepper
1 cup pitted dried prunes

Truss the fowl as for boiling. Cut up the beef into small pieces. Wash the leeks, cut into thin slices, using as much as possible of the green part. Put all ingredients except prunes in a large pot. Simmer for 3 hours, then add pitted prunes and simmer for 1 hour longer. Take up the fowl, remove skin, gristle, and bones; chop the meat small and return to the pot. Correct seasoning. The prunes should be left in the soup. Makes 5 quarts.

PRIDE OF ERIN SOUP

1 green cabbage (about 1 pound)
2 tablespoons butter
3 tablespoons chopped onion
¼ cup chopped raw potato
½ teaspoon ground mace
2 tablespoons all-purpose flour
2½ cups milk
2½ cups water or chicken bouillon
Salt and pepper
¼ cup heavy cream, whipped
2 tablespoons chopped parsley
2 tablespoons grated cheese (Parmesan preferably)

Quarter the cabbage; cut away the hard stalk. Cover with boiling water and leave for 5 minutes. Drain, pat dry, and shred. Melt the butter in a heavy pan over low heat and simmer the chopped onion until tender, but without browning. Add cabbage and potato and stir over low heat. Add mace. Stir in the flour to coat all ingredients, but do not brown. Add the liquids, bring to a boil, and simmer for 20 minutes, or until vegetables are tender. Rub through a sieve. Reheat and add salt and pepper to taste. If soup is too thick, add a little boiling milk. Serve with a spoonful of whipped cream on each serving. Sprinkle parsley and grated cheese on the cream. Makes about 7 cups.

WATERCRESS SOUP

3 cups milk
3 cups mashed potatoes
2 teaspoons salt
2 cups chopped watercress leaves
2 tablespoons butter

Combine boiling milk, mashed potatoes, and salt. Stir until smooth and boiling. Add watercress and cook for 5 minutes. Remove from heat and stir in butter. Makes about 7 cups.

FISH

DINGLE MACKEREL

6 small mackerel
¼ cup white vinegar
¾ cup water
Few grains of cayenne
6 peppercorns
1-inch piece of cinnamon stick
1 bay leaf
3 parsley sprigs
2 teaspoons salt

Cut off head and fins. Wash and clean mackerel, split, and remove backbones and tails. Roll up and place in a 1½-quart casserole. Bring vinegar, water, spices, bay leaf, parsley, and seasoning to boil and pour over fish. Cover and bake in preheated moderate oven (375° F.) for 45 minutes. Makes 6 servings.

LIFFEY TROUT WITH MUSHROOM SAUCE

I have known the delight of preparing and eating this dish after catching the trout myself in a leaf-dappled stretch of the Liffey. And, on the way home, I stopped at a field where *cuppeens* (little button mushrooms) nestled like fallen stars among the tufts of grass. There are few joys on earth to compare with gathering mushrooms in the early morning. Next best is to buy your trout and your mushrooms and to prepare the fish in this way:

4 small trout
6 tablespoons all-purpose flour
Pepper and salt
6 tablespoons butter
About 12 button mushrooms
1 cup half cream and half milk
1 tablespoon chopped parsley

Clean, wash, and dry the trout. Roll in ¼ cup of the flour seasoned with pepper and salt. Fry in ¼ cup of the butter. Drain, and keep hot. Wipe and slice the mushrooms and sauté in the same pan in which the trout were fried. Melt remaining butter in a small saucepan; stir in remaining flour. Add cream and milk and season to taste. Add mushrooms and reheat to serving point. Garnish the trout with parsley and serve sauce separately. Makes 4 servings.

MEAT AND POULTRY

STUFFED PORK FILLETS

2 fresh pork fillets or tenderloin
1 cup fine dry bread crumbs
1 parboiled onion, chopped
¼ teaspoon ground sage
Butter
Milk or chicken bouillon
Salt and pepper
Thick brown gravy
Apple sauce

Split fillets lengthwise and flatten them well. On half of each fillet place stuffing made as follows: Combine bread crumbs with onion, sage, 1 tablespoon melted butter, sufficient milk to bind, and salt and pepper to taste. Fold over each fillet and secure in place by sewing or skewering. Weigh. Place in baking pan, dot with butter, and roast in preheated moderate oven (350°F.) allowing 40 minutes to the pound. Serve with brown gravy and apple sauce. Makes 4 servings.

BEEF-AND-KIDNEY PUDDING

All-purpose flour
1 teaspoon baking powder
Salt
1 cup finely chopped beef suet
1 cup fine stale-bread crumbs
Water to mix
¾ pound round steak, cut into small pieces
¼ pound beef kidney, cut into small pieces
¼ pound mushrooms, sliced
2 tablespoons chopped onion
1 tablespoon chopped parsley
¼ teaspoon pepper
⅔ cup beef bouillon or water

Sift 1 cup flour with the baking powder and ½ teaspoon salt. Add suet and crumbs and mix well. Add enough water to make a stiff dough. Line a 1-quart casserole with half the dough. Put meats, mushrooms, onion, and parsley in layers in lined casserole, sprinkling each layer with 3 tablespoons flour, seasoned with 1 teaspoon salt and the pepper. Add the bouillon. Cover with remaining dough, moisten edges, and press together well. Cover with greased foil and steam for 3 hours. Makes 4 servings.

VEAL HOT POT

2 pounds lean veal
2 large onions
8 young carrots
¼ pound sliced bacon
¼ cup all-purpose flour
Salt and pepper to taste
2 tablespoons dry sherry
1 cup chicken bouillon or water

Dice veal, peel and slice onions, wash and slice carrots, dice bacon. Mix flour with salt and pepper; combine sherry with

*Irish Stew, Colcannon, Barmbrack,
and Irish Coffee*

bouillon. Put layer of onion and carrot in a greased 2-quart casserole; add a layer of bacon and veal. Repeat until all are used, sprinkling each layer with some seasoned flour. Add combined sherry and bouillon. Cover closely and cook in preheated very slow oven (275°F.) for about 2½ hours. Makes 4 to 6 servings.

BAKED LIMERICK HAM

Long ago a whole pig would have been baked in a pit lined with stones previously heated in the fire. Or it might have been cooked in one of the great bronze caldrons which were the most treasured possessions of well-to-do households. Pork was always the favorite meat of the Irish. Wasn't it as a swineherd that St. Patrick first came to us? When the meat was cooked the various cuts were served according to the social importance of the guests:

A thigh for a king and a poet;
A chine for a literary sage;
A leg for a young lord;
Heads for charioteers;
A haunch for a queen.

"The hero's morsel" was the choice tidbit reserved for the man who had performed the greatest or bravest exploit . . . and woe betide anyone who helped himself to it if he was not entitled to the honor. One of the biggest battles in Irish history occurred because a chieftain wrongfully appropriated "the hero's morsel."

1 Limerick ham (10 pounds)
1 tablespoon whole cloves
¾ cup honey
1 cup Madeira wine

Soak the ham in cold water for 12 hours. Place in a pot, cover well with fresh water, and bring slowly to a boil. Allow to simmer for 2 hours. Place the ham in a baking pan, remove the skin, and stick cloves over the entire surface. Pour the honey mixed with Madeira wine over the ham and bake in preheated moderate oven (350°F.) for 2½ hours, or until the knuckle bone can be removed. Makes about 20 servings.

SEVENTEENTH-CENTURY BEEF POT ROAST

1 cup very finely ground veal
1 egg white
3 pounds beef (select a thick solid piece)
4 slices of bacon
Pepper and salt
6 tablespoons all-purpose flour
3 tablespoons beef drippings
1½ cups water or beef bouillon
1 cup red wine
4 medium mushrooms, sliced

Mix veal and egg white. Make holes here and there in the beef and fill with veal mixture. Lay the strips of bacon on top and tie in place. Mix pepper and salt with 2 tablespoons of the flour; rub into the meat. In heavy pan sear meat quickly on all sides in smoking hot drippings. Add water, wine, and a sprinkling of salt and pepper. Cover and simmer until tender, about 3½ hours. When done, place meat on a platter, remove bacon and string, and keep the meat hot. Skim fat from the liquor and cook down until liquor measures about 2 cups. Add the sliced mushrooms, and thicken with remaining flour blended to a paste with a little cold water. Correct seasoning; serve the gravy separately. This beef is excellent cold. Makes 8 servings.

COCK OF THE NORTH

1 capon, about 6 pounds
Juice of 2 lemons
¼ cup all-purpose flour
Salt and pepper
1 cup butter
½ pound bacon, diced
5 small yellow onions
¾ cup Irish whisky
1 garlic clove
½ teaspoon ground allspice
1 cup dry red wine
1 cup water
2 egg yolks
2 tablespoons light cream
1 pound pearl onions
1 pound mushrooms

Cut up capon as for fricassee. Dip the pieces into lemon juice and then into 3 tablespoons of the flour, seasoned with salt and pepper. Brown in butter. Add bacon and small yellow onions; sprinkle with 1 tablespoon flour, and brown again. Flame the capon with Irish whisky. Add salt, pepper, garlic, and allspice. Cover with wine and water, and simmer gently for 45 to 60 minutes.

For the sauce make a broth with the neck, feet, and giblets. Strain off the liquor from the bird and add to the broth. Reduce to half by rapid boiling. Thicken with the raw egg yolks and cream.

Serve the capon in a dish garnished with the pearl onions and mushrooms, each cooked separately in water and lemon juice. Pour part of the sauce over the capon and serve the remainder separately. Makes 8 to 10 servings.

IRISH STEW

The original Irish stew was made with spareribs. Today we make it with mutton.

2 pounds neck of mutton or lamb
½ pound streaky bacon
3 pounds (9 medium) potatoes
10 to 12 small onions
Salt and pepper
2 cups cold water

Cut the meat into neat pieces and trim away as much fat as possible. Remove rind from bacon and cut into 1-inch pieces. Pare the potatoes and slice the onions. Place a layer of meat in a heavy stewpan, add a layer of bacon, onions, and potatoes, and sprinkle with seasoning. Repeat layers, finishing with potatoes. Add the water, let it come slowly to a boil, remove any scum, cover, and simmer gently for 2½ hours. The potatoes should be cooked to a pulp. Makes 4 servings.

◆ VEGETABLES ◆

BRAISED CABBAGE

1 medium Savoy cabbage
2 tablespoons butter
¼ cup chopped onion
2 large tomatoes, skinned, seeded, and chopped
1 tablespoon all-purpose flour
1 cup chicken bouillon
Salt and pepper to taste
2 teaspoons finely chopped parsley
¼ cup dairy sour cream

Quarter cabbage, remove most of stalk, cover with boiling water, and leave to blanch for 10 minutes. Drain and pat dry in a towel. Place in a glass baking dish. Melt butter over moderate heat and sauté onion until tender but not brown; add chopped tomatoes, stir in flour, add bouillon, and bring to a boil, stirring constantly. Add seasoning and parsley, mix well, and spoon the mixture over the quartered cabbage. Cook, covered, in preheated moderate oven (375°F.) for 30 minutes, basting occasionally. Stir several tablespoons of liquid from cabbage into sour cream. Pour over cabbage, and bake for 15 minutes longer. Makes 4 to 6 servings.

SLIEVE na mBAN CARROTS

The ruddy crest of *Slieve na mBan* (The Mountain of the Women) rising above its stole of milk-white mist gives its name to this dish of cream-wreathed carrots.

12 young carrots
3 tablespoons butter
½ cup milk
Salt and pepper to taste
½ cup heavy cream
2 egg yolks
1 teaspoon finely chopped parsley

Trim and wash carrots and halve lengthwise. Melt butter over moderate heat, add milk, season with salt and pepper, add carrots, and cook gently until tender. Remove from heat, stir in cream and beaten egg yolks, and reheat but do not boil, stirring until eggs thicken. Correct sea-

soning and add parsley. Makes 4 servings.

COLCANNON

This delectable mixture of buttered greens and potatoes is yet another way of foretelling the future at Halloween. A heaped portion is served on each plate. A well is made in the center of the heap to hold a generous amount of butter. The colcannon is eaten from around the outside of the heap, each person dipping his fork first into the colcannon and then into the melted butter. The perfect accompaniment is a glass of fresh buttermilk.

In the Midlands colcannon is called "Thump." In the North and West it is called "Champ." Here is a recipe for colcannon. Put the cooked potatoes through a sieve or ricer. Beat in a good lump of butter and enough hot cream or milk to make the mixture light and fluffy. Add to the potato mixture half its bulk of finely chopped cooked kale and 1 tablespoon minced onion. Add salt and pepper to taste, beat well, and reheat thoroughly. And don't forget the ring and that all-important silver coin.

HAGGERTY

- 3 medium potatoes
- 1 large onion
- 2 tablespoons bacon fat
- ¾ cup grated Cheddar cheese
  Salt and pepper to taste

Wash and pare potatoes, cut into paper-thin slices, and pat dry in a towel. Slice onion very thin. Heat half of bacon fat in a heavy frying pan and fill pan with alternate layers of potatoes and onion and cheese, finishing with potatoes. Sprinkle each layer with salt and pepper. Dot the top layer of potatoes with remainder of bacon fat. Cook over moderate heat until potatoes are almost tender. Turn the Haggerty carefully onto a platter, slip it, top side down, back into the pan, and continue cooking until done. To serve, cut into wedges. Makes 4 servings.

POTATO COLLOPS

There is no denying that the best way of all to cook potatoes is to boil or bake them in their jackets. And, notwithstanding the advice of foreign cooks, the skins of potatoes should not be gashed when being put to cook. If the skins should burst slightly in the boiling and subsequent drying (boiled potatoes should always be shaken for a minute or two over low heat after being drained) it is all to the good: there is no more appetizing sight than the floury "grin" of a burst boiled potato.

Admittedly, during the weeks before the new potatoes are ready for digging, last season's potatoes begin to show their age and sometimes need dressing up. And I know of few better potato dishes than Collops ("collop," by the way, means a small portion of any foodstuff). Originally "collope," the 16th century Irish referred to our famous rashers and eggs as "collopes and eggs."

- 3 medium potatoes
- 1 large onion
  Salt and pepper to taste
- 2 teaspoons chopped parsley
- ¼ pound raw bacon, diced (to be omitted on fast days)
- 2 tablespoons butter
- 1 cup milk, boiled
- 3 tablespoons grated cheese

Pare potatoes and cut into very thin slices. Chop onion. Place a layer of vegetables in a greased baking dish. Sprinkle with seasonings, parsley, and diced bacon (rind removed), and dot with butter. Repeat layers until all ingredients are used, finishing with potatoes. Pour in milk and sprinkle top with grated cheese. Cover and bake in preheated moderate oven (350°F.) for 45 minutes. Uncover and continue cooking until potatoes are done and top layer is brown. Makes 4 servings.

DESSERTS

APPLE PUDDENY-PIE

- 4 medium cooking apples
- 1 teaspoon ground cinnamon
- ½ teaspoon grated nutmeg
- ½ cup sugar
- ½ teaspoon salt
- ⅓ cup water
- 2 teaspoons fresh lemon juice
- 1 teaspoon grated lemon rind
- ½ teaspoon baking soda
- 1 cup quick-cooking oats
- ⅓ cup butter

Pare and core apples. Cut into eighths and place in greased baking dish about 10 x 6 inches. Sprinkle with combined spices, sugar, and a little of the salt. Mix water, lemon juice, and grated rind and pour over apples. Add baking soda and remaining salt to oats; work butter into this mixture until crumbly. Spread oatmeal mixture over apples and bake in preheated moderate oven (375°F.) for 40 minutes. Makes 4 to 6 servings.

LENTEN CAKE (EGGLESS)

- ½ cup butter
- 3 tablespoons molasses
- 1 cup milk
- 4 cups sifted all-purpose flour
- ¾ cup sugar
- 3 teaspoons ground allspice
- 2 teaspoons baking powder

- 1 teaspoon baking soda
- ½ teaspoon salt
- ½ cup raisins

Melt butter, add molasses and milk, and cool. Sift together flour, sugar, allspice, baking powder, baking soda, and salt. Stir butter mixture into dry ingredients. Add raisins and mix well. Pour into buttered pan (13 x 9 x 2 inches) and bake in preheated moderate oven (350°F.) for 30 minutes.

BARMBRACK

The term *barmbrack* for an Irish fruit loaf or cake does not derive from barm or leaven. It is a corruption of the Irish word *arán breac,* "speckled bread."

Halloween in Ireland would be unthinkable without barmbrack, the sweet and sticky-crusted loaf which foretells one's fortune for the coming year. Into the dough we knead (paper-wrapped to guard against choking or appendicitis) a ring for marriage, a silver coin for wealth, and a button for single blessedness.

- 7 cups sifted all-purpose flour
- 2 teaspoons ground allspice
- 1½ teaspoons salt
- 1 cup sugar
- 2 packages active dry yeast
- 3 cups warm milk and water (half and half)
- 6 tablespoons butter
- 2½ cup raisins
- ¾ cup dried currants
- ¾ cup chopped citrus peel

Sift flour, allspice, salt, and sugar into a large bowl. Dissolve yeast in half the warm milk and water. Add yeast and remaining liquid to dry ingredients, and mix thoroughly. Knead into a ball and turn out on a floured board. Knead until the dough no longer feels sticky and comes away clean from the board. Wash and grease the bowl, return the dough to it, cover, and let stand in a warm place until dough is double in bulk, about 1½ hours.

Turn the dough onto a floured board and flatten to a large round. Place butter, fruits, and peel in the middle, and work in these ingredients by squeezing and kneading until they are evenly incorporated in the dough. At this point, work in the paper-wrapped charms. Return the dough again to the greased bowl, cover, and leave to rise for about 45 minutes. Divide the dough into two parts and shape to fit 2 loaf pans (each 9 x 5 x 3 inches). Half fill the pans, cover, and leave in a warm place to rise to the top of pans. Bake in preheated hot oven (450°F.) for about 50 minutes, reducing the heat to 425°F. for the last 15 minutes

of baking. Five minutes before the barmbracks are done, brush with sugar and water in equal quantities. Makes 2 large barmbracks.

POTATO SEEDY CAKE

1½ cups sifted all-purpose flour
½ cup sugar
2 teaspoons baking powder
1 teaspoon salt
½ teaspoon ground allspice
¼ cup butter
1 teaspoon caraway seeds
½ cup dried currants
1 cup mashed potatoes
2 large eggs, well beaten

Sift together flour, sugar, baking powder, salt, and allspice; rub in the butter. Add caraway seeds. Add currants and mashed potatoes, mixing well. Add eggs. Place in a well-greased flat pan (8 x 8 inches), and bake in preheated hot oven (425°F.) for 30 minutes. Cut into squares and serve hot. Makes 9 squares.

PETTICOAT TAILS

This rather peculiar name is probably a corruption of *petite galette* (little cake).

1¼ cups butter
4 cups sifted all-purpose flour
¾ cup sugar
1 egg, beaten

Work butter into flour and mix in sugar. Add beaten egg and mix well. Although the mixture will be dry and crumbly, no other liquid should be added. The paste should be worked well with the hands to make it a cohesive mass. Cut it into 4 parts and roll each into a 9-inch round about ⅛ inch thick. In the center of each round stamp a circle with a 2½-inch pastry cutter. Cut the outside part into 8 equal segments. Lift carefully with a spatula onto a well-greased cookie sheet and bake in preheated moderate oven (350°F.) for 12 to 15 minutes. They should be very pale brown in color. Makes 36 pieces.

Note: If desired, brush cookies before baking with a little beaten egg white and sprinkle with a cinnamon-sugar mixture.

IRISH COFFEE

Pour 1 jigger Irish whiskey into a warmed goblet or coffee cup. Add 1 to 2 teaspoons sugar. Add hot strong coffee to within ½ inch of the top. Top with chilled sweetened whipped cream. Makes 1 serving.

IRISH MOSS or CARRAGEEN—

A species of small edible seaweed, varying in color from greenish yellow to purplish brown, named after Carragheen, Waterford County, Ireland. This seaweed is found along the coast of the British Islands, the rocky shores of continental Europe, and the eastern shores of the northern United States and Canada. The moss used domestically is obtained principally from New Hampshire and Massachusetts. The plants are washed in salt water and spread on the beach to dry and bleach, the process being repeated several times. The greater part of the supply is used for clarifying malt beverages. The remainder is retailed through druggists and health-food stores. It was formerly used in New England and still is, occasionally, to make a blancmange-type dessert.

IRISH MOSS BLANCMANGE

¾ cup Irish moss
Cold water
4 cups milk
Dash of salt
½ teaspoon lemon or vanilla extract
Sugar and cream

Soak moss in cold water for 5 minutes. Then tie moss in cheesecloth and put in top part of double boiler with milk and salt. Put over boiling water and cook, covered, for 30 minutes. Remove cheesecloth bag and add flavoring to milk mixture. Pour into bowl and chill until firm. Serve with sugar and cream, or with fruit. Makes 4 servings.

Italian Cookery

Italian cuisine is divided into butter and oil cooking. Northern Italy, cooler and pastoral, produces and uses excellent butter. Central and Southern Italy produce and use oil and cured pork fats, which do not suffer from the heat. Within these two basic divisions, the variety in foods is also very great, for historical, geographical, and economic reasons.

Italy's history has been one of independent tribes, cities, duchies, and kingdoms until the country was united, in 1870, into one nation. After the Second World War, the kingdom became a republic. In spite of the unification, an intensive local patriotism is part of the Italian character. Villages, towns, and regions look askance at each other, as exemplified in the Italian proverb of *moglie e buoi dei paesi tuoi,* "wives and cattle from your own locality."

This regional feeling has produced an independent, nonstandardized people and an infinite variety of architecture, customs, products, and cooking. Verona and Venice, for instance, are only a few hours' train journey apart, but their food is quite different.

Economically, the Italians have been until recently a very poor but imaginative people. In what other country have two simple ingredients, such as flour and water, resulted in so many pastas, food that is deliciously filling and an ideal stretcher of such expensive foods as meats and fats.

Throughout Italy the cooking is careful, with an instinctive feeling for flavor and texture combination. The laborer who eats his bread sprinkled with oil and chopped herbed tomatoes, the cook who can take a piece of cheese, put it between two slices of bread, fry it, and serve it with anchovy sauce, or transform a few little pieces of veal into dozens of delightful dishes are people who enjoy good food and are discriminating about it.

In Italy, it is always worthwhile to find out what foods and wines can be had locally, because many of them are not transported away from home, and many of them are strictly seasonal. Quite a number of dishes are made only in certain seasons or for certain holidays. Similar dishes turn up in many regions, but under various names and with their own special character. *Ravioli,* for instance, is called *ravioli* only in Piedmont and Genoa, and *tortellini, tortelli, agnolotti, anolini, cappelletti,* and *melfatti* in other places, and is everywhere filled with different stuffings.

No writing about Italian cookery would be complete without mention of Italian wines. All of Italy is a vineyard, and wine is part of the daily food, drunk at meals. The best-known Italian wine is red Chianti. But any Italian region, town, or village produces its own excellent wines, which should be savored by travelers in Italy.

 **APPETIZERS**

ANTIPASTO MISTO
(Antipasto Plates)

The *antipasto* (meaning "before the meal") platters and plates can be a little salad or a meal in itself. The idea is to combine vegetables, meats, fish, and eggs in as colorful an assortment as possible. Great care is taken in arranging the foods in an attractive and orderly way.

Antipasto Combinations

■ Arrange the following on a platter or plate: slices of Italian salami; rolled-up prosciutto or other ham; tuna in olive oil; black and green olives; eggs sliced or stuffed and topped, in both cases, with a parsley sprig or 3 capers; pickled mushrooms; radish roses; tomato slices, strips of red pimientos, and green peppers marinated in olive oil; celery stuffed with mashed Gorgonzola or other blue-veined cheese; eggplant salad; artichoke hearts marinated in a mixture of olive oil, white wine, basil or other herb, and salt and pepper; rolled anchovies, sardines, and any relishes such as pickled peppers, cauliflower, artichokes, labeled Italian style in food stores.

■ Cantaloupe or honeydew melon wedges wrapped in slices of prosciutto; pare chilled melon and cut into wedges; wrap with wafer-thin slices of prosciutto (allow 2 melon wedges for each person to be served); mushroom salad; anchovy-stuffed eggs; tomatoes; sliced fennel; slices of Italian salami; potato salad; pimiento marinated in olive oil; green olives; anchovies; sardines.

■ Meatless antipasto: overlapping slices of tomatoes and hard-cooked eggs, surrounded by chunks of tuna in olive oil and rolled anchovies, garnished with mayonnaise and decorated with parsley sprigs.

MEDAGLIONI DI MOZZARELLA
(Medallions of Mozzarella Cheese)

Cut medallions (diameter of fifty-cent piece and ½ inch thick) of Mozzarella or other cheese. Roll each piece of cheese in flour, well-beaten egg, and fine bread crumbs. Deep fry in ¼ inch of olive oil in skillet until golden-brown.

MELANZANE ALLA MARINARA
(Marinated Eggplant Appetizer)

1 large unpeeled eggplant, cut into 1-inch cubes
½ cup white vinegar (preferably wine vinegar)

1 teaspoon salt
½ teaspoon white pepper
1 garlic clove, minced
1 teaspoon dried oregano
½ teaspoon dried basil
¾ cup olive oil

Boil eggplant in boiling water to cover for 8 to 10 minutes. Drain. Cubes should be soft but retain their shape. Mix other ingredients except oil. Place drained eggplant in large bowl and pour marinade over. Toss thoroughly. Marinate overnight, or for at least 8 hours. Before serving, toss with oil. Makes 6 to 8 servings.
Note: This will keep for about 1 week in the refrigerator.

PROSCIUTTO WITH FRUITS

One of the most typical of Italian first courses for luncheon is the ham of Parma called prosciutto. This specially cured ham is eaten in thin slices. It is combined with various fruits and eaten with a little freshly ground black pepper and in some cases with a squeeze of lemon. These paper-thin slices of ham are always laid over the fruits they are to complement. Try them with:

■ Luscious ripe melon wedges
■ Quarters of peeled ripe pears
■ Wedges of ripe pineapple
■ Whole ripe figs with ham slices wrapped around them cornucopia fashion

Crisp bread and fresh butter go with this exciting appetizer.

  SOUPS

MINESTRONE MILANESE

¼ cup olive oil
1 garlic clove, minced
1 onion, minced
1 leek, washed and diced (when in season)
1 tablespoon chopped parsley
1 teaspoon dried thyme
1 tablespoon tomato paste
¼ cup water
3 canned or fresh tomatoes, peeled, seeded, and chopped
3 celery stalks, chopped
2 carrots, diced
2 potatoes, diced
¼ small cabbage, shredded
2 zucchinis, diced
6 cups hot water or bouillon
Salt to taste
½ teaspoon pepper
⅓ cup uncooked rice
1 to 1½ cups cooked and drained

dried beans
Grated Parmesan cheese

Put olive oil in large kettle. Add garlic, onion, leek, parsley, and thyme and cook until soft. Add tomato paste thinned with ¼ cup water and cook for 5 minutes. Add all remaining ingredients except rice, beans, and cheese. Simmer, covered, for 1 hour. Bring to boil, add rice, and cook until soft. Add beans; heat. Serve with cheese. Makes 3 quarts, or 6 servings.
Note: In this northern version of Italy's national soup, rice replaces pasta.

PAVESE
(Egg Consommé)

6 cups beef or chicken consommé
1 tablespoon minced parsley
3 eggs
3 tablespoons grated Parmesan cheese

Bring consommé to a boil. Beat parsley, eggs, and cheese together. Stir into consommé and cook, stirring, for a few seconds, or until eggs are set. Makes 1½ quarts, or 4 to 6 servings.

ZUPPA VENEZIANA DI PESCE
(Venetian Fish Soup)

3 pounds white-fleshed fish, including heads
3 cups water
1 onion, studded with 2 cloves
2 bay leaves
3 parsley sprigs
1 teaspoon salt
¼ teaspoon pepper
½ teaspoon crumbled dried marjoram
½ cup olive oil
1 garlic clove
½ cup dry white wine
1 cup stewed tomatoes

Trim fish and cut flesh into bite-size pieces. Reserve. Combine trimmings, including heads, water, onion, 1 bay leaf, parsley, salt, pepper, and ¼ teaspoon marjoram. Simmer, covered, for 30 to 40 minutes, stirring occasionally. Drain and reserve fish stock; there should be about 2 cups. Discard everything else. Fry fish pieces in the hot olive oil with remaining marjoram and bay leaf and the garlic. Add stock, wine, and tomatoes. Simmer, covered, for 15 minutes. Remove garlic. Makes 1½ quarts, or 4 to 6 servings.
Note: This fish soup is almost a stew.

MINESTRONE DI PASTA E FAGIUOLI
or PASTA FAZULA
(Thick Soup of Macaroni and Beans)

Wash 1 pound dried pinto or navy beans and soak overnight in 2 quarts water. Cook beans in the same water. Prepare sauce. Sauté ½ cup chopped salt pork, bacon, or ham with 1 minced garlic clove

Antipasto Misto

Minestrone Milanese

Prosciutto with Honeydew

or 2 tablespoons minced onion and a dash of chili pepper. Add to the beans and let cook until tender. Just before serving, add 1 pound cooked and drained *ditalini* (macaroni) and let simmer for 5 minutes. Stir well, and serve topped with grated Romano cheese. Makes 8 to 10 servings.

 FISH AND SEAFOOD

PESCE LESSO
(Poached Fish, Italian Style)

- 2 tablespoons minced parsley
- 1 garlic clove, minced
- 3 tablespoons olive oil
- 1 cup hot water
- 1½ pounds flounder fillets
- 1 teaspoon salt
- ⅛ teaspoon pepper
  Pinch of dried oregano

Cook parsley and garlic in olive oil in skillet for 3 minutes. Add hot water and bring to boil. Add fish and seasonings. Cover, bring again to boil, and cook for 5 to 10 minutes. Serve with the liquid. Makes 4 servings.

PESCE ALLA SICILIANA
(Sicilian Fish)

- 4 slices of halibut or swordfish (or other thick fish), 1¾ to 2 pounds
- ¼ cup olive oil
- 1 tablespoon chopped parsley
- 1 garlic clove, minced
- ½ cup white vinegar
- 2 pounds tomatoes, peeled, seeded, and chopped
  Salt and pepper to taste
- 1 package (10 ounces) frozen peas, thawed

In skillet brown fish in hot oil. Add parsley, garlic, and vinegar. Cook until liquid has almost evaporated. Add tomatoes, salt, and pepper. Simmer, covered, for 5 minutes. Add peas. Simmer, covered, for about 30 minutes. Put fish on hot platter and pour sauce over it. Makes 4 to 6 servings.

PESCE FRITTO
(Fried Fish Fillets, Italian Style)

- 4 medium fish fillets
- ½ cup all-purpose flour
- ½ cup olive oil
  Salt to taste
  Lemon wedges

Coat fillets with flour and fry in hot oil for about 8 minutes on each side. Drain on absorbent paper. Sprinkle with salt and serve with lemon wedges. Makes 4 servings.

Note: The olive oil gives fried fish a different flavor.

SCAMPI AI FERRI
(Garlic Broiled Shrimps)

- 2 pounds raw shrimps
- ½ cup olive oil
- 2 garlic cloves, minced
- 2 teaspoons salt
- ⅓ cup chopped parsley
  Lemon wedges

Split shrimp shells with scissors. Remove shells and devein shrimps. Arrange shrimps in shallow baking pan. Sprinkle with olive oil, garlic, salt, and half of parsley. Broil about 4 inches from source of heat for 5 to 7 minutes on each side, depending on size of shrimps. Sprinkle with remaining parsley and serve with lemon wedges. Makes 4 servings.

 **MEAT AND POULTRY**

SCALOPPINE DI VITELLO
(Veal Scaloppine)

- 1 pound veal scaloppine, cut very thin
- ⅓ cup all-purpose flour, seasoned with salt and pepper
- 6 tablespoons butter
- ¼ cup dry white wine

Coat scaloppine with flour. Sauté in hot butter for about 3 minutes on each side. Add white wine. Simmer for 2 minutes longer. Serve at once. Makes 3 or 4 servings.

COSTOLETTE ALLA PARMIGIANA
(Veal Chops Parmigiana)

- ½ cup fine dry bread crumbs
- ½ cup grated Parmesan cheese
- ¾ teaspoon salt
- ¾ teaspoon paprika
- 4 large loin veal chops (2 to 2½ pounds)
- 1 egg, beaten
- 3 tablespoons butter
- 4 thin slices of Mozzarella cheese
- 2 cups well-seasoned tomato sauce

Mix crumbs, Parmesan, salt, and paprika. Dip chops into egg and roll in crumb mixture. Heat butter and brown chops on both sides. Cover each with a slice of Mozzarella. Pour tomato sauce over chops. Cover and simmer for about 45 minutes. If sauce is too thick, add a little hot water. Makes 4 servings.

PETTO DI VITELLO
(Veal Breast)

- 3 pounds breast of veal
  Boiling water
- 2 teaspoons salt
- 1 celery stalk
- 1 carrot
- 1 onion
- ¼ teaspoon pepper
- ⅛ teaspoon ground nutmeg
- 1 tablespoon chopped parsley

- 3 tablespoons olive oil
- 3 tablespoons fresh lemon juice
- 2 eggs, beaten
- 1 tablespoon melted butter
  Fine dry bread crumbs

Simmer veal in boiling water to cover with salt, celery, carrot, and onion for 1 hour, or until tender. Remove meat and reserve broth for soup and other uses. Cool meat and cut into 1- or 2-inch strips. Combine pepper, nutmeg, parsley, oil, and lemon juice. Add meat and marinate for at least 2 hours, turning occasionally. Remove meat from marinade and dry with paper towels. Mix eggs and melted butter. Dip meat into mixture, roll in crumbs, and put in one layer in greased shallow baking dish. Bake in preheated moderate oven (375°F.) for 30 minutes, turning once after 15 minutes. Makes 4 servings.

ARROSTO DI AGNELLO
(Roast Lamb)

Taking a leg of lamb or an entire baby lamb, rub it well with garlic, rosemary leaves, and salt and pepper. Pour ½ cup olive oil into the roaster. Set lamb in it and roast, uncovered, in preheated moderate oven (350°F.), turning occasionally until practically done, allowing 30 minutes to the pound. Place peeled tiny new spring potatoes around meat and continue roasting until they are tender.

Note: Lamb prepared with a blend of herbs is an Easter delicacy throughout Italy, as is turkey on Thanksgiving in America.

AGNELLO ALLA CACCIATORA
(Lamb Cacciatora)

- 4 pounds shoulder or leg of lamb, trimmed of all fat and cut into 1½-inch cubes
- ⅓ cup olive oil
- 1 small garlic clove, minced
- 1 teaspoon crumbled dried rosemary
- ½ teaspoon crumbled dried sage
- 2 teaspoons all-purpose flour
- ½ cup white or wine vinegar
- ½ cup water
  Salt and pepper to taste

Brown meat in hot oil. Add garlic, rosemary, and sage. Sprinkle flour on meat. Add vinegar and water, stirring thoroughly. Cover and simmer for 1 hour, or until meat is tender. Season with salt and pepper. Stir frequently during cooking, and add a little hot water if necessary. Makes 6 servings.

MAIALE AFFOGATO
(Stewed Pork with Celery)

- 1 garlic clove
- 2 tablespoons olive or cooking oil

1 carrot, minced
2 pounds lean boneless pork, cut into bite-size pieces
1 cup dry red or white wine
1½ teaspoons salt
½ teaspoon pepper
2½ cups sliced celery
Bouillon or water
1 cup chopped fresh or canned tomatoes

Brown garlic in oil and discard garlic. Add carrot, pork, wine, and salt and pepper. Cook, covered, over low heat for 1½ hours. Cook celery in bouillon until almost tender. Drain. Add cooked celery and tomatoes to pork mixture for the last 15 minutes of cooking time. Makes 4 to 6 servings.

SALSICCIE E FAGIOLI
(Italian Sausages with Beans)

1 pound sweet or hot Italian sausages
2 tablespoons olive oil
2 tablespoons tomato paste
¼ teaspoon salt
⅛ teaspoon pepper (omit if hot sausage is used)
4 cups drained cooked kidney beans
¼ cup bean liquid or water

Prick sausages and put in skillet with cold water to cover. Cook over moderate heat until water evaporates. Then cook for 20 minutes, allowing sausages to brown on all sides. Remove from pan and keep hot. Add oil to fat in pan. Stir in tomato paste, salt, and pepper. Cook for 5 minutes. Add kidney beans, liquid, and sausages to pan. Simmer for 15 minutes, stirring occasionally. Garnish with parsley, if desired. Makes 4 servings.

Note: Use the sweet or hot variety of sausage, according to taste.

POLLO ALLA CACCIATORA
(Chicken Cacciatora)

¼ cup olive oil
1 chicken (2½ to 3 pounds), cut up
2 onions, sliced
2 garlic cloves, minced
2 cups (one 1-pound can) Italian tomatoes
1 can (8 ounces) tomato sauce
1 teaspoon salt
¼ teaspoon pepper
½ teaspoon celery seed
1 teaspoon crushed dried oregano
2 bay leaves
½ cup dry white wine

Heat oil in large deep skillet. Brown chicken in it. Remove chicken and keep hot. Cook onions and garlic in oil in skillet until tender. Add other ingredients except wine, and blend. Cook for 5 minutes. Return chicken to skillet. Cover and simmer for 45 minutes. Add wine and cook, uncovered, for about 15 min-

utes. Arrange on hot platter. Skim excess fat from sauce and remove bay leaves. Pour sauce over chicken. Makes 4 to 6 servings.

Note: Serve on spaghetti or noodles with a sprinkling of cheese.

PETTI DI POLLO ALLA PIEMONTESE
(Chicken Breast, Piedmont Style)

2 whole chicken breasts, boned and halved
2 tablespoons all-purpose flour
1 teaspoon salt
½ teaspoon white pepper
2 tablespoons butter
Slices of truffles or 4 large mushrooms, sliced and sautéed in butter
4 very thin slices of Swiss cheese

Trim chicken of skin, fat, and gristle. Put between sheets of wax paper and roll thin with a rolling pin. Coat with flour seasoned with salt and pepper. Heat butter and cook chicken until tender, about 5 or 6 minutes on each side. Remove to shallow baking pan. Arrange truffle slices on each breast and cover each with cheese. Put under broiler just long enough to melt cheese. Makes 4 servings.

FEGATINI DI POLLO ALLA SALVIA
(Chicken Livers with Sage)

Season chicken livers with salt and pepper and coat with chopped fresh or dried sage (about 1 tablespoon fresh sage or ½ teaspoon crumbled dried sage leaves per liver, depending on taste). Wrap chicken livers in strips of prosciutto or partly cooked lean bacon. Thread on small skewers. Broil over a campfire or an outdoor grill or a rotisserie or under the range broiler, turning occasionally. Allow about 8 to 10 minutes of broiling time. If livers are wrapped in prosciutto, baste with melted butter.

 **EGGS AND CHEESE**

UOVA IN PURGATORIO
(Eggs in Purgatory)

¼ cup chopped onion
¼ cup minced parsley
Salt and pepper to taste
1 tablespoon olive oil
2 cups chopped, peeled tomatoes (or canned)
8 eggs
4 slices of buttered toast

Sauté onion and parsley with salt and pepper in oil for 10 minutes. Add tomatoes and simmer for 30 minutes, stirring often. Bring to a boil, then care-

fully drop in the eggs, one at a time, to poach. Serve on buttered toast with the sauce. Makes 4 servings, allowing 2 eggs for each portion.

CROSTINI ALLA MOZZARELLA
(Italian Mozzarella Skewers)

Mozzarella originally came from the marshy farming districts around Naples, where buffaloes from India are used as beasts of burden. Their milk goes into cheese making. Our Mozzarella is more bland than the Italian and it is therefore a good idea to serve the *crostini* with anchovy butter.

Remove the crust from a loaf of French bread. Cut loaf into slices about ⅓ inch thick. Cut Mozzarella into slices the same size and thickness as bread. Place alternate slices of bread and cheese on a skewer until there are 3 of cheese and 4 of bread, beginning and ending with bread. Preheat baking dish and place skewers on it. Bake in a very hot oven (450°F. to 475°F.) just long enough for the cheese to melt and the bread to brown. Serve very hot with Anchovy Butter.

Anchovy Butter

Melt 1 cup butter. Chop 8 anchovy fillets and simmer in butter for 5 minutes. Pour sauce over each skewer serving.

PASTA, PANCAKES, AND RICE

SPAGHETTI CON LE POLPETTINE
(Spaghetti with Meatballs)

Tomato Sauce:

3½ cups (one 1-pound, 12-ounce can) tomatoes
3 cans (6 ounces each) tomato paste
4 cups water
1 onion, minced
1 garlic clove, minced
¼ pound salt pork, minced
2 tablespoons olive oil
2 tablespoons chopped parsley
2 teaspoons salt
½ teaspoon pepper
1 teaspoon sugar
½ teaspoon dried oregano
1 bay leaf, crushed
¼ cup grated Parmesan or Romano cheese

Meatballs:

½ pound each of ground beef, veal, and pork
2 eggs, beaten
1 teaspoon salt
¼ teaspoon pepper
¼ teaspoon dried oregano
½ cup grated Parmesan cheese

Salsiccie e Fagioli

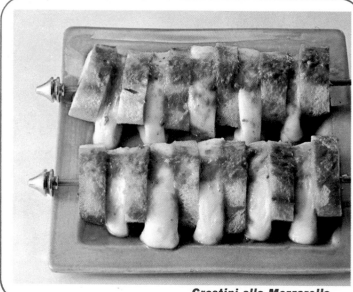

Crostini alla Mozzarella

Spaghetti con le Polpettine

Insalata Bandiera

Cassata Napolitana

2 tablespoons chopped parsley
2 teaspoons grated lemon rind
¼ cup fine dry bread crumbs
  Cooked spaghetti

Combine tomatoes, tomato paste, and water; bring to boil. Sauté onion, garlic, and salt pork in hot olive oil. Add to tomato mixture. Add remaining ingredients except cheese and simmer, covered, for about 1 hour, stirring frequently. Combine all meatball ingredients and mix thoroughly with hands. Shape into balls. Add to tomato sauce and simmer, covered, for about 40 minutes, stirring occasionally. Before serving, stir in the ¼ cup grated cheese listed in sauce. Pour over hot cooked spaghetti. Makes 6 servings.

SPAGHETTI AL QUATTRO FORMAGGI
(Spaghetti with Four Cheeses)
½ cup butter
⅔ cup shredded Mozzarella cheese
⅔ cup grated Gouda or Edam cheese
⅔ cup grated imported Swiss cheese
⅔ cup grated Parmesan cheese
1 pound spaghetti
  Salt and pepper

Melt butter in top part of a double boiler; have cheeses ready. Cook spaghetti to your taste in boiling salted water. Drain well and turn into a chafing dish or electric skillet turned to low. Add Mozzarella and Gouda and toss well. Then add half of butter and the Swiss cheese. Give it a thorough mixing and add freshly ground pepper. Finally add remaining butter and the Parmesan cheese. Toss again and serve very hot. Makes 4 servings.

LASAGNE CON LE POLPETTINE
(Lasagna with Meatballs)
¾ pound lean beef, ground
½ teaspoon salt
¼ teaspoon pepper
1 teaspoon grated lemon rind
2 tablespoons olive oil
3 cups favorite tomato sauce
1 pound lasagna, cooked and drained
1 pound ricotta or cottage cheese
1 pound Mozzarella cheese, cubed
1½ cups grated Parmesan cheese

Season beef with salt and pepper, add lemon rind, and shape into balls the size of a large marble. Brown in hot oil. Cover bottom of a large 2- to 3-inch-deep baking dish sparingly with tomato sauce. Line with lasagna. Dot with half of cheeses. Spread with half of remaining sauce; top with meat. Cover with remaining lasagna, sauce, and cheeses. Bake in preheated slow oven (325°F.) for about 45 minutes. Cool slightly. Makes 10 to 12 servings.

VERMICELLI ALLA PASTORA
(Fine Noodles for the Shepherdess)
1 pound vermicelli
1 pound ricotta, well creamed
1 cup hot water
3 tablespoons olive oil
  Salt and pepper to taste

While noodles cook in rapidly boiling water, dilute cheese with hot water and olive oil, stirring constantly. Strain noodles and mix them thoroughly with the cheese sauce. Season. Makes 6 servings.

CANNELLONI ALLA PARMIGIANA
(Stuffed Pancakes, I)
½ pound sausage meat, cooked and drained
1 package (10 ounces) frozen spinach, cooked and chopped fine
1 cup finely chopped cooked chicken
¼ cup grated Romano cheese
⅛ teaspoon ground thyme
⅛ teaspoon pepper
  Butter
1 cup milk
2 eggs, beaten
½ cup sifted all-purpose flour
1 teaspoon baking powder
½ teaspoon salt
  Parmesan Sauce

To make stuffing mix first 6 ingredients.

To make Cannelloni heat 2 tablespoons butter and the milk until butter is melted. Cool slightly. Add next 4 ingredients and mix until smooth. Drop by spoonfuls onto hot buttered skillet to form eighteen 3-inch pancakes. Fry until browned on both sides. Cool, and spread each with stuffing. Roll up and put in broilerproof shallow baking dish. Cover with Parmesan Sauce. Broil for 5 minutes. Makes 6 servings.

Parmesan Sauce
Melt 3 tablespoons butter; blend in 3 tablespoons flour. Add 1½ cups light cream; cook, stirring, until thickened. Stir in ½ cup grated Parmesan cheese. Season.

MANICOTTI
(Stuffed Pancakes, II)
1 cup sifted all-purpose flour
1 cup water
  Salt
7 eggs
2 pounds ricotta cheese
  Grated Parmesan or Romano cheese
¼ teaspoon pepper
½ pound Mozzarella, cut into 12 strips
3 cans (8 ounces each) tomato sauce

To make pancakes combine flour, water, and ¼ teaspoon salt; beat until smooth. Beat in 4 eggs, one at a time. Heat a 5- to 6-inch skillet and grease with a few drops of oil. Put about 3 tablespoons batter in hot skillet and roll around pan to distribute evenly. Cook over low heat until firm; do not brown. Turn, and cook lightly on other side. Continue making pancakes until all batter is used. This amount will make 12 to 14 pancakes. Do not grease skillet a second time.

To make filling mix ½ teaspoon salt, 3 eggs, ricotta, ¼ cup Parmesan, and the pepper. Put about 2 tablespoons filling and a strip of Mozzarella on each pancake and roll up. Pour 1 can tomato sauce into large shallow baking dish. Put pancakes, seam side down, in sauce. Cover with remaining 2 cans sauce and sprinkle with ½ cup Parmesan. Bake in preheated moderate oven (350°F.) for 45 minutes. Makes 6 generous servings.

RISOTTO ALLA MILANESE
(Rice, Milan Style)
¼ cup butter
¼ cup chopped beef marrow or 2 tablespoons butter
1 onion, minced
2 cups uncooked rice
½ cup dry white wine
  About 5 cups boiling chicken bouillon
½ teaspoon ground saffron, steeped in a little chicken bouillon
  Salt to taste
½ teaspoon white pepper
⅔ cup grated Parmesan cheese

In heavy saucepan melt butter and beef marrow. Cook onion in it until soft but not brown. Add rice and cook for 3 or 4 minutes, stirring. The rice must be transparent but not brown. Stir in wine and cook for 3 minutes. Add ½ cup boiling bouillon. Cook until bouillon is absorbed, stirring. Add remaining bouillon by half cups, allowing it to become absorbed after each addition, and stirring constantly. The cooking time should be 20 to 25 minutes after the bouillon has been first added, depending on the kind of rice used and the degree of doneness desired. (Italians eat it *al dente.*) After about 15 minutes of cooking time, add saffron, salt, and pepper. When done, stir in cheese. Serve with more cheese. Rice can be served plain or with chicken livers or mushrooms. Makes 4 to 6 servings.

Note: The finished product should be moist and creamy, not dry.

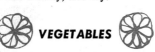 **VEGETABLES**

MELANZANE ALLA PARMIGIANA
(Eggplant Parmigiana)
2 cups olive oil, about

1 garlic clove, minced
1 large onion, chopped
5 cups canned Italian-style tomatoes
½ teaspoon dried basil
   Salt and pepper to taste
1 cup all-purpose flour
2 eggs, beaten
1 cup milk
2 medium eggplants, cut into ½-inch slices
1 cup grated Parmesan cheese
8 ounces Mozzarella cheese, diced
¼ cup butter

Heat ¼ cup of oil in skillet. Sauté garlic and onion in it until soft. Add tomatoes, basil, salt, and pepper. Cook, covered, stirring occasionally, for 30 minutes. Make batter with flour, eggs, and milk. Dip eggplant slices into batter and fry slices in remaining shallow hot oil until just browned on both sides. Add more oil after each frying. Arrange alternate layers of eggplant, sauce, and cheeses in casserole, sprinkling each layer with salt and pepper; dot with butter. Bake in preheated moderate oven (350°F.) for 30 minutes. Makes 6 to 8 servings.

PISELLI E PASTA
(Peas and Shell Macaroni)

¼ cup butter
¼ cup olive oil
1 onion, minced
1 garlic clove, minced (optional)
½ pound shell macaroni, cooked and drained
3 cups cooked peas
1 cup chopped parsley
½ cup finely cooked ham (optional)
   Grated Parmesan cheese
   Salt and pepper

Heat butter and oil. Sauté onion and garlic in it until onion is soft. Add other ingredients except cheese and season to taste with salt and pepper. Simmer, covered, for 10 minutes. Serve with cheese. Makes 4 to 6 servings.
Note: This dish is also served without the cheese in Italy.

PEPERONI CON PATATE
(Peppers and Potatoes)

1 pound sweet peppers
¼ cup olive oil
1 garlic clove, minced
1 onion, minced
5 potatoes, peeled and sliced or cubed
1 cup tomato juice
   Salt and pepper to taste

Trim peppers and cut into strips lengthwise. Heat olive oil and sauté garlic and onion in it. Add peppers and all other ingredients. Cook, covered, over low heat, for 30 minutes, or until potatoes are tender. Stir occasionally and add a little more tomato juice if necessary. Makes 4 servings.

Note: Served with eggs, this makes a good luncheon dish.

SPINACI STUFATI
(Steamed Spinach)

¼ cup olive oil
1 garlic clove, peeled
2 pounds fresh spinach or 2 packages (10 ounces each) frozen spinach
   Salt and pepper to taste

Heat oil and garlic; add spinach. Cook for 7 minutes, or until spinach is just tender. If too dry add ¼ cup water, although usually the water that clings to the spinach is enough to cook it. Season with salt and pepper; remove garlic clove before serving. Makes 4 servings.

ZUCCHINI AL BURRO
(Squash with Butter)

If squash is young, slice it without peeling. If skin is tough, peel it first. Cut into ½-inch slices. When all slices are in the skillet, add a large piece of butter, salt and pepper to taste, and a dash of ground cinnamon. Cover and simmer until done, stirring when necessary.

ZUCCHINI FRITTE
(Fried Squash)

8 small zucchinis, unpeeled
½ cup seasoned all-purpose flour
½ cup olive oil

Wash zucchinis, dry, and cut into ¼-inch rounds. Coat with flour. Fry in hot oil until crisp and golden. Drain on absorbent paper. Makes 4 to 6 servings.
Note: Wonderful with veal.

 SAUCES

SALSA PARMIGIANA
(Basic Tomato Sauce)

¼ cup minced onion
1 garlic clove, minced (optional)
¼ cup olive oil
¼ cup minced raw carrot
1 cup minced celery
¼ cup minced sweet basil
   Salt and pepper to taste
3 cups canned tomato sauce or two 6-ounce cans tomato paste diluted with 3 cans water

Sauté onion and garlic (if used) in oil until golden-brown. Add carrot, celery, sweet basil, and salt and pepper and continue cooking until vegetables are wilted. Add tomato sauce and simmer for 45 minutes, until tasty and thick. Serve this sauce over your favorite cooked pasta. Makes about 2¾ cups.

SALSA ALLA MARINARA
(Mariner's Sauce)

3 garlic cloves, minced
¼ cup minced parsley
½ cup olive oil
2 cups chopped, peeled tomatoes
1 teaspoon crumbled dried oregano
   Salt and pepper to taste

Sauté garlic and parsley in oil. When garlic is delicately brown, add tomatoes, oregano, and salt and pepper, and simmer for 30 minutes, or until well blended and thick. Makes about 1½ cups.
Note: For noodle-dough preparations.

SALSA DI VONGOLE
(White Clam Sauce)

3 tablespoons butter
1 garlic clove, minced
1 tablespoon all-purpose flour
2 cans (10½ ounces each) minced clams
¼ cup chopped parsley
   Salt and pepper to taste
¾ teaspoon dried thyme or basil

Heat butter and cook garlic in it for 1 minute. Blend in flour. Add other ingredients and simmer, covered, for about 10 minutes, stirring frequently. Makes 3 cups sauce.
Note: Serve over hot cooked spaghetti or linguine.

SALSA VERDE PICCANTE
(Piquant Green Sauce)

½ cup minced parsley
¼ cup chopped pignon nuts
2 tablespoons drained capers, chopped
½ cup fine dry bread crumbs
6 pitted black olives, minced
3 tablespoons olive oil
1 tablespoon wine vinegar
   Salt and pepper
1 teaspoon crushed chili pepper
1 teaspoon minced chives, onion, or garlic

Mix all ingredients thoroughly. Makes about 1 cup.
Note: Serve with fish.

SALSA DI ALICI
(Anchovy Sauce)

¼ cup olive oil
¼ cup butter
4 garlic cloves, minced
2 cans (2 ounces each) flat anchovy fillets, drained
¼ cup chopped parsley

Heat oil and butter and add garlic. Cook until garlic is soft, stirring. Add anchovies and cook, stirring, until anchovies have disintegrated. Stir in parsley. Makes about ¾ cup sauce.
Note: For fried Mozzarella, pasta, and boiled-fish dishes.

 **SALADS**

INSALATA DI FAGIOLINI E PATATE
(Green-Bean and Potato Salad)
4 large potatoes
1 pound fresh green beans (Italian preferred)
2 medium-size onions, chopped
  Salt and pepper
  Olive oil and wine vinegar

Wash potatoes and boil until tender; drain, peel, and cool. Boil beans in salted water until tender but firm; drain and cool. Slice or dice potatoes into a large bowl. Add beans, onions, and salt and pepper to taste and mix all carefully. Pour in about 3 tablespoons olive oil and 1 tablespoon wine vinegar, according to taste. Stir salad carefully; marinate in refrigerator for at least 2 hours. Stir again just before serving. Makes 6 to 8 servings.

INSALATA BANDIERA
(Flag Salad)
Fresh tomatoes, sliced or diced
Green beans, cooked, drained, cooled
Chopped carrots, raw or cooked and cooled
Florets of cauliflower, cooked, drained, cooled
Potatoes, cooked, peeled, and diced with a bit of chopped green onion
Red beets, cooked, peeled, and sliced or diced
Finely cut endive or other greens

In preparing Flag Salad, make your own choice among the vegetables, parboiling, straining, and cooling each vegetable separately. (Drop it into rapidly boiling salted water and leave it for just a few minutes, until cooked but firm.) Do not cook the tomatoes or members of the lettuce family (romaine, endive, chicory, escarole, dandelion). When each vegetable is cooled, sprinkle it with salt and pepper and salad dressing to taste. Toss well, and place in individual dishes of a Lazy Susan so that each dish is different from the others.

CANNELINI AL TONNO
(White-Bean and Tuna Salad)
5 cups (two 1-pound, 4-ounce cans) cannelini or 1 pound dried white beans
1 onion stuck with 2 cloves and 1 bay leaf (if using dried beans)
2 cans (7 ounces each) white-meat tuna fish
⅔ cup finely chopped scallions
½ cup finely chopped parsley
1 garlic clove, finely minced
  About ½ cup olive oil
  Vinegar or fresh lemon juice
  Salt and pepper

Open and drain the canned beans, or soak and prepare the packaged beans with onion and bay leaf and cook until tender. Cool. Combine with coarsely shredded tuna fish and other seasonings and dress to suit your taste with olive oil, vinegar, and salt and pepper. Chill before serving. This may be prepared while the beans are hot and eaten hot, although it is best when served cold for an appetizer or a luncheon salad. Makes 6 salad servings.

Note: Cannelini are long white beans which may be found canned or dried. If you do not find them in your locality, substitute white pea beans or small dried Limas.

 **SWEETS AND DESSERTS**

CASSATA NAPOLITANA
(Rich Dessert Cake)
One 9- or 10-inch spongecake or 2 sponge layers
1½ pounds ricotta cheese
⅓ cup sugar
½ cup light cream
1 teaspoon vanilla extract
¼ teaspoon almond extract
1 ounce (1 square) semisweet chocolate or ¼ cup semisweet chocolate pieces, chopped
¼ cup chopped toasted almonds
⅔ cup finely diced mixed candied fruit
¼ cup rum
  Frosting
  Candied cherries

If a whole cake is used, cut into 2 layers. Chill. Combine ricotta, sugar, light cream, and flavorings and mix well. Rub through a sieve or whip until smooth. Add chocolate, almonds, and fruit. Chill. Place 1 cake layer on serving plate and spread with filling. Top with remaining layer. Sprinkle with rum. Chill until shortly before serving time; then frost top. Reserve some of the Frosting to tint pink and use it for decorative swirls on cake. Decorate with cherries.

Frosting
1 egg white
2 cups confectioners' sugar
1 teaspoon almond extract
1 tablespoon fresh lemon juice

Mix all ingredients until smooth. If necessary, add a little water, ½ teaspoon at a time, to achieve right spreading consistency.

BUDINO DI RICOTTA
(Cream-Cheese Custard)
½ pound ricotta cheese
¼ cup grated milk chocolate
¼ cup finely chopped walnuts
2 tablespoons heavy cream (more if needed)

Cream the ricotta. Add chocolate and nuts and blend thoroughly. Add cream as needed for desired consistency. Serve in sherbet glasses. Makes 4 servings.
Note: This "custard" can also be used as a filling for many cakes and cookies.

FRAGOLE ALL' ITALIANA
(Italian Strawberries)
2 tablespoons sugar, or more, depending on berries
4 cups washed and hulled strawberries
⅔ cup dry white wine or fresh orange juice

Sprinkle sugar over strawberries and cover with wine. Chill before serving. Makes 4 to 6 servings.

GROSTOLI
(Crisp Cookies)
3 eggs, lightly beaten
5 cups sifted all-purpose flour
½ cup granulated sugar
1 teaspoon baking powder
1 cup milk
1 teaspoon salt
1 grated lemon rind (optional)
1 ounce of brandy (2 tablespoons)
  Lard
  Confectioners' sugar

Mix first 8 ingredients into smooth noodle dough and roll thin as a dime. With pastry cutter, form rectangles 2 by 3 inches. Deep fry in pure lard. Drain, and dust with confectioners' sugar. Makes about 8 dozen.

JAM—A preserve of fruit which is usually crushed, or may even be ground, cooked with sugar until thick, and stored in sterilized jars. The crushed particles of fruit remain in the finished product. The fruit used can be fresh, canned, frozen, or dried. Jam is sometimes made of fruits mixed with vegetables.

Making jam is one of the most satisfying branches of the ancient art of preserving foods. Before the general availability of canned and frozen foods and commercially made jams, homemade jams were the homemaker's pride and the joy of her family during many a long winter, when the jam's fragrance and sparkle brought summer sunshine to the cold dark season. Housewives slaved over hot stoves on many a summer day when the fruit was perfect for the purpose.

Success in jam making depends on the kind of fruit used, the cooking, handling, and storing. Because of the products available today, the homemaker has a choice of several methods for making jam:

☐ Jam Made without Added Pectin— (Pectin is a water-soluble substance present in plant tissue. It yields a jelly when it is properly combined with acid and sugar.) Some fruits contain enough natural pectin to eliminate the necessity for adding commercial fruit pectin. These fruits include tart apples, blackberries, cranberries, currants, gooseberries, Concord grapes, quinces, and raspberries.

Even when using them, however, some underripe fruits (they contain more pectin than ripe ones) should be included with the ripe fruits to insure the presence of enough pectin for gelling.

☐ Jams Made with Commercial Fruit Pectin—Liquid pectin is added to the cooked fruit and sugar after it is removed from the heat. Or powdered pectin is added to the unheated crushed fruit.

☐ Jams Made without Cooking—Some fresh, canned, or frozen fruits can be used without cooking if liquid or powdered fruit pectin is added and a long storage life is not desired. These fruits include blackberries, raspberries, strawberries, cherries, and peaches. No-cook jams cannot be stored at room temperature. If kept in the freezer, they will last up to one year; in the refrigerator their storage life is three to four months.

TO MAKE JAM

☐ Follow recipe directions for preparing and cooking fruit and for handling it after cooking.

☐ Stir well during cooking to prevent sticking and scorching.

☐ Remember that the mixture will thicken more as it cools. Jams made without added pectin take longer to cook than jams made with pectin, and it is more difficult to tell when the jam is finished. To determine this, use a candy and jelly thermometer, and cook mixture to 220°F. If you do not have a ther-

mometer, you can use the spoon, or sheet, test (the old "jelly test") although it is not absolutely dependable: Dip a cool metal spoon into the boiling mixture. Then raise it at least 1 foot above the kettle, out of the steam, and turn the spoon so that the syrup runs off the side. If the syrup forms drops that flow together and fall off the spoon as one sheet, the jam should be done.

☐ Prepare jars or glasses properly. Have them ready for use when jam is finished cooking. Jars and lids should be covered with hot, not boiling, water and brought to a boil. No further boiling is necessary. Keep hot in water or in a very slow oven until they are needed.

☐ To Seal Jam—Jam which will not be kept more than two months does not need any special sealing. Jam which will be kept longer should be kept in canning jars or sealed with paraffin.

Canning jars, such as the new all-purpose jars with two-piece metal screw-top lids, should be filled to the top, the rim wiped, and the clean hot metal lids placed on the jar with sealing compound next to the glass. The metal band is screwed on firmly, the jar cooled on a metal rack or folded cloth; then labeled, and stored in a cool, dry place.

If using paraffin to seal glasses, the paraffin should be kept hot without overheating. A double boiler is good for this. As soon as jam is in the glasses, filled to within ½ inch of top, cover immediately

with a ⅛-inch layer of paraffin. Be sure jam is completely covered by paraffin, and prick any air bubbles that may appear in the jam. A thin single layer of paraffin is preferable to either a thick or two thin layers as this gives a tighter seal with no chance for air bubbles.

JAMS MADE WITHOUT PECTIN

APRICOT-PINEAPPLE JAM

- 1 package (11 or 12 ounces) dried apricots
- 3½ cups (one pound, 14-ounce can) chunk-style pineapple
- 3½ cups water
- 1 jar (8 ounces) maraschino cherries
- 6 cups sugar

In large saucepan combine apricots, pineapple and syrup, water, and cherry syrup; let stand for 1 hour. Cook slowly until apricots are tender. Add sugar and cook slowly, stirring often, until thick and clear (216°F. on candy thermometer). Add cherries, cut into quarters; cook for a few minutes longer (220°F.). Pour into hot sterilized jars and seal. Makes six ½-pint jars.

SPICED BLACKBERRY JAM

- 4 cups canned blackberry pulp
- 1 teaspoon ground allspice or combination of ground spices
- 1¼ cups sugar*
- 2½ cups corn syrup
- 1 tablespoon fresh lemon juice

Bring pulp to boil in heavy 6-quart kettle. Boil hard for 15 minutes. Add spice, sugar, and syrup. Boil rapidly until jam forms thick jellied drops that adhere to edge of spoon, about 45 minutes. Add lemon juice. Cool slightly; stir; pour into sterilized glasses and seal. Makes four or five ½-pint jars.
*Or use 3 cups sugar, omitting syrup.

CRANBERRY AND FIG JAM

- 3 cups dried figs
- 3 cups water
- Grated rind of 1 orange
- 4 cups cranberries
- 3 cups sugar
- ¼ teaspoon salt

Wash figs and remove the hard stem ends. Put through food chopper, using medium blade. Add water and boil for 30 minutes, stirring frequently. Add rinds, cranberries, sugar, and salt and boil for another 30 minutes. Stir often to prevent burning. Pour into hot sterilized glasses and seal. Makes six ½-pint jars.

CRANBERRY, ORANGE, AND HONEY JAM

- 4 cups cranberries
- 2 cups boiling water
- Grated rind of 1 orange
- 1 cup sugar
- ¾ cup strained honey

Pick over, wash, and drain cranberries. Add water and orange rind; boil for 20 minutes. Force cranberries through a fine sieve. Bring to rapid boil and add sugar and honey, stirring until thoroughly mixed. Boil for 3 minutes longer. Pour into hot sterilized glasses or small molds and seal. Makes about four ½-pint jars.

SPICED GRAPE JAM

1½ pounds stemmed Concord grapes
    (2½ cups pulp and skins)
    Grated rind of 1 orange
½ cup water
2¼ cups sugar
½ teaspoon each of ground cloves
    and cinnamon

Wash grapes and slip skins from pulp. Heat pulp to boiling and rub through a coarse sieve to remove seeds. Add orange rind and water and cook for 10 minutes. Add grape skins, bring to boil, and add sugar and spices. Cook until thickened. Pour into hot sterilized jars and seal. Makes four or five ½-pint jars.

GRAPE AND PINEAPPLE JAM

2 pounds Concord grapes
1 lemon
    Dash of salt
1½ cups sugar
1 cup canned crushed pineapple

Wash grapes, drain, and stem. Slip skins from pulp and reserve. Heat pulp to boiling and rub through coarse sieve to remove seeds. Slice lemon thin and remove seeds. Add to grape pulp and skins; add salt, and cook over moderate heat for 15 minutes, stirring constantly. Add sugar and pineapple; cook to consistency of marmalade, about 20 minutes. Pour into hot sterilized jars and seal. Makes four or five ½-pint jars.

SPICED PEACH JAM

4 cups peach pulp
4 cups sugar
3 or 4 peach pits
1 tablespoon whole gingerroot
¾ teaspoon whole allspice
½ tablespoon whole cloves
1 cinnamon stick
    Juice of ½ lemon

Chop peach pulp; mix with sugar in preserving kettle. Crack peach pits; remove kernels and add to peach pulp. Add spices tied in a bag. Simmer until clear and thick, stirring occasionally to prevent sticking. Remove spice bag and add lemon juice. Fill hot sterilized jars; seal. Makes about four ½-pint glasses.

PINEAPPLE-STRAWBERRY JAM

8 cups hulled strawberries, quartered
4 cups chopped pineapple
4 cups sugar

Combine ingredients in large preserving kettle; let stand for 1 hour. Heat slowly until sugar is dissolved, stirring occasionally. Cook rapidly for 30 to 40 minutes, or until thick, stirring frequently to prevent sticking. Pour into hot sterilized

jars and seal. Cover and store. Makes five ½-pint jars.

PLUM-ORANGE JAM

1 large orange
½ pound seedless raisins
½ cup cold water
½ cup honey
24 large plums

Remove rind from orange in sections and discard all white membrane. Cut yellow rind into very small pieces or force through food chopper; dice pulp. Combine rind and pulp with raisins, water, and honey. Add plums which have been pitted and cut into eighths. (1 cup seedless grapes may be added if desired.) Cook over medium heat, stirring frequently, until thick, about 1 hour. Skim and pour into hot sterilized jars. Let cool slightly, and seal. If desired, ¼ cup chopped nuts may be added to the preserve just before jars are filled. Makes eight ½-pint jars.

RED-PEPPER JAM

Wash and seed 1 dozen large sweet red peppers. Force through medium blade of food chopper. Add 1 tablespoon salt and let stand overnight. Drain well, pressing out all liquid. Put in kettle with 2 cups white vinegar and 3 cups sugar. Cook, uncovered, for 45 minutes, or until of marmalade consistency, stirring frequently. Pour into hot sterilized jars and seal. Makes four or five ½-pint jars.

GOLDEN JAM

2 large oranges
6 cups diced rhubarb
3 cups ground raw carrots
3 cups light corn syrup
2 cups sugar*

Remove seeds and grind oranges. Combine with remaining ingredients and let stand overnight. Bring to a boil and cook slowly until rhubarb is transparent and mixture is thickened. Pour into hot sterilized jars and seal. Makes ten ½-pint jars.
*Or use 4 cups sugar, omitting corn syrup.

OLD-COUNTRY STRAWBERRY JAM

6 cups hulled strawberries
3 cups sugar

Put strawberries in a large heavy saucepan and mash. Cook over moderate heat until fairly thick, stirring frequently. Gradually add sugar; stir constantly over low heat until sugar is dissolved. Bring to boil and boil rapidly for 15 to 20 minutes, or until juice sheets from spoon, stirring occasionally to prevent sticking. Skim, and pour into hot sterilized jars. Seal. Makes four ½-pint jars.

TOMATO-APRICOT JAM

1 package (12 ounces) dried apricots
7 cups (two 1-pound, 12-ounce cans) tomatoes

1 teaspoon whole cloves
3 cinnamon sticks
1 teaspoon salt
7 cups sugar
    Juice of ½ lemon

Soak apricots overnight in tomatoes. Add spices, tied in a bag, and salt. Bring to boil and cook for 15 minutes. Add sugar and cook until clear and of consistency of marmalade. Remove spice bag; add lemon juice. Pour into hot sterilized jars and seal. Makes about five ½-pint jars.

QUINCE AND PEAR JAM

3 cups quince pulp
2 cups pear pulp
3½ cups sugar
    Salt
1 cup water

Wash and cut quinces; cover with water and cook until tender and mushy. Drain and use liquid for making Quince Jelly (page 984). Meanwhile wash and cut up pears and cook, covered, with water, until tender. Put through food mill, and measure. Put quinces through food mill to remove seeds and cores, and measure. Put measured pulp purée into kettle with sugar, salt, and water, and cook, stirring to prevent scorching, until thick. Pour into hot sterilized jars and seal. Makes four ½-pint jars.
Note: This is sometimes called Quince and Pear Honey.

RASPBERRY CURRANT JAM

2 cups currant pulp
2 cups crushed raspberries
3 cups sugar

To prepare currant pulp, cook currants (about 3 cups) until soft, press through a sieve or food mill. Measure pulp. Combine currant pulp, raspberries, and sugar. Bring slowly to boil, stirring occasionally until sugar dissolves. Cook rapidly to jellying point, about 30 minutes. As mixture thickens, stir frequently to prevent sticking. Pour, boiling hot, into sterilized jars and seal. Makes four ½-pint jars.

JAMS MADE WITH PECTIN

PINEAPPLE-MINT JAM

3½ cups (one 1-pound, 13-ounce can) crushed pineapple
¾ cup water
    Juice of 2 lemons
7½ cups sugar
1 bottle (6 ounces) liquid pectin
1 teaspoon peppermint extract
    Green food coloring

Mix first 4 ingredients. Bring to a boil, stirring. Boil for 2 minutes. Add pectin, peppermint, and coloring. Stir and skim for 5 minutes. Pour into hot sterilized jars and seal. Makes five ½-pint jars.

THREE-MINUTE STRAWBERRY JAM

2 cups mashed or sieved strawberries
4 cups sugar

1 box (1¾ ounces) powdered fruit
   pectin
1 cup water

Combine berries and sugar. Let stand for about 20 minutes, stirring occasionally. Stir pectin into water; bring to boil and boil rapidly for 1 minute, stirring constantly. Remove from heat, add berries, and stir constantly for about 2 minutes. Pour into sterilized jars; cover and let stand at room temperature for 48 hours, or until gelled. Seal and store in freezer, where jam will keep well for several months. Or it will keep for 6 to 8 weeks stored in refrigerator. Makes five ½-pint jars.

Note: To use liquid fruit pectin for this jam, omit powdered pectin and water and use ½ bottle liquid pectin (½ cup). It is not necessary to heat liquid pectin; just stir strawberry-sugar mixture into it and proceed as directed above.

TOMATO JAM

Scald, peel, and chop about 2¼ pounds ripe tomatoes. Bring to boil and simmer for 10 minutes. Measure 3 cups into large saucepan. Add 1½ teaspoons grated lemon rind, ¼ cup fresh lemon juice, and 6 cups sugar. Mix well and bring to a full rolling boil. Boil hard for 1 minute, stirring. Remove from heat and at once stir in 1 bottle (6 ounces) liquid pectin. Skim, then stir and skim by turns for 5 minutes. Ladle into hot sterilized jars and seal. Makes about seven ½-pint jars.

Note: Serve with any cold meat.

BERRY JAM

2 quarts blackberries, boysenberries,
   dewberries, strawberries, or
   youngberries or any mixture of these
7 cups sugar
½ bottle (6 ounces) liquid pectin or
1 box (1¾ ounces) powdered pectin

Wash berries and crush. If berries are very seedy, sieve half of berries to remove part of seeds. Combine 4 cups crushed berries and the sugar in saucepan. Mix well and bring to a full rolling boil. Boil for 1 minute, stirring constantly. Remove from heat and stir in pectin. Skim off foam and stir and skim alternately for 5 minutes. Fill hot sterilized jars and seal. Makes seven or eight ½-pint jars.

Note: If berries are lacking in tartness, substitute ¼ cup fresh lemon juice for ¼ cup of the fruit.

Loganberry or Red Raspberry Jam

Follow Berry Jam recipe, but use only 6½ cups sugar.

Gooseberry Jam

Follow Berry Jam recipe, but use only 6 cups sugar and grind berries instead of crushing.

BLUEBERRY JAM

Wash and pick over 1½ quarts ripe berries and crush; there should be 4½ cups. Combine in kettle with 2 tablespoons fresh lemon juice and 7 cups sugar; mix well. Bring to full rolling boil over high heat; boil hard for 1 minute, stirring. Remove from heat and stir in 1 bottle (6 ounces) liquid pectin. Skim off foam. Continue stirring and skimming for 5 minutes to prevent floating fruit. Ladle into hot sterilized jars and seal. Makes nine ½-pint jars.

RED-CHERRY JAM

2½ cups (one 1-pound, 3-ounce can)
   pitted red sour cherries
3½ cups sugar
½ bottle (6-ounce size) liquid pectin

Drain juice from cherries. Crush cherries thoroughly; add sugar, and mix in large preserving kettle. Bring quickly to a full rolling boil and boil rapidly for 1 minute, stirring constantly. Remove from heat, add pectin, and mix well. Skim, and pour into hot sterilized jars. Seal. Makes four ½-pint jars.

SOUR CHERRY JAM

1 quart ripe sour cherries, about
4 cups sugar
¾ cup water
1 box (1¾ ounces) powdered fruit
   pectin

Pit and grind the cherries and measure 2 cups into large bowl or pan. Add sugar to fruit, mix well, and let stand. Mix water and pectin in small saucepan. Bring to a boil and boil for 1 minute, stirring constantly. Stir into fruit mixture. Continue stirring for about 3 minutes. There will be a few remaining sugar crystals. Ladle quickly into glasses. Cover at once with tight lids. When jam is set, store in freezer. If jam will be used within 2 or 3 weeks, it may be stored in refrigerator. Makes about seven ½-pint jars.

PEACH JAM

3 cups canned sliced peaches
1 jar (8 ounces) maraschino cherries
1 large lemon
7½ cups sugar
1 cup liquid pectin

Drain peaches before measuring, then chop them. Add cherries, cut into quarters, juice from cherries, and juice of the lemon. Add peach syrup if necessary to make 4 cups of fruit mixture. Combine with sugar, bring to boiling point, and boil hard for 2 minutes. Stir almost constantly during the cooking. Remove from heat, stir in pectin, and let stand for 5 minutes, stirring frequently. Turn into hot sterilized jars and seal. Makes about six ½-pint jars.

PEAR-RASPBERRY JAM

Thaw 1 package (10 ounces) frozen raspberries. Peel and core about 2 pounds fully ripe pears and force them through medium blade of food chopper. Measure raspberries and enough ground pears to make 4 cups fruit. Put in kettle with ¼ cup fresh lemon juice, 1 tablespoon grated orange rind, and 6 cups sugar. Bring to full rolling boil over high heat; boil hard for 1 minute, stirring. Remove from heat and stir in half of 6-ounce bottle of liquid pectin. Skim off foam. Continue stirring and skimming for 5 minutes to prevent floating fruit. Ladle into hot sterilized jars and seal. Makes seven or eight ½-pint jars.

JAMS MADE WITHOUT COOKING

NO-COOK BLACKBERRY JAM

2 cups fully ripe blackberries (about 1
   quart)
4 cups sugar
2 tablespoons fresh lemon juice
½ bottle liquid pectin

Crush berries. (*For a less seedy jam, allow 1 more cup berries; strain half the berries and discard this half of the pulp.) Put fruit in large bowl and add sugar. Mix well. Combine lemon juice and pectin, and add to fruit. Continue stirring for 3 minutes. If a few sugar crystals remain they will do no harm. Pour into glasses or freezer jars. Cover with tight lids and let stand 24 hours to set. Store in freezer or for up to 3 weeks in refrigerator. Makes six ½-pint jars.

No-Cook Red-Raspberry Jam

Substitute red raspberries for blackberries in recipe above. Makes about six ½-pint jars.

No-Cook Strawberry Jam

Substitute 1¾ cups crushed strawberries for 2 cups berries in No-Cook Blackberry Jam recipe. Makes about five ½-pint jars.

No-Cook Peach Jam

2¾ cups peeled, pitted, and ground
   peaches (about 2¼ pounds, whole)
6½ cups sugar
⅓ cup fresh lemon juice
1 bottle liquid pectin

Proceed as in No-Cook Blackberry Jam recipe. Makes about nine ½-pint jars.

No-Cook Sour Cherry Jam

1¾ cups pitted and ground sour cherries
   (about 1 quart)
4 cups sugar
¼ cup fresh lemon juice
½ bottle liquid pectin

Proceed as in No-Cook Blackberry Jam recipe. Makes about five ½-pint jars.

JAMAICAN SOUPS

by Leila Hadley

Hearty and deliciously different, these soups capture the flavor of one of the loveliest islands in the Caribbean. Admittedly, there is something in my nature that finds much of the Caribbean cuisine unappealing. Roasted breadfruit sings no siren song for me. I have no truck with peanut stew, and I turn a rich shade of antique green when confronted with curried goat. Sweet-potato pone makes my teeth scream with anguish. To my notion, the best cooking is simply the best there is, but not necessarily the strangest or the most complicated or the most original.

And so, on coming to live in Jamaica, it was a matter of pure joy to find that no matter how disturbingly sweet and glutinous their pudding desserts, nor how scaringly seasoned their meat curries, the Jamaicans are masters at the preparation of fish and soup.

When fish and soup come together in a chowder, the combination is delectable and soul-warming. If you don't want to cope with anything more than a one-dish meal, yet feel like something more inventive than chicken, more delicate than steak, a fish chowder such as the one I'm about to describe is the perfect solution. At lunch or supper, accompanied by a green salad, hot buttered popovers, some fruit, or perhaps lemon sherbet with an extra tang of grated lemon, it makes a thoroughly delicious and satisfying meal. Jamaicans are connoisseurs of fish, and savor their fish bright-eyed and firm-fleshed, fresh from the sea. So in the morning, when the fishermen return in their dugout canoes, we go down to the beach to do our marketing. No matter how early we go, the higglers are there before us. The higglers (a polite corruption of the word hagglers) are the local peddlers. Traditionally, the fish higglers are women whose speech, colorful as their bright-printed cotton skirts, is shot through with startling endearments. "My darlin'," one of the women says, bargaining with a fisherman straight from his boat with a basket of fish, "you greedy as a old hog for make me pay such a price. Man, you two-face like a star-apple leaf. You is a real terrible t'ief for true."

She walks away, her hips penduluming with indignation, but the round wicker basket she balances on her head is nevertheless filled with fish. Purple doctorfish with curious smiling mouths, groupers, parrot fish—turquoise and shining—and red-spotted butterfish. After doing a little higgling myself, I buy shrimps, a lively lobster, a mirror-smooth kingfish, and a snapper the color of a pink sunset, all carefully weighed on a battered brass-pan scale.

Back home again in the kitchen, Miss Gladys, our cook, sets the final seal on my shopping pleasure by saying, "Them didn't rob you. Everything them lovely for true, Mistress." So now we are ready to make the chowder. By the way, if you live inland where fresh lobster and shrimps aren't available, there's no reason why you shouldn't use frozen seafood. Don't let the long list of ingredients put you off. The recipe, which appears on page 967, is actually simpler than it looks.

Another house specialty of ours is a Jamaican Pepperpot, and I'm sure that somewhere in the pot is a touch of white magic. For after that first spoonful has spread its influence on tongue and palate, strong taciturn men, previously all too plainly impervious to my charms as a temptress, have indicated in giddy phrases that I am the moon of all delight. Women, who would just as soon shred me into pieces and clap me into a Saratoga trunk, dimple at me sweetly, kowtow with fitting humility, and beg me to give them the recipe.

This Jamaican soup is an island specialty, and although there are innumerable ways of making it, this is the way it is prepared at the Myrtle Bank, the oldest hotel in Kingston, justly famed for its charm and comfort. In the evening, the tourists, unburdened of their complex of cameras, raffia-embroidered straw hats and baskets, souvenir shells and bundles of duty-free merchandise, sit out in the cool of the broad hotel veranda, listening to the palm trees clacking in the wind. Down by the bar, the band strikes up a Jamaican *mento*, or work song, soft and pleasing, and then sends out an animated Trinidadian calypso. A departing liner gives a resonant farewell hoot. The fireflies in the moonlit garden flash mating signals to each other. In a pleasantly lazy, calypso-collapse mood, you go in to dinner and, with a certain well-bred greediness, you wait for the pepperpot soup to appear.

MYRTLE BANK
JAMAICAN PEPPERPOT SOUP

2 pounds spinach (locally known by the fetching name of Callaloo!) or 2 packages (10 ounces each) frozen spinach, thawed
2 pounds beef, cut into 1-inch cubes
½ pound diced salt pork
3 onions, coarsely chopped
4 cups water
½ teaspoon dried thyme
3 scallions or chives, minced
1 seeded green pepper, minced
1 bay leaf
2 tomatoes, sliced
2 teaspoons salt
⅛ teaspoon cayenne or ½ teaspoon freshly ground black pepper
12 okras, stemmed
Butter
½ cup heavy cream
Paprika

Wash spinach, drain thoroughly, then chop coarsely. Put in large soup pot and add beef, salt pork, onions, and water. Bring these ingredients to the boiling point and then let simmer gently for 1 hour. Add thyme, scallions, green pepper, bay leaf, tomatoes, salt, and cayenne; allow to simmer for about 30 minutes. Slice okras into rings and sauté gently in butter. They musn't brown but must absorb the butter as flowers absorb the sun. Add them to the soup for last 10 minutes of cooking time. Just before serving, add cream. Sprinkle each serving with a wisp of paprika. Makes about 6 servings.

JAMAICAN SPLIT-PEA SOUP

2 cups split peas
2 onions, coarsely chopped
6 cups water
3 cups chicken or beef bouillon or consommé
Salt and pepper
4 strips of bacon, cooked and crumbled
Croutons

Boil split peas and onions in water for 30 minutes. Then simmer for 1½ hours. Whirl this purée in a blender for a few seconds. Return to pot and add bouillon. Season to taste. Garnish with crumbled bacon and croutons. Makes about 6 servings.

JAMAICAN CONGO-PEA
OR KIDNEY-BEAN SOUP

4 cups water
½ cup Congo peas (pigeon peas) or kidney beans
¼ pound salt pork or a ham bone with meat

1 bay leaf
4 peppercorns
Milk or light cream
Croutons
Chopped parsley

Bring water to a rapid boil. Drop peas in slowly so as not to lower boiling point. When last pea has been added, add meat, bay leaf, and peppercorns; simmer for about 2½ hours, or until peas are soft. Remove meat and mince finely. Whirl soup in a blender and return to the pot. Return meat. Thin soup as desired with milk. Garnish with croutons and parsley. Makes about 6 servings.

CHICKEN SOUP WITH SHERRY

Bones and scraps of 1 chicken
2 onions, chopped
2 teaspoons salt
½ teaspoon ground ginger
8 cups water
3 tablespoons sherry

Put chicken bones and scraps, onions, salt, and ginger in the pot with cold water and quickly bring to a boil. Reduce heat and simmer for 1½ hours. Add sherry and simmer for another 30 minutes. Strain, and serve. Very easy and very good. Makes about 6 servings.

JAMAICAN ONION SOUP WITH CHEESE

2 tablespoons soft butter
2 egg yolks
2 cups milk
1 can (10½ ounces) condensed consommé with enough water added to make 2 cups
1 cup sautéed, coarsely chopped onions
½ cup grated Gruyère cheese
Salt and pepper

Beat butter together with egg yolks. When thoroughly mixed, add milk and consommé. Bring to boiling point, stirring as you go. Reduce heat. Add onions, cheese, and salt and pepper to taste. Serve piping hot. Makes about 6 servings.

KINGSTON POTATO SOUP

6 tablespoons butter
6 leeks, sliced
2 onions, sliced
6 large potatoes, sliced
6 cups chicken bouillon
½ cup cooked green peas
Dash of cayenne
1½ teaspoons salt
1 cup milk
1 avocado, peeled and sliced

Melt butter in a saucepan. Add leeks and onions and sauté until golden-brown. Add potatoes and bouillon and let simmer for 30 to 40 minutes. When potatoes are well done, put soup through a sieve or whirl in a blender. Return to saucepan, add peas, cayenne, and salt, and cook for 5 minutes longer. Thin with heated milk. Place a slice or two of avocado in each soup plate and pour the soup over the avocado. Serve very hot. Makes about 6 servings.

JAMAICAN FISH CHOWDER
Fish

1 large or 2 small lobsters
1 pound shrimps
2 pounds fish fillets (cod or haddock)

Fish Stock

8 cups water
1 carrot, coarsely chopped
1 onion, coarsely chopped
1 celery stalk, coarsely chopped
1 garlic clove
1 bay leaf
1½ tablespoons salt
6 peppercorns
2 whole cloves
½ lemon

Chowder

½ cup olive oil
¾ cup sliced onions
1 tablespoon minced garlic
¼ cup parsley leaves
½ teaspoon dried basil
1 bay leaf
3 peppercorns
2 cups (one 1-pound can) solid-pack tomatoes
½ teaspoon salt
Pinch of ground saffron
¼ teaspoon grated lemon rind
1 cup dry white wine, or more

Garnish

3 tablespoons minced parsley

If you have brought home a live lobster, start by plunging it into enough boiling water to cover it generously. Add 2 tablespoons salt for each quart of water. When the water has returned to a rollicking boil, count the cooking time from this minute and allow 5 minutes for each pound of lobster. Remove the lobster from the water with kitchen tongs. When it is cool enough to handle, clip out the hard sac near the head, remove the dark intestinal vein, and draw out the meat from the shell. Cut the meat into serving pieces. If you've brought home a cooked lobster, all you have to do is remove the meat from the shell, discard the intestinal vein and the hard sac near the head, and cut the meat into serving pieces. Cover the chunks and put them in the refrigerator. Don't save the water in which the lobster was boiled in the hope you can use it for the stock. Take my word for it, you can't.

Now on to the shrimps, the fish, and the fish stock. Wash, shell, and devein the raw shrimps. Set aside. Cut the filleted fish into 2-inch cubes, wrap cubes in wax paper, and refrigerate until needed. Next step is to simmer for 10 to 15 minutes all the ingredients listed under Fish Stock. Then add the fish scraps, if you had a whole fish, and the shrimps. Let these simmer for 10 minutes. Let the shrimps cool in the stock. Remove shrimps and store them, covered, in the refrigerator until needed. Strain the stock and set aside.

Now then, get out a large soup pot. Pour in olive oil and place the pot over medium heat. Add sliced onions, minced garlic, and parsley leaves. Cook and stir until these are lightly browned. Then add basil, bay leaf, peppercorns, tomatoes, salt, and saffron. Simmer these ingredients, covered, for 30 minutes. You may want to place a slice of toast in each soup plate and, if so, now is a good time to make the toast. Some people prefer plain crackers with the chowder, but others prefer the chowder ladled over a slice of toast plus a liberal offering of popovers. After the soup has simmered for 30 minutes, add stock. Stir. Then add fish cubes, and do give these a last-minute pinch to find any bones that might have remained. Let fish simmer for 10 minutes. Then add lobster, shrimps, and lemon rind, and let this supreme concoction simmer for 5 more minutes. Add white wine, ladle the chowder into soup plates, garnish with minced parsley, and bring to the table at once! Makes about 6 servings.

PUMPKIN SOUP

Scooped-out chunks and pulp of a large pumpkin
2 onions, coarsely chopped
2 teaspoons salt
⅛ teaspoon cayenne
4 cups chicken bouillon
1 teaspoon grated onion
½ cup heavy cream, whipped
Pepper

Remove the seeds and strings from pumpkin. Add pumpkin, coarsely chopped onions, and salt and cayenne to bouillon and simmer until pumpkin is tender. Put soup through a sieve or whirl in a blender. Reheat to boiling point, but do not allow to boil. Just before serving, add grated onion. Top each serving with whipped cream and a grating of freshly ground black pepper. Makes 6 servings.

JAMBALAYA—A New Orleans Creole dish, made with combinations of ham, sausage, fowl, shrimps, oysters, tomatoes, onions, garlic, and other seasonings.

The origin of the dish is obscure, although it is evidently based upon elements of French and Spanish cooking. The Spanish *paella,* a mixture of rice, meat, and seafood, is a close relative. The origin of the name is obscure, too. It may derive from the French word for "ham," *jambon,* or it may come more directly from a Provençal word, *jambalaia* meaning "a dish of rice and fowl."

Jambalayas make excellent party dishes since they can be prepared beforehand. For a party, cook the jambalaya until it is almost done, refrigerate, and finish cooking just before serving. A green salad is a good accompaniment, and a creamy bland dessert provides a pleasant flavor contrast to the well-seasoned jambalaya.

CREOLE JAMBALAYA
    2 tablespoons butter
    1 pound raw smoked ham, coarsely
        diced
    2 large onions, chopped
    2 garlic cloves, minced
    1 medium green pepper, cut up
 4⅔ cups (two 1-pound, 3-ounce cans)
        tomatoes
    3 cups meat broth or 2 chicken cubes
        and 3 cups water
    1 bay leaf, crushed
  ½ teaspoon dried thyme
  ½ teaspoon chili powder
  ¼ teaspoon pepper
    2 cups long-grain rice
    1 pound fresh shrimps, cooked,
        shelled, and cleaned or 1 package
        (12 ounces) frozen shelled cleaned
        shrimps, cooked

Melt butter in top-of-stove casserole or Dutch oven. Add ham, onion, and garlic; cook until lightly browned. Add remaining ingredients except rice and shrimps and bring to boil. Gradually stir in rice. Cover and simmer for 30 minutes, or until rice is tender and liquid is absorbed. Add shrimps, and more seasoning if desired. Makes 6 servings.

JAPANESE COOKERY

a gourmet's
tour of
the exotic
and economical,
nutritious
and delicious
cookery of Japan.

Although some Japanese dishes seem very foreign to Americans, there are many of them that are ideally suited to our everyday life. They have many advantages, chief of which is their economy and healthfulness. Because meat is expensive in Japan, it is stretched with vegetables, and fish, which is plentiful, is used in many fascinating ways. Raw fish is eaten in the form of *sushi* and *sashimi* but it is more often served cooked. Few Japanese kitchens have ranges, as we have, so much of the food is cooked on a *hibachi* (a small grill) by broiling, steaming, boiling, and frying. Baked or roasted dishes are practically unknown.

One of the most entrancing things about Japanese food is its beauty. As much care is taken with the arrangement of the food, its color contrast, and even shape, as with the cooking and seasoning. This makes it especially appropriate for party food, when one wants the meal to look as attractive as possible. Also *nabe* cookery (cooking at the table) is wonderful for the busy hostess with no help. The guests do their own cooking and love it.

Japanese meals are served very differently from American ones. Not only because the guests sit on the floor, eat from low, usually individual, tables, and use chopsticks, but because the order in which the courses are served is very different from ours. For instance, although they have delicious soups, they do not necessarily come at the beginning of the meal. They don't have salads as we know them, and rice or noodles take the place of bread. Green tea is the national beverage, but beer is popular and sake, heated and served in tiny cups, is often served throughout the meal. Fruit is served as dessert, especially melons, berries, and tangerines, but the Japanese have sweets, usually made of bean paste, that are more appealing to Americans' eyes than to their palates. Pickles are very popular, as are salted plums (a breakfast treat), and vegetables. These and the other ingredients used in these recipes can be found in Japanese markets in large American cities. Recipes, unless otherwise noted, serve 6, and there is no reason in the world why they can't be incorporated into a meal that is otherwise typical of the United States.

GLOSSARY

JAPANESE INGREDIENT	TRANSLATION	SUBSTITUTE
Aburage	Fried soybean curd*	None
Ajinomoto	Monosodium glutamate	
Azuki	Japanese red beans	Red kidney beans
Beni-shoga	Pickled gingerroot*	Soak crystallized gingerroot in vinegar
Daikon	Japanese radish	Radish, perfectly white
Dashi	Japanese soup stock	Fish, chicken stock, consommé, or recipe at right
Ginko	Ginkgo nuts*	None
Kamaboko	Fish cakes *	Recipe, page 972
Katsuobushi	Dried bonito*	Dried shrimps
Konbu	Seaweed*	None
Matsutake	Wild mushrooms*	Regular mushrooms may be substituted, but the taste is not comparable
Mirin	Japanese wine	Sherry or whisky
Miso	Fermented bean paste*	Recipe at right
Nori	Seaweed in sheets*	None
Nou	Variety of seaweed*	None
Sake	Rice wine	Dry beer or dry white wine
Sashimi	Sliced raw fish	
Sembei	Soy-coated rice cracker*	None
Shichimi togarashi	Seven spices: mixture of pepper, poppy seed, cayenne, sesame, orange peel, hemp seed, and seaweed*	None
Shiitake	Mushrooms (a variety cultivated on trees)*	Regular mushrooms may be substituted, but the taste is not comparable
Shinsen-shoga	Fresh gingerroot*	Crystallized gingerroot, rinsed of sugar
Shirataki	Cellophane, transparent, or yam noodles*	Fine noodles or vermicelli
Shoyu	Japanese soy sauce	Soy sauce
Shungiku	Edible chrysanthemum*	None
Soba	Buckwheat noodles*	Fine noodles
Somen	Fine noodles	
Tofu	Soybean curd*	Tiny dumplings
Udon	Broad noodles	
Wasabi	Horseradish	
Yakidofu	Broiled bean curd*	None

* Available in Japanese food stores

EXAMPLES OF JAPANESE MEALS

BREAKFAST

Rice; *miso shiru* (bean paste soup); egg; *tsukudami* (fish cooked in *shoyu*); *konomono* (pickles); *umeboski* (salted plum); tea. The egg is usually raw, beaten with *shoyu* and poured over the hot rice.

NOON MEAL

Rice or any noodles (soba, udon, or somen); boiled vegetables; broiled fish; tea.

DINNER

Rice; *suimono* (clear soup); *sashimi* (raw fish); broiled or fried fish; *chawan mushi* (steamed custard); *tsukemono* (pickles); *tempura;* tea.

HOT TOWELS

This is a lovely Japanese custom, passed after any food is served. The towels (our fingertip terry towels are ideal) are wrung out in very hot water, rolled up tight, and passed to each guest while still steaming hot. A good way to do this is to wet the towels in hot water, twist each one into a figure eight, and keep on a hot tray, covered with foil, until time to serve.

DASHI
(Soup Stock)

This is the Japanese national soup stock, used in many recipes. It can be bought in little envelopes, like large tea bags, and made by boiling in water according to directions on the package.

4 cups water
Konbu
Shaved katsuobushi
½ teaspoon ajinomoto

Use a piece of *konbu* about 4 inches square. Put in the water and bring to a boil. Remove *konbu* and add shaved *katsuobushi,* available already shaved or in a rocklike piece; dried shrimps may be used instead. Add the amount specified on the package. Bring again to a boil and remove from heat. Add *ajinomoto.* When *katsuobushi* sinks to bottom of pot, pour off the clear liquid. This is *dashi,* and many of these recipes call for it. Makes about 4 cups.

MISO
(Fermented Bean Paste)

Miso is available in Japanese markets. If not available, this is a fairly reasonable facsimile

1 cup dried beans, white or pinto
2 tablespoons Japanese rice vinegar
2 tablespoons mirin
1 teaspoon salt

Cook beans in water to cover until they are very soft, adding more water to keep from sticking. Drain; mash smooth or whirl in a blender. Add remaining ingredients. Makes about 3 cups.

 ## SOUPS

SUIMONO
(Clear Soup)

This clear soup is simply *dashi,* sometimes with a few drops of *shoyu* added, with some beautiful garnish. The garnish may be almost anything: a few green peas, a thinly sliced mushroom, a chicken gizzard cut like a chrysanthemum (cut a half gizzard into squares, almost to the bottom; when cooked it will open up like a flower), a few slices of carrot cut with a tiny scalloped cutter, a lemon slice, a split shrimp or two, a triangle egg (drop a raw egg into the corner of a piece of greased foil folded into quarters, stand foil on point, and cook in boiling water), a few matchlike pieces of turnip, carrot, or onion, watercress leaves, shreds of chicken. Often two or three things are used. For instance, half a split shrimp, 2 slices of mushroom, 5 green peas. Whatever it is, it must look pretty!

TAMAGO SUIMONO
(Egg Soup)

    6 cups dashi (page 970)
    1 tablespoon shoyu
    4 eggs
    4 green onions, minced

Heat *dashi,* add *shoyu,* and bring to a boil. Beat eggs well, turn off heat under soup, and stir in eggs gradually, beating constantly. The eggs will set. Divide among 6 bowls and garnish each portion with a little of the minced onion. Makes 6 servings.

MISO SHIRU
(Bean Paste Soup)

    4 cups dashi (page 970)
    ½ pound (¾ cup) miso (page 970)

Heat *dashi* to a boil. Add *miso* and cook until *miso* is melted. Add almost anything—shredded *daikon* or sliced green onions, for instance. *Aburage* is often cut into squares and added. Makes 4 servings.

CHAWAN-MUSHI
(Steamed Custard)

This delicious dish may be served as a soup or a first course. In Japan, it's served warm, but when cold it is a delightful beginning for a summer meal. It is usually made with chicken or shrimps, often with both.

    1 chicken breast, boned (about 10 ounces)
    6 medium shrimps (optional)
    6 eggs
    3 cups dashi (page 970)
    2 tablespoons sake
    ⅓ cup shoyu
    3 medium-large mushroom caps
    ¼ cup cooked peas or 18 canned ginkgo nuts
    3 green onions, sliced thin
    3 water chestnuts, sliced thin or 6 thin slices of bamboo shoot
    6 spinach leaves or 6 small watercress springs

Use cooked chicken breast and shrimps or—and this is preferable—steam raw

shelled and cleaned shrimps and skinned and boned chicken breast over boiling water or *dashi* for 5 minutes. They will be firm enough to slice, but still juicy.

Beat eggs slightly and add cooled *dashi,* sake, and *shoyu;* mix well. Slice chicken and/or shrimps as thin as possible (or dice, if you prefer); slice mushrooms (if raw ones are used, they must be paper-thin); divide these ingredients evenly among six 1-cup bowls or custard cups. Add the other ingredients (any or all), cutting the greens into shreds and dividing everything as evenly as possible. Strain the egg mixture over all and steam over simmering water for 10 to 15 minutes, or until the custard is set. Overcooking will ruin the dish. Serve each bowl with a thin slice of lemon, if desired. Makes 6 servings.

 **FISH AND SEAFOOD**

CHIRINABE
(Fish Sukiyaki)

    6 cups dashi (page 970)
    ¼ cup sake
    2 pounds fish
    8 green onions, sliced
    3 squares tofu
    1 pound spinach or edible chrysanthemum
      Juice of 3 lemons
    1 ounce grated fresh gingerroot
    1 lemon, sliced

Heat *dashi* and sake in a chafing dish, electric skillet, or *sukiyaki cooker.* Cut fish into pieces, bones and all (the Japanese include head and tail). Add about one-fourth of it to stock. Add 1 of the onions, about one-fourth of *tofu* (each piece cut into 4 or 6 squares), and one-third of spinach leaves. Bring to a boil and add ingredients again, a few at a time. Each guest helps himself to a ladleful of the soup and uses his chopsticks to eat the solids directly from the common pot. They are dipped into the lemon juice and grated gingerroot, which are divided among the guests. The sliced lemon is a garnish. Makes 6 servings.

SASHIMI
(Sliced Raw Fish)

This is just raw fish without benefit of *sushi* rice. The fish, which must be very very fresh, is boned and sliced ¼ inch thin or thinner, then cut into pieces about 1 by 2 inches. Serve with grated horse-radish, *daikon,* and gingerroot, *shoyu* and

mustard. Each guest mixes his own sauce and dips fish into it with chopsticks. Bonito, albacore, shrimps, and scallops are popular for *sashimi,* although other fish are also used.

NIGIRI SUSHI
(Raw Fish Rice Ball)

    Raw tuna fish
    Grated fresh horseradish
    Cooked Sushi Rice
    Shoyu

Slice the tuna ¼ inch thick and cut into pieces 2 inches long and 1 inch wide. Sprinkle a little grated horseradish (or grated gingerroot) on it. Then pick up some of the rather gooey rice (about 2 tablespoons) and form it into an oval. Put a slice of fish on top and mold as symmetrically as possible. Serve with *shoyu.* Mackerel, clams, whitefish, prawns, and other fish can be used the same way. If you can't bear the idea of raw fish, use smoked salmon.

Sushi Rice

    1 pound polished rice
    2½ cups water
    1¼ cups white vinegar
    3 tablespoons salt

Wash rice 3 hours before cooking. Boil water, add rice, and bring to a rolling boil. Then lower heat and cook until rice is tender and water absorbed. Spread out in a shallow bowl. Cool quickly by fanning. (If you have an electric fan, fine!) Mix in 1¼ cups white vinegar (preferably Japanese) and 3 tablespoons salt. You now have *sushi* rice.

TEMPURA
(Tempura)

Many Americans think of *tempura* as shrimps dipped into batter and fried in deep fat. That is one form, and a very good one, but in Japan all kinds of seafood and vegetables are also used. Some, such as ginkgo nuts in little edible seaweed baskets and shoots of young ginger, are impossible for us to find. The food should be fried at the table and served immediately. An electric skillet or deep fryer is fine, or a *tempura nabe* (cooker), which must be used over an electric plate.

Ingredients (use any or all):

    Shrimps, shelled and cleaned
    Small fish, cleaned but whole
    Clams, scallops, mussels, or oysters, shelled but whole
    Lobster, cut into slices across the grain
    Fillet of fish, cut into strips with the

grain
Mushrooms, sliced if large, whole if small
Spinach, whole perfect leaves
Carrots, cut into thin diagonal slices
Green onions, cut into thin diagonal slices or whole if small
Celery, cut into thin diagonal slices
Chinese or snow peas, whole, strings removed
Eggplant, cut like French-fried potatoes
Sweet potatoes, cut into thin slices
Watercress, whole sprigs
String beans, whole, cooked for 5 minutes

Batter:

2 eggs
¾ cup all-purpose flour
1 cup water
1 tablespoon cornstarch
½ teaspoon salt
½ teaspoon baking powder
Peanut or other cooking oil

Beat eggs until fluffy, add remaining ingredients, and mix—a few lumps are of no concern to the Japanese. Have plenty of oil heated to 350°F. on a frying thermometer and have all ingredients dry. Dip into batter; shrimps may be held by their tails; spinach, watercress, and small green onions by the stems; other ingredients may be dropped into the batter, then lifted out with a slotted spoon or tongs and allowed to drain for a second before putting into the fat. The batter coating should be very thin. The Japanese sometimes shake a few extra drops of the batter onto the food in the fat, using their chopsticks. This makes little beads of crispness on the food. Small pieces of food, such as string beans or snow peas, are usually dipped and fried 2 or 3 at a time. The food is turned so that it will brown evenly, then drained; the tempura cooker has a perforated shelf for this purpose; a cake rack on a plate does nicely. The food should be served on a paper napkin, to absorb extra fat, as soon as it is done. Each guest should dip his portion into the Sauce (below) and eat at once. (If preferred, *shoyu* alone may be used for sauce.) The hostess may officiate at the cooking, or guests may take turns cooking while the others eat. Usually one variety of food is cooked and served at a time, as shrimps, fish, mushrooms, beans, etc. Makes enough batter for 6 servings.

Sauce

1 cup dashi (page 970)
⅓ cup shoyu
⅓ cup sake
Sugar to taste (optional)

Combine all ingredients and mix well. Each guest should be given a small dish of sauce, and grated radish and grated fresh gingerroot should be on hand to add to it.

Note: In Japan, small amounts of anything left—not enough to go around—are chopped, stirred into the remaining batter, then dropped by spoonfuls into the fat—a mixed fritter!

TENDON, short for TEMPURA DOMBURI
(Tempura over rice served in a covered casserole)

Tendon, in its simplest form, is shrimps or lobster fried like *tempura,* but served on a bed of rice. Sometimes watercress or other vegetables are cooked like *tempura* and added to the shrimps and the sauce is poured over all. Instead of rice, the Japanese noodles (*udon*) or buckwheat noodles (*soba*) may be used.

TEMPURA SEMBEI
(Cracker-Fried Shrimps)

This is very appealing to the occidental palate. It can be made with any fish or shellfish, but is perhaps best made with jumbo shrimps.

2 pounds jumbo shrimps or prawns
2 eggs
1 teaspoon shoyu
1 cup sembei crumbs (see note)
Fat for deep frying

Shell shrimps, split down the back, remove veins, and open. Beat eggs slightly; add *shoyu.* Roll *sembei* or whirl in the blender to make crumbs. Dip shrimps into egg mixture, then into crumbs, and allow to dry for 30 minutes. Fry in deep fat (360°F. on frying thermometer) until nicely browned, 2 to 3 minutes. Serve with *tempura* sauce. Makes 4 servings.

Note: *Sembei* are Japanese crackers. There are many varieties, but the one to use here is the small salty one with a shiny varnished look.

TEMPURA SOBA
(Fried Shrimps with Noodles)

This is very good. Cook a bundle (10 to 12 ounces) of *soba* until tender. Put in a *domburi* (casserole) and top with small strips of lemon peel and with *tempura* of small shrimps, *Kamaboko* (see recipe below), shellfish such as clams, and assorted vegetables. Serve with *Kakejiru* (see recipe at right above)

Kamaboko
(Fish Cakes)

Kamaboko are available in Japanese markets. If you can't get them, here is a recipe.

1 pound fillet of any white fish
2 tablespoons cornstarch
1 teaspoon sugar
½ teaspoon ajinomoto
Water

Grind fish, add cornstarch, sugar, *ajinomoto,* and just enough water to make a thick paste. Knead well, form into a sausage-shape, or mound on a narrow clean board so that you have a half-cylinder, and steam for 15 minutes. Slice before dipping into batter for *tempura.* Makes 6 to 8 servings.

Kakejiru
(Sauce)

3 cups dashi (page 970)
3 tablespoons shoyu
½ teaspoon sugar
½ teaspoon ajinomoto

Heat *dashi,* add other ingredients, and serve.

ONIGARI YAKI
(Broiled Shrimps)

These are delicious and make a delicious appetizer served before an occidental meal. Allow 6 medium-size shrimps for each person. Leave them whole, with the shells on, and thread 3 on each bamboo skewer, putting the skewer first just below the head (or where the head would have been), then near the tail, so that each shrimp is U-shape. Cook together ¾ cup shoyu, ½ cup *mirin,* and 2 teaspoons sugar (the sugar can be omitted to appeal more to American palates) for 4 or 5 minutes. Soak shrimps in this mixture, then broil over charcoal or in the oven, basting with the marinade. Don't overcook—5 or 6 minutes should suffice.

Note: You and your guests may be happier if the shrimps are shelled before cooking, but if they're not, be sure to serve hot towels after this dish has been eaten.

NUTA
(Seafood Salad)

1 pound raw scallops
3 bunches green onions, sliced
1 teaspoon salt
¼ cup miso
1 tablespoon sugar
2 tablespoons vinegar
2 tablespoons ajinomoto
1 large head celery
2 cups shredded daikon or sliced radish
Lettuce

Cut scallops into thin slices; use raw, or cook for 2 minutes. Blanch green onions. Mix salt, *miso,* sugar, vinegar, and *ajinomoto.* Combine with vegetables and scallops. Serve cold on shredded lettuce. Makes 4 to 6 servings.

Sashimi   Onigari Yaki
Butaniku-Teriyaki

Nuta
Tempura Sembei

MEAT

JYUNIKU-TERIYAKI
(Broiled Beef)
2 pounds beef tenderloin
1 tablespoon grated fresh gingerroot
¼ cup shoyu
1 garlic clove, mashed
¼ cup mirin
2 tablespoons peanut oil

The meat may be cut into individual steaks; or cut into ⅛-inch slices and then into strips, then woven on bamboo skewers; or it may be cut into ¾-inch cubes and strung on skewers. Mix gingerroot, *shoyu*, garlic, and *mirin* and marinate skewered meat for 1 hour. Brush with oil and broil or sauté, basting with the marinade. The meat should be shiny when done, but not dried out. Time of cooking varies with the thickness of the meat. This may be used as an appetizer or an entrée. Makes 6 to 8 servings.
Note: Although *teriyaki* may be made with fish or chicken, beef is the most popular.

BUTANIKU-TERIYAKI
(Broiled Pork)
2 pounds lean pork, cut into ¾-inch cubes
½ cup shoyu
¼ cup sake
2 tablespoons sugar
1 garlic clove, crushed (optional)
½ ounce fresh gingerroot, sliced

Marinate meat in other ingredients for 1 hour, turning once. Broil over charcoal or in a broiler, basting with the marinade and turning so that all sides become brown and shiny. Cook until pork is thoroughly done, but not dry, for 20 to 25 minutes. Makes 6 to 8 servings.

UMANI
(Meatballs)
½ pound ground beef or pork
1 tablespoon water
Cornstarch
1½ cups water
3 tablespoons shoyu
½ teaspoon sugar
½ teaspoon ajinomoto
1 cup sliced carrots
1 cup cooked string beans

Mix meat with water and 1 tablespoon cornstarch and form into small balls. Combine water, *shoyu*, sugar, and *ajinomoto* and cook meatballs in it for 10 minutes. Remove meatballs and cook carrots in same sauce. Return meatballs to mixture and add beans. Heat, and serve. Makes 4 servings.

NABE RYORI
Nabe ryori means "cooking at the table," and is an ancient form of Japanese cookery, which is growing in popularity in this country. Called "friendship dishes," the best known is *sukiyaki*, but there are many others, some included here. *Mizutaki*, originally just chicken, precooked in the kitchen and finished at the table, is now made with other meats and can include vegetables. A *hokotsu*, or copper cooker with a chimney for charcoal, surrounded by a moat for the cooking food, is used in Japan, but a Japanese casserole or *domburi*, placed on a charcoal burner or electric plate, is also used. An electric skillet makes a fine table cooker.

SUKIYAKI
(Plough-Roasted)
This is the Japanese dish best known to Americans. It can be made in many different ways, and is. It is inexpensive, low in calories, and good eating. This basic recipe may be varied to suit, and American vegetables can take the place of Japanese ones.

1 cup mirin
1 cup shoyu
1 teaspoon ajinomoto
2 pounds beef tenderloin or sirloin
1 cup beef suet
2 large onions
6 green onions
1 or 2 bamboo shoots
1 can tofu
1 small can shirataki
 Optional: Spinach, mushrooms, carrots, Chinese cabbage, celery, eggplant, bean sprouts, watercress, snow peas
 Sugar
6 raw eggs

First make the *warishita*, which is the cooking mixture, by combining *mirin*, *shoyu*, and *ajinomoto*. Some people use *shoyu* and sugar, thinned with *dashi*. Have mixture in a pitcher at the table. The beef is preferably tenderloin or sirloin, but as it is sliced paper-thin, it does not have to be top grade. It is easier to slice if it is partially frozen, but Japanese markets sell it sliced. Arrange it tastefully. Cut suet into 3 or 4 pieces. Cut onions into halves from top to bottom, then slice ⅜ inch thick. Cut green onions into 2-inch pieces. Slice bamboo shoot. Cut *tofu* into 1-inch cubes. Drain *shirataki* (if dried *shirataki* is used, soak in cold water for 2 hours and cut into 4-inch lengths). The optional vegetables are sliced thin, except spinach leaves and watercress which are stemmed, and snow

peas, which are trimmed of tips and strings. Arrange all these attractively as possible on bamboo trays or dishes. Use electric skillet or put *sukiyaki* pan on the table over heat. Using chopsticks, put the suet in the pan and rub around so that it melts. Add about ¼ of ingredients at a time, keeping them in separate little heaps and turning with chopsticks as they cook. Sprinkle 2 teaspoons sugar over the mixture. Stir lightly. Add about ½ cup of the *warishita* and when everything is almost done, add the beef. As soon as it loses color, serve the guests with some of each ingredient and repeat the procedure. Each guest breaks his own egg into a small bowl, beats it with his chopsticks, and dips his food into it before eating, to cool food and coat it with a bland sauce. Makes 6 servings.
Note: Many Japanese start with beef, then add the *warishita* and other ingredients, but this way there is no danger of overcooking the beef.

BATAYAKI
(Butter-Cooked Meat)
1 pound beef tenderloin, sliced thin
2 onions, cut into ¼-inch slices
1 daikon, sliced
1 cucumber, sliced
4 green onions, cut into 2-inch lengths
1 bamboo shoot, sliced thin
 Sliced tofu (optional)
 Sliced mushrooms, spinach, or cooked shirataki (optional)
 Butter or beef suet
1 cup sake
½ cup shoyu
 Sugar (optional)

Batayaki is like *sukiyaki* except that it is marinated in sauce, then cooked in butter or suet. Many Americans prefer it to *sukiyaki*. Arrange beef and next 7 ingredients attractively and symmetrically on trays or plates. Heat butter in *sukiyaki* pan or electric skillet and add a few of the ingredients at a time, cooking until done to your liking. If the beef is added last, it can be cooked rare. Add more butter as needed. As soon as one batch is cooked, serve it, and add more ingredients to the pan to cook while guests are eating. For sauce to serve with *batayaki*, in small cups, combine sake, *shoyu*, and sugar to taste. Grated *daikon*, *shoyu*, mustard, and "7 spices," available at Japanese markets, are also put on the table for seasoning the sauce. Makes 4 servings.

JYUNIKU NO MIZUTAKI
(Table-Boiled Beef)
2 pounds beef, tenderloin or sirloin,

sliced paper-thin
1 Chinese cabbage
1 pound spinach
1 bamboo shoot, sliced, or one 5-ounce
   can, drained
1 tofu, cut into cubes
6 green onions, sliced diagonally
3 carrots, sliced diagonally
3 celery stalks, sliced diagonally
6 large mushrooms, sliced thin
8 cups dashi (page 970) or water
   Junidanya Sauce

Have beef sliced as for *sukiyaki* and arrange on a plate. (To make meat easier to handle, freeze until hard and then slice.) Steam Chinese cabbage and spinach until just wilted. Cool, and put a layer of the cabbage leaves on a cloth (the Japanese use a bamboo mat); on top of this put a layer of spinach leaves. With the help of the cloth, roll the long way, so that the cabbage will roll around the spinach. Press out all the moisture, then slice the roll into ½-inch slices and arrange on a plate. Also arrange, as attractively as possible, next 6 ingredients and put on the table, surrounding the cooker. Heat *dashi* in the kitchen and start charcoal outside. When ready to eat, bring hot *dashi* and glowing charcoal (in bucket with long-handled tongs) to the table. Pour about two thirds of *dashi* into cooker and immediately fill chimney with charcoal. (If you put charcoal in ahead of liquid, the solder may melt.) Now add (or have the guests add) about one third of ingredients. As the ingredients cook, the guests help themselves. The second batch is started while the guests are dipping their food into the sauce and eating it, and when that's done, the broth, now enriched, is served in cups. After the rest of the *dashi* and the ingredients are cooked, each guest mixes the remaining broth with what's left of his sauce. This is highly relished. This sounds complicated, but the ritual is the part that is most delightful, although the dish is delicious. Makes 6 servings.

Junidanya Sauce
½ cup sesame seeds
1 cup dashi (page 970)
½ cup shoyu
1 tablespoon vinegar
   Cayenne
1 tablespoon peanut oil
   Garlic (optional)

Toast the sesame seeds in a heavy dry pan, shaking until lightly browned. Grind to a paste in a mortar, or whirl in a blender. Add *dashi, shoyu,* and vinegar, stirring well. Add cayenne in judicious

amounts to the oil (Mr. Nishigaki, the originator, uses dry red peppers). If garlic is used, crush or purée it and add to taste. Each guest is given a small cup of this sauce. Also have finely minced green onions, grated gingerroot, and, if you wish, Japanese chili powder on hand for those who want to add them to the sauce. Makes about 1¼ cups.

 **POULTRY**

KUSHI-KATSU
(Fried Chicken on Skewers)
2 broiler-fryers (2½ to 3 pounds each)
1 cup sake
3 tablespoons shoyu
6 small onions
½ teaspoon salt
¼ cup all-purpose flour
2 eggs
1 cup sembei crumbs
   Deep fat
   Shoyu

Skin and bone chicken and cut meat into pieces. Marinate in sake and *shoyu* for 30 minutes. Cut onions into sixths from top to bottom. String chicken on bamboo skewers, alternating pieces with onion. Mix salt and flour and beat eggs slightly. Dip skewers into flour, then into egg, then roll in crumbs. Let stand for 30 minutes, then fry in deep fat (350°F. on a frying thermometer) until crisp and tender. Serve with *shoyu* and, if you wish, grated gingerroot and minced green onion. Makes 8 servings.

TORI NO MIZUTAKI
(Boiled Chicken)
2 broiler-fryers (2½ to 3 pounds each)
10 cups water
½ teaspoon ajinomoto
2 teaspoons salt

Sauce:
2 cups dashi (page 970)
2 tablespoons mirin
⅔ cup shoyu

Condiments:
Minced green onions
Grated gingerroot
Lemon juice

Have chicken chopped into 2-inch pieces, bones, skin, and all. Cover with water in a large pot, add *ajinomoto* and salt, and simmer, covered, until tender. Bring to the table and transfer to the cooker. You may have to do this a little at a time. Each guest helps himself to chicken with his chopsticks, dips chicken into the

sauce, and adds such condiments as desired. The sauce is made by mixing the *dashi, mirin,* and *shoyu;* each guest is given a small cupful. At the end of the meal, the delicious broth from the chicken is served to the guests in cups. Makes 6 servings.

Note: This is *mizutaki* at its simplest. In recent years many vegetables are added: sliced mushrooms, sliced onions or leek, Chinese cabbage, spinach, sliced carrots, etc.

YOSE-NABE
(Mixed Cooked Foods)
This is cooked in a *hoko-nabe,* or Japanese cooker with a chimney for hot charcoal surrounded by a "moat" in which the food is cooked. It can be a mixture of almost anything, but the following is typical.

½ pound raw shrimps
½ pound skinned and boned raw
   chicken (about 1 pound before
   skinning and boning)
2 bamboo shoots
6 green onions
½ pound fresh mushrooms or three
   4-ounce cans sliced mushrooms
1 pound spinach
2 cups dashi (page 970)
   Ponzu

Shell and clean shrimps and split. Slice chicken as thin as possible (if you steam it for a few minutes, it's easier). Slice bamboo shoots, green onions, and mushrooms. Steam spinach until limp, stack in a neat pile, and cut into ½-inch slices. Arrange ingredients attractively on a platter. Heat *dashi* and put in cooker; add hot charcoal to chimney with tongs (lacking the cooker, an electric skillet can be used). The hostess or guests add the ingredients to the hot *dashi* with chopsticks and remove them as soon as they're done. The food is dipped into *Ponzu* and eaten at once. When all the food is eaten, the by now rich soup is ladled into bowls and drunk. This amount makes 4 servings—enough for *nabe* cooking.

Ponzu
(Dipping Sauce)
½ cup shoyu
½ cup fresh lime juice
2 tablespoons grated fresh gingerroot
2 tablespoons minced green onion
2 tablespoons grated daikon

Combine *shoyu* and lime juice. Divide among 4 bowls and pass other ingredients in tiny dishes, for guests to add at will.

RICE, NOODLES, AND VEGETABLES

GOHAN
(Rice)

Wash rice very well under running water. Put in a heavy kettle with a tight-fitting lid. Add 1¼ cups cold water for each cup of rice. Cover and bring rapidly to a hard boil. Turn heat to medium-low and cook for about 12 minutes, then turn heat as low as possible for another 15 minutes. Turn off heat and let stand, still covered, for another 10 minutes before serving. If you wish, you may add ½ teaspoon salt for each cup rice at beginning of cooking.

Note: In Japan the water content of rice varies during the year and allowance for that is made in the amount of cooking water. Japanese rice is sticky, not in separate grains, to make it easier to pick up with chopsticks. The bland flavor of rice is used to offset the spicy flavor of other foods.

CHAZUKE

This is the lowliest of dishes, made with leftover rice with very hot tea poured over it—the Japanese version of milk toast. Here is a more elaborate version.

NORI-CHAZUKE
(Rice with Seaweed)
8 cups hot cooked rice
5 cups hot dashi (page 970) or tea
1 tablespoon wasabi, or to taste
Shoyu to taste
5 sheets toasted nori
2 tablespoons toasted sesame seed

Put rice in a 1½-quart *domburi*. Season *dashi* with *wasabi* and *shoyu*. Sprinkle with *nori* and sesame. Pour liquid over all and serve at once. Makes 6 to 8 servings.

Note: To toast sesame seed, cook in a heavy deep skillet, stirring, until it begins to color. Toast *nori* under the broiler until crisp. If using dried *wasabi*, moisten it in a little water first.

ODAMAKI-MUSHI
(Egg Custard Noodles)
1 pound udon
1 chicken breast, steamed
2 tablespoons shoyu
About 1 bamboo shoot, sliced (½ of 5-ounce can, or as much as needed for design)
2 green onions, sliced diagonally
3 cups dashi (page 970)
2 eggs, beaten

Cook *udon* in salted water until just tender, drain, and rinse. Divide among 6 soup bowls. Slice chicken breast thin and marinate in *shoyu* for 10 minutes. Arrange on top of *udon* along with bamboo and onions, making a design. Mix *dashi* with eggs, and divide among the bowls. Set bowls on a rack over simmering water, cover, and steam for 10 minutes. Serve at once. Makes 6 servings.

SOBA
(Buckwheat Noodles)
The Japanese are very fond of these noodles, which are delicious. They are available in Japanese markets in 14- and 16-ounce packages. Drop noodles into boiling water. When it again comes to a boil, stir, and add ½ cup cold water to stop boiling. Bring again to a boil and again add cold water. Do this 4 times altogether. Cover, turn off heat, and let stand for 15 minutes; then rinse well with cold water. Serve cold with *shoyu*. These noodles are also delicious served hot with butter.

HITASHIMONO
(Boiled Greens)
Any tender young greens such as spinach or lettuce or young turnip greens may be used. Cook them without salt in a minimum of water until tender but still green. Serve in small bowls with a mixture of 1 cup *dashi* (page 970) and ¼ cup *shoyu*.

MATSUTAKI DOBIN
(Steamed Mushrooms)
6 large mushrooms
1 teaspoon salt
2 tablespoons sake
1 chicken breast
½ pound fillet of sole or other white fish
1 bunch of watercress
¼ cup canned ginkgo nuts
1½ cups dashi (page 970)
1 tablespoon shoyu
1 tablespoon fresh lemon juice

Slice mushrooms thin and soak in salt and sake for 10 minutes. Steam chicken and fish for 8 minutes. Remove skin and bones from chicken and then slice chicken and fish. Remove stems from watercress and chop leaves. Divide mushrooms, chicken, fish, watercress, and ginkgo nuts among 6 bowls with covers. Mix *dashi*, remains of sake, *shoyu*, and lemon juice and divide among the cups. Cover and steam for 20 minutes. Makes 6 servings.

Note: *Mutsutaki*, Japanese mushrooms, look like corks from opened champagne bottles. They are available dried in some Japanese stores and may be used in this recipe. They must be soaked before using.

Canned ones are also to be found; they need no soaking. In Japan this dish is steamed in individual *dobin*, or teapots, hence the name. The juice is poured from the spout into little cups and drunk. Makes 6 servings.

OSHITASHI
(Spinach with Sesame)
1 pound spinach
¼ cup sesame seeds
¼ cup shoyu

Pile spinach evenly in stacks of 6 to 8 leaves. Lay in a skillet and pour boiling water over them. Cook for 2 minutes, or until wilted. Drain, rinse with cold water, and press all moisture from the leaves. Cut piles in 1-inch pieces. Toast sesame seeds in a dry pan until they begin to color, then crush in a mortar or whirl in a blender. Add *shoyu* and pour over spinach. Serve cold. Makes 4 servings.

NOPPE JIRU
(Vegetable Stew)
3 cups dashi (page 970) or consommé
½ cup diced daikon
¼ cup diced carrot
¼ cup diced turnip
½ cup peas
1 tablespoon shoyu
4 teaspoons cornstarch
¼ cup cold water
¼ teaspoon ajinomoto

Combine *dashi* with vegetables and cook until barely tender. Add *shoyu* and cornstarch, mixed with water and *ajinomoto*. Cook until thickened, and serve. Makes 4 servings.

GOMA-ZU
(Sauce for Vegetables)
This can be used on vegetables such as bean sprouts, spinach, cucumbers, or watercress. As the vegetables are usually served cold, the dish is comparable to a salad.

1 cup cider vinegar
1 tablespoon shoyu
1 teaspoon salt
2 tablespoons sugar, or to taste
¼ teaspoon ajinomoto
⅓ cup ground toasted sesame seeds
¼ cup mirin

Mix well before serving. Makes about 1⅔ cups.

SALADS

JUJU GAKUAN
(Salad)
Chop 3 green onions and mix with 1 large peeled and chopped cucumber. Add

Sukiyaki

2 cups mashed bean curd (cottage cheese may be substituted) and season with salt and pepper. Mix with mayonnaise (widely used in Japan) or with oil and fresh lemon juice. Makes 4 to 6 servings.

KYURI-MOMI
(Vinegared Cucumber)

1 cucumber or daikon
2 tablespoons salt
2 tablespoons sugar
3 tablespoons vinegar

Peel cucumber and slice thin. Sprinkle with salt; let stand for 30 minutes. Drain and rinse. Add sugar and vinegar, and chill. Makes 2 servings.

 DESSERTS

AWAYUKI-KAN
(Snow Gelatin)

1 envelope unflavored gelatin
1 cup water
1 cup sugar
2 egg whites
2 tablespoons fresh lemon juice

Stir gelatin into water. Let stand for 5 minutes. Heat, stirring, until gelatin is dissolved. Add sugar and stir until dissolved. Chill until it begins to thicken. Beat egg whites until stiff. Fold egg whites and lemon juice into gelatin mixture. Pour into an 8-inch square pan and, when set, cut into 2-inch squares. Makes 16 squares.

Nishiki-Kan
(Two-Tone Jelly)

Follow recipe for *Awayuki-kan,* but divide gelatin-sugar mixture, after it has thickened slightly, into 2 parts. Mix one part with 2 beaten egg whites and pour into a moistened pan. Chill until firm. Mix the other part with 2 beaten egg yolks and pour on top of white mixture when it is firm. When set, cut into pieces.

CHAKIN SHIBORI
(Sweet-Potato Dessert)

1 cup well-drained canned fruit (pineapple, mandarin oranges, plums, etc.)
2 cups mashed cooked sweet potatoes
½ cup sugar
½ teaspoon salt

Cut fruit into cubes (mandarin sections may be left whole). Mix mashed potato with sugar and salt and cook over low heat, stirring, until moisture disappears and potato is very thick. Cool. Place about 3 tablespoons on a square of clean cloth, put a piece of drained fruit on top, bring cloth up around, and twist into a ball. Remove cloth. You should have a round of potato paste stuffed with fruit. Serve at once. Makes about 10.

YOKAN
(Bean Cakes)

1 pound red Japanese beans
8 cups water
1½ cups sugar
2 envelopes unflavored gelatin
½ cup cold water

Buy Japanese red beans if possible, otherwise use kidney beans. Cook in water until very soft. Mash through a strainer or whirl in a blender. Add sugar, and gelatin dissolved in cold water (a little salt will make it more palatable to Americans). Cook until thick and pour into 8-inch square pan. When cold, cut into squares. Fancy-shape cookie cutters may be used. Sometimes these bean cakes are wrapped in cherry leaves before serving. Makes 3 dozen.

TSUJIURA
(Japanese Fortune Wafers)

⅓ cup butter
1¾ cups sugar
1 egg
¼ cup milk
2 cups all-purpose flour
1 teaspoon baking powder
¼ teaspoon salt
1 teaspoon almond extract or 2 teaspoons vanilla extract

Cream butter until light and fluffy. Beat in sugar. Add egg and mix well. Stir in milk. Sift flour with baking powder and salt. Add to batter and stir until smooth. Add flavoring. Spread as thinly as possible on the bottom of baking pans. Bake in preheated moderate oven (350°F.) for 8 to 10 minutes, or until very lightly browned. Working quickly, cut into 3½-inch squares, or cut into rounds with a 3-inch cutter, and while still warm put a "fortune" written on a piece of paper in the center. Fold and press edges together firmly. If the cakes cool, slip them back in the oven before attempting to roll. If rolled properly thin, this will make 6 dozen.

JELLIED—This adjective describes: 1) A semitransparent, semisolid, and somewhat elastic consistency of foods, due to the presence of such substances as agar, gelatin, Irish moss, isinglass, or pectin; 2) A completed dish containing, or covered with, gelatin such as jellied eggs, jellied salads, jellied meats, etc.

Jellied dishes include soups, aspics, molded salads, and desserts. They are extremely popular because they are colorful, attractive, and delicious to eat. Also, foods with a jellied coating do not dry out.

Jellied dishes should be stiff enough to hold their shape when unmolded, but they should be tender. Since they can be prepared in advance of serving, they are used a great deal for entertaining.

The gelling agents most often used in home cookery are gelatin and pectin. Gelatin is a protein substance made from animal tissues. It is available unflavored in granular form and in sheets, and fruit- and vegetable-flavored in granular form. It is combined with a liquid which can be fruit or vegetable juice, milk, or broth. The gelatin-liquid mixture can be used plain; it can have solids such as chopped meat, chicken, fish, vegetables, or fruit added; and it can be used to coat other foods. One of the characteristics of such jellied dishes is that the gelatin mixture retains its translucence.

When a richer mixture is desired, beaten egg whites and/or whipped cream are folded into the gelatin mixture and cloud it: Spanish cream, chiffon pies, charlottes, sherbets, and Bavarians are examples of this type of dish.

The second most widely used gelling agent is pectin, a water-soluble substance present in plant tissue which yields a jelly when properly combined with acid and sugar. Some fruits, such as tart apples, blackberries, cranberries, and quinces contain enough natural pectin, particularly when slightly unripe, to gel without the addition of any artificial gelling agent when they are properly cooked. Commercial liquid and dry pectins are available and are used in the making of jams, jellies, and preserves.

Agar, made from various kinds of algae or seaweed, bleached and dried; Irish moss, made from dried and bleached carrageen, a dark-purple seaweed; and isinglass, a semitransparent whitish gelatin prepared from the air bladders of certain fish, including carp, cod, and sturgeon, are other gelling agents. Their use in home cookery today is very limited and they are not widely available. Agar can be found in drugstores; Irish moss and isinglass in some health-food stores and perhaps in some country food stores.

A few jellied dishes gel because of the gelatin present in the original substance. Head cheese is an example of such a dish. Jellied soups and meats may be made by boiling meat and bones which are rich in gelatin. When the broth is strained and cooled, the mixture solidifies.

RUBY-GLAZED CHICKEN-LIVER PÂTÉ

½ pound chicken livers
2 tablespoons butter or margarine
2 hard-cooked eggs
2 packages (3 ounces each) cream cheese
2 tablespoons chopped parsley
¾ teaspoon salt
 Dash of cayenne
1 tablespoon brandy
1 can (10½ ounces) consommé madrilene, undiluted

Sauté chicken livers in butter until lightly browned. Put chicken livers and eggs through fine blade of food chopper or blend in electric blender. Cream cheese with next 4 ingredients. Blend mixtures thoroughly. Pack into refrigerator dish. Pour consommé over pâté to cover. Refrigerate. Makes 1½ cups.

JELLIED CONSOMMÉ MADRILENE

3 envelopes unflavored gelatin
½ cup cold water
2 cups tomato juice
2 cups clear chicken bouillon
½ teaspoon grated onion
2 tablespoons dry sherry
 Lemon wedges

Soften gelatin in cold water. Heat tomato juice, bouillon, and onion. Pour over gelatin, stirring until gelatin is dissolved. Add sherry, strain out onion, and chill consommé until firm. Beat slightly with a fork before serving. Garnish with lemon wedges. Makes 4 servings.

JELLIED FRUIT SOUP

½ cup each of dried prunes and apricots
½ cup seedless raisins
1 cinnamon stick
2 cooking apples, peeled
2 fresh pears, peeled
2 cups (one 1-pound can) unsweetened sour red cherries
1 box (3 ounces) cherry-flavored gelatin
1 cup boiling water
 Lemon slices

In large kettle soak prunes, apricots, and raisins in 3 cups cold water for 1 hour. Add cinnamon stick, sliced apples and pears. Cover and simmer for 15 minutes, or until fruit is tender. Add undrained cherries and bring to boil. Dissolve gelatin in boiling water; stir gently into fruit. Chill overnight. Serve with lemon. Makes 8 servings.

MOLDED CRABMEAT SALAD

1 envelope unflavored gelatin
1 cup cold water
½ cup hot water
2 cans (6½ ounces each) crabmeat
½ cup mayonnaise or salad dressing
¼ cup ketchup
 Juice of 1 lemon
½ cup diced celery
2 tablespoons each of chopped sweet pickle and stuffed olives
¼ teaspoon salt
 Salad greens

Sprinkle gelatin on cold water and let stand for 5 minutes. Add hot water and stir until dissolved. Add remaining ingredients except salad greens. Chill until mixture begins to set. Stir well and pour into 1½-quart mold. Chill until firm. Unmold on greens. Makes 4 servings.

CLAM-ASPIC SALAD

1 envelope unflavored gelatin
1 tablespoon cold water
1 cup tomato juice
2 tablespoons fresh lemon juice
½ teaspoon salt
1 can (10½ ounces) minced clams, drained
2 hard-cooked eggs, chopped
2 tablespoons chopped sweet pickle
1 tablespoon grated peeled raw cucumber
½ cup diced celery
½ cup cubed avocado
 Lettuce
 Mayonnaise
6 stuffed olives, sliced

Soften gelatin in cold water for 5 minutes. Combine tomato juice, lemon juice, and salt in saucepan; bring to boil. Stir in softened gelatin; remove from stove and allow to cool. Chill until gelatin has the consistency of unbeaten egg white. Fold in clams, eggs, pickle, cucumber, celery, and avocado. Pour into a lightly oiled 1-quart loaf pan or ring mold. Chill until firm. Slice, and serve on lettuce; garnish with mayonnaise and olives. Makes 4 to 6 servings.

SAVORY SHRIMP MOLD

2 envelopes unflavored gelatin
½ cup cold water
1 cup boiling water
2 bouillon cubes
¼ cup mayonnaise
1 teaspoon horseradish
1 teaspoon instant minced onion
1 tablespoon minced parsley
2 tablespoons fresh lime or lemon juice
 Dash each of Worcestershire and hot pepper sauce
1 pound shrimps, cooked, peeled, cleaned, and diced
½ cup heavy cream, whipped
 Seasoned salt and pepper to taste
 Salad greens

Soften gelatin in cold water; add boiling water and bouillon cubes; stir until gelatin and cubes are dissolved. Chill until slightly thickened. Fold in remaining ingredients except greens. Pour into 1-quart mold. Chill until firm. Unmold on greens. Makes 6 servings.

PORK AND VEAL HEAD CHEESE

1 pig's head, quartered
1 pound lean pork
1 pound veal
4 cups meat stock or bouillon
2 bay leaves
2 sprigs of fresh thyme
¼ teaspoon powdered cloves
2 teaspoons salt
8 peppercorns
1 teaspoon grated lemon rind
3 onions, peeled and sliced
1 carrot, peeled and sliced
1 celery stalk, sliced

Wash head thoroughly, remove ears, brains, eyes, tongue, and most of the fat. Soak in cold water for 12 hours, changing water several times. Combine head, ears, and tongue with remaining ingredients in large kettle; bring to a boil and simmer for about 4 hours or until the meat is falling from the bones. Cook brains for about 15 minutes in a little stock; cool, and dice. Separate the meat from the bones; discard bones. Dice ears. Slice pork, veal, tongue, and meat from head and alternate sliced and diced meats in a mold. Pour stock over meat. Cover with a cloth and put a weight on top. Chill. Serve cut into slices. Makes 10 to 12 servings.

JELLIED MEAT LOAF

1 envelope unflavored gelatin
1 cup chicken bouillon
½ medium green pepper, sliced
1 tablespoon diced onion
12-ounce can luncheon meat
½ cup undiluted evaporated milk
 Dairy sour cream
 Horseradish

Soften gelatin in ¼ cup of bouillon for 5 minutes. Put over low heat and stir until dissolved. Put gelatin mixture, remaining bouillon, pepper, and onion in container of electric blender; blend until smooth. Add luncheon meat and milk and blend well. Pour into lightly oiled loaf pan (9 x 5 x 3 inches). Chill until firm. Unmold; serve with sour cream seasoned with horseradish. Makes 6 servings.

JELLIED CHICKEN MOLD

5-pound fowl
4 cups boiling water
1 onion
2 celery stalks
1 bay leaf
 Salt
 Cooking oil
 Pepper
 Mayonnaise
 Chopped fresh or crumbled dried herbs

Have fowl cut into pieces. Wash; put in kettle; add boiling water, onion, celery, bay leaf, and 1 teaspoon salt. Cover; bring to boil and simmer for 2½ hours, or until fowl is tender. Drain, reserving liquid. Cool fowl; remove meat from bones and cut into coarse pieces. Arrange in 6 oiled individual molds or 1½-quart mold. Skim fat from liquid; strain; reduce to 2 cups by boiling, uncovered. Season to taste with salt and pepper, and pour over chicken. Cool; then chill overnight, or until set. Unmold, and serve with mayonnaise seasoned with herbs. Makes 6 servings.

JELLIED COTTAGE-CHEESE AND TOMATO SALAD

1 envelope unflavored gelatin
¼ cup cold water
½ cup boiling water
½ teaspoon salt
1 onion, grated
2 tablespoons cider vinegar
½ pound cottage cheese
1 can (8 ounces) tomato sauce
 Coleslaw
 Green-pepper rings

Soak gelatin in cold water, add boiling water, and stir until dissolved. Add salt, onion, and vinegar. Add 3 tablespoons of this gelatin liquid to cottage cheese. To remaining gelatin liquid add tomato sauce. Pour half of tomato mixture into lightly oiled 1-quart mold; chill until set. Meanwhile keep cottage cheese and remaining tomato mixture at room temperature. Add cottage-cheese mixture to jellied tomato layer and chill until set. Then cover with remaining tomato mixture and chill once more. To serve, unmold on slaw; garnish with pepper rings. Makes 4 to 6 servings.

JELLIED VEGETABLE RING

1 envelope unflavored gelatin
¼ cup cold water
1½ cups boiling water
3 tablespoons sugar
¼ cup cider vinegar
1 teaspoon salt
½ teaspoon curry powder
 Dash of pepper
1 tablespoon minced onion
1 cup celery strips
¾ cup finely shredded cabbage
¼ cup diced cooked beets
 Salad greens
 Mayonnaise or salad dressing

Soften gelatin in cold water for 5 minutes; then dissolve in boiling water. Add sugar, vinegar, seasonings, and onion. Chill until slightly thickened; stir and fold in vegetables. Pour into 1-quart ring mold. Chill until firm. Unmold on salad greens and serve with mayonnaise. Makes 4 to 6 servings.

JELLIED PEAR AND CREAM-CHEESE SALAD

1 box (3 ounces) lemon-flavored gelatin
 Hot water
½ teaspoon salt
2 canned pear halves or 1 fresh pear, diced
1 banana, diced
4 maraschino cherries, cut up
1 package (3 ounces) cream cheese, softened
½ cup broken nut meats
 Salad greens

Dissolve gelatin in 2 cups hot water. Add salt and chill until mixture begins to set. Divide gelatin. To one half add diced pear, banana, and cherries. Turn into 1-quart mold and chill until firm. Beat remaining gelatin until fluffy. Beat in cream cheese and fold in nut meats. Pour over first gelatin layer. Chill until firm. Unmold on salad greens. Makes 4 servings.

ASPIC GLAZE FOR SANDWICHES

1 envelope unflavored gelatin
½ cup cold water
1 cup boiling water
1 chicken bouillon cube

Soften gelatin in cold water for 5 minutes. Add boiling water and bouillon cube and stir until cube and gelatin are dissolved. Chill until thickened to the consistency of unbeaten egg white.

■ To Glaze Sandwiches—Place openface sandwiches in refrigerator and chill for 30 minutes. Spoon gelatin mixture over sandwiches to completely cover. Chill for about 30 minutes. Makes enough glaze for 12 open-face sandwiches.

STRAWBERRY CHIFFON PIE

1 box (3 ounces) strawberry-flavored gelatin
⅔ cup boiling water
⅛ teaspoon salt
2 tablespoons fresh lemon juice
1 package (10 ounces) frozen sliced strawberries, thawed
3 egg whites
⅓ cup sugar
 Ladyfinger Crust

Dissolve gelatin in boiling water. Add salt, lemon juice, and strawberries. Chill until thickened but not firm. Beat egg whites until foamy; gradually add sugar and beat until stiff but not dry. Fold into gelatin. Pile in Ladyfinger Crust and chill until firm. Makes 6 to 8 servings.

Ladyfinger Crust

Split 12 ladyfingers. Use some to line bottom of deep 9-inch pie pan. Cut some into halves crosswise and arrange around edge of pan. Break remainder into small pieces and fill in spaces in bottom of pan. Melt 2 tablespoons butter and pour over ladyfingers in bottom. Chill. Makes one 9-inch pie shell.

Raspberry Chiffon Pie

Use recipe for Strawberry Chiffon Pie, substituting raspberry gelatin for strawberry and 1 package raspberries for the strawberries.

VANILLA BAVARIAN CREAM

1 envelope unflavored gelatin
½ cup sugar
¼ teaspoon salt
4 eggs, separated
1 cup milk
1 teaspoon vanilla extract
1 cup heavy cream, whipped

Combine gelatin, ¼ cup sugar, and salt in saucepan. Beat egg yolks with milk; add to gelatin mixture. Cook over low heat, stirring constantly, until gelatin is dissolved. Remove from heat; add vanilla. Chill until mixture mounds slightly when dropped from spoon. Beat egg whites until foamy. Gradually beat in ¼ cup sugar, 1 tablespoon at a time, continuing to beat until stiff. Fold meringue and then whipped cream into

gelatin mixture. Pour into 2-quart mold. Chill for at least 4 hours, or until firm. Unmold. Serve plain or with fruit or crème de menthe, if desired. Makes 8 servings.

COFFEE-BANANA BAVARIAN

1 envelope unflavored gelatin
½ cup milk
1 cup strong hot coffee
⅓ cup sugar
⅛ teaspoon salt
1 teaspoon rum extract
1 cup heavy cream, whipped
1 ripe banana, diced
½ cup chopped nuts

Soften gelatin in milk for 5 minutes. Add coffee and stir until gelatin is dissolved. Add sugar, salt, and flavoring. Chill until slightly thickened. Fold in remaining ingredients. Chill until firm. Makes 6 servings.

SPANISH CREAM

4 eggs, separated
½ cup sugar
2 cups hot milk
1 envelope unflavored gelatin
¼ cup cold water
½ teaspoon vanilla extract

Beat yolks until thick and lemon-colored. Gradually beat in sugar. Gradually stir in hot milk. Cook over low heat, stirring constantly, until mixture coats a spoon. Soak gelatin in cold water. Let stand for 5 minutes. Add gelatin to hot custard mixture. Stir over ice until mixture is slightly thickened. Beat egg whites until stiff and fold into custard mixture. Add flavoring. Pour mixture into 1-quart mold. Chill until firm. Unmold by dipping mold into lukewarm water for a few seconds. Serve plain or with whipped cream, fresh or cooked fruit, or berries, if desired. Makes 6 servings.

ORANGE-HONEY SHERBET

1½ teaspoons unflavored gelatin
¾ cup cold water
½ cup honey
 Grated rind of 2 oranges
1½ cups fresh orange juice
2 egg whites
 Few grains of salt

Soften gelatin in ¼ cup cold water. Mix ½ cup water, the honey, and orange rind together; boil for 5 minutes. Add softened gelatin and stir until dissolved. Cool, add orange juice, and pour into freezing tray. Freeze until thick and mushy. Remove to well-chilled bowl and beat with rotary beater until mixture is smooth and fluffy. Fold in stiffly beaten egg whites and salt. Beat again with rotary beater, return to freezing tray, and freeze until firm, stirring occasionally. Makes 6 to 8 servings.

TROPICAL MARMALADE

1 orange
1 lemon

1 tangerine (or another kind of orange)
1 cup water
2½ cups, about (one 1-pound, 4-ounce can) crushed pineapple
1 package powdered pectin
5 cups sugar
½ teaspoon salt
½ teaspoon ground ginger

With 2-blade vegetable peeler, shave peel of fruits into strips. Then cut peel into thin slivers, ⅛ inch or less. Simmer for 20 minutes in water. Cut fruit into halves; with curved grapefruit knife scoop out pulp. Squeeze out juice; add with pulp to peel. Simmer for 10 minutes. Measure all fruit into saucepan, adding water to make 3½ cups. Add powdered pectin; bring to boil. Add remaining ingredients. Stir constantly. When mixture comes to rolling boil, remove from heat after 1 minute. Cool; ladle into hot sterilized jars; seal. Makes seven 8-ounce jars.

JELLY—A mixture of fruit juice, sugar, acid, and pectin, either natural or added, cooked to the stage at which gelation occurs. The resulting product is clear and bright-colored. It is firm enough to hold its shape when turned out of the container in which it was stored. Jelly has a quivering quality and is easily spooned; it should never be syrupy, sticky, gummy, or tough.

Unlike jams, which require only one cooking, jellies require two: one cooking prepares the fruit for juice extraction; in the second cooking the juice is mixed with sugar and cooked to the gelation stage. The first cooking can be eliminated, of course, by the use of frozen or canned juices.

Specific amounts of fruit juice, pectin, acid, and sugar are necessary to make a successful jelly.

The fruit gives the jelly its flavor and color, and supplies, at least in part, the pectin and acid needed. The fruit also has mineral salts which add to the flavor and aid gelation. Fruits with definite or distinctive flavors are best for jelly making because the flavor is diluted by the large proportion of sugar needed for proper consistency and good keeping quality.

Pectin, a water-soluble gelling agent, is found naturally in fruits; when accompanied by an acid and sugar in correct proportions, it makes the jelly gel. It also helps prevent recrystallization of the sugar. Some fruits have enough natural pectin, others do not; and all fruits have less pectin when they are fully ripe, hence fruit used for making jelly should be only ripe enough to be firm, or some underripe fruit should be included. Commercial fruit pectins are available in liquid or powdered form. These may be used with any fruit whether it is naturally high in pectin or not and the fruit may be fully ripe. The cooking time for these jellies is shorter, the formulas standardized, so there is no question about when the jelly has cooked enough. Also the amount of yield is greater.

Some acid is necessary for flavor in jelly making; also the acid aids the pectin to precipitate out, thus forming the jelly. There is a great variation in the amount of acid in various kinds of fruit, and in relation to acid, too, underripe fruit has more than ripe. If fruit is ripe, the acid in the recipe is increased by adding lemon juice or citric acid.

Sugar in the correct amounts is the last of the elements which together are responsible for the formation of the jelly. Sugar also serves as a preserving agent and contributes to the flavor.

Beet or cane sugar may be used in jelly making for they have the same composition. Sometimes corn syrup or honey may be used in place of part, but not all, of the sugar. Usually ¾ cup sugar to each 1 cup juice is the proportion; however, this may vary with the ripeness of the fruit and the amount of pectin present.

There are several ways to make jelly, and because of the products and facilities available today, jelly can be made successfully at any time of year.

☐ Jellies Made without Added Pectin—The juice of fruits known to be high in natural pectin should be selected. Among such fruits are tart apples, blackberries, cranberries, currants, gooseberries, Concord grapes, quinces, and raspberries. It is usually best to have part of the fruit underripe. One fourth underripe to three fourths ripe is the ratio most commonly recommended to assure sufficient pectin. To find out whether or not fruit juice has enough natural pectin, add 4 to 5 tablespoons alcohol to 1 tablespoon fruit juice. If the pectin coagulates in a solid mass, the juice has enough.

☐ Jellies Made with Commercial Fruit Pectin—In this method, liquid pectin is added to the boiling juice and sugar mixture. Use only recipes designed for this form. Fully ripe fruit may be used.

When powdered fruit pectin is used, it is mixed with the unheated fruit juice. Use only recipes designed for this form. Fully ripe fruit may be used.

☐ Jellies Made without Cooking—These may be made with powdered or liquid fruit pectin if they can be stored in a freezer, or used within three to four months if kept in the refrigerator.

TO MAKE JELLY

☐ In addition to the standard items found in most kitchens the following equipment is needed for making jelly: A large, broad-bottomed, wide-topped kettle, large enough so fruit juice will not boil over; a jelly bag or several thicknesses of cheesecloth, firm unbleached muslin, or Canton flannel (used with nap side in), to strain the juice; a stand for the jelly bag, or a colander; if making jelly without commercial pectin, a jelly and candy, or a deep-fat thermometer is helpful, as is a clock with a second hand, and household scales for weighing fruit.

☐ Have glasses ready when they are needed. Glasses, or jars, and lids should be covered with hot, not boiling, water, and brought to a boil. No further boiling is necessary. Keep hot in water or in a very slow oven until they are needed.

☐ To Prepare Juice—You can have the luxury of freshly made jelly in the winter by freezing or canning the juice when fruit is in season.

Select fruit of uniform ripeness; avoid either very green or overripe fruit, both of which may cause trouble. Use a 4- or 6-quart kettle with wide bottom. Sort, wash, and drain fruit; it is not necessary to remove stems, pits, or skins. Crush with potato masher. Add a small amount of water. Heat to simmering; if needed, simmer for 5 to 12 minutes to soften fruit; stir often. Pour fruit into dampened jelly bag or into two thicknesses of cheesecloth over bowl. Let drip for at least 1 hour. Bag may be pressed very lightly with back of spoon to extract juice.

To Freeze—Pour juice into liquid-tight containers, leaving 1-inch headspace for expansion. Freeze at 0°F.

To Can—Add sugar in the proportion of 1 cup sugar to 1 gallon juice. Reheat to simmering and pour into hot clean jars to within ½ inch of top. Seal according to manufacturer's instructions. Process in simmering water (180°F.) for 20 minutes. Label juice, giving kind, date canned, and the amount of sugar used in preparing. Store in cool, dry, dark place. If crystals form, strain before making jelly.

☐ If making a jelly without added pectin, cook mixture at a rapid boil until it reaches 220°F. on a candy and jelly thermometer. If you do not have one you can use an old standby jelly test, the spoon, or sheet, test, although it is not as reliable as a thermometer: Dip a cool metal spoon into the boiling jelly mixture. Then raise it at least 1 foot above the kettle, out of the steam, and turn the spoon so that the syrup runs off the side. If the syrup forms drops that flow together and fall off the spoon as one sheet, the jelly should be done.

☐ To Seal Jelly—See To Seal Jam, page 961.

JELLIES MADE WITHOUT PECTIN

APPLE JELLY

3 pounds tart red apples
4 cups water
3 cups sugar

Wash apples, cut out any blemishes and the stem and blossom ends, but do not peel or remove the core. Cut apples into eighths. Put fruit in a flat-bottomed saucepan and add water. Cover and simmer until the juice flows freely, about 15 minutes. Strain through a damp jelly bag or several layers of dampened cheesecloth. For crystal-clear jelly, do not squeeze or press the bag. Measure juice into a deep saucepan. (There should be 4 cups.) Boil for 5 minutes. Stir in the sugar and boil rapidly to the jelly stage, 220°F. on a candy and jelly thermometer. Skim any foam from mixture and pour into hot sterilized jars; seal. Makes four or five ½-pint jars.

SPICED APPLE AND BLUEBERRY JELLY

2½ quarts green apple parings or apples
1 cup blueberries
Rind of 1 orange
1 teaspoon ground mace
Few whole cloves
¼ cinnamon stick
2 cups sugar

Cook apple parings and cores, removing only blossom ends, with blueberries, orange rind, and spices in water barely to cover until juice is extracted. Strain through flannel cloth. There should be from 2½ to 3 cups juice. Add sugar and cook until juice sheets from spoon. Jelly should be skimmed several times during cooking. Pour into hot sterilized jars, and seal. Makes about four ½-pint jars.

CRANBERRY JELLY

2 cups cranberries
1 cup boiling water
1 cup sugar

Pick over and wash cranberries; drain. Add water and boil for 20 minutes; rub through sieve. Cook pulp for 3 minutes. Add sugar, mix well, and cook for 2 minutes longer. Pour into jelly glasses or small molds and chill for at least 24 hours. Makes 6 servings.

CONCORD LIME JELLY

4 pounds Concord grapes
Grated rind and juice of 5 small limes
Sugar

Wash grapes, drain, and stem. Put into large preserving kettle and crush slightly. Do not add water. Cook for about 30 minutes, stirring occasionally. Pour into flannel jelly bag and let drain for several hours; do not squeeze. Measure grape juice; bring to boil and boil rapidly for 5 minutes. Add lime rind, juice, and sugar, allowing ¾ cup sugar to each 1 cup

juice. Cook until jelly sheets from spoon. Pour into hot sterilized jars, and seal. Makes four or five ½-pint jars.

GRAPE JELLY

3 pounds Concord grapes
About 2½ cups sugar

Crush grapes. Bring to boil and cook for 15 minutes. Strain juice through flannel jelly bag; chill. Dip out juice; do not use sediment at bottom as it may cause crystals to form. Add sugar, using 5 parts sugar to 4 parts juice by measure. Stir until sugar is completely dissolved; do not heat. Pour into hot sterilized jars, and seal. Makes about three ½-pint jars.

MINT JELLY

Use any apple jelly recipe, cooking 1 cup chopped mint leaves with each 1½ pounds apples when preparing juice for jelly. Color a delicate green with vegetable coloring.

QUINCE AND CRANBERRY JELLY

12 large quinces
2 pounds cranberries
Sugar

Wash fruit. Cut quinces into quarters, cover with water, and cook until tender. Add cranberries and cook until skins burst. Strain through jelly bag. Measure juice. For each 1 cup juice, measure ¾ cup sugar. Boil juice for 12 minutes; add sugar, stirring until well mixed. Boil until jelly sheets from spoon. Pour into hot sterilized jars, cool slightly, and seal. Makes about twelve ½-pint jars.
Note: Save this recipe until you find quinces and cranberries in the market in the fall.

JELLIES MADE WITH PECTIN

AROMATIC APPLE JELLY

2 cups apple juice
3½ cups sugar
1 tablespoon aromatic bitters
Juice of 1 lemon
Red food coloring
½ bottle (6-ounce size) liquid pectin

Put juice and sugar in large kettle and bring to boil. Add bitters, lemon juice, and few drops of coloring; bring to boil. Stir in pectin; when mixture boils, let boil for one minute, stirring. Skim, and pour into hot sterilized jars. Seal. Makes about four ½-pint jars.

BERRY JELLY

About 2½ quarts ripe blackberries, boysenberries, dewberries, loganberries, red raspberries, strawberries, or youngberries
7½ cups sugar
1 bottle (6 ounces) liquid pectin

Wash berries and crush thoroughly. Place in jelly cloth or bag, press out juice, and

measure. Pour 4 cups juice into very large saucepan and add sugar. Mix well and bring to a full rolling boil, stirring constantly. Add liquid pectin and boil hard for 1 minute, stirring constantly. Remove from heat and skim off foam with a metal spoon. Pour quickly into hot sterilized jars, and seal. Makes about eight ½-pint jars.
Note: If berries are lacking in tartness substitute ¼ cup fresh lemon juice for ¼ cup fruit juice.

Black Raspberry Jelly

Use 3 cups juice, 5 cups sugar, and ½ bottle pectin. Heat crushed berries until the juice flows. Cover and simmer for 15 minutes. Place in jelly bag and press out juice. Combine 3 cups juice and ¼ cup fresh lemon juice in large saucepan. Proceed as with basic recipe above. Makes six ½-pint jars.
Note: This jelly may set slowly. Allow a week or longer.

BLACKBERRY-JUICE JELLY

2 cups canned unsweetened blackberry juice
1 tablespoon fresh lemon juice
½ package (1¾-ounce size) powdered fruit pectin
1¼ cups sugar*
¾ cup corn syrup

Strain juices through fine cloth into large kettle. Place over high heat; heat almost to boiling point; stir in dry pectin and let jelly come to a full boil. Add sugar and corn syrup; mix well and boil rapidly until jelly sheets from spoon. Remove from heat, skim, and pour at once into hot sterilized jars. Cool slightly; seal. Makes about three ½-pint jars.
* Or use 2 cups sugar and omit syrup.

CIDER-AND-SAGE JELLY

½ cup boiling water
3 tablespoons dried sage
1½ cups sweet cider
3¾ cups sugar
Yellow vegetable coloring
½ cup liquid fruit pectin

Pour boiling water over sage. Cover and let stand for 15 minutes. Strain through cheesecloth. Add more water, if needed, to make ½ cup. Add cider and sugar, and heat to boiling. Add enough coloring to tint mixture light yellow. Add pectin, stirring constantly. Boil rapidly for 1 minute. Skim, and pour into hot sterilized jars. Seal. Makes about four ½-pint jars.

GRAPE JELLY

3 pounds ripe Concord grapes
5¾ cups sugar
¾ cup water
1 box (1¾ ounces) powdered fruit pectin

Thoroughly crush the grapes, place in jelly cloth or bag, and squeeze out juice. Measure 3 cups into a large bowl or pan. Add sugar to juice and mix well. Mix water and pectin in small saucepan. Bring to a boil and boil for 1 minute, stirring constantly. Stir into fruit juice. Continue stirring for about 3 minutes. There will be a few remaining sugar crystals. Quickly pour into glasses. Cover at once with tight lid. When jelly is set, store in freezer. If jelly will be used within 2 or 3 weeks, it may be stored in the refrigerator. Makes about eight ½-pint jars.

Note: For best results in making grape jellies, squeeze crushed grapes through 4 thicknesses of dampened cheesecloth.

GRAPE-JUICE JELLY

6½ cups sugar
2½ cups water
1 bottle (6 ounces) liquid pectin
3 six-ounce cans (2¼ cups) frozen concentrated grape juice

Stir sugar into water. Place over high heat and, stirring constantly, bring quickly to a full rolling boil that cannot be stirred down. Boil hard for 1 minute. Remove from heat and stir in pectin. Add thawed concentrated grape juice and mix well. Pour immediately into hot sterilized jars, and seal. Makes about nine ½-pint jars.

GRAPE-AND-BASIL JELLY

½ cup boiling water
1 tablespoon dried basil
1½ cups grape juice
3 cups sugar
½ cup liquid pectin

Pour boiling water over basil. Cover and let stand for 5 to 10 minutes. Strain through cheesecloth. Add more water, if needed, to make ½ cup. Add grape juice and sugar and heat to boiling. Add pectin, stirring constantly. Boil for half minute. Skim, and pour into hot sterilized jars. Seal. Makes about four ½-pint jars.

Note: Dried thyme may be used in place of basil.

GRAPEFRUIT-AND-SAVORY JELLY

½ cup boiling water
2 tablespoons dried summer savory
1 cup grapefruit juice
3¼ cups sugar
Green vegetable coloring
½ cup liquid pectin

Pour boiling water over savory. Cover and let stand for 15 minutes. Strain through cheesecloth. Add more water, if needed, to make ½ cup. Add grapefruit juice and sugar. Heat to boiling. Add enough coloring to tint mixture light green. Add pectin, stirring constantly. Boil rapidly for ½ minute. Skim, and pour into hot sterilized jars. Seal. Makes three ½-pint jars.

ORANGE JELLY

6 medium oranges
4 medium lemons
4½ cups sugar
½ bottle (6-ounce size) liquid pectin

Extract juice from oranges and lemons and strain. There should be 2½ cups juice. Put in large kettle, add sugar, and

mix well. Bring to a boil over high heat and add pectin, stirring constantly. Then bring to a full boil and boil for half minute. Skim, and pour into hot sterilized jars. Seal. Makes four or five ½-pint jars.

ORANGE-GRAPEFRUIT-JUICE JELLY

3¼ cups sugar
1 cup water
3 tablespoons fresh lemon juice
½ bottle (6-ounce size) liquid pectin
1 six-ounce can (¾ cup) frozen concentrated orange-and-grapefruit juice

Stir sugar into water. Place over high heat and, stirring constantly, bring quickly to a full rolling boil that cannot be stirred down. Add lemon juice and boil hard for 1 minute. Remove from heat and stir in pectin. Add thawed concentrated orange-and-grapefruit juice and mix well. Pour immediately into hot sterilized jars, and seal. Makes about four ½-pint jars.

PLUM JELLY

5 pounds ripe tart plums
1½ cups water
1 box (1¾ ounces) powdered fruit pectin
7½ cups sugar

Crush plums thoroughly. Do not peel or pit. Add water, bring to a boil, and simmer, covered, for 10 minutes. Put in jelly bag and press out juice to make 5½ cups. Combine with pectin in kettle and mix well. Bring to a hard boil over high heat, stirring. Add sugar and again bring to a full rolling boil. Boil hard for 1 minute, stirring. Remove from heat, skim off foam, and pour into hot sterilized jars. Seal at once. Makes nine ½-pint jars.

QUINCE JELLY

3 pounds ripe quinces
¼ cup strained fresh lemon juice
7½ cups sugar
½ bottle (6-ounce size) liquid pectin

Remove cores and blossom and stem ends from quinces, but do not peel. Put through food chopper. Add 4½ cups water, bring to boil, and simmer, covered, for 15 minutes. Put in jelly bag and press out juice to make 4 cups. Combine in kettle with lemon juice and sugar; mix well. Bring to boil over high heat, stirring. Add pectin, bring to a full rolling boil, and boil hard for 1 minute, stirring. Remove from heat, skim off foam, and pour into hot sterilized jars. Seal. Makes eight ½-pint jars.

RED RASPBERRY JELLY

2¼ quarts fully ripe red raspberries
6 cups sugar
¾ cup water
1 box (1¾ ounces) powdered fruit pectin

Thoroughly crush the raspberries, place in jelly cloth or bag, and squeeze out juice. Measure 3 cups into a large bowl

or pan. Add sugar to juice and mix well. Mix water and pectin in small saucepan. Bring to a boil and boil for 1 minute, stirring constantly. Stir into fruit juice. Continue stirring for about 3 minutes. There will be a few remaining sugar crystals. Quickly pour into jars. Cover at once with tight lids. When jelly is set, store in freezer. If jelly will be used within 2 or 3 weeks, it may be stored in the refrigerator. Makes about eight ½-pint jars.

JELLIES MADE WITHOUT COOKING

NO-COOK BLACKBERRY JELLY

1¾ quarts ripe blackberries
5 cups sugar
2 tablespoons fresh lemon juice
½ bottle liquid pectin

Crush blackberries and put in jelly cloth or bag. Squeeze out juice and measure 2½ cups into bowl. Add sugar and mix well. Mix lemon juice and liquid pectin; then stir into blackberry juice. Continue stirring for 3 minutes. If a few sugar crystals remain they will do no harm. Pour into glasses or freezer jars. Cover with tight lid. Let stand for 24 hours to set. Store in freezer or for up to 3 weeks in refrigerator. Makes about seven ½-pint jars.

NO-COOK GRAPE JELLY

2 pounds ripe Concord grapes
4 cups sugar
2 tablespoons water
½ bottle liquid pectin

Crush grapes and put in jelly cloth or bag. Squeeze out juice and measure into bowl. Add sugar and mix well. Mix water and liquid pectin; then stir into grape juice. Continue stirring for 3 minutes. If a few sugar crystals remain they will do no harm. Pour into glasses or freezer jars. Cover with tight lids. Let stand for 24 hours to set. Store in freezer or for up to 3 weeks in refrigerator. Makes about six ½-pint jars.

NO-COOK RED RASPBERRY JELLY

1½ quarts ripe red raspberries
5 cups sugar
2 tablespoons water
½ bottle liquid pectin

Crush raspberries and put in jelly cloth or bag. Squeeze out juice and measure 2½ cups into bowl. Add sugar and mix well. Mix water and liquid pectin; then stir into raspberry juice. Continue stirring for 3 minutes. If a few sugar crystals remain they will do no harm. Pour into glasses or freezer jars. Cover with tight lids. Let stand for 24 hours to set. Store in freezer or for up to 3 weeks in refrigerator. Makes about seven ½-pint jars.

NO-COOK STRAWBERRY JELLY

1½ quarts ripe strawberries
4 cups sugar
2 tablespoons fresh lemon juice
½ bottle liquid pectin

Crush strawberries and put in jelly cloth or bag. Squeeze out juice and measure 1¾ cups into bowl. Add sugar and mix well. Mix lemon juice and liquid pectin; then stir into strawberry juice. Continue stirring for 3 minutes. If a few sugar crystals remain they will do no harm. Pour into glasses or freezer jars. Cover with tight lids. Let stand for 24 hours to set. Store in freezer or for up to 3 weeks in refrigerator. Makes about six ½-pint jars.

JERUSALEM ARTICHOKE—This tuber, *Helianthus tuberosus*, is a native of North America and a hardy sunflower perennial which will grow from six to twelve feet in height. The tubers, which grow underground, vary in shape from oblong to elongated, in one piece or branched, and weigh three to four ounces. Their skin is very thin and the color ranges from light beige to a deep yellow, or to brown, reddish, or purplish tinges. The flesh of the Jerusalem artichoke is white and crisp, with a pronounced sweetish flavor of its own. The tubers shrivel quickly when exposed to air.

The Jerusalem artichoke is not even remotely related to the globe artichoke, nor does it resemble an artichoke in appearance. It was probably called an artichoke because its taste vaguely resembles that of the globe artichoke. What is more, it has nothing to do with the city of the Holy Land. The "Jerusalem" in its name is an adaptation of the Italian word for sunflower, *girasole*.

The American Indians cultivated it for centuries. Samuel de Champlain reported seeing the Jerusalem artichoke about 1605 in the gardens of Indians on Cape Cod, and it was introduced to Europe in 1616.

Availability—From October to March in specialty food stores.

Purchasing Guide—Select artichokes with a fresh appearance, free from blemishes.

Storage—Store in a cool dry place. When cooked, store in refrigerator.

☐ Refrigerator shelf: 4 to 5 days

Caloric Value

☐ 3½ ounces, raw = 70 calories

Basic Preparation—Wash and scrub well. Can be eaten raw: sliced and salted like radishes. Jerusalem artichokes are usually cooked with skins on since the skin is thin; however, they may be pared before cooking if preferred.

☐ **To Boil**—Wash and scrub well. Cook, covered, in boiling water to cover for 20 to 30 minutes, or until tender. Check artichokes during cooking period. Overcooking causes the tubers to become mushy. When tender, rub off skin. Season with salt and pepper and serve with melted butter.

Jerusalem artichokes can also be creamed after boiling, or prepared au gratin. They can be cooked, chilled, and cubed for a salad. Prepare as fritters by dipping cooked artichokes into batter, then frying. They can also be made into croquettes or French-fried.

☐ **To Mash**—Boil until tender. Rub off skin. Mash artichokes and season as desired.

☐ **To Fry**—Parboil artichokes and rub off skin. Cook thin slices in very hot deep fat until golden-brown. Drain. Season with salt and pepper. Serve immediately.

☐ **To Bake**—Wash and scrub well. Bake in preheated hot oven (400°F.) for 30 to 40 minutes, or in moderate oven (350° F.) for 40 to 60 minutes. Avoid overcooking.

JERUSALEM ARTICHOKES WITH TOMATOES

2 tablespoons butter
2 tablespoons olive oil
1 cup canned tomatoes
  Salt and pepper
½ teaspoon crumbled dried basil
2 cups sliced cooked Jerusalem artichokes

Heat butter and olive oil. Add tomatoes and salt and pepper to taste. Stir in basil. Cook over low heat, stirring constantly, until very hot. Add artichoke slices and reheat until hot. Serve immediately. Makes 4 servings.

JEWISH COOKERY

by Violet Leonard Kanfer

A varied and representative collection of favorite Jewish dishes, plus a special group of holiday recipes.

Many foods mentioned in the Bible are still used by Jewish people. This is especially true of dishes which are part of holiday tradition, for example the unleavened bread or matzo which is eaten during Passover. Honey, written of frequently in the Old Testament, is still served on the New Year table.

After the exodus from the Holy Land, Jews were scattered to communities throughout the world. In each country where they found themselves, the Jewish homemakers adapted the local produce and cuisine to the special requirements of their Dietary Laws (see below). Except for the foods proscribed by these laws, and the foods specifically associated with religious holidays, Jewish cookery is influenced by the country in which the Jews are or were living. For instance, French Jews ate food much influenced by French cookery, while the food of the German Jews was definitely German in character.

Dishes associated with Jews in the United States are mostly eastern European in origin since most of the American Jews came from eastern Europe. These foods were often modified by family taste and by local availability of ingredients. An illustration of the way in which a recipe traveled is cited by the 11th-century French-Jewish Biblical commentator and scholar, Solomon ben Isaac Rashi, who wrote that the Sabbath dish called *cholent* or *shalet* derived from the French word *chaud*. The dish, he speculates, came from Rome. From France this dish was carried to Germany, to Russia, and thence to Poland. It was brought to America by immigrants from these countries. This dish is served on the Sabbath, or Day of Rest. Since cooking is forbidden on this day, a blend of starches and meat is cooked slowly in the oven, and kept warm overnight. It is still served in homes and restaurants here.

WHAT IS KOSHER AND WHAT ARE THE DIETARY LAWS?

The act of eating is considered by Jews who observe their religious laws to be a religious experience. For this reason a prayer of thanksgiving is said over each meal, or between-meal snack. Blessings are invoked on bread, on wine, and on other foods, such as the first fruits of the season. This food is hallowed as a sacrament, and accepted as one of God's blessings.

The regulations as to the types of food which may or may not be eaten derive from Bible laws. Some theories have been set forth that the rules arose from early recognition of the importance of cleanliness and health and hygiene needs. However, these laws are also a rigid religious discipline which according to the philosopher Maimonides "train us to master our appetites, and accustom us not to consider eating and drinking as ends of man's existence."

Permitted foods are called "kosher" which means "fitting or proper." This includes ritually slaughtered herbivorous animals which "chew the cud and have cloven hooves," and specified birds. There are strict proscriptions against birds and animals of prey, scavengers, creeping insects, and reptiles, all seafood except those with scales and fins, and the blood of all animals (Leviticus 11:1-47). Blood is always extracted from meat and poultry. Even in the case of eggs, any with blood spots are unfit. In addition, meat from the hind quarters of all animals is prohibited. Kosher foods of all kinds are readily available in Jewish and many non-Jewish stores. They are often marked by a *U* in a circle, or by a *K* alone or in a circle. The first means that the foods are endorsed by the Union of Orthodox Jewish Congregations of America, the largest food-endorsing body in the country. The *K* means that other endorsing agencies guarantee that the food is kosher.

In addition, the mixing of meat and milk products is strictly forbidden. This stems from the Biblical injunction "thou shalt not seethe a kid in his mother's milk" (Deuteronomy 14:21). All dishes and utensils used in the preparation of meat and dairy dishes are kept separate.

However, there are foods that are *parve,* or neutral, which means they can be eaten with both meat or dairy dishes. Eggs, vegetables, and fish belong to this neutral group. In order to distinguish quickly such foods from others, their packages are often marked "parve."

The laws governing the slaughter of animals are based upon sparing the animals' suffering. The functionary is a respected person, especially trained, and uses a special knife.

JEWISH FOOD CUSTOMS

"There is no festive celebration without eating and drinking"—Talmud.

All Jewish holidays and holy days are associated with specific food traditions. The Sabbath, which starts at sundown Friday, is marked with an elaborate meal, the best of the week. Traditionally a fine loaf of unsliced twisted white bread called *challah* is blessed by the master of the house. It is then broken and passed to each person at the table, so that all are literally "breaking bread together." A blessing is pronounced over wine or grape juice. The menu is then at the homemaker's discretion, and depends on the locale and economic situation. It is always the finest that can be provided. Since cooking is forbidden until the following sundown, it is customary to serve dishes which can be kept warm in the oven.

All other holiday meals are based on the model of the Sabbath. The exception is the Passover, a spring festival which celebrates the exodus of the Israelites from bondage under the Pharoahs in Egypt. During the eight days of this holiday no bread or other leavened baked goods may be eaten. Nor may beans, peas, corn, rice, or other grains be used. This is a reminder of the haste with which these ancient people fled their homes, and of their privations during their sojourn in the wilderness. All leavening is removed from the house, and special utensils and dishes are used.

Passover—The week of Passover starts with a special ceremonial meal known as a *seder* or "order of service." The story of the Exodus is read and explained. Food symbols are tasted by everyone at table. These are:

1. Three matzos (unleavened bread) symbolizing the three groups into which each Jewish community was divided.

2. A roasted bone, usually lamb or chicken, which represents the sacrificial paschal lamb offered on the eve of the exodus.

3. Bitter herbs, usually horseradish root and watercress, as a reminder of the bitterness of slavery.

4. A roasted or hard-cooked egg, recalling the individual offering at the Temple; also a symbol of life.

5. A green vegetable, usually parsley

or celery tops, as a suggestion of spring's rebirth.

6. Salted water into which these greens are dipped as a token of the tears shed for suffering and persecution.

7. A blend of chopped apple, nuts, and wine called *charoses* which represents the bricks made without straw by the Israelites who were slaves in Egypt.

8. Wine, which is served in goblets four times during the ceremony, to symbolize the promise of redemption made four times in the Bible.

In addition, a large goblet of wine is placed on the table for the prophet Elijah, for whom a door is left ajar. Legend has it that this messenger of the Messiah may arrive at anyone's table during the Passover seder as a harbinger of peace and freedom throughout the world.

Special Passover dishes such as fried matzos and nut cakes are prepared throughout the week.

Other Holiday Food Traditions—Rosh Hashanah, New Year's Day, is in the autumn. Honey and apples are served as a wish for a sweet year to come. Other sweets are served.

Yom Kippur, Day of Atonement, is a day of strict fasting, and prayer. No food or drink is partaken of for twenty-four hours of penitence. Traditionally the fast is preceded by a festive meal, and the fast is broken with fish dishes to symbolize fruitfulness and plenty.

Sukkot, Harvest Festival, is celebrated by decoration with fruits and vegetables and by serving sweets. A citrus fruit and branches of myrtle, palm, and willow are part of the ceremony. In many countries a stuffed cabbage or vine leaves is traditional. Also, so is strudel.

Shevout, Giving of the Law, is celebrated by serving dishes prepared with milk and honey symbolizing the "sweetness of Torah (Ten Commandments and other laws) and the nutrition of learning." It is a time of confirmations and consecration of the children and many parties are given.

Hanukkah celebrates the heroism of Mattathias and his sons the Maccabees, who defied Antiochus in the 2nd century B.C. At this time a miracle occurred. It was thought that there was only sufficient oil for one night's illumination, but the oil was found to last for eight nights. Candles are kindled each night in cele-

bration, and games and gifts are usual. *Latkes,* potato pancakes, are traditional.

Purim, the Feast of Esther, commemorates the rescue of her people by Esther, the Jewish Queen, wife of Xerxes or Ahasuerus of Persia, whose evil Prime Minister Haman had plotted to kill all the Jews in the kingdom. This is a gay holiday celebrated with masquerades and fetes. Foods associated with the festival are triangular cakes filled with poppy seeds or fruits, often prunes and nuts. These are called *Hamantaschen* or Haman's pockets. Strudels and cookies are also served.

 APPETIZERS AND SOUPS

CHOPPED CHICKEN LIVERS

½ pound chicken livers
Salt
1 medium onion
2 hard-cooked eggs
1 teaspoon salt
⅛ teaspoon pepper
Rendered chicken fat
Lettuce and tomato

Score chicken livers with a sharp knife. Wash, drain, and sprinkle with salt. Broil chicken livers for 3 to 5 minutes, or until cooked. Grind livers finely with onion and hard-cooked eggs. Add salt and pepper. Add enough chicken fat to make a mixture that is smooth and has the consistency of mashed potatoes. Serve on lettuce with a wedge of tomato. Makes 4 appetizer servings.

CHICKEN FAT AND GRIBENES
(Cracklings)

2 cups fat and skin of raw chicken, duck, or goose
1 onion, chopped

Cut fat and skin into small cubes. Fry slowly, stirring occasionally, in a skillet over medium heat. Drain fat as it fills pan. When fat is almost rendered, add onions and continue cooking until onions are golden-brown. Drain through a fine sieve. Store fat and use as rendered chicken fat. Reserve *gribenes* and use mixed into chopped chicken livers as a spread on bread to be served with soup, or as a snack tidbit. Makes 1 cup clear rendered chicken fat.

MUSHROOM BARLEY SOUP

6 dried mushrooms
¼ cup pearl barley
2 quarts water
2 teaspoons salt
¼ teaspoon pepper

2 onions, chopped
3 tablespoons butter
2 tablespoons flour
¾ cup milk

Soak mushrooms in cold water for 10 minutes. Slice. In a saucepan combine mushrooms with barley, water, salt, and pepper. Cover and simmer for 1 hour. Sauté onions in butter. Add to soup. Cook for an additional 30 minutes. Gradually, while stirring, mix flour with milk. Add mixture to soup. Cook, stirring, for 15 minutes. Makes 8 servings.

GOLDENE YOICH
(Golden Chicken Broth)

1 stewing chicken (4 to 5 pounds), and giblets
Boiling water
1 tablespoon salt
1½ cups diced carrots
¾ cup chopped celeriac or celery
½ cup diced parsnip

Use a fresh-killed fowl with a yellow skin with plenty of fat. Use gizzard, heart, and chicken feet if they are available. To clean chicken feet scald them in boiling water. Peel off membranes. Quarter chicken. Place chicken with gizzard, heart, and chicken feet in a large kettle. Cover with boiling water. Add salt and vegetables. Cover and simmer slowly. Do not remove scum. Simmer for 2 to 3 hours, or until fowl is tender. Remove chicken and serve separately; or place chicken pieces in a soup bowl and spoon soup over the top. Before serving soup, remove excess chicken fat and season to taste. Noodles may be added if desired. Makes 6 to 8 cups.

KNAIDLACH
(Matzo Balls)

2 eggs
¼ cup chicken or goose fat or shortening
1 scant cup matzo meal
¼ to ½ cup water (approximately)
1 teaspoon salt
Dash of ground ginger or cinnamon

Combine eggs, fat, and matzo meal and beat well. Add water and salt, stirring to make a stiff batter. Add seasoning, cover, and chill in refrigerator for at least 2 hours. About 30 minutes before serving, wet hands with cold water to prevent sticking and form balls of the batter. Drop the dumplings into boiling salted water, cover, and cook for 30 minutes. Drain, and serve with clear soup or as a substitute for potatoes.

■ **Variations**—Add 2 tablespoons chopped liver or 2 tablespoons finely chopped parsley to batter before chilling.

SCHAV
(Sorrel Soup)

1 pound schav (sorrel or sour grass)
2 onions, minced
8 cups water
2 teaspoons salt
1 tablespoon fresh lemon juice

Festive Tzimmes   **Gefilte Fish**

¼ cup sugar (optional)
2 eggs
Dairy sour cream

Wash sorrel, and shred. Place sorrel, onions, water, and salt in a large deep saucepan. Bring to a boil, lower heat, and simmer, covered, for 45 minutes. Add lemon juice and sugar, if desired. Beat eggs and gradually beat into soup. Chill; serve garnished with sour cream. Makes 1½ quarts.

 FISH

GEFILTE FISH

3 pounds fresh fish (1 pound each of whitefish, pike, and carp)
2 large onions, peeled and sliced
6 cups water
2 carrots, sliced
2 teaspoons salt
½ teaspoon white pepper
2 eggs
6 tablespoons ice water
1½ tablespoons matzo meal or cracker meal
Horseradish

Have fish filleted but reserve head, skin, and bones. Place head, skin, and bones in a large saucepan. Add onions, water, carrots, salt, and pepper. Bring to a boil, lower heat, and simmer until fish is ready. Grind fish fillets finely. Put fish into a bowl; correct seasoning. Add eggs, ice water, and matzo meal. Chop until mixture is smooth and well blended. With wet hands, shape fish mixture into balls about the size of a small baking potato. Place balls into fish stock carefully, cover, and simmer slowly for 1½ hours. Remove cover during the last 30 minutes of cooking. Cool fish slightly and place on a platter or put in a bowl. Strain stock over fish. Place carrots around fish. Chill. Serve with horseradish, white or red. Makes 6 generous servings.

JELLIED FISH

1 whole fish, 4 to 5 pounds (haddock, carp, or other fish)
2 medium onions, sliced
1 bay leaf
1 carrot, sliced
½ lemon, sliced
1½ teaspoons salt
6 cups water

Clean fish; remove head and tail. Put head and tail in kettle with remaining ingredients. Cover and cook for 1½ hours. Strain broth and return to kettle. Add the fish, cut into 1-inch slices. Simmer for 15 minutes, or until fish is done. Remove pieces carefully and put in shallow serving dish. Continue boiling broth until liquid has reduced to about 1½ cups. Pour over fish. Chill until firm. As fish chills, spoon stock over fish so that fish is completely covered. Serve garnished with lemon, black olives, and mayonnaise. Makes 4 to 6 servings.

Passover Nut Cake   **Charoses**

SWEET-AND-SOUR FISH

2 onions, thinly sliced
2 lemons, sliced
¼ cup firmly packed light brown sugar
¼ cup seedless raisins
1 bay leaf
6 slices of whitefish or pike
1½ teaspoons salt
2 cups water
1 cup gingersnaps, crushed
¼ cup cider vinegar
Slivered blanched almonds

Combine first 8 ingredients in a sauce-pan. Cover and simmer for 25 minutes. Remove fish with a spatula and place on a platter. Add gingersnaps and vinegar to pan juices. Cook over low heat, stir-ring constantly, until smooth and well blended. Pour sauce over fish, and sprin-kle with nuts. Serve warm or cold. Makes 6 servings.

 MEAT

CHOLENT
(Jewish Sabbath Meal-in-One)

2 onions, diced
2 tablespoons vegetable shortening or chicken fat
½ pound dried Lima beans, soaked overnight in cold water
½ cup barley
6 to 8 potatoes, pared and quartered
2 pounds brisket of beef, in one piece
2 tablespoons flour
Salt, pepper, and paprika to taste
Boiling water

Brown onions in shortening in the bot-tom of a large Dutch oven or other heavy pan with a lid. Pour in presoaked beans, barley, and potatoes. Make a space in the center and sink the meat in this space. Mix flour and seasonings and sprinkle over other ingredients. Add enough boiling water to come almost to the top of pan. Cover tightly and simmer very slowly, using an asbestos pad over the heat. Cook for 5 hours or overnight. Do not stir, but shake the pot from time to time to prevent sticking. This dish may be cooked in the deep well of a stove or in an electric beanpot. In that case, set control to 150°F. and cook overnight. May also be cooked in an automatic oven at very slow (200°F.) overnight. Makes 6 servings.

POT ROAST

4 pounds beef chuck, boneless and in one piece
Salt and pepper

3 tablespoons rendered chicken fat
4 onions, peeled and sliced
2 cups canned tomatoes
8 medium potatoes, peeled and cut into halves
8 carrots, cut into 2-inch lengths
2 tablespoons flour, lightly browned

Sprinkle meat with salt and pepper. Melt fat in a Dutch oven and brown meat in it on all sides. Add onions and tomatoes. Cover and simmer for 3 hours, turning meat occasionally and adding more to-matoes to keep meat from sticking. About 30 minutes before meat is ready, add potatoes and carrots and cook until tender. Remove meat and vegetables. Slice meat and keep warm. Mix browned flour with a little water to make a smooth paste. Add to pan juices. Cook over low heat, stirring constantly, until sauce is smooth and thickened. Pour sauce over meat and vegetables. Serve with dump-lings if desired. Makes 8 servings.

BRISKET OF BEEF

2- pound boneless fresh brisket of beef
Fat or shortening
2 cups dried beans, navy or Lima, soaked overnight
Salt and pepper
1 bay leaf
1 large onion, chopped

Brown meat in fat. Add drained beans. Add salt and pepper to taste, bay leaf, and onion. Add enough water just to cover the beans. Cover tightly and cook over low heat at a slow simmer, stirring occasionally, until meat and beans are tender, approximately 2 to 2½ hours. Can also be baked, tightly covered, in moderate oven (350°F.) for 2 to 3 hours. Makes 8 servings.

FESTIVE TZIMMES
(Main-Dish Meat and Vegetables)

5 large carrots, scraped
5 white potatoes, peeled
3 sweet potatoes, peeled
2½ pounds brisket or short ribs of beef
1 pound dried prunes, rinsed
1 teaspoon salt
½ cup honey or brown sugar
1 onion
Cold water to cover
2 tablespoons shortening or chicken fat
2 tablespoons flour

Slice vegetables 1 inch thick. Sear meat on all sides in a heavy Dutch oven or any other heavy saucepan. Add vege-tables and prunes to meat. Add salt, honey, onion, and water to cover. Bring to the boiling point and skim. Reduce

heat to simmer. Cook, uncovered, for 2½ to 3 hours, or until the meat is very tender to the fork. Do not stir, but shake the pot to prevent sticking. More water may be added if required. Remove onion. Taste and correct seasoning. Make a *roux* of the fat and flour and add to the mixture. Turn into a casserole or baking dish and bake in preheated moderate oven (350°F.) for 30 minutes, or until brown on top. Makes 8 servings.

TONGUE WITH SWEET-AND-SOUR SAUCE

Pickled beef tongue (4 to 5 pounds)
Water
1 onion, sliced
1 garlic clove
1 bay leaf
3 tablespoons shortening
1 onion, chopped
2 tablespoons flour
⅓ cup cider vinegar
⅓ cup honey
½ teaspoon ground ginger
¼ cup seedless raisins
¼ cup slivered blanched almonds
1 lemon, thinly sliced

Wash pickled tongue. Cover with water; add sliced onion, garlic, and bay leaf. Cover and simmer for about 3 hours, or until tongue is tender. Drain, and reserve 2 cups broth. Skin tongue and discard root and other bones. Slice, and keep warm. Melt shortening and sauté chopped onion until golden. Stir in flour. Grad-ually stir in reserved broth. Add re-maining ingredients and cook over low heat, stirring constantly, until smooth and thickened. Pour sauce over sliced tongue. Makes 6 servings.

STUFFED BREAST OF VEAL

6 pounds breast of veal
1 tablespoon salt
½ teaspoon pepper
1 teaspoon garlic powder
Bread Stuffing
¼ cup fat or shortening

Have butcher cut a pocket in the veal. Sprinkle meat inside and out with salt, pepper, and garlic powder. Lightly fill the pocket with Bread Stuffing. Fasten with skewers or sew opening. Melt fat in a roasting pan. Put veal in pan and roast in a slow oven (325°F.) for 3 hours, or until meat is tender. Baste every 30 min-utes with the pan juices. Add water to the pan to keep meat from sticking, if necessary. Makes 8 servings.

Bread Stuffing

3 tablespoons fat
1 onion, minced

Challah   Holishkes   Cholent   Knaidlach in Goldene Yoich

1 green pepper, seeded and chopped
½ cup chopped celery
8 slices of white bread
  Salt, pepper, crumbled dried thyme
1 teaspoon paprika
1 egg, well beaten

Melt fat and sauté vegetables for 10 minutes, stirring constantly. Soak bread in cold water for 5 minutes. Squeeze out all excess moisture. Mix bread with vegetables and salt, pepper, and thyme to taste. Stir in paprika and egg. Mix well.

SALAMI AND EGGS
16 slices of salami (kosher salami)
 8 eggs
   Salt and pepper
¼ cup water

Cut salami into strips and place in a large skillet. Sauté over low heat until salami is well heated and bottom of pan is well greased with the fat from the salami. Beat eggs, add salt and pepper to taste, and beat in water. Pour mixture over salami and cook as you would an omelet. Makes 4 servings.

 POTATOES, PASTA, AND PANCAKES

KARTOFFEL LATKES
(Potato Pancakes)
4 potatoes
1 tablespoon grated onion
1 large egg
⅓ cup all-purpose flour
¾ teaspoon salt
  Fat or oil

Peel potatoes and grate very finely; there should be about 3 cups grated. Squeeze out some of the moisture in the grated potatoes. Add onion, egg, flour, and salt. Beat until well blended. Put ½ inch of fat in the skillet. Drop batter by heaping tablespoonfuls into hot fat and fry until crisp and brown on both sides. Remove pancakes and drain on absorbent paper. Serve hot with sour cream, hot applesauce, cream cheese, or apricot or prune purée, if desired. Makes 4 servings.

POTATO KNISHES
2½ cups sifted all-purpose flour
 1 teaspoon baking powder
½ teaspoon salt
 2 eggs
½ cup cooking oil
 2 tablespoons water
   Potato Filling

Sift flour with baking powder and salt. Make a well in the center and add eggs, oil, and water. Mix with the hands and then knead on a lightly floured board until smooth. Roll out dough on a lightly floured board as thin as possible. Cut into 3-inch rounds. Place 1 tablespoon Potato Filling on each round. Moisten edges of dough and pull together to enclose filling completely and to form a ball. Place pinched side down on an oiled cookie sheet. Bake in preheated moderate oven (350°F.) for 35 minutes, or until brown. Makes about 2 dozen.

Note: Knishes can also be filled with pot cheese, ground meat or chicken, or with cooked and seasoned buckwheat groats.

Potato Filling

1 cup chopped onions
⅓ cup chicken fat
2 cups mashed potatoes
1 egg, well beaten
1 teaspoon salt
⅛ teaspoon white pepper

Sauté onions in fat until golden-brown. Beat in remaining ingredients.

KARTOFFEL CHREMSEL
(Potato Fritters)

4 potatoes, about 1½ pounds
2 egg yolks
1 teaspoon salt
⅛ teaspoon pepper
1 tablespoon potato starch
2 egg whites
Butter or fat

Cook potatoes and peel. Press potatoes through a ricer, or mash. Beat in egg yolks, salt, pepper, and potato starch. Beat egg whites until stiff but not dry. Fold egg whites into potato mixture. Heat butter in a skillet to depth of ½ inch. Drop mixture by tablespoonfuls into hot butter. Fry until crisp and golden-brown on both sides. Serve with sour cream or applesauce, if desired. Makes 6 servings.

FALAFEL (Chick-Pea Croquettes)

2 cups thick puréed cooked chick-peas
½ teaspoon salt
¼ teaspoon white pepper
¼ teaspoon mixed ground herbs—basil, marjoram, thyme
¼ teaspoon hot pepper sauce
Fine dry cracker or bread crumbs
2 eggs
2 tablespoons melted shortening or olive oil
Shortening for deep frying

Canned or cooked chick-peas should be drained and mashed. Grind chick-peas through the fine blade of a food chopper. Add salt, pepper, herbs, hot pepper sauce, and 2 tablespoons cracker or bread crumbs. Beat eggs and stir into mixture. Stir in 2 tablespoons melted shortening. Shape mixture into 2½- to 3-inch fingers about 1 inch in diameter. Roll each in dry cracker or bread crumbs. Fry a few at a time in deep hot shortening (360°F. on a frying thermometer) for 2 to 3 minutes, or until golden brown. Remove with a slotted spoon and drain on absorbent paper. Serve hot. Makes 18 to 20.

KASHA VARNISHKAS
(Buckwheat Groats with Noodles)

1 egg
1 cup buckwheat groats
½ teaspoon salt
2 tablespoons rendered chicken fat

2 cups boiling water
2 cups cooked bowknot noodles
Salt and pepper to taste

Combine unbeaten egg, groats, and salt. Place chicken fat in skillet and add groat mixture and boiling water. Cover tightly and cook over low heat, stirring occasionally, until kasha is tender, about 15 minutes. Add additional water or meat broth to keep mixture from sticking. Mix kasha with cooked noodles. Add salt and pepper to taste and reheat until piping hot. Serve with meat. Makes 6 servings.

KAESE BLINTZES
(Rolled Cheese Pancakes)

1 package (7 ounces) dry cottage cheese (farmer cheese)
1 carton (12 ounces) pot cheese
2 packages (3 ounces each) cream cheese
Sweet butter
8 eggs
1 tablespoon sugar
2 teaspoons salt
1½ cups sifted all-purpose flour
1½ cups milk
Parve margarine
Dairy sour cream

To make filling, beat cheeses, 1 tablespoon soft butter, 2 eggs, sugar, and ½ teaspoon salt together.

To make batter, beat 6 remaining eggs until frothy; add remaining 1½ teaspoons salt. Add flour, ½ cup at a time, stirring to make a smooth paste. Gradually add milk, stirring constantly. Heat a heavy 6½-inch skillet and grease well. Have a piece of brown paper and some *parve* margarine handy for greasing skillet when frying rest of pancakes. Into the hot skillet pour enough batter (2 to 3 tablespoons) to cover bottom when batter is quickly rolled around. Tilt pan to distribute batter. Cook until pancake is firm and browned on one side. Put on buttered plate, browned side up. Grease skillet if necessary and fry another pancake the same way. While second one is cooking, spoon about 1 tablespoon filling right on edge of first pancake. Fold up once, fold over two sides, and make one more turn. Put on buttered plate. Continue until batter and filling are used up. Should pancakes develop empty spaces during frying, fill spaces with a little batter.

When ready to serve, heat a small amount of butter in large skillet. Fry blintzes until golden-brown on all sides. Serve at once with sour cream. Fry only the number of filled blintzes desired for one meal. Unfried blintzes keep well for a day or two in the refrigerator. Or they can be wrapped in vapor-proof paper and frozen until ready to use. Makes about 2 dozen.

Cherry Blintzes

Mix 1½ cups drained canned pitted red sour cherries, 1½ tablespoons flour, ⅛

teaspoon ground cinnamon, and sugar to taste. Substitute for cheese filling in Blintzes recipe.

Blueberry Blintzes

Mix 1½ cups blueberries, 1½ tablespoons flour, ⅛ teaspoon ground cinnamon, and sugar to taste. Substitute for cheese filling in Blintzes recipe.

 BREADS

CHALLAH
(Sabbath or Holiday Twist Bread)

1 package active dry yeast or 1 cake compressed yeast
2 tablespoons sugar
1½ cups lukewarm water*
About 5 cups sifted all-purpose flour
2 teaspoons salt
2 eggs
2 tablespoons oil
1 egg yolk
2 tablespoons poppy seeds

Combine yeast, sugar, and ¼ cup water. *Use very warm water (105°F. to 115°F.) for dry yeast; use lukewarm water (80°F. to 90°F.) for compressed yeast. Let stand for 5 minutes. Sift flour and salt into a large bowl. Make a well in the center and drop in eggs, oil, remaining warm water, and finally yeast mixture. Work liquids into the flour. Knead on a floured board until dough is smooth and elastic. Place in a bowl, brush top with oil, cover with a towel, and let stand in a warm place to rise for 1 hour. Punch down, cover, and let rise to double in bulk. Divide dough into 3 equal parts. Between lightly floured hands, roll dough into 3 strips of even length. Braid these and place on a greased cookie sheet. Cover and let rise to double in bulk. Brush with egg yolk and sprinkle with poppy seeds. Bake in preheated moderate oven (375°F.) for 45 to 50 minutes, or until golden-brown. This recipe makes 1 very large loaf or 2 smaller loaves. It may be used as a pan loaf or for rolls instead of for twisted bread.

MANDELBROT
(Almond Bread)

1½ cups sifted all-purpose flour
¼ teaspoon salt
1 teaspoon baking powder
4 eggs
1 cup sugar
3 tablespoons cooking oil
1 teaspoon vanilla extract
1 cup chopped blanched almonds
1 tablespoon ground cinnamon

Sift flour with salt and baking powder. Beat eggs until thick and lemon-colored. Gradually beat in sugar. Stir in oil and vanilla. Stir in flour and almonds. Grease and flour two loaf pans (9 x 5 x 3 inches). Cover the bottoms of the pans with batter. Sprinkle with cinnamon. Add another layer of batter and cinnamon and con-

tinue layering until all cinnamon and batter are used. Bake in preheated moderate oven (350°F.) for 25 minutes, or until cake is golden-brown. Breads will only be 2½ inches high. Remove from pans, and cool. With a sharp knife cut breads into ½-inch slices. Place slices on greased cookie sheet and brown in preheated hot oven (400°F.) for 5 to 6 minutes.

 ## PICKLES

PICKLED PUMPKIN
2 pounds pumpkin
1 cup firmly packed dark brown sugar
½ cup cider vinegar
¼ teaspoon ground allspice
½ teaspoon salt

Remove skin and cut pumpkin into small wedges. Combine brown sugar, vinegar, allspice, and salt. Cook until sugar is dissolved. Add pumpkin and continue simmering until pumpkin is tender. Spoon mixture into sterilized glass jars. Seal. Makes about 1½ pints.

GARLIC HALF-SOUR PICKLES
48 medium cucumbers about 4 inches long
Coarse salt
Garlic cloves
Mixed pickling spices
Dill sprigs

Wash cucumbers and place in an upright position in sterilized jars. To each quart of cucumbers add 1 teaspoon salt, 4 garlic cloves, and ¼ teaspoon pickling spices. Place 1 sprig of dill with seed heads on top of each jar. Fill with cold water and let stand for 5 minutes before sealing. Store in cool place for about 2 weeks. Makes 48.

PICKLED GREEN TOMATOES
48 small green tomatoes
Salt
Water
Dill
Garlic cloves
1 tablespoon pickling spices
1 cup cider vinegar

Wash tomatoes and use whole. Do not remove stem end. Put into a brine solution made by adding 1 cup salt to each 4 cups water. Let stand overnight. Drain. Arrange tomatoes in a large crock or earthenware bowl. Layer tomatoes with sprigs of fresh dill with seed heads. Place 1 garlic clove on each layer of tomatoes. Tie pickling spices in cheesecloth bag.

Add vinegar, spices, and 6 quarts water to the tomatoes. Make sure all tomatoes are covered by lacing a weighted cover on them to keep them under liquid. Cover loosely with cheesecloth. Let stand for 2 weeks. Then pack into sterilized jars with liquid covering them; store in cool place for later use. Makes 48.

 ## DESSERTS AND CAKES

FRUIT COMPOTE
¼ pound each of dried apricots, peaches, and pears
1 juice orange
Pinch of ground allspice
2 tablespoons honey
2 tablespoons sugar
¼ cup walnuts or blanched almonds

Cover fruits with water and cook until tender. Drain juice from fruit and reserve it. Peel yellow rind from the orange and cut rind into slivers. Add rind to juice drained from fruit and cook over low heat until liquid simmers. Add spice, honey, and sugar. Continue to simmer until juice is slightly thickened. Pour syrup over fruit. Serve in compote dishes and sprinkle with nuts. Makes 4 servings.

LOKSHEN KUGEL
(Noodle Pudding)
3 tablespoons shortening or oil
½ pound broad noodles, boiled and drained
3 eggs, separated
1 teaspoon ground cinnamon
¼ teaspoon ground nutmeg
½ cup sugar
¼ teaspoon salt
¾ cup raisins (optional)
½ cup chopped nuts (optional)

Add fat to noodles. Beat egg yolks and add. Blend in spices, sugar, and salt. Beat egg whites until stiff but not dry and fold in. Pour into greased 1½-quart baking dish, adding one third of mixture at a time, alternating with raisins and nuts, if desired. Bake in preheated moderate oven (350°F.) for 45 minutes, or until set. Serve hot, with or without any desired pudding sauce, as a side dish with meats or as a dessert. Makes 6 servings.
Note: This is often varied with the addition of apples, chopped dried fruits, dates, etc.

LEKAH
(Honey Cake)
4 eggs
1 cup sugar

1 cup honey
½ cup strong black coffee
2 tablespoons oil
3½ cups sifted all-purpose flour
1½ teaspoons baking powder
1 teaspoon baking soda
½ teaspoon salt
1 teaspoon ground cinnamon
½ teaspoon ground ginger
¼ teaspoon ground nutmeg
Dash of ground cloves (optional)
½ cup chopped nuts
½ cup raisins
¼ cup finely cut citron or other candied fruit
2 tablespoons brandy (optional)

Beat eggs until light. Gradually beat in sugar until mixture is fluffy. Dilute honey with hot coffee and cool to lukewarm. Add oil. Blend into eggs and sugar alternately with sifted dry ingredients. Add nuts and fruits. Blend well, but do not overbeat. Add brandy. Pour into a well-greased and paper-lined pan (9 x 13 x 2 inches). Bake in preheated slow oven (300°F.) for 1 hour, or until a tester inserted in the center comes out clean of crumbs. Invert on a rack to cool before cutting into squares of desired size.

PRUNE PIROSHKIS
2 cups sifted all-purpose flour
½ teaspoon salt
⅔ cup shortening
1 egg yolk
¼ cup ice water
Prune Filling

Sift flour with salt. Cut in shortening until mixture resembles coarse cornmeal. Beat egg yolk with water and add to flour mixture. Stir until dough forms a ball. Roll out dough on a lightly floured board to ⅛-inch thickness. Cut into 3-inch rounds. Top each round with a spoon of Prune Filling. Moisten edges of dough and pull dough over the filling, forming a half-moon shape. Place on a greased cookie sheet. Bake in preheated hot oven (400°F.) for 15 minutes, or until brown. Makes about 2 dozen.
Note: Piroshkis can also be filled with chopped chicken livers, chopped fish, chopped mushrooms, or cheese.

Prune Filling
¼ cup honey
⅔ cup fresh orange juice
2 teaspoons fresh lemon juice
1 pound pitted prunes
2 teaspoons grated orange rind

Mix honey with orange and lemon juice and cook at a slow boil for 5 minutes. Add prunes, cover, and cook for 15 minutes. Drain and chop prunes. Stir in orange rind. Cool mixture before filling piroshki.

TAYGLACH MIT NESHOMAS
(Nut and Honey Sweetmeats)
3 cups sifted all-purpose flour
1 teaspoon baking powder
4 eggs
¼ teaspoon salt
Filling
Syrup

Sift flour with baking powder. Beat eggs with salt. Stir in flour. Knead lightly until smooth. Roll out on a lightly floured board to ⅛-inch thickness and cut into 1½-inch rounds. Place 1 teaspoon Filling on each round and fold dough around Filling to form a ball. Drop *tayglach* into hot Syrup and simmer for 15 minutes, or until Syrup has been absorbed. Shake pot occasionally to prevent dough from sticking. Place *tayglach* on a platter sprinkled with confectioners' sugar. Separate while still warm. Let cool and dry.

Filling
Mix 1 cup finely chopped or grated nuts and raisins with 1 teaspoon fresh lemon juice.

Syrup
Combine 1 cup honey with 1 cup sugar, ½ cup water, and ½ teaspoon ground ginger. Bring to a boil, lower heat, and drop in *tayglach*.

HOLIDAY SPECIALTIES

PASSOVER

PESACH RUSELL
(Passover Fermented Beet Juice)
10 to 12 pounds beets
Water

Wash beets, peel, and cut into quarters. Place beets in a clean crock of stoneware or earthenware. Cover beets with water and cover crock with cheesecloth. Let stand at room temperature for 1 week. Uncover and remove all scum. Stir well and re-cover. Let stand for 2 to 3 weeks, or until liquid is scarlet and clear. Makes 2 to 3 quarts of *rusell*.
Note: The *rusell* liquid and beets are used in borscht, to cook pot roast, as a drink, and to make beet horseradish.

RUSELL CHRAIN
(Passover Horseradish with Fermented Beet Juice)
Peel horseradish root and grate very finely. Add just enough rusell liquid (above) to moisten and tint the desired color. Season with salt and sugar to taste.

CHAROSES
4 tart apples, cored and grated
1½ cups blanched shelled almonds, ground
¼ cup walnuts, ground
3 tablespoons sugar
½ teaspoon each of ground cinnamon and ginger
1½ teaspoons grated lemon rind
3 tablespoons fresh lemon juice
Passover red wine

Combine all ingredients and blend with enough wine to give a spreading consistency. Makes 8 to 10 servings.

RUSELL BORSCHT
4 cups rusell liquid (at left)*
1 cup chopped rusell beets*
1 medium onion, chopped
Salt, sugar, and fresh lemon juice

Heat *rusell* liquid with beets and onion. Cook over low heat until beets are tender. Add salt, sugar, and lemon juice to taste. Makes 4 servings.
■ **Variation**—Sliced hard-cooked egg may be added to borscht when served either hot or cold. Or, when borscht is hot and ready to be served, beat 2 eggs until well blended. Gradually beat borscht into the eggs. Reheat slightly but do not boil. *If *rusell* liquid and beets are not available, fresh cooked or canned beets may be used with their juice. Add extra lemon juice for the tartness required.
Note: When served hot, add hot boiled potato and sour cream to borscht. When served cold, add chopped cucumbers, scallions, and sour cream.

RUSELL FLEISCH IN BORSCHT
(Meat Cooked in Fermented Beet Juice)
4 cups rusell liquid (at left)
2 cups chopped rusell beets
3 cups water
⅔ cup chopped onions
3 pounds boneless brisket or chuck of beef
Beef marrow bones
2 teaspoons salt
¼ teaspoon pepper
Sugar and fresh lemon juice
1 egg
Boiled potatoes

Place liquid and beets in a Dutch oven or deep kettle. Add water, onions, meat, bones, salt, and pepper. Cover and simmer for 2 to 3 hours, or until meat is tender. Remove meat, slice, and keep warm. Season broth to taste with sugar and lemon juice. Beat egg slightly and gradually beat broth from meat into egg. Spoon some of the sauce over the meat and serve the remainder in soup bowls. Serve boiled potatoes with the borscht in bowls. Makes 6 to 8 servings.

VEGETABLE CUTLETS
1¼ cups finely chopped cooked green pepper
1¼ cups tightly packed grated raw carrot
1¼ cups tightly packed chopped raw spinach
3 medium potatoes, boiled and mashed
1 tablespoon grated raw onion

1 tablespoon minced parsley
3 eggs
1½ teaspoons salt
1¼ cups matzo meal
Melted fat or shortening

Mix vegetables and parsley. Beat eggs with salt and add to vegetables, beating until mixture is well blended and smooth. Stir in matzo meal and let stand for 30 minutes. Form into patties about 3 inches in diameter and fry in shallow fat until golden-brown on each side. Drain on absorbent towels. Makes 8 servings.

MATZO BRIE
(Fried Matzos)
4 eggs, well beaten
1 cup water
Salt
4 matzos
Shortening or fat

Beat eggs with water and a little salt. Break matzos into small bite-size pieces. Soak in water; drain. Stir matzos into eggs and let stand for 5 minutes. Pour mixture into a skillet with a thin layer of hot shortening. Fry over moderate heat until golden-brown on one side. Turn and brown the other side, stirring occasionally to break up the pieces. Can be served for breakfast or lunch. Makes 4 servings.

MATZO KUGEL
(Matzo-Meal Pudding)
3 matzos
Water to cover
1 teaspoon salt
2 tablespoons melted chicken fat, shortening, or oil
3 eggs, separated
1 cup sugar
Grated rind of 1 lemon
Juice of 1 lemon
1 cup chopped apples
½ cup chopped nuts
Matzo meal
¼ teaspoon ground cinnamon

Soak matzos in water to cover until they are soft. Squeeze out excess liquid. Stir until creamy. Add salt and melted fat. Beat egg yolks with sugar, rind, and juice. Blend into matzo mixture. Fold in stiffly beaten egg whites. Alternate the batter with apples and nuts in a greased 2-quart pudding dish, starting and ending with batter. Sprinkle with matzo meal and cinnamon. Bake in preheated moderate oven (350°F.) for 30 minutes, or until lightly browned and set. May be served with fruit or wine sauces, or garnished with berries. Serve warm. Makes 6 servings.

CHREMSLACH
(Matzo-Meal Fritters)
1 cup matzo meal
2 tablespoons chopped blanched almonds
2 teaspoons granulated sugar
¼ teaspoon salt
1 cup chicken bouillon, boiling
4 eggs, separated
Fat or oil for deep frying

Confectioners' sugar
Honey

Mix matzo meal with almonds, sugar, and salt. Stir in boiling bouillon. Add mixture gradually to beaten egg yolks. Blend well. Beat egg whites until stiff but not dry. Use hands to fold egg whites into batter. Drop mixture by teaspoonfuls into deep hot fat (360°F. on a frying thermometer). Fry until golden-brown, 2 to 3 minutes. Drain on absorbent paper and sprinkle with confectioners' sugar. Serve with honey. Makes about 5 dozen.

PASSOVER NUT CAKE

  6 eggs
  6 tablespoons sugar
  6 tablespoons matzo cake meal
  1 tablespoon fresh lemon juice
  2/3 cup finely chopped almonds or walnuts
  1/8 teaspoon salt
  Confectioners' sugar

Separate eggs and beat egg yolks until thick and lemon-colored. Beat in sugar and continue beating until thick and creamy. Gradually stir in matzo cake meal. Stir in lemon juice and nuts. Beat egg whites with salt until stiff but not dry and fold them into cake batter. Pour mixture into an ungreased tube pan (9 x 3 inches). Bake in preheated slow oven (300°F.) for 45 minutes; increase heat to 325°F. for 15 minutes, or until top of cake springs back when lightly touched. Remove from oven and invert pan. Cool thoroughly, and then cut out of pan. Sprinkle with confectioners' sugar. Makes one 9-inch cake.

  SUKKOT

MEAT KREPLACH (Dumplings)

  2 cups sifted all-purpose flour
  1/2 teaspoon salt
  2 eggs
  2 to 3 tablespoons cold water
  Meat Filling

Sift flour with salt, and make a well in the center of the flour. Add eggs and water. Mix with the hands until dough becomes a compact ball. Knead on a lightly floured board until smooth and elastic. Let stand for 1 hour. Roll out on a lightly floured board as thin as pos-

sible. With a sharp knife cut dough into 2-inch squares. Top each square with a small ball of Meat Filling. Moisten edges of dough, bring opposite corners together, and press firmly to shape a triangle. Then bring the other two opposite corners together to form caplike *kreplach*. Drop *kreplach,* one at a time, into boiling salted water. Simmer slowly for 15 to 20 minutes. *Kreplach* will rise to the top when they are done. Serve with gravy or in chicken soup. Makes 2 to 3 dozen.

Meat Filling

Mix 1½ cups finely ground cooked meat or chicken with 1 well-beaten egg and 1 teaspoon grated onion. Shape mixture into small balls about the size of a small olive.

HOLISHKES (Meat-Stuffed Cabbage)

  2 pounds beef chuck, ground
  3/4 cup cooked rice or kasha
  2 eggs
  1/4 cup grated onion
  1/3 cup grated carrot
  1/2 teaspoon salt
  20 to 24 large green cabbage leaves
  1/2 cup cider vinegar or 1/4 teaspoon sour salt (citric acid crystals)
  3/4 cup firmly packed dark brown sugar
  1 can (8 ounces) tomato sauce

Mix meat with rice, eggs, onion, carrot, and salt. With a sharp knife carefully slice off the back of the tough rib of each cabbage leaf, keeping surface of leaf in one piece. Pour boiling water over cabbage leaves and let stand until wilted. Drain. Place a ball of meat about the size of a small plum at one side of the leaf. Roll the cabbage tightly around the meat to enclose the filling completely. Place filled rolls in a heavy Dutch oven or deep saucepan. Add remaining ingredients mixed together. Cover and simmer for 50 minutes to 1 hour. Add water if necessary to prevent sticking. Makes 8 to 10 servings.

 **SHEVUOT**

MAMALIGA (Cornmeal Mush)

  2 cups yellow cornmeal
  1 cup cold water

  1 teaspoon salt
  4 cups boiling water
  1/2 cup butter or margarine
  1 cup grated cheese or 2 cups pot cheese

Mix yellow cornmeal with the cold water. Add salt to boiling water. Stir in paste and cook over low heat, stirring constantly, for 30 minutes. Add butter and cheese and stir until butter is melted. Serve with additional butter, and jam, sugar, or preserves if desired. Makes 12 servings.

 PURIM

HAMANTASCHEN

  2½ cups sifted all-purpose flour
  1 tablespoon baking powder
  1 teaspoon salt
  1/4 cup sugar
  1 egg, beaten
  3/4 cup milk
  1/3 cup melted butter or margarine
  Poppy-Seed Filling or lekvar (puréed prune butter in a jar)
  1 egg yolk, beaten

Sift flour with baking powder, salt, and sugar. Beat egg with milk and mix with melted butter. Pour mixture into the center of the flour and stir until a soft dough is formed. Knead on a lightly floured board until smooth and not sticky. Roll to 1/4-inch thickness. Cut into 3-inch circles. Top each with a small spoon of Poppy-Seed Filling. Moisten edges of circle and fold the three sides over the filling, leaving the filling exposed in the center and shaping the pastry into a tricorn shape. Brush with egg yolk and place on a greased cookie sheet. Bake in preheated moderate oven (350°F.) for 20 to 25 minutes. Makes 15 to 18.

Poppy-Seed Filling

Mix 1 cup finely ground poppy seed with 1 egg yolk, 2 tablespoons honey or sugar, 1½ teaspoons fresh lemon juice, and 3 tablespoons finely chopped nuts. Blend well.

JULEP—An alcoholic drink made with spirits, most often bourbon, but sometimes rum or brandy; and sugar, crushed ice, and mint. The name is of Arabic origin but the drink is associated with the southern United States, especially Kentucky.

The proper construction of a mint julep has produced a great deal of controversy. It would, therefore, be imprudent and presumptuous to give a final formula for this exquisite, cooling, decorative, and consoling concoction. Suffice it to say that most people agree that the classic julep is one made with bourbon. As to whether the mint in a julep should be crushed or not, and the drink sipped from a straw or directly from the glass, each to his own choice. To quote the English writer Charles Dickens who traveled in the American southern states in 1842: "the mounds of ices, and the bowls of mint julep and sherry cobbler that they make in these latitudes, are refreshments never to be thought of afterwards, in summer, by those who would preserve contented minds."

KENTUCKY MINT JULEP

Chill silver julep mugs, goblets, or tumblers in frozen-food compartment of refrigerator. For each mug, dissolve 1 lump sugar or 1 teaspoon sugar in a little water. Reserve. Fill mug with finely crushed ice. Pour in 1½ ounces of bourbon. Stir in dissolved sugar. Stir until the mug is heavily frosted on the outside. Garnish with 6 sprigs of fresh mint, tucked into the ice so that they protrude. Serve with or without a straw.

GEORGIA MINT JULEP

Proceed as above, but substitute equal parts of brandy and peach brandy for the bourbon.

RUM MINT JULEP

Proceed as above, but substitute dark or light rum for the bourbon.

JULIENNE—The term, of French origin, refers first to food cut into thin matchlike strips. Vegetables, meats, poultry, and cheese can be cut in this manner. Julienne strips of food are used in soups, salads, and many other dishes. These strips of food should be cut with a sharp knife and handled carefully during preparation and cooking to prevent breaking.

The second meaning of the culinary term julienne is a clear consommé to which a mixture of finely shredded vegetables has been added. The vegetables are first cooked slowly in a little butter and then added to the hot consommé. Consommé Julienne is highly thought of in French cookery, since it makes an excellent light soup to precede a substantial dinner.

CONSOMMÉ JULIENNE

Mix 3 cans condensed consommé and 2 cans water; simmer for a few minutes. When ready to serve, pour consommé into bowls and garnish with some of each of the following cooked vegetables cut julienne style: carrot, white turnip, green pepper, leek, mushroom, celery, green cabbage, and lettuce. Sprinkle each serving with a little chopped parsley or chervil. Makes 6 servings.

JUNIPER BERRY—The fruit of the evergreen *Juniperus communis,* a small tree or shrub. The berries, which vary in size from one-fifth to one-half inch in diameter, are purple in color with a greenish bloom. The berries of the common juniper plant are too pungent to be eaten raw. They are dried for cooking, which makes them black, and used to flavor meats, game, stuffings, sauces, and marinades. They remove the strong flavor of game and give foods an interesting taste. They should be crushed before using, since this releases the flavor. The flavor of freshly dried juniper berries is intense but it dissipates fairly quickly so that dried juniper berries should not be kept too long. They are available in specialty food stores.

Juniper berries are an inseparable part of gin. They were first used, it is said, by the 17th-century nobleman, the Comte de Moret, son of the French king Henry IV. The very name "gin" comes indirectly from juniper berries, for the French name for gin was *genievre,* corrupted into "Geneva" in Holland. Gin is still called *genievre* in France.

The juniper tree and berry have traditionally been associated with the protection of people. It is said that when the Virgin Mary and Jesus were trying to escape from the punishment of King Herod by fleeing into Egypt, they hid behind the juniper bush's spreading branches and were saved. And Elijah, the prophet, while escaping from the wicked Queen Jezebel, wife of Ahab, was protected by an angel of God when he slept under a juniper tree in the wilderness.

The Romans burned juniper trees to protect themselves from harm. Virgil, the Latin poet of the 1st century A.D., instructs: "But learn to burn within your sheltering rooms/Sweet Juniper." In India, the juniper tree, there the drooping juniper, is a sacred shrub. The twigs are burnt as incense.

In America juniper berries were one of the foods of the Indians, used both as spices and dried and ground into meal.

JUNIPER POT ROAST IN BURGUNDY

  1 pot roast, about 5 pounds (rump, chuck, bottom round, or brisket of beef)
    Salt
10 juniper berries, crushed, or more to taste
  6 onions, peeled
  6 parsnips, peeled
  2 cups of 1½-inch pieces of celery
  6 carrots, scraped
  2 cups Burgundy or dry red wine
  2 cups boiling water or beef bouillon

Rub pot roast with salt and juniper berries. Put roast in a Dutch oven and surround with vegetables. Pour wine and water over roast. Cover tightly and simmer over low heat, turning meat occasionally, for 3 to 4 hours. (Meat can also be roasted, covered, in slow oven, 325° F., for 3 to 4 hours.) Remove meat and keep warm on a platter. Strain sauce and vegetables through a sieve or whirl all in a blender. Slice meat and serve with the sauce and hot sauerkraut. Makes 6 to 8 servings.

JUNIPER-BERRY SAUCE

  2 tablespoons butter
2½ tablespoons all-purpose flour
  2 cups beef bouillon
  1 bouillon cube
  ½ cup Madeira
    Salt and pepper to taste
  2 teaspoons ground juniper berries

Melt butter and stir in flour. Gradually stir in bouillon. Add bouillon cube and Madeira. Add salt and pepper to taste if necessary. Stir in juniper berries. Cook over low heat, stirring constantly, until sauce is smooth and slightly thickened. Serve with roast meats, fowl, and game. Makes about 2½ cups.

KABOB—The word, also spelled "kebab" and "cabob," means a small piece of roasted meat. The addition of the word *shish,* or "skewer," means that the meat was threaded on a skewer and then roasted.

In American usage, kabobs are small pieces of meat, fish, or poultry, with or without cubes of vegetables or fruits, which are sometimes marinated in a spicy sauce before being threaded on skewers. The skewers may be bamboo, wood, or metal. The food is then broiled or roasted until golden-brown and brushed with the marinade, if any, during cooking.

Kabobs are of Near Eastern origin and are a feature of the cuisines of Turkey, Iran, Iraq, Lebanon, Syria, and India.

LAMB SHISH-KABOB
2 pounds shoulder lamb chops,
   1½ inches thick
8 small onions, peeled
2 medium green peppers, cut into
   eighths
4 tomatoes, quartered

½ cup cooking oil
1 teaspoon salt
¼ teaspoon pepper
1 teaspoon crumbled dried marjoram
2 teaspoons fresh lemon juice

Bone chops and cut meat into cubes. Put meat and vegetables in bowl. Mix remaining ingredients and pour over contents of bowl. Store in refrigerator for at least 1 hour before starting to cook. Have ready some long metal skewers or firm slender green sticks. Push pieces of lamb and vegetables onto skewers or sticks, alternating meat with vegetables. Hold skewers over hot coals, turning to brown all sides. Take care not to burn sticks. Shish-kabob should be done in 10 to 15 minutes. Makes 4 servings.

SKILLET KABOBS
1½ pounds sirloin steak
2 tomatoes, each cut into 8 wedges
2 green peppers, cut into 1-inch pieces
1 can (8 ounces) onions, drained
   Salt and pepper to taste
   Cooking oil

Cut steak into 1-inch pieces. Thread meat and vegetables alternately on 8 short or 4 long skewers and sprinkle with salt and pepper. Heat small amount of oil in large skillet and brown kabobs quickly on all sides. Reduce heat, cover, and cook for 5 to 10 minutes, or until foods are of desired doneness. Serve on or off skewers, or hold food between toasted frankfurter rolls and pull out skewers. Makes 4 servings.

SPICY PORK KABOBS
2 pounds lean boneless pork
¼ cup smooth peanut butter
1 teaspoon ground coriander
1½ teaspoons salt
½ teaspoon cayenne
1 teaspoon ground cuminseed
½ teaspoon pepper
4 onions, grated
1 garlic clove, minced
1½ tablespoons fresh lemon juice
1 tablespoon brown sugar
3 tablespoons soy sauce

Cut pork into 1½-inch cubes. Mix remaining ingredients and add pork; stir until well coated. Cover, and refrigerate for several hours. Thread on skewers and broil in broiler or over coals for 20 to 25 minutes. Makes 6 servings.

PINEAPPLE-FRANKFURTER KABOBS

Cut frankfurters into 1-inch lengths. String on skewers alternately with drained pineapple chunks. Mix equal parts of prepared mustard and pineapple syrup; brush on frankfurters and pineapple chunks. Broil until sizzling hot. Serve with toasted split rolls.

SHRIMP KABOBS

Peel jumbo shrimps and remove veins. String on skewers, alternating with squares of bacon and pitted large ripe olives or cubes of pineapple. Dip into melted butter or oil and broil for 4 minutes on each side.

KALE—This member of the *Brassica* genus or cabbage family is also called "borecole," "cole," or "colewort." There are a number of varieties of the vegetable, ranging from dwarf to tall sizes, with leaves that vary from green to reddish or purplish. Kale is grown for its large curled or smooth leaves. It has a very high vitamin content. Kale can be cooked in any of the ways spinach is cooked, but the leaves should be chopped.

Availability and Purchasing Guide—Kale is most plentiful and inexpensive during the winter months. Look for crisp, clean leaves of good color.

Kale is also available canned and frozen.

Storage—Keep in refrigerator in moisture-proof bag or covered container.

☐ Refrigerator shelf, raw: 3 to 8 days
☐ Refrigerator shelf, cooked and covered: 4 to 5 days
☐ Refrigerator frozen-food compartment, cooked, prepared for freezing: 2 to 3 months
☐ Freezer, cooked, prepared for freezing: 1 year
☐ Canned, kitchen shelf: 1 year

Nutritive Food Values—Kale is a good source of vitamins A and C, and contains calcium, some riboflavin, and iron.

☐ 3½ ounces, raw = 38 calories
☐ 3½ ounces, cooked = 28 calories

Basic Preparation—Remove the tough stems and midribs; cut large leaves into pieces.

☐ **To Cook**—Add kale to 1 inch of boiling salted water; simmer for 10 to 15 minutes, until just tender. Drain. Season with salt, pepper, and butter. May be sprinkled with diced salt pork or bacon which has been cooked until brown and crisp.

☐ **To Freeze**—Wash kale thoroughly and remove tough stems and wilted leaves. Chop. Blanch in boiling water for 2 minutes. Drain. Chill in cold water for 5 minutes. Drain. Pack into containers, leaving ½-inch headspace. Seal.

KALE, COUNTRY STYLE

Cook 2 pounds of kale in 2½ cups of boiling salted water for 15 minutes, or until tender. Drain, and chop; put back in saucepan and add 3 tablespoons bacon fat and 1 tablespoon pickle relish. Heat well; season. Makes 3 servings.

KALE, BACON, AND OATMEAL

¼ pound bacon, diced
2½ cups water
2 pounds kale, washed, stemmed, and chopped
1 cup cooked oatmeal

Cook bacon over low heat until crisp; add water and kale. Cook for about 15 minutes, or until tender. Add cooked oatmeal; mix well. Season to taste with salt and pepper. Makes 6 servings.

KETCHUP—This highly seasoned, thick condiment sauce is also called "catchup" or "catsup." These two words derive from colloquial pronunciations of the real name, which comes from a Malay word *kechap* for spiced fish sauce.

Ketchup is a smoothly textured and brightly colored sauce, usually made with red-tomato pulp. It can also be made from green tomatoes, fruits, berries, vegetables, and even seafood.

Originally, ketchup meant a sauce in which the important ingredient was salted spiced mushrooms. In Great Britain, mushroom ketchup has been known for centuries and it is still widely used.

When making ketchup, the ingredients can be cooked until tender and then puréed through a sieve or food mill. Or the ingredients can be whirled in a blender before cooking and then cooked to the proper thickness. The two most important points to remember are first, to use a deep kettle to allow the mixture to "plop" without splattering the kitchen and second, to stir constantly when the mixture has cooked to a thick purée, to prevent sticking and scorching. Pour mixture while hot into sterilized jars, seal, cool, and store.

Ketchup can also be "cooked" in the oven. This eliminates watching and stirring. Bake mixture, uncovered, in preheated slow oven (325°F.) until volume is reduced by half. The length of time varies with the amount of moisture in the original purée.

Commercially made tomato ketchups are available, some more highly seasoned than others.

TOMATO KETCHUP

1 cup white vinegar
1½ teaspoons whole cloves
1½ teaspoons coarsely broken cinnamon stick
1 teaspoon celery seed
8 pounds (about 24) fully ripe tomatoes
2 cups water
1 tablespoon instant minced onion

½ teaspoon cayenne
1 cup sugar
4 teaspoons salt

Bring first 4 ingredients to boil and remove from heat. Scald and crush tomatoes. Put tomatoes in kettle with water, onion, and cayenne. Bring to boil and cook for 15 minutes. Put through food mill. Combine purée and sugar in kettle; cook, stirring frequently, for 45 minutes, or until reduced by half. Strain vinegar, discarding spices, and add with salt to tomato mixture. Continue cooking, stirring almost constantly, for 30 minutes, or until thick. Ladle into 4 hot sterilized ½-pint jars, and seal.

Note: To help retain color, wrap individual jars in brown paper before storing.

TOMATO COCKTAIL AND TOMATO KETCHUP

8 quarts tomatoes
4 celery stalks, minced
1 green pepper, minced
7 teaspoons salt
2 onions
1¼ cups sugar
1½ cups cider vinegar
1 teaspoon each of ground cinnamon and allspice
½ teaspoon ground cloves
¼ teaspoon pepper
Dash of cayenne

Wash, scald, peel, and quarter tomatoes. Simmer until very juicy. Strain juice through wire strainer or cheesecloth without pressing through any of the pulp. Reserve pulp for ketchup. To the juice add celery, green pepper, 4 teaspoons salt, and 1 onion, minced. Heat to simmering and strain into hot clean jars. Seal, and process in hot-water bath for 10 minutes.

Put tomato pulp through a sieve. Add sugar, vinegar, and remaining 3 teaspoons salt. Put spices and remaining onion, sliced, in a small muslin bag; tie securely and cook with tomato mixture. Cook until thickened, stirring often. Discard spice bag and pour ketchup into sterilized jars; seal. Makes about 4 quarts tomato cocktail and 1½ pints ketchup.

MUSHROOM KETCHUP

4 pounds mushrooms
Coarse salt (1 to 2 tablespoons)
1 cup vinegar
1 medium onion
1 garlic clove
1 teaspoon mixed pickling spice
¼ teaspoon nutmeg

Remove stems and peel mushrooms. Sprinkle undersides with salt, and let stand for 1 hour. Wipe with a paper towel. Wash stems and put stems and mushrooms in bowl. Sprinkle with salt and let stand in cool place for 3 days, stirring frequently with a wooden spoon. Put in kettle and add remaining ingredients. Simmer, covered, for about 1 hour, adding a little water or vinegar, if necessary. Strain, and put in hot sterilized bottles with screw tops. Fasten corks

loosely and stand bottles in pan of water reaching to tops of bottles. Bring slowly to boil and keep at this temperature for 20 minutes. Remove from water, insert corks, and screw on caps. Makes about 4 cups.

FRUIT KETCHUP

6 tart apples, cored and sliced
1 medium onion, chopped
½ cup sugar
½ teaspoon each of white pepper, salt, powdered mustard, and ground cloves and cinnamon
Pinch of allspice
¾ cup white vinegar
¼ cup water

Cook apples in enough water to cover until tender. Press apples through sieve and add remaining ingredients. Cook over low heat, stirring occasionally, until thick, about 2 hours. Pour into sterilized jars, seal, and cool. Makes about 1 pint.

GRAPE KETCHUP

5 pounds Concord grapes
½ cup water
5 cups sugar
2 cups cider vinegar
1 teaspoon salt
½ cup mixed pickling spices tied in a cheesecloth bag

Remove grapes from stems. Cook grapes with water at a boil until grapes are tender. Press grapes through a sieve or food mill. Add remaining ingredients and cook over low heat, stirring occasionally, until mixture is thick. Remove spice bag. Pour ketchup into sterilized jars, seal, cool, and store. Makes about 4 pints.

KID—This is the meat of a young goat slaughtered before being weaned. Kid is a surprisingly bland and delicate meat, which is prized in the cooking of Latin countries in Europe and South America. It is often served as an Easter dish as a substitute for the traditional Easter lamb. The reason for this is that lambs can grow into sheep and yield precious wool, while goats are less expensive and easier-to-raise animals. In any case, kid can be prepared like any young lamb.

ROAST KID

1 cup vinegar
2 medium onions, minced
1 teaspoon dried thyme
1 garlic clove, minced
1 bay leaf
1 teaspoon salt
4 pounds kid, cut into serving pieces
½ pound salt pork, sliced

Mix first 6 ingredients, and pour over kid meat in bowl. Let stand to marinate for 1 hour. Drain, and put meat in roasting pan. Cover with sliced pork. Roast in preheated moderate oven (350°F.) for about 2 hours, basting occasionally with drippings in pan, and adding a little water if necessary to prevent drying out. Makes 4 to 6 servings.

100 Menus
to help you plan more varied meals for your family with the recipes in this volume

*Recipes for all starred dishes found in this volume.

BREAKFAST

Sliced Oranges
with Cranberry Sauce
Broiled Kippered Herring*
Mamaliga (Cornmeal Mush)*
Butter

Sauerkraut Juice
Phillip's Ham and Eggs*
Buttered Thin Rye Toast
Blueberry Jam*

Grapefruit Sections
Crisp Sausage Links
Huckleberry Griddle Cakes*
Whipped Cream Cheese
Honey

Applesauce
Sonkás Palacsinta
(Pancakes Layered
with Minced Ham)*
Fried Tomatoes

Pears Stewed in Grape Juice
Crisp Bacon
Pecan Waffles
Honey Topping*

Pineapple Juice
Tortilla con Jamon
(Spanish Omelet with Ham)*
Hominy and Cheese*

Stewed Apricots
Fried Salt Pork
and Milk Gravy
on Hominy Grits*
Eggs Parmesan*
Hot Biscuits

Tomato Cocktail*
Haddock-Potato Patties*
with Poached Eggs
Old-Fashioned Hoecake*
Red-Cherry Jam*

LUNCH OR SUPPER

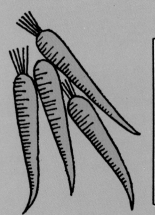

English Ham and Egg Cakes*
Broiled Peach Halves
Corn Bread Squares
Whipped Butter

Sliced Bananas
in Cranberry Juice
Huevos Escalfados Fritos
(Poached Eggs and Ham, Fried)*
Toasted English Muffins

Apple and Apricot Juice
Corned-Beef Hash
with Creamed Eggs*
Broiled Tomato Slices
and Mushrooms
Hard Rolls

Melon and Berries in Cream
Grilled English Herring*
Home-Fried Potatoes
Crumpets
Tomato Jam*

Jamaican Split-Pea Soup*
Cheese-Nut Burgers*
on Toasted Buns
Whole Apples or Pears

Quiche de Bourbonnaise
(Ham and Swiss Cheese Pie)*
Insalata Bandiera
(Flag Salad)*
Chocolate Fudge
or Brownies

Savory Shrimp Mold*
Insalata di Fagiolini
e Patate (Green-Bean
and Potato Salad)*
Assorted Crisp Breads
Orange-Honey Sherbet*

Jamaican Congo-Pea
or Kidney-Bean Soup*
Molded Crabmeat Salad*
Cracked Wheat Toast
Plum Jelly*

Baked Pea Beans
Boston Brown Bread
Pickled Green Tomatoes*
Jellied Pear and
Cream-Cheese Salad*

Rollmops*
Jellied Vegetable Salad
Pumpernickel Bread
Sweet Butter
Honey-Date Bars*

Tuna Salad with Sour-Cream
Horseradish Sauce*
Dill Pickles   Cherry Tomatoes
Crackers
Honey-Orange-Almond Cake*

Honeydew Rings
with Shrimp Salad*
Hominy Puffs*
Chocolate or Coffee
Ice Cream Sodas*

Kingston Potato Soup*
Pizza con Uova e Prosciutto
(Ham and Egg Pizza)*
Strawberries à la Mode*

Grilled Frankfurters
or Hamburgers
Buttery Garlic Grits*
Tomato Lettuce Salad
Apple and Grape-Juice Ice*

Eggs Zurlo*
Pickled Beets on Greens
Ice-Cream-Sundae*

———————◆———————

Minestrone Milanese*
Toasted Italian Bread
Banana Splits*

Goldene Yoich
(Golden Chicken Broth)*
Sour Rye Bread
Garlic Half-Sour Pickles*
Passover Nut Cake*

———————◆———————

Crabmeat Stuffed Mushrooms*
Jellied Cottage-Cheese
and Tomato Salad*
Melba Toast
Cantaloupe Ice*

Ruby-Glazed
Chicken-Liver Pâté*
Crisp Rye Wafers
Cucumber Cups*
Huckleberry Cottage Pudding*
with Lemon Hard Sauce*

———————◆———————

Jamaican Onion Soup
with Cheese*
Ham and Corn Fritters*
Waldorf Salad

Roast Fresh Ham*
Succotash
Baked Yams
Red Cabbage Slaw
Pocket Book Rolls
Strawberry Sundae

———————◆———————

Mushroom Barley Soup*
Spiced Ham and Bananas*
Oshitashi
(Spinach with Sesame)*
Ice-Cream Shadow Cake*

Curried Ham
and Fresh-Pork Loaf*
Spicy Cranberry Sauce*
Braised Cabbage*
Green Beans and Celery Salad
Corn Sticks   Butter
Taylach mit Neshomas
(Nut and Honey Sweetmeats)*

———————◆———————

Savory Stuffed Heart*
Broccoli Vinaigrette
Vienna Bread   Butter
Apricot Ice-Cream Pie*

Magyar Guylás
(Hungarian Goulash)*
Buttered Noodles
with Caraway Seeds
Honeyed Beets*
Celery Hearts
Rum-Raisin Ice Cream*
Petticoat Tails*

———————◆———————

Pavese (Egg Consommé)*
Haddock Plaki*
Deviled Eggs* on Lettuce
Sliced Tomatoes
Challah
Szilvás Gombóc
(Plum Dumplings)*

Veal Hearts
with Fruit Stuffing*
Risotto alla Milanese
(Rice, Milan Style)*
Green Beans
Sliced Cucumber Salad
Almond Ice Cream*

———————◆———————

Pachadi (Yogurt Salad)*
Pickled Pumpkin*
Keema Matar
(Chopped Meat with Peas)*
Steamed Spinach
Sesame Crackers
Fresh Coconut Ice*

Consommé Julienne*
Stuffed Pork Fillets*
Squash Casserole*
Cabbage, Green and
Red-Pepper Salad
Rolls
Pineapple Ice Cream*

———————◆———————

Tomato Juice
Flaked Haddock, Newburg*
on Squares of
Grits Batter Bread*
Green Bean, Onion, and
Cucumber Salad
Blueberry Parfait*

Veal Hot Pot*
Gohan (Rice)*
Green Pepper Salad
Squash Muffins*
Strawberry Chiffon Pie*

———————◆———————

Gefilte Fish*
Red Horseradish
Festive Tzimmes
(Main Dish
Meat and Vegetables)*
Coleslaw
Dark Pumpernickel Bread
Watermelon Granité*
Lekah (Honey Cake)*

Pride of Erin Soup*
Seventeenth-Century
Beef Pot Roast*
Mashed Yellow Turnips
Pepper Hash*
Soda Bread*   Butter
Honeyed Pears*

———————◆———————

Cock of the North
(Capon with Pearl Onions
and Mushrooms)*
Potato Collops*
Kale
Currant-Jelly and
Raspberry Ice*
Lenten Cake*

Beef-and-Kidney Pudding*
Green Beans
with Horseradish Sauce*
Sliced Tomatoes
Irish Moss Blancmange*
Grostoli (Crisp Cookies)*

———————◆———————

Irish Stew*
(Mutton or Lamb)
Buttered Cabbage
Cucumber, Carrot and
Green Pepper Sticks
Crispy White Rolls
Apple Puddeny-Pie* Topped
with Vanilla Ice Cream*

Uova in Purgatorio
(Eggs in Purgatory)*
Crostini alla Mozzarella
(Italian Mozzarella Skewers)*
Mixed Green Salad
Ice 'n Cream* Cookies
Espresso

———————◆———————

Anchovy Eggs* on Chicory
Scaloppine di Vitello
(Veal Scaloppine)*
Potato Pastry Shells*
Filled with Cream
Green Peas
Finocchio and Plum Tomatoes
Cassata Napolitana (Cake)*

Fegatini di Pollo alla
Salvia (Chicken Livers
with Sage)*
Spaghetti al Quattro
Formaggi (Spaghetti with
Four Cheeses)*
Escarole and Green Pepper
Salad with Italian Dressing
Honeydew and Orange Dessert*
Cookies

———————◆———————

Smoked Salmon with Capers
Myrtle Bank Jamaican
Pepperpot Soup*
Hot Cornbread Squares
Coffee-Chocolate Pie*

Indian Broiled Shrimps*
Moong Ki Dal (Mung Beans)*
Dahi Bhath
(Rice with Buttermilk)*
Mango Chutney
Tangerine Ice
in Orange Shells*

———————◆———————

Soowar Ka Gosht Vindaloo
(Sour Pork Curry)*
Rice   Spiced Peach Jam*
Crisp Rolls
Honey Mousse*
Sliced Mangoes
Darjeeling Tea

Pickled Herring*
Csirke Paprikás
(Chicken Paprika
with Sour Cream)*
Makos Tészta
(Noodles with Poppy Seed)*
Cseresznye Kisütve
(Deep-Fried Cherries)*

———————

Jellied Fruit Soup*
Holishkes
(Meat-Stuffed Cabbage)*
Wilted Cucumbers with Dill
Pumpernickel   Sweet Butter
Diós Tekercs (Hungarian
Walnut Roll)*

———————

Grapefruit Avocado Cup
Stuffed Ham Slices*
Corn Pudding
Buttered Green Lima Beans
Hot Biscuits
Cranberry and Fig Jam*
Mocha Parfait*

———————

Melanzane alla Marinara
(Eggplant Marinara
Appetizer)*
Pollo alla Cacciatora
(Chicken Cacciatora)*
Spaghetti with Parmesan
Cheese   Bread Sticks
Instant Blender Lemon Ice*

———————

Sarson Bhara Kekda
(Shrimps with Mustard)*
Murgha Kari (Chicken Curry
with Tomatoes)*
Rice   Raw Cauliflower
Salad with Sesame Seed
Banana Ice Cream*

———————

Chopped Chicken Livers*
Tongue with Sweet-and-
Sour Sauce*
Cabbage Strudel*
Waldorf Salad
Coffee Ice Cream with
Chocolate-Covered
Coffee Beans*

———————

Cold Fresh Ham*
Sweet Pickled Peaches
Tejfeles Baffözélek
(Dried Beans in Sour Cream)*
Hearts of Romaine or
Belgian Endive
Chakin Shibori
(Sweet-Potato Dessert)*

———————

Crabmeat Cocktail
Roast-Beef Hash Casserole*
Red-Pepper Jam*
Stewed Tomatoes
and Celery
Corn Muffins
Dutch Honey Cake*

———————

Bárány Pörkölt Árpakásával
(Lamb and Barley Stew)*
Squash Baked in Shells*
Green Bean Salad
Sour Rye Bread
Applesauce   Huszárcsok
(Hussar's Kisses)*

———————

Broiled Haddock Fillets*
with Fresh Grapefruit
Sections
Peperoni con Patate
(Peppers and Potatoes)*
Watercress-Radish Salad
Jelly-Roll Sandwiches*
with Ice Cream

Clam and Tomato Juice
Cocktail
Roast Duck
Honey-Glazed Apples*
Onions with Peas
Red and Green Cabbage Salad
Poppy-Seed Strudel*

———————

Ham and Corn Potato Soup*
Jellied Chicken Mold*
Tomato, Cucumber, and
Avocado Salad
Peach Ice*
Brown-Sugar Hermits*

———————

Celery and Sweet Pickles
Cock-a-Leekie Soup*
Haggerty*
Mince Pie   Tea

———————

Hamburger Princess*
Salt Pork, Beans,
and Hominy*
Shredded Carrot and
Cabbage Salad
Fruit-Juice Ice*
Hickory Nut Cake*

———————

Hamburger Guacamole*
Mexican Hominy*
Fresh Pineapple and
Mixed Greens Salad
Crisp Toast
Cinnamon Chocolate Parfait*

———————

Chicken Hash à la Ritz*
Fresh Asparagus
Wild Rice
Tomatoes Stuffed with
Cucumbers and Green
Onion Salad
Garlic French Bread
Frozen Crêpes*

———————

Turkey Noodle Soup
Jellied Meat Loaf*
Carrot Curls·
Toasted Split French Rolls
with Parmesan Cheese   Butter
Cherry Strudel*

———————

Cold Rusell Borscht*
Hot Sweet and Sour Fish*
Kartoffel Latkes
(Potato Pancakes)*
Toasted Bagels
Sweet Butter
Hickory Crescents*
Muscatel Ice*

———————

Fruit Cup
Disznókaraj Magyarosan
(Hungarian Pork Chops)*
Kasha Varnishkas (Buckwheat
Groats with Noodles)*
Jerusalem Artichokes
with Tomatoes*
Nut Strudel*

———————

Ham-Lima Bean Soup*
Canadian Hamburger Pie*
Avocado-Melon Salad*
Chocolate Ice Cream Roll*
with Chocolate Fudge Sauce*

———————

Jellied Consommé Madrilene*
Baked Ham with Spicy Sauce*
Baked Yams
Buttered Spinach
Pear, Cranberry, and Lettuce
Salad
Rolls   Butter
Chocolate Ice Cream*

———————

Ham-Stuffed Chicken*
Quince and Cranberry Jelly*
Baked Potatoes
Wilted Spinach Salad
Hot Buttermilk Biscuits
Margarine
Gajar Halwa (Carrot Dessert)*

———————

Prosciutto with Fruits*
Cannelloni alla Parmigiana
(Stuffed Pancakes)*
Mixed Green Salad
with Plum Tomatoes
Italian Dressing
Wholewheat Italian Bread
Butter
Chocolate-Rum Sundae*

———————

Wild West Hamburger*
Potatoes Hashed in Cream*
Tomatoes, Green Peppers, and
Cucumbers in Vinegar
Sourdough or French Bread
Huckleberry Shortcake*

Knaidlach
(Matzo Balls)*
in Consommé
Pesce alla Siciliana
(Sicilian Fish)*
Cooked Mixed
Vegetable Salad
Hard Rolls
Orange Ice*   Cookies

◆

Meatball Shepherd's Pie*
Kale, Country Style*
Lettuce Hearts and
French Dressing
Spanish Cream*
Mincemeat Hermits*

Kreplach* in Chicken Soup
Brisket of Beef*
with Lima Beans
Tomato and Watercress Salad
Sour Rye Bread
Meringues Glacées* with
Rhubarb Ice*

◆

Juniper Pot Roast
in Burgundy*
Kartoffel Chremsel
(Potato Fritters)*
Zucchini al Burro
(Squash with Butter)*
Escarole-Beet Salad
Mocha Sundae*

Head Cheese*
Liffey Trout with Mushroom
Sauce*
Duchess Potatoes
Coleslaw
Blueberry Ice Cream*
Molasses Hermits*

◆

Chicken Soup with Sherry*
Corned-Beef Hash Lyonnaise*
Tomato Ketchup*
Brussels Sprouts
Apple and Celery Salad
Ladyfinger Ice-Cream Cake*

Vegetable Juice Cocktail
Clam Pastries*
Creamed Hamburger
and Cabbage*
French-Fried Potatoes
Celery and Cucumber Sticks
Fresh Pineapple Ice*
Cookies

◆

Ham Croquettes*
with Hazelnut
and Mushroom Sauce*
Whole Carrots with Honey
Glaze*   Brown Rice
Asparagus, Pimiento Salad
Raspberry Chiffon Pie*

Broiled Cod Steaks with
Salsa Verde Piccante
(Piquant Green Sauce)*
Shoestring Potatoes
Orange and Grapefruit Salad
Toasted Corn Bread
Vanilla Bavarian Cream*

◆

Maiale Affogato
(Stewed Pork with Celery)*
Whipped Potatoes
Marinated Carrots and Peas
on Lettuce
Seeded Hard Rolls
Coffee-Banana Bavarian*
Salted Almonds

Barbecued Halibut Steaks*
New Potatoes in Cream
Peas and Mushrooms
Grape and Orange Salad
Buttered Parkerhouse Rolls
Harlequin Crinkle Cups*

◆

Suimono (Clear Soup)*
Vegetable Tempura
and Sauce*
Chirinabe (Fish Sukiyaki)*
Kyuri-Momi
(Vinegared Cucumber)*
Chakin Shibori
(Sweet Potato Dessert)*
Green Tea

Miso Shiru
(Bean Paste Soup)*
Sashimi (Sliced Raw Fish)*
Jyuniku-Teriyaki
(Broiled Beef)*
Soba (Buckwheat Noodles)*
Oshitashi
(Spinach with Sesame)*
Awayuki-Kan (Snow Gelatin)*

◆

Ham Baked in Claret*
Succotash   Baked Yams
Spinach-Red Onion Salad
Huckleberry Cream-Cheese
Pie*

Beef Loaf, Farmer Style*
Mushroom Ketchup*
Hominy au Gratin*
Panned Mixed Greens
Radishes   Green Onions
Strawberry Ice*
Chocolate-Diamonds
with Hazelnuts*

◆

Beef and Rice Casserole*
Buttered Mixed Vegetables
Wholewheat Rolls
Pear and Mandarin Orange
Salad
Molasses Chip Sundae*

Melon Wedges Wrapped
in Prosciutto*
Lasagne con le Polpettine
(Lasagna with Meatballs)*
Tossed Green Salad with
Ripe Olives
Lemon Frappé*

◆

Spicy Pork Kabobs*
Wheat or Rice Pilaf
Sesame Wafers
Apple, Olive and Celery
Salad
Hazelnut Cream*

Tennessee Hamburger*
Baked Hominy Grits*
Mustard Greens
or Swiss Chard
Hot Corn Sticks   Butter
Perfection Salad
Strawberry-Honey Bavarian*

◆

Meatballs with Almond–
Mushroom Noodles*
Zucchini Fritte
(Fried Squash)*
Green Pepper, Pimiento and
Cabbage Salad
Plum Ice*   Poundcake

Tomato-Avocado
Hors-d'Oeuvre*
Dingle Mackerel*
Slieve na mBam Carrots*
Hard Rolls   Butter
Honey-Nut-Apple Pie*

◆

Pumpkin Soup*
Pork Fricassee Filipino*
Curried Rice
Banana and Macadamia Nut
Salad
Coconut Cake

Pork and Veal Head Cheese*
Sweet Pickles
Mellanzane alla Parmigiana
(Eggplant Parmigiana)*
Chicory and Romaine Salad
Italian Bread Sticks
Fresh or Stewed Figs in
Tokay Wine

◆

Watercress Soup*
Pot Roast*
Vegetable Cutlets*
Zeller Salatá (Celery-
Root Salad)* on Greens
Pumpernickel Toast
Cherry Strudel*

Petto di Vitello
(Veal Breast)*
Vermicelli alla Pastora
(Fine Noodles for the
Shepherdess)*
Marinated Tomatoes and
Cucumbers
Fresh Fruit Cup

◆

Turkey Hash*
Shoestring Potatoes
Broccoli with Hollandaise
Sauce*
Tomato Aspic on Lettuce
Seeded Hard Rolls
Hazelnut Tarts*

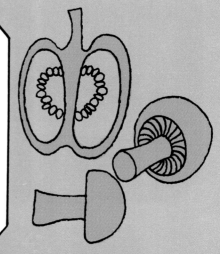

*Recipes for all starred dishes found in this volume.

GENERAL INFORMATION

The Ingredients and Measurements Used in Recipes

All recipes in this book have been tested in the Woman's Day Kitchens with standard American measuring cups (8 ounces = 16 tablespoons), measuring spoons (1 tablespoon = 3 teaspoons), and other standard kitchen equipment. All measurements are level. Liquids are measured in standard 8-ounce glass measuring cups, at eye level.

All sugar is granulated white sugar unless otherwise specified.

All flours, cake and all-purpose, are sifted before measuring unless otherwise specified. No self-rising flour is used.

All baking powder is double-acting baking powder.

All brown sugar is firmly packed when measured.

All confectioners' sugar is sifted before measuring.

All pepper is ground black pepper unless otherwise specified.

Fats and shortening are measured at room temperature, packed firmly into measuring cup and leveled with a straight knife. They are scraped out with a rubber spatula.

Salted butter or margarine, packed in ¼-pound sticks, is used unless otherwise specified. 1 stick = ½ cup = 8 tablespoons = ¼ pound.

1 tall can evaporated milk (14½ ounces) contains 1⅔ cups undiluted evaporated milk. Sweetened condensed milk is an entirely different product, and cannot be used interchangeably with evaporated milk.

⅓ to ½ teaspoon dried herbs can be substituted for each tablespoon fresh herbs. Crumble herbs before using to release flavor.

Before starting to cook or to bake, read the recipes carefully. Assemble all ingredients and equipment. Follow recipe exactly. Do not increase or decrease recipe unless you are a skilled enough cook to recognize what adjustments must be made as to ingredients, pan sizes, and/or cooking time.

Cooking Temperatures and Times

Cooking temperatures and times are approximate for meat. They depend not only on the weight and kind of meat, but also on its shape, temperature, and its bone and fat contents. A meat thermometer was used in testing.

Cooking times for meats are as recommended by the National Live Stock and Meat Board, 36 Wabash Avenue, Chicago, Illinois 60603.

Oven Temperatures

TEMPERATURES (Degree F.)	TERM
250 to 275	VERY SLOW
300 to 325	SLOW
350 to 375	MODERATE
400 to 425	HOT
450 to 475	VERY HOT
500 to 525	EXTREMELY HOT

Important—Preheat oven for 10 to 15 minutes before placing food in it. Many a cake has been spoiled by being placed in a barely heated oven. Baking times are based on the assumption that the oven is already at the stated temperature.

Check the oven temperature control frequently, especially if baking times vary from those given in recipes. (This can be done with a portable oven thermometer.) If a control is consistently off, call your public utility. They should be able to reset the oven temperature control.

Caloric Values

The caloric values, where mentioned, for each food are based on 100 grams, about 3½ ounces edible portion, as mentioned in Composition of Foods, Agriculture Handbook No. 8, Agricultural Service of the United States Department of Agriculture, Washington, D. C., revised December 1963.

APPETIZERS

Anchovy Eggs 912
Antipasto Misto (Antipasto Plates) .952
Apple Slices, Savory 913
Avocado Hors-d'Oeuvre 913
Banana-Ham Rolls, Glazed 856
Charoses .994
Cheese Olive Puffs 913
Chicken-Liver Pâté, Ruby-Glazed. .979
Chicken Livers, Chopped 987
Clam Pastries 912
Crabmeat Stuffed Mushrooms . . .913
Cucumber Cups 913
Cucumbers and Onions, Wilted . .912
Curry Puffs. 912
Deviled Eggs 912
Fegatini di Pollo alla Salvia
  (Chicken Livers with Sage) 955
Ham
  Canapés, Smithfield Ham 852
  Frenched Ham and Swiss 913
  Ham-and-Cheese Appetizers . . .852
  Ham and Egg Butter 866
  Ham and Egg Piroshki (Little
    Russian Pies) 864
  Ham Dip 852
  Ham Turnovers. 852
  Potted Ham and Eggs 866
  Prosciutto with Fruits 952
Herring
  Herring Butter 903
  Herring in Sour Cream 903
  Herring Salad 913
  Pickled Herring 903
  Rollmops 903
Kyuri-Momi (Vinegared
  Cucumber) 978
Medaglioni di Mozzarella
  (Medallions of Cheese) 952
Melanzane alla Marinara
  (Marinated Eggplant Appetizer) .952
Mushroom Pastries 912
Nigiri Sushi (Raw Fish Rice Ball) .971
Quiche de Bourbonnaise (Ham and
  Swiss-Cheese Pie) 862
Sashimi (Sliced Raw Fish) 971
Shrimps, Indian Broiled 913
Tempura .971
Tempura Sembei (Cracker-Fried
  Shrimps) 972
Tomato-Avocado Hors-d'Oeuvre . .913

BEVERAGES

Ice-Cream Sodas 932
Irish Coffee. 950
Mint Julep, Georgia 996
Mint Julep, Kentucky 996
Mint Julep, Rum 996
Pesach Rusell (Passover Fermented
  Beet Juice) 994

BREADS, PANCAKES, DUMPLINGS

Challah (Twist Bread) 992
Chapatis .939
Diós Tekercs (Walnut Roll) 922
Dumplings
  Ham Dumplings 852
  Knaidlach (Matzo Balls) 987
  Meat Kreplach (Dumplings) . . .995
  Potato Knishes 991
Pancakes
  Cannelloni alla Parmigiana 958
  Huckleberry Griddle Cakes 915
  Kartoffel Latkes (Potato
    Pancakes) 991

Manicotti (Stuffed Pancakes) . . .958
Sonkás Palacsinta (Pancakes
  Layered with Minced Ham) . . .919
Pizza con Uova e Prosciutto
  (Ham and Egg Pizza) 864
Quick Breads
  Batter Bread, Grits 907
  Boxty-on-the-Griddle 944
  Boxty-on-the-Pan 944
  Buns, Hazelnut Cinnamon 882
  Hamantaschen 995
  Hoecake, Old-Fashioned 904
  Mandelbrot (Almond Bread) . . .992
  Matzo Brie (Fried Matzos) 994
  Muffins, Squash. 915
  Nut Bread 904
  Soda Bread, Basic Recipe for 944

CAKES

Barmbrack 949
Cassata Napolitana (Rich Dessert
  Cake) .960
Hickory Nut Cake 904
Honey Cake, Dutch 911
Honey-Orange-Almond Cake 910
Lekah (Honey Cake) 993
Lenten Cake (Eggless) 949
Nut Cake, Passover 995
Potato Seedy Cake 950

CANDIES AND CONFECTIONS

Buttered Honey Nuts 911
Hickory Nut Creams 904
Pennies from Heaven 910
Tayglach mit Neshomas (Nut and
  Honey Sweetmeats) 994

CASSEROLES

Beef and Rice Casserole 872
Beef Casserole with Almonds. 873
Beef, Potato, and Bean Casserole. .873
Corned-Beef Hash and Tomatoes,
  Baked .881
Cottage Pie 876
Festive Tzimmes (Main Dish and
  Vegetables) 990
Frankfurter, Hominy, and Green-
  Pea Casserole 907
Hake Casserole. 847
Ham-and-Bean Bake 853
Ham and Broccoli Casserole 853
Ham and Cabbage with Tomatoes. .855
Ham and Green-Noodle Casserole. .853
Ham and Potatoes au Gratin. 853
Ham and Sweets 855
Hamburger-Macaroni Casserole . .872
Hamburger Pie, Canadian. 872
Ham Fleckerl, Viennese (Ham and
  Noodle Casserole) 865
Lasagne al Forno 873
Lasagne con le Polpettine
  (Lasagne with Meatballs) 958
Roast-Beef Hash Casserole 881
Tempura Domburi (Tendon) 972
Tempura Soba (Fried Foods with
  Noodles) 972
Wiener Eierkuchen (Egg Cake) . . .865

CEREALS AND PASTA

Hominy
  Baked Hominy Grits 907
  Buttery Garlic Grits 907
  Fried Hominy Grits 907
  Hominy and Cheese 907
  Hominy au Gratin 907
  Hominy Puffs 907

  Mexican Hominy 907
  Salt Pork, Beans, and Hominy . . .907
  Salt Pork and Milk Gravy on
    Hominy Grits, Fried 907
Macaroni and Cheese, Ham-
  Asparagus Rolls with 858
Mamaliga (Cornmeal Mush) 995
Noodles
  Diós Tészta (Boiled Noodles
    with Walnuts 920
  Kasha Varnishkas (Buckwheat
    Groats with Noodles) 992
  Makos Tészta (Boiled Noodles
    with Poppy Seeds) 920
  Odamaki-Mushi (Egg Custard
    Noodles) 976
  Soba (Buckwheat Noodles) 976
  Vermicelli alla Pastora
    (Fine Noodles for the
    Shepherdess) 958
Piselli e Pasta (Peas and Shell
  Macaroni) 959
Rice
  Chazuke 976
  Dahi Bhath (Rice with
    Buttermilk) 942
  Fried Rice with Ham 865
  Gohan (Rice) 976
  Ham Fried Rice 858
  Nori-Chazuke (Rice with
    Seaweed) 976
  Risotto alla Milanese 958
  Sushi Rice 971
Spaghetti alla Carbonara
  (Spaghetti and Eggs on Ham) . .862
Spaghetti al Quattro Formaggi
  (Spaghetti with Four Cheeses) . .958
Spaghetti con le Polpettine
  (Spaghetti with Meatballs) 955

COOKIES

Brown-Sugar Hermits 901
Chocolate Diamonds with
  Hazelnuts 882
Grostoli (Crisp Cookies) 960
Hickory Crescents 904
Honey-Date Bars 911
Huszárcsók (Hussar's Kisses) 922
Mincemeat Hermits 901
Molasses Hermits 901
Petticoat Tails 950
Prune Piroshkis 993
Tsujiura (Fortune Wafers) 978
Yokan (Bean Cakes) 978

DESSERTS

Blintzes, Blueberry 992
Blintzes, Cherry 992
Blintzes, Kaese (Rolled Cheese
  Pancakes) 992
Chremslach (Matzo-Meal Fritters) .994
Frozen
  Banana Split 934
  Crêpes, Frozen. 934
  Harlequin Crinkle Cups 934
  Ice-Cream Cake 932
  Ice-Cream Shadow Cake 932
  Jelly-Roll Sandwiches 934
  Ladyfinger Ice-Cream Cake 932
  Melon à la Mode 934
  Meringues Glacées 934
  Mousse, Honey 910
  Pie, Apricot Ice-Cream 934
  Pie, Coffee-Chocolate 934
  Roll, Chocolate Ice-Cream 932

Sherbet, Orange-Honey 980
Snowballs, Summer 934
Strawberries à la Mode 934
Fruit
Apples, Honey-Glazed 910
Compote, Fruit 993
Cseresznye Kisütve (Deep-Fried
Cherries) 921
Fragole all'Italiana
(Strawberries) 960
Gajar Halwa (Carrot Dessert) . . .942
Honeydew and Orange Dessert . .911
Pears, Honeyed 910
Ice Cream
Almond Ice Cream 929
Banana Ice Cream 929
Blueberry Ice Cream 929
Chocolate Freezer Ice Cream 929
Chocolate Ice Cream 929
French Vanilla Ice Cream 929
Peach Ice Cream 929
Pineapple Ice Cream 929
Raspberry Ice Cream 929
Rum-Raisin Ice Cream 929
Strawberry Ice Cream 929
Strawberry Ice Cream, Fresh . . .929
Vanilla Ice Cream 929
Ice-Cream Bonbons 934
Ice 'n Cream 929
Ices
Apple and Grape-Juice Ice 925
Apricot Ice 925
Cantaloupe Ice 925
Coconut Ice, Fresh 925
Coffee Ice with Whipped Cream . .925
Currant-Jelly and Raspberry Ice . .925
Fruit-Juice Ice 925
Lemon Frappé 925
Lemon Ice, Instant Blender 925
Muscatel Ice 925
Orange Ice 925
Peach Ice 926
Pineapple Ice, Fresh 926
Plum Ice 926
Rhubarb Ice 926
Strawberry, Apricot, Raspberry,
or Peach Frappé 926
Strawberry Ice 926
Tangerine Ice in Orange Shells . . .926
Three-Fruit Ice 926
Watermelon Granité 926
Parfaits
Blueberry Parfait 930
Cherry Parfait, Two-Tone 930
Cinnamon Chocolate Parfait 930
Mocha Parfait 930
Strawberry Parfait 930
Puddings
Apple Puddeny-Pie 949
Blancmange, Irish Moss 950
Budino di Ricotta (Cream-
Cheese Custard) 960
Chakin Shibori (Sweet-Potato
Dessert) 978
Huckleberry Cottage Pudding . . .915
Lokshen Kugel (Noodle
Pudding) 993
Matzo Kugel (Matzo-Meal
Pudding) 994
Szilvás Gombóc (Plum
Dumplings) 920
Refrigerator
Awayuki-Kan (Snow Gelatin) . .978

Bavarian, Coffee-Banana 980
Bavarian Cream, Vanilla 980
Bavarian, Strawberry-Honey . . .909
Hazelnut Cream 882
Heavenly Hash 879
Nishiki-Kan (Two-Tone Jelly) . . .978
Spanish Cream 980
Shortcake, Huckleberry 915
Sundaes
Arabian Sundae 932
Brandied Fruit Sundae 932
Brittle Sundae 931
Candied Fruit Sundae 932
Cereal Sundae 932
Chocolate-Mint Sundae 931
Chocolate-Rum Sundae 932
Coconut Sundae 932
Cookie Sundae 932
Cranberry-Orange Sundae 932
Ginger Sundae 931
Hot Caramel Sundae 931
Jam or Preserves Sundae 932
Junior Sundae 932
Maple-Rum Sundae 931
Marshmallow Sundae 931
Mincemeat Sundae 932
Mocha Sundae 932
Molasses Chip Sundae 932
Nutmeg Sundae 931
Orange and Blue Sundae 931
Orange Sundae 932
Oriental Sundae 931
Party Pink Sundae 932
Peach Sundae 931
Pineapple-Ginger Sundae 932
Pineapple Sundae 932
Stop-and-Go Sundae 931
Tropical Sundae 932
Zippy Sundae 932

DESSERT SAUCES
Basic Hard Sauce 877
Brandy Hard Sauce 877
Brown-Sugar Hard Sauce 878
Cherry-Nut Patties 878
Creamy Hard Sauce 878
Fluffy Hard Sauce 878
Honey-Cream Sauce 911
Ice Cream as a Dessert Sauce . . .934
Ice Cream, Sauces for 930
Lemon Hard Sauce 878
Mocha Hard Sauce 878
Orange Hard Sauce 878
Sherry Hard Sauce 877
Spicy Hard Sauce 878
Vanilla Sugar 904

EGGS
Cakes, English Ham and Egg 862
Custard, Swedish Ham 865
Eggs Carmen 864
Eggs Fu Yung 865
Eggs Parmesan 861
Eggs Zurlo 865
Fried Eggs à l'Américaine 861
Fried Eggs, Devonshire 865
Ham and Eggs, Phillip's 861
Huevos en Toledo (Eggs in Toledo) 865
Huevos Escalfados Fritos (Poached
Eggs and Ham, Fried) 862
Oeufs Cocottes au Jambon
(Eggs in Ramekins with Ham) . .861
Oeufs sur le Plat à l'Andalouse
(Andalusian Egg Platter) 862
Pie, Ham and Egg 862

Quick Ham and Egg Dishes 865
Tarhonya (Egg Barley) 919
Tart, Ham and Egg 862
Timbales, Ham 865
Tortilla con Jamon (Spanish
Omelette with Ham) 861
Uova in Purgatorio (Eggs in
Purgatory) 955

FISH
Bhaji Malida Machli (Stuffed Fish
with Greens) 942
Chirinabe (Fish Sukiyaki) 971
Cisco, Broiled 903
Gefilte Fish 989
Haddock Fillets, Broiled 845
Haddock, Newburg, Flaked 846
Haddock Plaki 846
Haddock-Potato Patties 846
Hake, Curried 847
Hake, Sesame Baked 847
Halibut
Baked Whole Halibut 848
Barbecued Halibut Steaks 848
Deviled Halibut Steaks 848
Halibut with Creamy Mustard
Sauce 848
Pesce alla Siciliana (Sicilian
Fish) 954
Planked Halibut Steaks 848
Poached Halibut Steaks with
Curry Sauce 848
Herring, Broiled Kippered 903
Herring, Fried Smoked 903
Herring, Grilled English 903
Jellied Fish 989
Kamaboko (Fish Cakes) 972
Mackerel, Dingle 945
Pesce Fritto (Fried Fish Fillets) . .954
Pesce Lesso (Poached Fish) 954
Sweet- and Sour-Fish 990
Tejfeles Sült Ponty (Pike Baked in
Cream) 919
Trout, Liffey, with Mushroom
Sauce 945

JAMS, JELLIES, AND PRESERVES
Honey Butter 909
Honey-Fruit Butter 909
Honey Topping 911
Jams
Apricot-Pineapple Jam 963
Berry Jam 965
Blackberry Jam, No-Cook 965
Blackberry Jam, Spiced 963
Blueberry Jam 965
Cranberry and Fig Jam 963
Cranberry, Orange, and Honey
Jam 963
Golden Jam 964
Gooseberry Jam 965
Grape and Pineapple Jam 964
Grape Jam, Spiced 964
Loganberry or Red Raspberry
Jam 965
Peach Jam 965
Peach Jam, No-Cook 965
Peach Jam, Spiced 964
Pear-Raspberry Jam 965
Pineapple-Mint Jam 964
Pineapple-Strawberry Jam 964
Plum-Orange Jam 964
Quince and Pear Jam 964
Raspberry Currant Jam 964
Red-Cherry Jam 965

Red-Pepper Jam 964
Red-Raspberry Jam, No-Cook ...965
Sour Cherry Jam 965
Sour Cherry Jam, No-Cook 965
Strawberry Jam, No-Cook ...965
Strawberry Jam, Old Country ..964
Strawberry Jam, Three-Minute ..964
Tomato-Apricot Jam 964
Tomato Jam 965
Jellies
  Apple Jelly 982
  Apple Jelly, Aromatic 982
  Apple and Blueberry Jelly, Spiced .982
  Berry Jelly 982
  Blackberry Jelly, No-Cook 984
  Blackberry-Juice Jelly 982
  Black Raspberry Jelly 982
  Cider-and-Sage Jelly 982
  Concord Lime Jelly 982
  Cranberry Jelly 982
  Grape-and-Basil Jelly ...983
  Grapefruit-and-Savory Jelly ...983
  Grape Jelly 982
  Grape Jelly, No-Cook 984
  Grape-Juice Jelly 983
  Mint Jelly 982
  Orange-Grapefruit-Juice Jelly ...984
  Orange Jelly 983
  Plum Jelly 984
  Quince and Cranberry Jelly 982
  Quince Jelly 984
  Red Raspberry Jelly 984
  Red Raspberry Jelly, No-Cook ..984
  Strawberry Jelly, No-Cook 984
  Lemon-Honey Spread 911
  Marmalade, Tropical 980

MEATS
  Beef
  Barbecued Beef Hash 881
  Batayaki (Butter-Cooked Meat) ..974
  Beef-and-Kidney Pudding 945
  Brisket of Beef 990
  Cholent (Jewish Sabbath Meal-
    in-One) 990
  Corned-Beef Hash Lyonnaise 881
  Corned-Beef Hash, Maine 879
  Corned-Beef-Hash Mounds,
    Broiled 881
  Corned-Beef Hash O'Brien 881
  Corned-Beef Hash with Creamed
    Eggs 881
  Corned-Beef Hash with Mustard
    Sauce 881
  Hash-Stuffed Cabbage Rolls 881
  Hash with Mushrooms 879
  Holishkes (Meat-Stuffed
    Cabbage) 995
  Jyuniku No Mizutaki (Table-
    Boiled Beef) 974
  Jyuniku-Teriyaki (Broiled Beef) .974
  Magyar Gulyás (Hungarian
    Goulash) 918
  Pot Roast 990
  Pot Roast in Burgundy, Juniper ..996
  Pot Roast, Seventeenth-Century
    Beef 948
  Skillet Kabobs 997
  Sukiyaki (Plough-Roasted) 974
  Umani (Meatballs) 974
  Frankfurter Hash 879
  Frankfurter Kabobs, Pineapple ...998
  Ham
  Baked Cranberry Ham Cubes 853

Baked Ham-and-Pork Balls 855
Baked Ham with Cumberland
  Sauce 858
Baked Ham with Spicy Sauce 852
Baked in Claret, Ham 853
Baked Limerick Ham 948
Cold Fresh Ham 851
Croquettes, Ham 856
Fritters, Ham and Corn 856
Frizzled Ham with Piquant
  Sauce 858
Glazed Cold Ham 853
Ham à la Crème 858
Ham Biscuit Roll with Cheese
  Sauce 856
Ham Corn-Bread Ring with
  Creamed Peas 856
Ham Hawaiian 856
Ham in Cider 853
Ham Kedgeree 858
Hash, Ham 858
Huevos con Tortillas y Jamon
  (Ham and Eggs with Tortillas) .861
Leftover Ham, 50 Ways to Use ...859
Loaf, Curried Ham and Fresh-
  Pork 856
Loaf, Ham and Veal 856
Loaf, Orange-Glazed Ham 856
Pork Fricassee Filipino 851
Roast Fresh Ham 851
Soufflé, Ham 865
Spiced Ham and Bananas 853
Stuffed Ham Slices 853
Hamburger
Bacon Nutburgers 869
Beef and Noodle Platter 872
Beef-and-Tomato Loaf 870
Beef, Carrot, and Olive Loaf 870
Beef Loaf, Farmer-Style 870
Beef-Stuffed Cabbage Rolls 873
Cheeseburgers de Luxe, Beef 869
Cheese-Nut Burgers 869
Creamed Hamburger and
  Cabbage 872
Hamburger 877
Hamburger and Kidney Pie 872
Hamburger-Corn Skillet Dinner ..873
Hamburger Princess 868
Hamburgers, Polish Style 868
Hamburgers with Sherry-Cheese
  Sauce 869
Hamburger-Zucchini Skillet
  Dinner 873
Hawaiian Hamburgers 868
Lemon Pie-Pan Steak 868
Meatball Shepherd's Pie 872
Meatballs, Chili 870
Meatballs in Curried Tomato
  Sauce 870
Meatballs, Königsberger 870
Meatballs with Almond-
  Mushroom Noodles 870
Meatballs with Raisin Sauce,
  Burgundy 869
Meat Loaves, Orange-Glazed 870
Paprika Hamburgers 869
Peanut Hamburger Balls 870
Pepper-Ring Burgers 868
Picadillo 877
Pizza-Burgers 868
Salisbury Steak with Mushroom
  Sauce 868
Sauerbraten Hamburgers 869

Smothered Hamburger Steaks
  and Onions 868
Stir-Fry Ground Beef 876
Stuffed Hamburger Patties 869
Surprise Hamburgers 877
Sweet-and-Sour Hamburgers 868
Tennessee Hamburger 869
Texas Sombreros 872
Wild West Hamburger 876
Hasenpfeffer 878
Hét Vezér Tokány (Seven
  Chieftains' Tokany) 918
Kid, Roast 999
Lamb
  Agnello alla Cacciatora 954
  Arrosto di Agnello (Roast) 954
  Keema Matar (Chopped Meat
    with Peas) 939
  Palak Gosht (Lamb with
    Spinach) 939
  Rogan Gosht (Lamb Curry) 939
  Shish-Kabob, Lamb 997
Meat Loaf, Jellied 979
Pork
  Butaniku-Teriyaki (Broiled
    Pork) 974
  Disznókaraj Magyarosan
    (Hungarian Pork Chops) 918
  Head Cheese 882
  Head Cheese, Pork and Veal 979
  Salsiccie e Fagioli (Italian
    Sausages with Beans) 955
  Soowar Ka Gosht Vindaloo
    (Sour Pork Curry) 939
  Spicy Pork Kabobs 997
  Stuffed Pork Fillets 945
Salami and Eggs 991
Székely Gulyás (Székely
  Sauerkraut Goulash) 919
Variety
  Beef Heart with Vegetables 883
  Fried Heart Slices 883
  Savanyu Ökörfarok (Sour Oxtail
    Ragout) 918
  Savory Stuffed Heart 883
  Scotch Heart Patties 883
  Tongue with Sweet-and-Sour
    Sauce 990
  Veal Hearts, Danish 883
  Veal Hearts with Fruit Stuffing ..883
Veal
  Borjú Pörkölt (Veal Paprika) ...918
  Breast of Veal, Stuffed 990
  Costolette alla Parmigiana (Veal
    Chops Parmigiana) 954
  Hash, Veal 879
  Hot Pot, Veal 945
  Petto di Vitello (Veal Breast) 954
  Scaloppine di Vitello (Veal
    Scaloppine) 954

PICKLES AND RELISHES
Fruit Ketchup 999
Garlic Half-Sour Pickles 993
Grape Ketchup 999
Green Tomatoes, Pickled 993
Mushroom Ketchup 999
Pepper Hash 879
Pumpkin, Pickled 993
Rusell Chrain (Passover Horse-
  radish with Fermented Beet Juice) 994
Tomato Cocktail and Tomato
  Ketchup 999
Tomato Ketchup 999

PIES, TARTS, AND PASTRIES

Almásrétes (Apple Strudel) 921
Cheese Strudel 922
Cherry Strudel 922
Hazelnut Tarts 882
Honey-Nut-Apple Pie 910
Huckleberry Cream-Cheese Pie ..915
Ladyfinger Crust 980
Nut Strudel 922
Poppy-Seed Strudel 922
Potato Pastry Shells 912
Raspberry Chiffon Pie 980
Squash Pie, Company 915
Strawberry Chiffon Pie 980

POULTRY

Ham-Stuffed Chicken Legs 852
Chicken Hash à la Ritz 879
Chicken in Ham Blankets 855
Chicken Mold, Jellied 979
Cock of the North 948
Csirke Paprikás (Chicken Paprika
  with Sour Cream) 919
Kushi-Katsu (Fried Chicken on
  Skewers) 975
Murgha Kari (Chicken Curry with
  Tomatoes) 939
Petti di Pollo alla Piemontese
  (Chicken Breast, Piedmont Style).955
Polla alla Cacciatora (Chicken
  Cacciatora) 955
Tori No Mizutaki (Boiled Chicken).975
Turkey Hash 879
Yose-Nabe (Mixed Cooked
  Foods) 975

SALADS

Avocado-Melon Salad 911
Cannelini al Tonno 960
Cottage-Cheese and Tomato Salad,
  Jellied 980
Ham and Egg Salad 864
Ham and Eggs in Aspic 861
Ham Fruit Salad 858
Ham Salad 858
Ham Salad, Broiled 858
Ham Salad, Molded 858
Honeydew Rings with Shrimp
  Salad 911
Insalata Bandiera (Flag Salad) ...960
Insalata di Fagiolini e Patate
  (Green-Bean and Potato Salad)..960
Juju Gakuan (Salad) 976
Mousse de Jambon (Ham Mousse) 865
Nuta (Seafood Salad) 972
Pachadi (Yogurt Salad) 939
Pear and Cream-Cheese Salad,
  Jellied 980
Vegetable Ring, Jellied 980
Zeller Saláta (Celery-Root Salad)..919
Zöld Paprika Saláta (Green-Pepper) 919

SANDWICHES

Croque Monsieur (Fried Sandwich) 862
Crostini alla Mozzarella (Skewers).955
Cuscinetti Filanti al Prosciutto
  (Pillows with Italian Ham) 862
Ham and Cheese Bites 852
Ham and Egg Smørrebrød 862
Ham and Potato-Salad Sandwiches.859
Hamburger Guacamole 868
Hamburger Sandwiches, French-
  Fried 873
Ham-Cheese Rolls, Hot 859
Ham Salad Boats 859
Western Long Boys 859

SAUCES, GLAZES, AND GRAVIES

Anchovy Butter 955
Aspic Glaze for Sandwiches 980
Cranberry Sauce, Spicy 859
Curry Sauce 848
Dressing, Fruit 859
Goma-Zu (Sauce for Vegetables)..976
Ham Glazes 850
Hazelnut and Mushroom Sauce ...882
Hollandaise 905
Honey Glazes 909
Horseradish Sauce 914
Horseradish Sauce, Creamy 859
Horseradish Whipped-Cream Sauce 914
Junidanya Sauce 975
Juniper-Berry Sauce 996
Kakejiru (Sauce) 972
Mustard Sauce 881
Mustard Sauce, Hot 859
Orange Juice Glaze 856
Parmesan Sauce 958
Ponzu (Dipping Sauce) 975
Salsa alla Marinara 959
Salsa di Alici (Anchovy Sauce) ...959
Salsa di Vongole (White Clam
  Sauce) 959
Salsa Parmigiana (Basic Tomato
  Sauce) 959
Salsa Verde Piccante (Piquant
  Green Sauce) 959
Sour-Cream Horseradish Sauce,
  Tuna Salad with 914
Stuffing, Bread 990

SHELLFISH

Clam-Aspic Salad 979
Crabmeat Salad, Molded 979
Kekda Bengali (Bengali Crab) 942
Onigari Yaki (Broiled Shrimps) ..972
Sarson Bhara Kekda (Shrimps with
  Mustard) 942
Scampi ai Ferri (Garlic Broiled
  Shrimps) 954
Shrimp Kabobs 998
Shrimp Mold, Savory 979

SOUPS AND STEWS

Creole Jambalaya 968
Dashi (Soup Stock) 970
Fish Chowder, Jamaican 967
Fruit Soup, Jellied 979
Kömèny Leves (Caraway Soup) ...917
Meat
  Bárány Pörkölt Árpakásával
    (Lamb and Barley Stew) 918
  Chawan-Mushi (Steamed Custard) 971
  Chicken Fat and Gribenes
    (Cracklings) 987
  Chicken Soup with Sherry 967
  Cock-a-Leekie Soup 945
  Consommé Madrilène, Jellied ..979
  Goldene Yoich (Chicken Broth).987
  Gulyásleves (Goulash Soup) 917
  Ham and Corn Potato Soup 852
  Hamburger Stew 868
  Ham-Lima Bean Soup 852
  Heart Stew 883
  Irish Stew 948
  Maiale Affogato (Stewed Pork
    with Celery) 954
  Majorannás Tokány (Beef Stew
    with Marjoram) 918
  Rusell Fleisch in Borscht (Meat
    Cooked in Fermented Beet Juice) 994
  Suimono (Clear Soup) 970

Szegedi Csirke Paprikás (Chicken
  Stew) 919
Pavese (Egg Consommé) 952
Pepperpot Soup, Myrtle Bank
  Jamaican 966
Tamago Suimono (Egg Soup) 971
Vegetable
  Congo-Pea or Kidney-Bean Soup,
    Jamaican 966
  Consommé Julienne 996
  Minestrone di Pasta e Fagiuoli
    or Pasta Fazula (Thick Soup of
    Macaroni and Beans) 952
  Minestrone Milanese 952
  Miso Shiru (Bean Paste Soup)...971
  Mushroom Barley Soup 987
  Onion Soup with Cheese,
    Jamaican 967
  Potato Soup, Kingston 967
  Pride of Erin Soup 945
  Pumpkin Soup 967
  Rusell Borscht 994
  Schav (Sorrel Soup) 987
  Sóska Leves (Sorrel Soup) 917
  Split-Pea Soup, Jamaican 966
  Watercress Soup 945
Zuppa Veneziana di Pesce
  (Venetian Fish Soup) 952

VEGETABLES

Beans
  Green Beans with Horseradish
    Sauce 914
  Miso (Fermented Bean Paste) ..970
  Moong Ki Dal (Mung Beans) ...942
  Pongal 942
  Tejfeles Baffözelék (Dried Beans
    in Sour Cream) 919
Beets, Honeyed 909
Cabbage, Braised 948
Cabbage Strudel 922
Carrots, Slieve na mBan 948
Channa Kari (Chick-Pea Curry) ..942
Falafel (Chick-Pea Croquettes) ...992
Hitashimono (Boiled Greens) 976
Jerusalem Artichokes with
  Tomatoes 985
Kale, Bacon, and Oatmeal 999
Kale, Country Style 999
Matsutaki Dobin (Steamed
  Mushrooms) 976
Mellanzane alla Parmigiana (Egg-
  plant Parmigiana) 958
Noppe Jiru (Vegetable Stew) 976
Oshitashi (Spinach with Sesame) ..976
Potatoes
  Colcannon 949
  Haggerty 949
  Hashed in Cream, Potatoes 879
  Kartoffel Chremsel (Potato
    Fritters) 992
  Peperoni con Patate (Peppers and
    Potatoes) 959
  Potato Collops 949
  Rakott Krumpli (Potato and Egg
    Casserole) 919
Spinaci Stufati (Steamed Spinach) .959
Squash
  Squash Baked in Shells 914
  Squash Casserole 914
  Squash Patties 915
  Zucchini al Burro (with Butter) ..959
  Zucchini Fritte (Fried Squash) ..959
Vegetable Cutlets 994